Land and the Mortgage

The Human Economy

Series editors:
Catherine Alexander, Durham University
Horacio Ortiz, CNRS, CEFC, and East China Normal University

Those social sciences and humanities concerned with the economy have lost the confidence to challenge the sophistication and public dominance of the field of economics. We need to give a new emphasis and direction to the economic arrangements that people already share, while recognizing that humanity urgently needs new ways of organizing life on the planet. This series examines how human interests are expressed in our unequal world through concrete economic activities and aspirations.

Volume 9
Land and the Mortgage
History, Culture, Belonging
Edited by Daivi Rodima-Taylor and Parker Shipton

Volume 8
Commerce as Politics
The Two Centuries of Struggle for Basotho Economic Independence
Sean M. Maliehe

Volume 7
Credit and Debt in an Unequal Society
Establishing a Consumer Credit Market in South Africa
Jürgen Schraten

Volume 6
Money at the Margins
Global Perspectives on Technology, Financial Inclusion, and Design
Edited by Bill Maurer, Smoki Musaraj, and Ivan V. Small

Volume 5
Money in a Human Economy
Edited by Keith Hart

Volume 4
From Clans to Co-ops
Confiscated Mafia Land in Sicily
Theodoros Rakopoulos

Volume 3
Gypsy Economy
Romani Livelihoods and Notions of Worth in the 21st Century
Edited by Micol Brazzabeni, Manuela Ivone Cunha, and Martin Fotta

Volume 2
Economy for and against Democracy
Edited by Keith Hart

Volume 1
People, Money, and Power in the Economic Crisis
Perspectives from the Global South
Edited by Keith Hart and John Sharp

Land and the Mortgage

History, Culture, Belonging

Edited by
Daivi Rodima-Taylor and Parker Shipton

berghahn
NEW YORK • OXFORD
www.berghahnbooks.com

First published in 2022 by

Berghahn Books

www.berghahnbooks.com

© 2022, 2026 Daivi Rodima-Taylor and Parker Shipton
First paperback edition published in 2026

All rights reserved. Except for the quotation of short passages
for the purposes of criticism and review, no part of this book
may be reproduced in any form or by any means, electronic or
mechanical, including photocopying, recording, or any information
storage and retrieval system now known or to be invented,
without written permission of the publisher.

Library of Congress Cataloging-in-Publication Data

A C.I.P. cataloging record is available from the Library of Congress
Library of Congress Cataloging in Publication Control Number: 2021057371

British Library Cataloguing in Publication Data

A catalogue record for this book is available from the British Library

EU GPSR Authorized Representative

LOGOS EUROPE, 9 rue Nicolas Poussin, 17000, LA ROCHELLE, France
Email: Contact@logoseurope.eu

ISBN 978-1-80073-348-0 hardback
ISBN 978-1-83695-685-3 paperback
ISBN 978-1-80758-733-8 epub
ISBN 978-1-80073-349-7 web pdf

https://doi.org/10.3167/9781800733480

Contents

List of Illustrations vii

Acknowledgments ix

Introduction. Land, Finance, Technology: Perspectives on Mortgage Lending 1
  Daivi Rodima-Taylor

Part I. Situating Land Mortgage in Time and Space

Chapter 1. The Glittering Mortgage, the Vanishing Farm: Enticement, Entrustment, Entrapment 37
  Parker Shipton

Chapter 2. A Brief Legal and Social History of Mortgage 66
  David J. Seipp

Chapter 3. Land Tenure: From Fiscal Origins to Financialization 74
  Michael Hudson

Part II. Mortgage as Cultural Export: Land, Family, and the State

Chapter 4. Inheriting Debt: Legal Pluralism, Family Politics, and the Meaning of Wealth in Ghana 95
  Sara Berry

Chapter 5. Tales of Mortgage, Risk, and Taxation in Rural Senegal 119
  Kristine Juul

Chapter 6. Signs of Trouble: Land, Loans, and Investments in Post-conflict Northern Uganda 144
  Mette Lind Kusk and Lotte Meinert

Part III. Old Rules and New Twists: Reinventing and Resisting Land Financialization

Chapter 7. Reinventing Land Mortgage in Postsocialist Europe: The Romanian Case   161
Stefan Dorondel, Daivi Rodima-Taylor, and Marioara Rusu

Chapter 8. Distressed Publics: Circumventing the Mortgage from South Africa to Ireland   188
Nate Coben and Melissa K. Wrapp

Chapter 9. Governing the Old City: Land Records, Digitization, and Liquidity in Lahore   216
Tariq Rahman

Part IV. Coming Full Circle: Hopes, Ideologies, and Life on the Ground

Chapter 10. Mortgage Credit as an Instrument of Economic Growth in Colonial Massachusetts, 1642–1777   233
Winifred B. Rothenberg

Chapter 11. When Land Takes Wing: The Concentration of Holdings and the Human-Animal Dimension   261
Parker Shipton

Conclusion. Envoi   280
Parker Shipton

Index   293

Illustrations

Figures

5.1. Many loans are used for fattening rams for the annual Eid el Kabir celebration. © Kristine Juul. 126

5.2 and 5.3. Despite taxation, public waste management is lacking and infrastructure and sanitation at the weekly livestock market remain very poor. © Kristine Juul. 133

5.4. Registration and issuing a birth or marriage certificate requires payment of a fee to the municipality. © Kristine Juul. 135

6.1. Borrowing money from the bank. Drawing by Mette Lind Kusk. 148

6.2. James sells off customary land to repay his bank loan. Drawing by Mette Lind Kusk. 149

6.3 and 6.4. Not-for-sale signs from Gulu town and the surrounding parishes. © Mette Lind Kusk. 153

6.5. The fenced plot bought by the foreign company for testing the feasibility of building wind turbines. © Lotte Meinert. 156

7.1. The moving border stick marking the land dispute between neighbors (June 2004). © Stefan Dorondel and Thomas Sikor. 174

7.2. Land fragmentation in a hilly village, Davideşti, Argeş County (2010). © Stefan Dorondel. 176

7.3. A ruined pump station in Bistretu village, Dolj County (July 2014). © Stefan Dorondel. 179

8.1. Exterior of the Western Cape Department of Human Settlements building. © Melissa K. Wrapp. 197

Tables

7.1. The evolution of bank credits for agriculture in Romania in 2005–2020. Source: Authors' aggregation based on monthly National Bank of Romania bulletins. 177

10.1. Number of mortgages by occupation of the parties. © Winifred B. Rothenberg. 240

10.2. Mean nominal loan amount by occupation of the parties, in £s. © Winifred B. Rothenberg. 240

10.3. Mortgages discharged and undischarged, by occupation of the debtor. © Winifred B. Rothenberg. 243

10.4. Discharged and undischarged mortgages, by percent urban/rural. © Winifred B. Rothenberg. 243

10.5. Two sub-samples: Differences of means of selected variables. © Winifred B. Rothenberg. 243

Acknowledgments

We want to extend our sincere gratitude to the individuals and organizations who have helped so much to bring this much-needed scholarly endeavor to its fruitful completion. We thank the participants of our symposium "Mortgage across Cultures: Land, Finance and Epistemology," held at the African Studies Center of Boston University in April 2016, and co-funded by the BU Department of Anthropology, African Studies Center, and Center for the Finance, Law and Policy.

Daivi Rodima-Taylor is thankful for the chance to further develop these conversations at the March 2019 Title Working Group's workshop at the Department of Anthropology of the University of California, Irvine and is grateful to its organizers Bill Maurer, Nathan Coben, and Melissa Wrapp. Parker Shipton's research on this project benefited from his Andrew W. Mellon fellowship at the Center for Advanced Study in the Behavioral Sciences at Stanford University, in 2014–15. We also thank the participants of the triple panel on Land Disputes and Displacement at the November 2014 African Studies Association annual meeting in Indianapolis and co-organized by Lotte Meinert and Daivi Rodima-Taylor and subsequent discussions at the Symposium on Land and Conflict at the Institute of Peace and Strategic Studies of Gulu University, Uganda, that took place in January 2015. Our special thanks go to the late Professor John Harris, founding director of Boston University African Studies Center and participant of several of our workshops, for his inspiring contributions and eager encouragement for our research project.

For their invaluable help in preparing this book for publication, we thank our two anonymous reviewers, editors of the Berghahn Human Economy Series Keith Hart and Theodoros Rakopoulos, editors of Berghahn Books Tom Bonnington and Anthony Mason, and production editor Elizabeth Martinez. We also thank copyeditor Ilana Brown and indexer Larry Sweazy. Our gratitude also goes to the American School of Classical Studies at Athens for permitting us to include part of *Horoi: Studies in Mortgage, Real Security, and Land Tenure in Ancient Athens* (*The American Excavations in the Athenian Agora. Hesperia:* Supplement IX) by John V. A. Fine. Last, but most, we extend our heartfelt thanks to Polly Steele and Christopher Taylor.

INTRODUCTION

Land, Finance, Technology
Perspectives on Mortgage Lending

DAIVI RODIMA-TAYLOR

Land has served as a primary means of sustenance, but also as a vehicle for wealth and power throughout the ages. Lending against land has taken diverse forms in different societies and time periods. Oftentimes a risky practice, mortgage has been treated in scholarly literature primarily as an economic or legal contract. This book calls for a fuller, culturally sensitive, and human-centered exploration of this age-old, but continuously reinvented institution.

Today, lending against real property is occurring in significant volumes globally. Mortgage loans in the OECD[1] countries increased from 20 percent to 64 percent of GDP between 1914 and 2010 (Proskurovska and Dorry 2018). In the United States alone, mortgage debt reached $10.44 trillion at the end of June 2021, according to the Federal Reserve Bank of New York.[2] Homeownership remains a principal means of wealth creation for most Americans – more than a financial asset, it allows access to schools, jobs, and other opportunities (Faber 2018). Mortgage lending is also an important part of land titling reforms that seek to enhance agricultural productivity and rural entrepreneurship in the Global South. The outcomes of such initiatives have been uneven and ambiguous, and remain a hotly debated policy issue.

Advances in information technology have significantly changed mortgage lending. The 2007 subprime crisis revealed the pitfalls of some of the new financial instruments – such as mortgage-backed securities that enabled the sale of the debt on secondary markets and integrated home loans with speculative global finance. The subsequent foreclosure crisis deprived millions of homeowners of their property and savings worldwide – with particularly grave effects for low-income populations. New digital technologies for the management of housing markets may denote a new "technological phase" of housing financialization marked by data collection and analysis with the help of algorithms – with data turned into a marketable commodity and people profiled and ranked for profit in the ever-growing digital "information dragnet" (Fields 2019: 17–18; Fourcade and Healy 2017). At the same time, abstract and depersonalized financial flows entailed in commercialized housing debt paradoxically involve persistent personalized sentiments of reciprocity and mutuality, and conversations about individual responsibility and moral behavior (Langley 2008; Maurer 2006; Samec 2018; Stout 2019a). The embeddedness of mortgage loans in familial patterns of reciprocity and intergenerational cycles of exchange may render mortgage holders even more vulnerable to dispossession and disempowerment.

New technologies such as digital mortgage processing offer hope for previously underserved populations, while bringing along new challenges and vulnerabilities. Lending assisted by financial technology (FinTech) could expand credit for those with limited access to traditional financial markets by facilitating easier and less costly services, while lessening discrimination resulting from personal interactions. The digital take-off has been rapid. The market share of FinTech lenders[3] in US mortgage lending has grown from 2 to 8 percent between 2010 and 2016 (Fuster et al. 2018).[4] On the other hand, the algorithm-empowered mortgage also introduces significant fair lending concerns and may reinforce racial and economic inequalities (Allen 2019; Courchane and Ross 2019). Drawing on the historical legacies of discriminatory redlining,[5] the predictive models of algorithms may introduce new, difficult-to-detect biases that call for novel approaches to housing policy and ethics.

This chapter argues that the ambiguous and uneasy partnerships of the formal and informal, public and private have resided in mortgage and titling institutions throughout history. With a focus on the evolution of legal norms and institutions for mortgage credit and land titling in the non-Western and Western world, it relates these continuities to new practices and technologies in the mortgage space. In an era of intensifying population mobility, resettlement and political transitions in many parts of the world, these questions carry broader social and political import. Postsocialist settings have become a testing ground for land titling and financialization reforms after the era where real property rights did not exist. Attempts to institute mortgage lending in these societies testify, however, to the endurance of preexisting authority patterns and recombinant property forms that mix frameworks from different periods and property regimes. Reforms that institute exclusive land rights may exacerbate political conflicts, power struggles, and economic inefficiencies.

It is therefore important to study local and global perspectives of financialization as interlinked, exploring the ways in which local economies interact with large corporations and governments (see Hart 2017; Hart, Laville, and Cattani 2010). Hart calls for a more detailed study of the complementary potential and dialectical movement of bureaucracy and informality, and the specific, cultural embeddedness of both. Setting out to study mortgage lending from a human economy perspective, this chapter contends that the impact of new financial technologies should be evaluated within the particular historical and socio-cultural contexts of mortgage institutions. Land and the mortgage are frequently central to broader struggles over belonging and identity, calling attention to an increasing plurality of real property forms, entitlements, and calculative practices in the Global South and North – as well as the historical continuities in broader, racialized relations of inequality shaping the mortgage lending. The institutional and technological advances in global mortgage markets continue to intersect with interpersonal networks of reciprocity and expectations of mutuality among mortgage borrowers – while building on the social imaginaries and public representations of housing credit as a safeguard of one's biological survival and social continuity.

Pledging, Contracting, and Mortgaging in Historical Perspective

The Social Embeddedness of Land

Land has historically been situated in the nexus of wealth and power, and land transactions have been shaped by attempts to keep up existing social and political hierarchies. Early land pledges took variable forms and served diverse functions, while also fortifying the positions of the powerful, including chiefs and hereditary landed estate owners. At the same time, as histories from early Africa and Europe reveal, land credit has also been deeply embedded in interpersonal networks, informal agreements, and patterns of mutuality that often may have contradicted the written word of legal contract – if such could be found.

Land pledging in Africa has existed since pre-colonial times and varied greatly historically and geographically, but also featured some important regularities. Called a multitude of names – "pawning," "pledging," "promising," "secured agreement" – it has served as an important source of credit, but also functioned as a form of land sales in places where these have been illegitimate (Delville et al. 2002). Pledging is a process where a borrower grants another person the right to use his or her farmland until the repayment of the borrowed sum. The transaction was often highly personal and based on complementary interests between parties with unequal access to productive resources (2002: 63). The duration and form of the arrangement have varied widely, depending on factors such as customary land rights and patterns of settlement, social recognition of open-ended loans, interpersonal relations and patterns of reciprocity, and urgency of credit needs. Such land transfers often served to integrate newcomers into local communities with the emergence of new cash crops: in early twentieth-century Ghana, cultivation of cocoa and groundnuts opened up frontier areas where new settlers provided labor assistance to farmers for access to land (Mireku et al. 2016). That solidified chiefly authority over land allocation in the form of land "leases" that has persisted through postcolonial times (Berry 2013).

Therefore, land pledging has features in common with other customary contracts – it could be renegotiated or revoked and often depended on the consent of third parties such as family and kin (Ghai 1969). As landholding was frequently subject to multiple and overlapping user rights, property law was concerned with obligations between people in respect to things, rather than rights of persons over things (Gluckman 1965). Jural rights emanated from multiplex social ties between people, including kinship, but also territoriality and co-residence and the history and frequency of mutual support (Moore 1998). Land pledging thus featured as an integral part of a complex web of reciprocal obligations and exchanges among people related by kin, territory, and other modes of affinity.[6]

Pledging or pawning land was thus part of "informal" land tenure where ancestral or kin-group land was held in trust and defined by a variety of use rights and long- and short-term obligations. The rise of the institution of formal mortgage in much of the non-Western world has been associated either with colonial-era land grabs of settler economies (see Shipton 2009 for Kenya), or with post-colonial land titling reforms that have seen varied success at best. It has been estimated that more than 70 percent of the world's population lacks access to legally registered land titles.[7] Formal land titling reforms are based on the "freehold-mortgage" nexus – the assumption that individually owned and freely transferable landholding easily translates into agricultural credit, and the creditor has a full and inalienable right to the forfeited land (Shipton 2009). Proponents of land titling in the Global South have viewed registration as a means to protect marginalized farmers from land grabs and dispossession or advocated it as facilitating entrepreneurship by turning land into tradable asset and mortgage collateral. Although land registration can thus be viewed as a "pro-poor legal empowerment strategy," such reforms may have divisive and destabilizing effects – considering that most land titling initiatives tend to involve profound shifts and transformations in existing rights (Boone 2019: 384). Both claims on land and their reinforcement are embedded in institutions, many of which are broader than strictly economic or legal spheres – and can include lineage, family, age-sets, and community (2019: 395). Land property has been at the center of the interaction between custom and statutory law in Ghana where informal negotiations of inheritance and credit transactions continue to abound (Berry, this volume). Land pledges have constituted a source of continuity as well as conflict in financial and social relations, partly also due to their ambiguity and open-endedness. Boundaries between informal pledges, land sales, and formal mortgages are increasingly blurred, creating new challenges for mortgaging inherited property. Many recent land titling initiatives in Africa and elsewhere in the Global South have fueled speculative investment and land concentration in the hands of the wealthy.

In societies undergoing violent conflicts, resettlement, or regime transitions, land property can become central in broader struggles over belonging and identity (Shipton and Rodima-Taylor 2015). Formalization of land claims becomes a contested and political process where new normative and institutional frameworks for land titling and transacting may arise locally and in parallel to official frameworks (Benjaminsen and Lund 2003; Geschiere 2009; Lund 2013; Meinert and Rodima-Taylor 2017). In post-conflict northern Uganda, resistance and contestation surround the growing monetary transactions involving familial land (Kusk and Meinert, this volume). Post-socialist settings in particular have become a testing ground for land titling reforms aiming to bring about broad-based social and economic restructuring. Many countries in Eastern Europe experienced an almost complete elimination of real property rights during the socialist era, and new land privatization policies view land credit as a primary vehicle in rendering land a mobile and productive asset. Not many landholders, however, are exercising their right to use land as collateral: its market value remains low, compounded by unclear ownership records and conflicting claims, ineffective foreclosure procedures, and incomplete legal frameworks (European Bank for Reconstruction and Development 2007; Giovarelli and Bledsoe 2001). The rights-based models that seek to restore land to former owners have often failed to consider the multiple use rights and intermediate nodes of administrative control that characterize the lived experience in agrarian communities (Humphrey 1983; Sikor 2006; Rodima-Taylor and Shipton 2017; Verdery 2003). Local power relations and informal hierarchies have persisted throughout the post-socialist era, often replicating the pre-reform patters of differentiation and inequality (see Dorondel, Rodima-Taylor and Rusu, this volume).

The Contractual Features of Medieval European Mortgage

The institution of mortgage shaping people's present-day realities through global financial markets as well as government policies largely results from the historical development of the concept in Western jurisprudence. An important feature in the evolution of the early mortgage in Europe is the gradual shift in the legal documents from the credit aspect of mortgage contract to land and title transfers that introduced an arbitrary element of harshness. In medieval England, mortgage involved a physical transfer of the property to the creditor. First described by Randulf de Glanvill,[8] Chief Justiciar of England in the twelfth century, the term depicted an arrangement where profits and fruits from the land could be kept by the creditor in addition to full loan repayments. Known as mortgage or "dead pledge" in Norman French, the name referred to the fact that it provided no profit to the owner (Shanker 2003: 71).

Lenders' possession of the landholding could be seen as a protective measure in the absence of the land titling system, while also circumventing the Church's prohibition on charging interest on debts (Burkhart 1999: 252). In the absence of a valid title system, both Glanvill's gage and its thirteenth-century derivative, Bractonian mortgage, left it to the lender to provide proof about the loan and valid title. Littleton's gage, which emerged in the fifteenth century and similarly entailed possession by the mortgagee, sought to address this issue by granting legal title to the lender immediately after the loan transaction, while the borrower was able to recover the land automatically after timely debt repayment (Berman 2005: 85). Mortgage was therefore legally structured as a contractual arrangement obligating the mortgagor to fully forfeit their property in case of default – and reinforced unconditionally by early common law courts that considered the "freedom of contract" paramount (Shanker 2003: 72). The Littletonian gage was thus a "culmination of a process by which the borrower and lender's relationship increasingly shifted from its true character and invested the lender with greater rights in the borrower's land" (Burkhart 1999: 255). Most of the mortgages, however, did not serve their modern purpose of financing property purchase, but functioned mostly as a last source of credit for risky borrowers (Waddilove 2018). The finality of land forfeiture in case of loan default created a disconnect between the legal structure of the mortgage, and the underlying purpose of the debt transactions where land featured merely as a collateral security for a loan, with its value often exceeding the loan amount (Berman 2005).

Equity of Redemption and the Beginning of Modern Mortgage

The present-day mortgage originates from the seventeenth century, when equity law[9] took it over from common law courts. Applying to mortgages its repertoire of equitable principles, equity courts instituted mortgagor's equity of redemption that prohibited the lender benefiting from the mortgaged property once the debt had been repaid. Mortgage law thereby became a distinct body of equity law, while earlier it had been governed by general contract law and conveyance law – and where it had been bound by the actual terms of agreement that may have often been guided by the superior bargaining power of one party over another (Shanker 2003: 69–73). The equity courts thus started to follow the content of the transaction, which was a debtor-creditor relationship. In order to protect the interests of the lender, a foreclosure proceeding was developed that required the borrower to exercise his or her right of redemption by a full payment within a reasonable time period (2003: 76).

This introduced a novel situation where the mortgagor continued to hold the land, despite the lack of legal title, and was eligible to repay the loan and redeem property until the point when equity of redemption was foreclosed by the court (Waddilove 2018). As a result, mortgages became widespread since the late seventeenth century. Discussing the social origins of equity of redemption, David Waddilove mentions the increasing unfairness of mortgage terms to mortgagors as well as the attempts by the Chancery to help hereditary aristocracy "unlock the capital value of their prime asset" with a lesser likelihood of losing it (2018: 119). He argues, however, that there might have been another important reason behind equity of redemption that the history of jurisprudence has not yet recognized. This is the widespread informality that governed the relationships between mortgagors and lenders – who often knew each other and were connected by multiple ties of reciprocity. Despite strict legal terms of mortgage contracts, practices that enabled delayed mortgage payments might have been a cultural norm (see also David J. Seipp, this volume, about the development of legal doctrines underpinning mortgages in Anglo-American law). Situated in such social context, equity of redemption appears as an "enforcement of prevailing social views of proper mortgage dealings irrespective of legal technicality" (2018: 142). This demonstrates the central importance of broader social norms and networks of credit and debt in the evolvement of real property mortgage in Western jurisprudence – not just in non-Western societies.

Equity of redemption also affected the development of mortgage law in British North American colonies,[10] with the mortgagor retaining the ability to grant additional liens to other creditors – known as junior lenders (Berman 2005: 89). In recent decades, however, real estate finance has profoundly changed, and junior mortgage debt is increasingly converted into alternative contracts and arrangements. The economic depression of the 1930s that forced many lenders to withdraw from mortgage lending precipitated the rise of a secondary mortgage market[11] and securitization of mortgages. This market remained largely inactive until the 1970s and 1980s when an acceleration of mortgage-backed securities occurred (Berman 2005: 93) – partly fueled by the entry of semi-private banks and insurance firms into the residential mortgage market as well as advances in information technology.

The new financial instruments demonstrate a growing tension between contract law and property law, suggests Andrew Berman. These include arrangements such as mezzanine loans[12] and preferred equity investments for corporate bodies – frequently at the heart of commercial mortgage-backed securities – which could lead to heightened risk-taking by market participants (2005). Sjef Van Erp points out that this significant blurring of boundaries occurring between equity law and contract law is accompanied by a "growing category of intermediary rights." While both of these legal fields regulate relationships between private citizens, contract law has historically focused on the person of the citizen, whereas property law pertained to his or her rights against other subjects in regards to an object (2013: 2). At the center of the nineteenth-century contract law was the autonomy and freedom to contract, while property law was more complex.[13] Transfers of contractual claims almost did not exist at that time, and if they occurred, it was between natural persons rather than "financial conglomerates" – a far cry from the mortgage securitization of the present day (2013: 3).

Van Erp suggests that the rise of digital technologies and possibilities for electronic cross-border commerce situates the institutional and legal frameworks governing real property transactions increasingly "on the borderline of contract and property" (2013: 7). This can be seen in the case of MERS (Mortgage Electronic Registration System), a privately held company in the United States set up by banks and the government-sponsored enterprises involved in housing loans, which claims to hold title to approximately half of the mortgaged homes in the United States (2013: 12).[14]

It records transfers and modifications to servicing rights and ownership of the loans. In that privately controlled electronic registry where MERS is registered as mortgagee for at least half of the mortgages, the system is able to transfer mortgages to registered banks in a way that is only visible to system participants (2013: 13). By promising its users commercial certainty, MERS has afforded mortgage titles an "unprecedented level of liquidity" (Keenan 2019: 20).

Contemporary Mortgage Markets: Financialization, Depersonalization, and Persisting Mutualities

Over the past half century, housing markets have become increasingly dependent on the performance of global and anonymous financial markets. Originally designed as credit markets to finance house purchasing, mortgage markets, while facilitating loans, also drove up housing prices – expanding the market while lenders relaxed mortgage requirements. In the early twentieth-century United States, homeownership was viewed as a relatively risk-free and profitable investment: mortgage markets became "important routes to homeownership, equity and economic growth" (Aalbers 2008: 153; see also Aalbers 2012). The creation of three government-sponsored agencies – Federal National Mortgage Association (Fannie Mae), Federal Home Loan Mortgage Corporation (Freddie Mac), and Government National Mortgage Association (Ginnie Mae) – that functioned as securitizers, buying mortgages from lenders and then repackaging and selling these mortgage-backed securities to investors, led to further institutionalization of mortgage markets. Neoliberal deregulation aided the expansion of secondary markets that connected mortgage loans to stock markets and added to their volatility. In 2005, secondary markets represented two-thirds of the country's mortgage markets (Aalbers 2008: 155). While the "originate-to-distribute" business model of institutional lenders facilitates the expansion of real property markets, its intersection with global financial markets makes it possible to expand the demand for real property beyond homeowners' income or capital circulating in the domestic economy (Proskurovska and Dorry 2018: 4). Mortgage portfolios on secondary markets are grouped and priced by risk categories for lenders and investors. Credit scoring as well as other anticipatory technologies are used to predict borrowers' behavior. Such automated credit-scoring models reduce individuals to homogenized members of assumed groups, while concealing their socio-geographical characteristics and local expertise – facilitating a "redefinition" of the family home as an "object of speculation and credit" (Aalbers 2008: 156–57).

Standardization of mortgages as mortgage-backed securities (MBS) thus makes the product more transparent to investors and ties mortgage loans further to global capital markets. The growing loan securitization may therefore be viewed as an instance of financialization – a pattern of accumulation where "profit-making occurs increasingly through financial channels rather than through trade and commodity production" (Aalbers 2008: 148; see also Kalb 2013 about financialization as reproducing a large-scale institutionalized system of unequal exchange). Turning the financial sector from serving other sectors into an independent growth industry (Aalbers 2008: 148; Engelen 2002), financialization involves non-financial sectors of the economy in capital and money markets – and housing constitutes one of the primary areas where these connections occur. Before the 2007 financial crisis, the fastest growing part of the secondary mortgage market were subprime MBS – those with high-risk credit scores from borrowers with less than perfect credit. Such MBS attracted predatory lenders who practiced higher than normal fees, abusive terms, and targeted marginalized and inexperienced borrowers. This resulted in an explosive combination.

The mortgage foreclosure crisis that followed the 2007 financial crash deprived around 9 million households in the United States of their homes, while triggering a cycle of "downward mobility" among many middle-class Americans (Stout 2019a: 4). The questionable public-private partnerships continued in the aftermath of the mortgage crisis in the form of homeowner assistance programs where "corporate loan modification bureaucracies" – largely involving the same lenders who had profited from subprime mortgages – reframed the political nature of the mass-scale bank seizures as "technical and bureaucratic." Between 2009 and 2015, 70 percent of applicants for home loan modification were denied assistance (Stout 2019a: 8–10). The abysmal performance of mortgage modification programs exacerbated widespread moral critiques of the lenders and a refusal of blame for default among the borrowers (Jefferson 2013: 92).

The foreclosure crisis of 2008 reverberated globally leading to hundreds of thousands of foreclosures and evictions in Spain alone, with tremendous costs in human health and labor (Garcia-Lamarca and Kaika 2016). It challenged the popularly held premises of reciprocity entailed in mortgage debt, adversely affecting relationships between commercial mortgage lenders and customers, but also upsetting the perceived balance of rights and duties between citizens and the state (Sabaté 2016). This highlights the relevance of studying mortgage loans and foreclosures as lived experience – as an arena where the familial and social interacts with impersonal financial markets. Tomas Samec (2018) describes housing mortgages in post-socialist Czech Republic as being closely tied to familial exchanges and generational reciprocity, with intergenerational money transfers from parents to children serving as an important means of payment. That has resulted from inadequate lending institutions and regulatory policies to finance housing loans, but is also shaped by cultural norms and social expectations. These informal loans and kin-based circles of mutuality interact with the "circulation of formal debts" and contribute to the social embodiment of the highly formalized mortgage (2018: 550). Samec contends that such attachments of the "semi-financialized subjectivity" (2018: 549) can be more easily taken advantage of by the formal sector lenders in their "social regulation of poverty," playing on family-related emotions, fears, and obligations. With the spread of high-risk subprime lending, the practices of financial markets have thus extended from "high finance" into everyday "routines and rhythms" of the mortgage borrowers, as Paul Langley suggests (2008: 472). By capturing the informal practices and social networks of the poor and financially underserved and formalizing these through credit scores and other devices, such lending serves to create responsible, self-sufficient subjects "on the edges of the financial system" (Kear 2016: 261).

Emerging experiments with alternative financing strategies such as housing microfinance that have proliferated particularly in the Global South make promises toward new affordable and incremental housing strategies, while remaining fraught with challenges and unknowns (Grubbauer and Mader 2021). Recent retreat of the state from providing housing to low-income groups and the rise of private housing investment have rendered such populations even more vulnerable to the "financial inclusion" agendas advanced by multinational organizations and financial institutions (2021: 469). As Rodrigo Fernandez and Manuel Aalbers (2020) suggest, "subordinated financialization of housing" in the Global South remains shaped by the dynamics of the integration of peripheries in the "hierarchical global monetary structures" (681). Mortgage alternatives such as housing microfinance may therefore deepen the structures of inequality and dispossession, while normalizing the calculative logics of formal financial discipline and encouraging risk-taking among the vulnerable in the guise of "debt-free narratives of financial inclusion" (Grubbauer and Mader 2021: 471).

New Technologies for Titling and Mortgaging: Promises and Pitfalls

The historical evolvement of land title qualification procedures has involved a gradual disarticulation of land from its everyday use and ownership practices. Historically, two main types of title qualification procedures have emerged, each evolving from particular historical situations and political rationales: recording and registration. These systems differ in the management of uncertainty around the transfer of property rights (Proskurovska and Dorry 2018: 14). The recording procedure that originated in old English law and was prevalent in common law countries[15] noted down the conveyances as well as all claims and liabilities relating to a plot of land. The purpose of the record was not to validate ownership but provide public information about the transaction. Relying on tracing the histories of ownership through long chains of paper deeds, conveyancing was anchored in physical possession of land. Based on the feudal tenure system and the Crown as an overarching holder of land, the possession-based title was relative rather than absolute, as deed-based ownership could be contested and negotiated (Bouckaert 2010).

The registration procedure that originated in Roman law became widespread in countries influenced by German civil law. Registration produces a "constitutive effect" as the procedure assures that the title has been vetted for possible defects (Bouckaert 2010). These two distinct qualification practices gave birth to the three main styles of real property registration systems: the German, Torrens/English, and French/Latin approach. The Torrens title system,[16] which arose as a modification to the common law system at the time of the global industrial revolution, was a shift away from the relativity of possession-based common law title toward a more "market-friendly" registration-based title that sought to turn land into a liquid asset. This also shifted the legal basis of the title from histories of prior possession to the singular act of registration. The title registration system could be seen as part of the growing line of new record-keeping technologies such as double-entry bookkeeping that enabled efficiently balancing growing amounts of data about commercial transactions (Keenan 2019). Such financial instruments strove to create one-to-one correspondence between written registry and reality in order to convey an immediately existing value to the holder of the financial instrument – a hallmark of many credit instruments to come (Keenan 2019; see also Riles 2011).

New technology applications are being increasingly explored for large-scale data coordination and management and novel transparent solutions to titling and mortgaging (see also Tariq Rahman in this volume on efforts to digitize the land revenue system in Lahore, India). In the development of land and real estate markets, several stages have been identified based on the degree of separation between land and land-derivative.[17] This entails the creation of increasingly abstract commodities through a chain of contracts that produce re-classifications, moving from simple commodities such as ownership and mortgages, to complex ones such as mortgage-backed certificates, land-based securities or insurance products (Proskurovska and Dorry 2018: 12; Wallace and Williamson 2006). For functioning mortgage credit markets to develop, mechanisms have to be in place for physical parcels to be reclassified into such tradable assets (see also Bouckaert 2010). Increasing volumes of transactions and new forms of intermediaries give rise to new inefficiencies, such as growing costs, information asymmetries, and speculative behavior.[18] Innovations in land administration systems have aimed at standardizing the qualification practices[19] to harmonize land derivatives both nationally and internationally (MSCI 2018). New information technologies such as blockchain, artificial intelligence, and big data enable easier validation and synchronization of information pertaining to real property (Graglia and Mellon 2018; Peiro and Martinez Garcia 2017).

Some of the new technologies hold particular promise for land registries as these involve vast amounts of supporting documents and data, and are typically organized as centralized databases. It has been reported that about a third of the countries globally have some sort of digital land database (Shang and Price 2018). Blockchain technology has been eyed as facilitating more transparent and tamper-resistant land registries. Records on blockchain are widely distributed and verified by a multitude of nodes in a peer-to-peer digital network, affording such property records system transparency and resilience (De Filippi and Wright 2018). Blockchain-based land registries are currently being developed in countries such as Georgia, Ghana, and Sweden, with variable success (see Rodima-Taylor 2021). The application also poses challenges. Not unlike other digital registries, blockchain registries leave out significant details that do not fit into their strict parameters—therefore legitimizing a single perspective or version of events. Digital land registries often fail to convey a multisided representation of lateral use practices with their extended kin implications, cutting out the element of negotiation and disputing that has traditionally served as an important part of both oral and written contracts. Furthermore, as blockchain land registries often entail partnerships with private technology companies, the owners of the blockchain may end up becoming private owners and traders of public data (see Van Erp 2016; Vos 2017).

Such technology innovations may thus enable new spheres of accumulation and profiting. Helping investors establish a new asset class based on "bundled rental checks" for cheaply accumulated foreclosed single-family homes, now converted into multi-apartment rentals, digital innovations have provided the owners with new ways to aggregate income flows and interact with capital markets (Fields 2019). By means of the "automated landlord," properties and tenants are "not only mediated, but governed, by smartphones, digital platforms, and apps, and the data and analytics these devices ... enable" (2019: 1). Helping landlords manage their geographically dispersed property portfolios, digital technologies become part of the ongoing strategies of financial accumulation of contemporary capitalism, while grounded in material life and existing power relations (2019: 17).

There have also been increasing attempts to digitize the mortgage lending process. The digital turn has been further propelled by a search of mortgage lenders for new solutions with steadily growing loan production costs[20] and the recent decline in the volume of mortgage loan originations (2016–2018).[21] While many mortgage lenders utilize new technologies to some degree, FinTech lenders have fundamentally streamlined and automated their mortgage origination processes, with an "end-to-end online mortgage application platform and centralized mortgage underwriting ... augmented by automation" (Fuster et al. 2018: 6). The role of such technology-based mortgage lenders offering online application processing is growing in the mortgage market, taking over customers from nonbanks (independent mortgage finance companies), community banks, as well as larger banks. FinTech lenders profess to offer customers cost savings and efficiency through reduced processing times and easy online access. FinTechs are also increasingly important in refinancing that has become a key part of the mortgage markets in the recent years. Andreas Fuster and his colleagues suggest that the emergence of several stand-alone FinTech lenders[22] in the past few years may mark the rise of a new business model, particularly as the uptake of new technologies for established lenders with branch-based loan origination is not a smooth process.[23] While the operations of the latter are less flexible as compared to specialized nonbank lenders[24] due to organizational and regulatory complexity, advantages include low-cost deposit funding and cross-selling opportunities. However, the shift to online lending involves economies of scale necessary for maintaining an online platform, and this may result in a more concentrated mortgage market (Fuster et al. 2018).

The digital uptake for some FinTech mortgage lenders has been quick and impressive. One of such novel companies, Quicken Loans, recently announced a four-year partnership as the first ever "official mortgage sponsor of the NFL."[25] The company's first ad aired during Super Bowl 2016 promised house-hunters loan approval in as little as eight minutes: "PUSH BUTTON. GET MORTGAGE." The memorable commercial was a success. Quicken's *Rocket Mortgage* quickly became the largest mortgage lender in the United States with its $25 billion worth of mortgages in the fourth quarter of 2017, overtaking San Francisco-based bank Wells Fargo as the largest of the nation's thirty thousand home lenders.[26] The Detroit-based Quicken is reaching borrowers online in all fifty states out of its three hubs. Professing to have been "FinTech before FinTech was cool,"[27] the company that was founded in the 1980s is now part of a growing range of firms and startups offering mortgage digitally.

A recent report by Boston Consulting Group points out that while the digital initiatives are expected to lead to an increase in the volumes and cost-effectiveness of mortgage originations, implementation for many companies been more challenging: successful applications have "interwoven digital into the fabric of the entire organization, including marketing, sales, back-office operations, technology, risk and compliance, and integrations with third party partners" (Jindal, Hart, and Levin 2019: 2). The uptake of digital mortgage technology has accelerated with the COVID-19 pandemic, which set limitations on face-to-face meetings of borrowers with loan officers. At the same time, the pandemic has adversely affected low-income and minority communities and households, straining care and solidarity networks, and fueling mortgage and rent defaults due to income loss (Rogers and Power 2020). FinTech lending could expand credit for those with lower access to traditional financial markets, by facilitating competition, reducing the cost of obtaining information and discrimination resulting from personal interactions. Minority borrowers are often at a disadvantage when applying for a mortgage as they are "less attached to traditional financial institutions, are less likely to shop for a mortgage, and are residentially concentrated in lower income neighborhoods." On the other hand, the digital technology introduces new data sources and processing methods, and alternative ways of credit modeling that can exacerbate fair lending risk (Courchane and Ross 2019: 784–88).

Redlining in Mortgage Lending before and after the Algorithm

The mortgage industry has a history of inhibiting racial and ethnic minorities from generating home equity, systematically reproducing spatial segregation and dispossession. Racially restrictive covenants that have been part of the housing history in the United States have frequently found expression in discriminatory restrictions around mortgage lending. The federal housing policies, formulated by the National Housing Act of 1934 and aimed at making housing more accessible in the wake of the Great Depression, ended up fostering residential segregation. The newly formed Federal Housing Administration established racially oriented restrictions on eligibility for mortgages (Rothstein 2017). The practice of "redlining" was introduced through the racial and wealth maps of US cities of the Home Owners' Loan Corporation that financed federally backed government home loans in the 1930s and soon became a nationwide "risk-evaluation" standard (Allen 2019: 221). The color-coded maps encouraged mortgage lending in more affluent and White areas, while inhibiting it in areas populated by racial minorities and recent immigrants – where financially qualified community members were often denied credit (2019: 236). The federal backing of housing loans that was limited to White Americans reinforced the lines between segregated neighborhoods and separated impoverished inner cities from affluent suburbs for decades to come.

The Fair Housing Act, part of the Civil Rights Act of 1968, prohibited discrimination around the sale, rental, and financing of housing, and the Equal Credit Opportunity Act of 1974, Home Mortgage Disclosure Act of 1975, and Community Reinvestment Act of 1977 aimed to further safeguard fair lending practices to marginalized and minority communities. The fair housing and lending laws, however, have not managed to completely undo the long history of formal racial redlining as well as more subtle informal practices of biased lending that have limited income generation and housing improvement for entire neighborhoods[28] – and thus continue to define those "high-risk" areas as new technologies for housing finance emerge.

Many of the historically "redlined" communities were infused with predatory subprime credit in the 1990s–2000s, resulting in massive foreclosures. The mortgage industry profited from the subprime loans, with lenders facing increasing pressures from securitizers to provide them. Much of that profitability was due to high fees on loans and exorbitant interest rates that extracted capital from low-income and minority neighborhoods (Hammel and Nilsson 2019: 547). Subprime loans target borrowers with weak credit histories and limited ability to make down payments – borrowers who have historically been excluded from fixed-price loan markets. Risk-based loan pricing for these groups takes advantage of large historical performance data sets (Frame, Wall, and White 2018: 12).

High-cost mortgage lending has been on the rise in minority communities also after the 2008 subprime crisis. A recent meta-analysis of existing studies assessing discrimination in US mortgage lending markets over the four decades before 2016 found that Black and Hispanic borrowers were more likely to be rejected when applying for a mortgage loan and more likely to receive a high-cost mortgage (Quillian, Lee, and Honore 2020: 25). Based on Home Mortgage Disclosure Act data from 2014, Jacob Faber showed that compared to 71 percent of White applicants approved for home loans, those rates were lower for Asian (68 percent), Latinx 63 percent), and Black borrowers (54 percent). Black and Latinx borrowers were about three times more likely to receive higher cost loans (2018: 215–16). The largest differences between White and minority outcomes were observed in areas where subprime lending had been common prior to the crisis, and where foreclosures accumulated in its aftermath. While seen as presently too risky for mortgage loans by many mainstream lenders, these neighborhoods should be viewed as a product of a long-term, problematic relationship of neglect and rent seeking (Hammel and Nilsson 2019: 547).

These legacies of inequality thus still define access to financial services in many neighborhoods. Since the financial crisis of 2008, low- and moderate-income communities have suffered from bank branch closures – between 2008 and 2016, metropolitan areas across the United States lost 15 to 20 percent of their bank branches (Velasquez 2020). There are high costs of being underbanked, with people forced to use the products of "fringe finance" such as check cashing, money orders, and prepaid cards. The need for mortgage and small loan products in these communities, and their historically poor experience with formal banks, are fueling the demand for FinTech services (Velasquez 2020).

The impact of FinTech-empowered mortgage lending to racial disparities has not been clear-cut, however, while raising challenging questions about the potentially discriminating effects of algorithmic decision-making. In a recent study of Home Mortgage Disclosure Act data that assessed mortgage lending disparities between populations of different racial composition, Tyler Haupert (2020) found that both FinTech as well as traditional lenders were likely to offer subpar terms to non-White applicants, while FinTech-mediated loans resulted in higher rates of subprime loans for Black applicants as compared to their similarly qualified White counterparts. In another recent study that investigated the effects of FinTech mortgage lending on racial disparities, Robert Bartlett, Adair Morse, Richard Stanton, and Nancy Wallace (2019) found that discrimination in mortgage loan pricing was present both in cases of traditional, face-to-face lenders, and platform lenders offering complete online contracting.[29] Accepted Latinx and African American borrowers paid 7.9 and 3.6 basis points more in interest for home-purchase and refinance mortgages than similarly qualified White borrowers – with the lending discrimination costing to the minority borrowers $765 million in extra interest per year. A reduction in price discrimination against minority borrowers of about 40 percent was observed with FinTech lending (2019: 5–6). While FinTech may remove some "face-to-face biases," FinTech lenders were found to use "pricing strategies and data analytics that nevertheless produce discriminatory pricing" (2019: 29).

With the change of technology in the mortgage industry, the nature of discrimination may thus change from human racism and in-group biases to "statistical discrimination" that can effect disparate impact[30] through the use of Big Data variables (Bartlett et al. 2019: 30). James Allen (2019) argues that the history of segregation has resulted in creating massive data sets consisting of "decades of information built on exclusion and discrimination," and therefore affect the emerging algorithmic decision-making – with "pencil redlining" giving way to "algorithmic redlining" (2019: 234). The historical redlined maps have informed computational procedures for loan risk evaluation and cartography and shaped the funding of public works and private sector investment (2019: 236; see also Light 2011).

Machine learning brings new dimensions into credit scoring processes. While traditional credit scoring employs statistical analysis to "derive a fixed formula based on a defined set of credit history attributes," the flexible algorithms of machine learning models can change with exposure to new data. Machine learning enables identification and utilization of "subtle and difficult-to-observe relationships among disparate data elements from many different sources that can be combined to better predict consumer behavior" (Courchane and Ross 2019: 785–86). Such alternative modeling combined with an expanded set of data elements can broaden credit access to new consumers, including the unbanked. Automated lending can still pose fair lending risk. The use of alternative data sources in lending decisions may lead to "correlations with prohibited factors" that pose disparate impact risk: for example, school attended or geographical location can be correlated with race and ethnicity. When processing large amounts of legitimate risk variables, algorithmic predictive models could therefore proxy race in ways that are not easy to detect. The combination of alternative data sources with machine learning may perpetuate historical biases inherent in those sources – for example, data about banking behavior could underrepresent minority groups (2019: 786–87).

Algorithmic decision-making is not neutral, but inevitably reflects the values and intentions of the designer – thereby institutionalizing those values in code (Mittelstadt et al. 2016: 7). Algorithmic bias arises from pre-existing social values from which the technology emerges, technological constraints (e.g., alphabetical lists) and errors, and newly emerging contexts of use in the decision-making architecture (2016: 7). Human interpretation of the algorithmic decisions and correlations can further add to the subjectivity. The strategies to prevent discriminatory redlining by "sensitive attributes and proxies" may include the integration of anti-discrimination criteria into the classifier algorithm, construction of various metrics of fairness between data subjects, and other techniques (2016: 8–9). In order to counteract the dangers of algorithmic redlining, James Allen (2019) suggests more attention to the transparency of algorithmic risk evaluation and its auditing. That entails disclosing data inputs used to formulate credit scores and mortgage rates, as well as monitoring the effects produced for bias. These measures are complicated, however, due to the increasingly proprietary nature of the software and the complexity of machine learning where bias can emerge during the process rather than reside in the code. The poor transparency of complex systems and limited ability of humans to interfere highlights the difficulties of applying traditional notions of responsibility to algorithm-empowered decision-making. It is therefore not easy to replace human professionals with implicit and local knowledge with automated decision-makers – ones whose degree of accountability and moral agency remains unclear (Mittelstadt et al. 2016: 11). The challenges involved in automated decision-making may call for new approaches that transcend existing epistemic and regulatory solutions.

Big data is increasingly playing a foundational role in organizing our society and economic relations, and opaque data analysis by corporate and state actors undermines accountability and civil liberties, argue Benedetta Brevini and Frank Pasquale (2020). Highlighting the discrimination residing in the real world in which algorithms operate, Anupam Chander suggests that the transparency of algorithms should be combined with "algorithmic affirmative action" in a world "permeated with the legacy of discriminations past and the reality of discriminations present" (2017: 1025). Considering the limits of transparency in complex machine learning systems, Daniel Innerarity (2021) advises attention to the "strategies of non-transparency" by those exercising power and the ways to construct alternative strategies of "explainable artificial intelligence" (2021: 1). The new "architectures of control" for a critical review of artificial systems should be spearheaded by public organizations and similar actors, and based in collectivities: auditing algorithms thus becomes a "collective task and public responsibility" rather than one centered on the rights of an individual user (2021: 7). Such a relational and socio-politically embedded view of algorithmic transparency would entail novel approaches to algorithm audits with a joint engagement between community members and activists, regulatory authorities and planners, as well as new forms of partnerships between FinTech lenders and disadvantaged communities (see Allen 2019; Velasquez 2020). Policy reforms may be required in areas such as intellectual property, data protection, and internet law that could facilitate disclosures from both public and private agencies utilizing algorithmic decision-making (Allen 2019: 262).

The machine learning technologies in the mortgage space today draw on a longer history of computerization of consumer credit. Information technology advances in the 1990s enabled automatic mortgage underwriting, resulting in important changes for the borrowers (Foote, Loewenstein, and Willen 2019). Advances in data storage and information processing allowed faster and less costly mortgage origination and out-of-state competition. Technology changed the ways mortgage lenders evaluated risk. It enabled coders to include large data-sets of loan records to construct empirical default models, with new additions such as credit scores – while weakening the relevance of some others such as the debt-to-income ratio. It thus minimized the role of "intuitive human judgement" that had been relevant particularly in marginal cases (2019: 3). These developments echoed the increasing centrality of consumer credit scoring systems with the digital advances in the 1980s–1990s that was accompanied by a gradual downgrading of empirical knowledge gained through personal interactions. The distribution channels of retail banks became more centralized and virtualized while information about customers and ways to obtain it became standardized, and private credit-scoring consultancies emerged as major actors in retail banking. As Andrew Leyshon and Nigel Thrift suggest, the credit-scoring technologies led to a "quantitative revolution" designed to evaluate and predict customer behavior at a distance (1999: 450). Branch closures were particularly significant in low-income, inner city areas. Foregrounding the profitability of the customer to the bank, the new values imparted through code and "new monetary networks of inclusion and exclusion" became increasingly less accessible to review and interrogation (1999: 452–54).

The availability of Big Data has changed the way consumer behavior is measured, shifting focus on measuring action (often in real time) and expressing it in scores and ratings associated with good or bad decisions – revealing an emerging "economy of moral judgement" (Fourcade and Healey 2017: 24). Emerging from the bureaucratic forms of administration based on standardized categories and routines, the "roboprocesses" mediated by computerized record-keeping and adjudication may amplify the unaccountability of bureaucracy by rendering it automatic, suggests Hugh Gusterson (2019: 4). The technological advances of the 1980s that combined standardized routines with computer code coincided with the global spread of extractive neoliberalism, skewing the algorithmic processes "in favor of corporate profit-making" and perpetuating racial and economic inequalities (2019: 7). The automated calculative systems of mortgage modification programs employed at the wake of the 2008 subprime crisis provide a vivid illustration of such automated bureaucracy, argues Noelle Stout (2019b). Designed to maximize profits for the investors, these automated processes introduced errors and prevented meaningful human intervention, leading to an "unparalleled numbers of bank seizures of American homes" (2019b: 32). Even more importantly, algorithmic decision-making undermined human agency and accountability, inducing humans to act like automatons in charge of "pushing through" the processes "programmed to work against homeowners' interests" (2019b: 41).

On Evolving Mortgaging and Titling

The historical evolvement of mortgage lending and land titling institutions examined in this chapter revealed two broad and conflicting tendencies. First, throughout history and across the world, real property claims and transactions have been embedded in interpersonal networks, and socio-cultural norms and expectations of mutuality – but also in hierarchies of inequality. Second, legal and administrative devices to manage real property have evolved toward growing exclusion of lateral claims, use rights, and ownership histories. This imbalance has a potential to deepen dispossession and disempowerment of low-income mortgagors globally who use their informal networks to manage their formal credit obligations and extend their everyday norms of mutuality to the anonymous mortgage markets managed through algorithms. The "new" mortgage borrowers in the Global South may be especially vulnerable.

The histories of pledging and mortgaging in early Africa and early Europe revealed that such land transactions have been deeply intermeshed with other forms of credit and debt, often functioning as part of existing interpersonal networks and obligations. While early land pledges took variable forms, they often served to fortify the positions of the powerful, including chiefs, village headmen, and landed estate owners. In medieval Europe where land titles were not easily reinforced, early mortgages often involved a transfer of the land property to the creditor. A concurrent conceptual shift from debt to landholding took place in legal documents with simple cash debts easily leading to land loss to the borrower. However, delayed mortgage payments might have been an informal "cultural norm" at the time (Waddilove 2018). The early mortgage, despite the rigid stipulations of the law books, may thus have been subject to considerable interpersonal renegotiation. When the Chancery courts took over from the common law the administration of mortgage law, borrower's equity of redemption was instituted allowing the submission of a full payment within a reasonable time period after the missed deadline. The impact of this legal reform varied contextually. While this was intended as a device that served the borrower's interests, experience from the colonial United States shows that the introduction of the clearly defined foreclosure proceedings may have also rendered the land more liquid and facilitated the dispossession of indigenous populations (Park 2016).

The popularity of a housing mortgage as a private investment strategy has been growing over the past half century, with mortgage loans becoming dependent on the performance of global, anonymous financial markets. That is also reflected in developments in title registration systems that have gradually shifted their legal basis from histories of prior possession to a singular act of registration, making it easier to sell and purchase land. This has culminated in the mortgage securitization technologies of the present day that render real property a financial instrument to be traded in global markets.

Empirical evidence from different parts of the world shows that the seemingly depersonalized transactions have been frequently shaped by "non-commercialized" norms of mutuality and embedded in familial and intergenerational exchanges and expectations. That embeddedness may render mortgage holders more vulnerable to dispossession and disempowerment. Policy reforms seeking to introduce exclusive land rights in transitional or conflict-related settings similarly testify to the endurance of existing authority patterns and recombinant property forms that mix normative frameworks from different time periods and property regimes.

The emerging FinTech mortgage market aims to make it easier for the borrowers to access mortgage loans, but it may also facilitate smoother access of low-income consumer groups to overpriced and unsuitable financial products – and encourage a further intrusion of formal finance into the everyday "routines and rhythms" of these borrowers (Langley 2008). The rise of algorithmic decision-making in credit-scoring and mortgage processing involves novel challenges to transparency and inclusion. The new credit-scoring infrastructures, designed to evaluate and predict customer behavior at a distance, have reinforced the divisions of exclusion, while rendering them increasingly inaccessible to interrogation (Leyshon and Thrift 1999). While partly drawing on historical but biased datasets and methods, algorithmic predictive models can proxy race and other prohibited categories in new and opaque ways – with "pencil redlining" giving way to "algorithmic redlining" (Allen 2019). Algorithmic scorecards integrate personal information of mortgage borrowers, making moral judgments about their behavior and creditworthiness, while turning the data into a marketable commodity for the profit of private investors and technology companies. Increasingly, calls can be heard for novel approaches to collective action and public oversight of algorithmic mortgage lending that involves new partnerships between borrowers, community activists, policy makers, and the financial industry.

Excessive household indebtedness has brought along a moral condemnation of debt and diverse forms of resistance that include debt cancellation campaigns, calls for legislative changes, and alternative lending institutions (Sabaté 2020). Numerous social movements that attempt to reimagine the unequal indebtedness of racialized capitalism have emerged in the United States since the financial crisis, argues Hannah Appel (2019). The Debt Collective and Rolling Jubilee have successfully challenged existing policy frameworks around household debt and inspired broader conversations about debt forgiveness and the colonial histories of exclusion (Appel 2019). New relational forms of financial practice that emerged from the networks of artists and activists of Strike Debt/Occupy Wall Street have incorporated the "everyday distress generated by the debts" into creative popular confrontation with the abstract complexity of financial instruments (Aitken 2015: 862; see also Haugerud 2012 on theatrical political activism to protest wealth disparities). Increasing instances of collective housing debt with the rise of mutual-aid housing cooperatives in the Global South have opened new frontiers for contesting relations between creditors and debtors that often remain invisible due to power disparities, argues Lorenzo Vidal, calling attention to "debt as a power relation" (2018: 1205). Collective institutions such as debtors' unions have demonstrated the potential to renegotiate illegitimate debts as well as build reparative social relations (Appel 2019).

Contributions to the Volume

Our book aims to study the human economy of mortgage as constructed and remade by people in their daily practices. It unveils the inextricable intermingling of local forms of mutuality and solidarity with larger bureaucracies: mortgaging is shown to relate directly to inheritance, insurance, taxation, as well as local politics. Most of the existing scholarly literature on land and mortgages has been written by economists and legal specialists, reflecting the perspectives of their disciplinary traditions. Lacking are assessments from a wider range of disciplines in the social sciences and humanities, drawing upon historical experiences, cultural meanings, and locally informed perspectives, including those of mortgagors themselves. This anthology, drawing on empirical research in different parts of the world, is meant to help fill that gap. The chapters in this volume bring together interdisciplinary perspectives and scholarly expertise from anthropologists, historians, legal scholars, and economists, and present a multifaceted analysis of historical and contemporary cases of mortgage and land titling from diverse parts of the world – including Africa, Asia, the United States, and East and West Europe.[31]

A few chapters of the anthology examine the still little-explored topic of embeddedness of land pledging and mortgaging in African countries in vernacular and formal bureaucracies. Sara Berry's chapter elaborates on the ways social groupings, such as families and polities, mediate debt and property. Family land property in Ghana has prolonged the endurance of family as a "micropolitical arena" for contesting claims over wealth and belonging between individuals. Although certain formalization of inheritance transactions has occurred recently, these legal changes may have reinforced the "corporate character" of the Asante family, widening the circle of kin-based inheritors. Land pledges have constituted a source of continuity as well as conflict in social relations, partly due to their ambiguity and open-endedness. Kristine Juul's chapter inquires whether clearly defined property rights could lead to economic growth by enabling both land mortgaging and taxation in the rural communities of Senegal. Juul contends that these reforms have not yet led to enhanced financial stability for the local people who tap into multiplying formal and informal credit instruments to meet their mortgage obligations. In both cases – land mortgage and taxation – the payment of what is owed, either to the state or financial company, can be used to manipulate property rights, as well as validate and reconstruct one's belonging and identity.

Several chapters of the volume caution against the assumption that land privatization and financialization is a panacea for economic insecurity in regions undergoing transition and resettlement. The study by Mette Kusk and Lotte Meinert explores contested land sales in northern Uganda after the long-lasting armed conflict between Lord's Resistance Army and government forces. In areas where people have returned after decades-long interruptions, family land property is affected by disputes and arguments centering on the new phenomenon of land sales – often to outsiders and foreigners. The authors investigate what the proliferation of "not-for-sale" signs across the local landscape may tell us about the land market and property relations in that particular place. Focusing on a different transitional context, the chapter by Stefan Dorondel, Daivi Rodima-Taylor, and Marioara Rusu explores the reinvention of land mortgage after a fifty-year interruption caused by the socialist regime in Romania. The analysis situates the post-socialist rural financialization within the histories of diverse tenure reforms in the Romanian countryside, and among a multiplicity of formal and informal actors that shape economic practices in local communities. It highlights the importance of undertaking systematic ethnographic and policy-oriented research into rural lending in post-socialist societies – an area of inquiry that still often remains in the shadows. The micro-politics of resistance is central in the chapter by Nate Coben and Melissa Wrapp that compares the cases in South Africa and Ireland where rural landholders devise strategies to evade mortgage offers from formal financial institutions while relying heavily on informal social networks. The study explores two large-scale public projects: provisioning of post-apartheid social housing in South Africa and the fiscal resolution of an unprecedentedly large mortgage market crisis in Ireland. The two cases reveal stirrings for more self-evidently status-based relations, hierarchies, and asymmetries. These are captured in the concept of "distressed publics": as movements, activities, and aesthetics that represent imaginings and condemnations of prior modes of governance as well as critiques of the inequalities of modern innovation. These chapters call attention to new ways of resistance and novel political imaginaries around mortgages and their failures to solve social problems.

Tariq Rahman's contribution discusses the recent state-led, World Bank-inspired effort to digitize the land revenue system in Lahore, India. Rahman's ethnographic perspectives into the struggle to digitize land records in the Old City of Lahore suggest that concerns about the centralizing capacities of e-governance may be premature. Although land records have been scanned and made accessible to the public at computerized service hubs, *patwari* – the traditional land revenue officials – remain central to the land revenue system. As objects that hold together entangled histories and longstanding social networks, plots of land defy comprehension by digital interfaces alone. Rahman demonstrates that governing land property in the old city remains both a social and material practice – and one deeply embedded in vernacular knowledge and hierarchies.

The contributions by Parker Shipton explore mortgage as a uniquely human institution deriving from particular cultures and forms of reasoning. Shipton examines some of the many imaginative ways, including metaphor and euphemism, in which humans seek to comprehend this institution with its risks and promises. Offering glimpses of the mortgage in Eurasian and North American history, Shipton warns of risks to farming people and communities as the mortgage spreads to rural tropical settings. His second chapter outlines the effects of land loss by family farmers, entailed in the takeover by corporations engaged in industrial animal farming, and the effects on animal well-being.

Historical perspectives from ancient Mesopotamia and Egypt, medieval England, and colonial United States further illuminate the foundations and variations of the mortgage institution. The chapter by Michael Hudson describes land tenure in the ancient Near East, while highlighting its fundamentally political dimensions. Hudson elaborates on the histories of the early struggles to control the usufruct from land and their implications to the development of money and agrarian debt. The chapter relates these historical contestations between rulers and creditors over the control of the rental value of land to contemporary debates over land taxation and financialization. In his chapter about the history of mortgage as a legal device in Anglo-American law, David Seipp discusses the development of mortgage in medieval and early modern England. With the examples of common types of mortgages that provided cases in England's Court of Chancery in late sixteenth-early seventeenth centuries, Seipp points out the gamble-like features of the early modern mortgage and strong social pressures against forfeiture. He argues that the nature and purpose of mortgages have profoundly changed in contemporary modern Anglo-American society with its housing markets and social expectations of individual self-sufficiency: it has become a formalized financial tool with a primary goal of acquiring property. Winifred Rothenberg's chapter examines, using archival records and other sources, more than a century of the first recorded mortgages in colonial Massachusetts and the part they played in the financialization of an economy. The chapter highlights the contributions of mortgage credit to reducing landlessness and poverty in the largely rural region of the United States. Mortgages backed paper money, a novelty at the time. Both borrowers and lenders invested in the mortgage and the colony in paper money, with enough confidence to change the nature and scale of the colonial economy.

Tracing origins of land titling, pledging, and the mortgage in periods over millennia, our book thus explores effects of colonial policies, state impositions, and locally rooted understandings as they have combined and recombined in diverse regions across the world. Our hope is that this collection will prompt other scholars to devote more attention to the peculiar and culture-bound institution of mortgage and compel them to rethink the premises of land property, finance, and trust in new and productive ways.

Daivi Rodima-Taylor is a social anthropologist, and researcher and lecturer at the African Studies Center of the Pardee School of Global Studies of Boston University. Her research explores the social meanings of property and finance, the morality and regulation of credit and debt, and the intersection of digital technologies with local economies in the Global South. She was educated at Tartu University and Brandeis University, and her work has been supported by the Wenner-Gren Foundation for Anthropological Research. She has been leading a Boston University interdisciplinary task force on migrant remittances and human security, and directs the BU ASC Diaspora Studies Initiative. She has conducted longitudinal field research in East Africa, co-edited special issues, and published articles in journals such as *Africa*, *African Studies Review*, *American Anthropologist*, *Global Networks*, *Social Analysis*, *American Ethnologist*, *Journal of International Relations and Development*, *Geoforum*, *Global Policy*, and *Review of International Political Economy*.

NOTES

1. The Organisation for Economic Co-operation and Development.
2. Center for Microeconomic Development. "Household Debt and Credit Report." *Federal Reserve Bank of New York*. Retrieved 10 August 2021 from https://www.newyorkfed.org/microeconomics/hhdc.html.
3. Companies that utilize new financial technology such as specialized software and algorithms to improve and innovate financial services.
4. As the 2018 report of the New York Fed points out, the FinTech innovation "has improved the efficiency of financial intermediation in the U.S. mortgage market," with FinTech lenders able to offer faster and less costly services than traditional lenders, and manage better application volatility (Fuster et al. 2018: 21–25).
5. Redlining is a discriminatory practice of denying access to financial services such as mortgage loans based on race and ethnicity. Redlining in the United States originated in the housing policies of the 1930s and prevented people of color from buying or renovating houses in certain areas.
6. Many present-day institutions and norms of mutuality in African communities creatively combine age-old patterns of sharing and reciprocity with new resources and values (Rodima-Taylor 2014). That calls for more research into claims, disputes, and user networks that surround land-based credit arrangements in the present day.

7. The World Bank. "Why Secure Land Rights Matter." *The World Bank*, 24 March 2017. Retrieved 27 March 2021 from https://www.worldbank.org/en/news/feature/2017/03/24/why-secure-land-rights-matter.
8. Glanvill is considered the probable author of *Tractatus de legibus et consuetudinibus regni Anglie* (The treatise on the laws and customs of the Kingdom of England), which is the earliest treatise on the laws of England.
9. The rules of equity arose in England where the strict limitations of common law prompted the King to set up courts of chancery (equity) to provide remedies through royal power. Such activities included correction of property lines, taking possession of assets, imposing liens, dividing assets, or injunctive relief to prevent irreparable damage. "Equity." Law.com. Retrieved 3 April 2021 from https://dictionary.law.com/Default.aspx?selected=646.
10. The emergence of the legal instrument of foreclosure in the colonial history of the United States had a profound significance in altering the relationships between money and land in indigenous communities. As K-Sue Park points out, land became easily exchangeable with money and was used as loan collateral only after mortgage foreclosure was authorized by law: "Colonists began to use land like money and . . . call money 'Coined Land'" (2016: 1008).
11. Marketplace where mortgages are sold by the loan originators, packaged into grouped loans or mortgage-backed securities, to investors such as insurance companies, pension and hedge funds.
12. A mezzanine loan is secured by the borrower's equity in other entities – often subsidiaries that actually own the underlying real property. The same underlying parcel of land usually also serves as mortgage collateral for a conventional borrower who is the direct owner of the property. While a mezzanine loan is subordinate to a senior mortgage lender's collateral, it is also senior to the borrower's equity investment in the real property (Berman 2005: 4–5). The mezzanine lender's right to foreclose on the equity interests is therefore riskier and of limited value as the underlying real property remains subject to the senior mortgage (2005: 37–38).
13. The central tenets of property law included the optimal standardization of *numerus clausus* principle (a concept of property law that limits the number of types of property rights that are recognized legally), the transparency principle, as well as a body of ground rules governing the application of property rights (Van Erp 2013: 5).
14. MERS as a private alternative of land records infrastructure operates without much centralized oversight, and many of its records tend to be invalid or dated (De Filippi and Wright 2018: 115).
15. Under the common law system, past legal precedents and rulings are used to decide cases at hand. Countries that use common law systems include the United Kingdom, United States, Australia, Canada, India, Hong Kong, and New Zealand.
16. Torrens title is a land registration and land transfer system in which a state creates and maintains a register of land holdings that serves as the conclusive evidence of title of the person recorded on the register as the proprietor and of all other interests recorded on the register.

17. A derivative is a "contract that derives its value from the performance of the underlying land or property" (Proskurovska and Dorry 2018: 12).
18. Services such as price determination, risk assessment, and contract negotiation have become particularly expensive and time consuming (Proskurovska and Dorry 2018: 17).
19. In order to construct abstract property rights expressed through land derivatives, the parcel of land thus needs to be defined in relation to the rest of the land, but also in the context of the relationships of the land to its owners and other stockholders of land derivatives. Yuval Millo (2007) calls this interactive process "qualification," which re-establishes relationships around various derivatives every time a derivative is traded while using land as collateral against a bank loan by agents, such as lenders, notaries, and valuators. These stakeholders build on previous qualifications kept in different databases, while forming a consensus for new qualifications in the emerging chain of derivatives. Among these actors from administrative, legal, fiscal, and other realms, conflicts can arise, and consensus processes depend on effective synchronization between classifications.
20. The Mortgage Bankers Association reported in its Annual Mortgage Bankers Performance Report that in 2018, independent mortgage banks and mortgage subsidiaries of chartered banks faced the lowest net production income per loan since 2008. Adam Desanctis. "Independent Mortgage Bankers' Production Volume and Profits Down in 2018." Mortgage Bankers Association, 17 April 2019. Retrieved 25 March 2021 from https://www.mba.org/2019-press-releases/april/independent-mortgage-bankers-production-volume-and-profits-down-in-2018.
21. The US mortgage market saw a 26 percent decline in origination volume from 2016 to 2018 (Jindal, Hart, and Levin 2019: 3).
22. Similar to other nonbanks, most FinTech lenders sell their loans through channels supported by government guarantee programs.
23. For instance, Bank of America launched a digital mortgage application in 2018: Penny Crosman. "Bank of America Launches a (Mostly) Digital Mortgage." *American Banker*, 11 April 2018. Retrieved 2 April 2021 from https://www.americanbanker.com/news/bank-of-america-launches-a-mostly-digital-mortgage.
24. See also Lux and Greene (2015) on the rise of non-banks (financial institutions that are unaffiliated with depository institutions) in mortgage lending.
25. Terry Lefton. "Quicken Loans Becomes NFL's First Official Mortgage Sponsor." Sports Business Journal, 7 January 2020. Retrieved 20 June 2020 from https://www.sportsbusinessdaily.com/Daily/Issues/2020/01/07/Marketing-and-Sponsorship/Quicken-Loans-NFL.aspx.
26. Samantha Sharf. "Quicken Loans Overtakes Wells Fargo as America's Largest Mortgage Lender." *Forbes*, 5 February 2018. Retrieved 26 May 2021 from https://www.forbes.com/sites/samanthasharf/2018/02/05/quicken-loans-overtakes-wells-fargo-as-americas-largest-mortgage-lender/#37bde091264f.
27. J. D. Alois. "Fintech Before Fintech Was Cool: QuickenLoans is Rebranding as Rocket." *Crowdfund Insider*, 31 January 2019. Retrieved 21 March 2021 from https://www.crowdfundinsider.com/2019/01/143957-FinTech-before-FinTech-was-cool-quickenloans-is-rebranding-as-rocket/.

28. Walter F. Mondale. "The Civil Rights Law We Ignored." *New York Times*, Op-Ed, 10 April 2018. Retrieved 25 March 2021 from https://www.nytimes.com/2018/04/10/opinion/walter-mondale-fair-housing-act.html.
29. The study drew upon "never-before-linked information at the loan level on income, race, ethnicity, loan-to-value ratios, debt-to-income ratios, all contract terms, and indicators for whether the lender-of-record primarily used algorithmic scoring" within the Government Sponsored Enterprises' pricing grid (Bartlett et al. 2019: 5). It investigated whether interest rates offered by the lenders were greater than those required for the sale of loans to Fannie Mae and Freddie Mac.
30. Disparate impact occurs when a "bank applies a racially or otherwise neutral policy or practice equally to all credit applicants, but the policy or practice disproportionately excludes or burdens certain persons on a prohibited basis" (The Office of the Comptroller of the Currency 2010: 8).
31. The discussion of the chapters of the collection began at the symposium "Mortgage across Cultures: Land, Finance and Epistemology" at Boston University African Studies Center in April 2016 (see Rodima-Taylor and Shipton 2017).

REFERENCES

Aalbers, Manuel. 2008. "The Financialization of Home and the Mortgage Market Crisis." *Competition and Change* 12(2): 148–66.

———. 2012. *Subprime Cities: The Political Economy of Mortgage Markets*. Hoboken, NJ: John Wiley & Sons.

Aitken, Rob. 2015. "Everyday Debt Relationalities." *Cultural Studies* 29(5–6): 845–68.

Allen, James. 2019. "The Color of Algorithms: An Analysis and Proposed Research Agenda for Deterring Algorithmic Redlining." *Fordham Urban Law Journal* 46(2): 219–70.

Appel, Hannah. 2019. "Debtors of the World, Unite!" Retrieved 7 August 2021 from http://bostonreview.net/class-inequality/hannah-appel-debtors-world-unite.

Bartlett, Robert, Adair Morse, Richard Stanton, and Nancy Wallace. 2019. *Consumer Lending Discrimination in the FinTech Era*. Working Paper 25943, National Bureau of Economic Research.

Benjaminsen, Thor, and Christian Lund. 2003. *Securing Land Rights in Africa*. London: Frank Cass.

Berman, Andrew. 2005. "'Once a Mortgage, Always a Mortgage': The Use (and Misuse) of Mezzanine Loans and Preferred Equity Investments." *11 Stan. J.L. Bus. & Fin.* 76: 1–55.

Berry, Sara. 2013. "Question of Ownership: Proprietorship and Control in a Changing Rural Terrain; A Case Study from Ghana." *Africa* 83(1): 36–56.

Boone, Catherine. 2019. "Legal Empowerment of the Poor through Property Rights Reform: Tensions and Trade-offs of Land Registration and Titling in Sub-Saharan Africa." *The Journal of Development Studies* 55(3): 384–400.

Bouckaert, Boudewjin. 2010. "Title Systems and Recordation of Interests." In *Encyclopedia of Law and Economics*, ed. Boudewjin Bouckaert, 191–203. Cheltenham: Edward Elgar.

Brevini, Benedetta, and Frank Pasquale. 2020. "Revisiting the Black Box Society by Rethinking the Political Economy of Bid Data." *Big Data & Society* 7(2). https://doi.org/10.1177/2053951720935146.

Burkhart, Ann. 1999. "Lenders and Land." 54 *Case W. Res. L. Rev.* 69 (2003–2004): 149–315.

Chander, Anupam. 2017. "The Racist Algorithm." *Michigan Law Review* 115(6): 1023–46.

Courchane, Marsha, and Stephen Ross. 2019. "Evidence and Actions on Mortgage Market Disparities: Research, Fair Lending Enforcement, and Consumer Protection." *Housing Policy Debate* 29(5): 769–94.

De Filippi, Primavera, and Aaron Wright. 2018. *Blockchain and the Law: The Rule of Code.* Cambridge, MA: Harvard University Press.

Delville, Philippe, Camilla Toulmin, Jean-Philippe Colin, and Jean-Pierre Chauveau. 2002. *Negotiating Access to Land in West Africa: A Synthesis of Findings from Research on Derived Rights to Land.* London: International Institute for Environment and Development.

Engelen, Evald. 2002. "Corporate Governance, Property, and Democracy: A Conceptual Critique of Shareholder Ideology." *Economy and Society* 31: 391–413.

European Bank for Reconstruction and Development. 2007. *Mortgages in Transition Economies.* London: EBRD.

Faber, Jacob. 2018. "Segregation and the Geography of Creditworthiness: Racial Inequality in a Recovered Mortgage Market" *Housing Policy Debate* 28(2): 215–47.

Fernandez, Rodrigo, and Manuel Aalbers. 2020. "Housing Financialization in the Global South: In Search of a Comparative Framework." *Housing Policy Debate* 30(4): 680–701.

Fields, Desiree. 2019. "Automated Landlord: Digital Technologies and Post-Crisis Financial Accumulation." *EPA: Economy and Space.* https://doi.org/10.1177/0308 518X19846514

Foote, Christopher, Lara Loewenstein, and Paul Willen. 2019. *Technological Innovation in Mortgage Underwriting and the Growth in Credit, 1985–2015.* Working Paper 19–11. Federal Reserve Bank of Boston.

Fourcade, Marion, and Kieran Healy. 2017. "Seeing Like a Market." *Socio-Economic Review* 15(1): 9–29.

Frame, Scott, Larry Wall, and Lawrence White. 2018. *Technological Change and Financial Innovation in Banking: Some Implications for FinTech.* Working Paper 2018–11. Federal Reserve Bank of Atlanta.

Fuster, Andreas, Matthew Plosser, Philipp Schnabl, and James Vickery. 2018. *The Role of Technology in Mortgage Lending.* Federal Reserve Bank of New York Staff Report no. 836. 75 pp.

Garcia-Lamarca, Melissa, and Maria Kaika. 2016. "'Mortgaged Lives': The Biopolitics of Debt and Housing Financialisation." *Transactions of the Institute of British Geographers* 41: 313–27.

Geschiere, Peter. 2009. *The Perils of Belonging: Autochthony, Citizenship, and Exclusion in Africa and Europe.* Chicago: University of Chicago Press.

Ghai, Jash. 1969. "Customary Contracts and Transactions in Kenya." In *Ideas and Procedures in African Customary Law*, ed. Max Gluckman, 333–46. London: Routledge.

Giovarelli, Renee, and David Bledsoe. 2001. *Land Reform in Eastern Europe: Western CIS, Transcaucuses, Balkans, and EU Accession Countries*. Seattle, WA: FAO.

Gluckman, Max. 1965. *The Ideas in Barotse Jurisprudence*. New Haven, CT: Yale University Press.

Graglia, Michael, and Christopher Mellon. 2018. "Blockchain and Property in 2018." *Innovations: Technology, Governance, Globalization* 12(1–2): 90–116.

Grubbauer, Monika, and Philip Mader. 2021. "Housing Microfinance and Housing Financialisation in a Global Perspective." *International Journal of Housing Policy* 21(4): 465–83.

Gusterson, Hugh. 2019. "Robohumans." In *Life by Algorithms: How Roboprocesses Are Remaking Our World*, ed. Catherine Besteman and Hugh Gusterson, 1–30. Chicago: The University of Chicago Press.

Hammel, Daniel, and Isabelle Nilsson. 2019. "Mortgage Foreclosures, Race, and Postrecession Lending." *The Professional Geographer* 71(3): 536–50.

Hart, Keith. 2017. *Money in a Human Economy*. New York: Berghahn.

Hart, Keith, Jean-Louis Laville, and Antonio Cattani. 2010. "Building the Human Economy Together." In *The Human Economy*, ed. Keith Hart, Jean-Louis Laville, and Antonio Cattani, 1–20. Cambridge: Polity Press.

Haugerud, Angelique. 2012. "Satire and Dissent in the Age of Billionaires." *Social Research* 79(1): 145–68.

Haupert, Tyler. 2020. "The Racial Landscape of Fintech Mortgage Lending." *Housing Policy Debate*. https://doi.org/10.1080/10511482.2020.1825010.

Humphrey, Caroline. 1983. *Karl Marx Collective: Economy, Society and Religion in a Siberian Collective Farm*. Cambridge: Cambridge University Press.

Innerarity, Daniel. 2021. "Making the Black Box Society Transparent." *AI & Society*. https://doi.org/10.1007/s00146-020-01130-8.

Jefferson, Anna. 2013. "Narratives of Moral Order in Michigan's Foreclosure Crisis." *City & Society* 25(1): 92–112.

Jindal, Micah, Billy Hart, and Nate Levin. 2019. *How Digital Mortgage Solutions Can Help Win the War against Margin Compression: US Mortgage Industry White Paper*. Boston: Boston Consulting Group.

Kalb, Don. 2013. "Financialization and the Capitalist Moment." *American Ethnologist* 40(2): 258–66.

Kear, Mark. 2016. "Peer Lending and the Subsumption of the Informal." *Journal of Cultural Economy* (3): 261–76.

Keenan, Sarah. 2019. "From Historical Chains to Derivative Futures: Title Registries as Time Machines." *Social & Cultural Geography* 20(3): 283–303.

Langley, Paul. 2008. "Sub-Prime Mortgage Lending: A Cultural Economy." *Economy and Society* 37(4): 469–94.

Leyshon, Andrew, and Nigel Thrift. 1999. "Lists Come Alive: Electronic Systems of Knowledge and the Rise of Credit-Scoring in Retail Banking." *Economy and Society* 28(3): 434–66.

Light, Jennifer. 2011. "Discriminating Appraisals: Cartography, Computation, and Access to Federal Mortgage Insurance in the 1930s." *Technology and Culture* 52: 485–522.

Lund, Christian. 2013. "The Past and Space: On Arguments in African Land Control." *Africa* 83(1): 14–35.

Lux, Marshall, and Robert Greene. 2015. "What's Behind the Non-Bank Mortgage Boom?" Harvard Kennedy School, M-RCBG Associate Working Paper Series, No. 42.

Maurer, Bill. 2006. *Pious Property. Islamic Mortgages in the United States.* New York: Russell Sage Foundation.

MSCI. 2018. *Global Methodology Standards for Real Estate Investment.* Retrieved 7 August 2021 from https://www.msci.com/documents/1296102/1378010/MSCI+Global+Methodology+Standards+for+Real+Estate+Investment+-+November+2017.pdf/e5a263f1-e79c-4cfe-b8de 532e87f9a639.

Meinert, Lotte, and Daivi Rodima-Taylor. 2017. "ASR Forum: Land Disputes and Displacement in Postconflict Africa." *African Studies Review* 60(3): 7–17.

Millo, Yuval. 2007. "Making Things Deliverable: The Origins of Index-Based Derivatives." *The Sociological Review* 55(2): 196–214.

Mireku, Kwaku, Elias Kuusaana, and Joseph Kidido. 2016. "Legal Implications of Allocation Papers in Land Transactions in Ghana: A Case Study of the Kumasi Traditional Area." *Land Use Policy* 50: 148–55.

Mittelstadt, Brent, Patrick Allo, Mariarosaria Taddeo, Sandra Wachter, and Luciano Floridi. 2016. "The Ethics of Algorithms: Mapping the Debate." *Big Data & Society* (July–December): 1–21.

Moore, Sally. 1998. "Changing African Land Tenure: Reflections on the Incapacities of the State." *The European Journal of Development Research* 10(2): 33–49.

The Office of the Comptroller of the Currency. 2010. *Fair Lending: Comptroller's Handbook.* Retrieved 7 August 2021 from https://www.occ.gov/publications-and-resources/publications/comptrollers-handbook/files/fair-lending/pub-ch-fair-lending.pdf.

Park, K-Sue. 2016. "Money, Mortgages, and the Conquest of America." *Law & Social Inquiry* 41(4): 1006–35.

Peiro, Nicholas, and Eduardo Martinez Garcia. 2017. "Blockchain and Land Registration Systems." *European Property Law Journal* 6(3): 296–320.

Proskurovska, Anetta, and Sabine Dorry. 2018. *Is a Blockchain-Based Conveyance System the Next Step in the Financialisation of Housing? The Case of Sweden.* Working Paper No 2018-17. LISER, Luxembourg. 44 pp.

Quillian, Lincoln, John Lee, and Brandon Honore. 2020. "Racial Discrimination in the U.S. Housing and Mortgage Lending Markets: A Quantitative Review of Trends, 1976–2016." *Race and Social Problems* 12: 13–28.

Riles, Annelise. 2011. *Collateral Knowledge: Legal Reasoning in the Global Financial Markets.* Chicago Series in Law and Society. Chicago: University of Chicago Press.

Rodima-Taylor, Daivi. 2014. "Passageways of Cooperation: Mutuality in Post-Socialist Tanzania." *Africa* 84(4): 553–75.

———. 2021. "Digitalizing Land Administration: The Geographies and Temporalities of Infrastructural Promise." *Geoforum* 122: 140–151.

Rodima-Taylor, Daivi, and Parker Shipton. 2017. *Mortgage across Cultures: Land, Finance, and Epistemology.* Boston University, Land Mortgage Working Group Research Report 03/2017. 72 pp.

Rogers, Dallas, and Emma Power. 2020. "Housing Policy and the COVID-19 Pandemic: The Importance of Housing Research during This Health Emergency." *International Journal of Housing Policy* 20(2): 177–83.

Rothstein, Richard. 2017. *The Color of Law: A Forgotten History of How Our Government Segregated America*. New York: Liveright.

Sabaté, Irene. 2016. "The Spanish Mortgage Crisis and the Re-Emergence of Moral Economies in Uncertain Times." *History and Anthropology* 27(1): 107–120.

———. 2020. "Overindebtedness and Resistance." In *Oxford Research Encyclopedia in Anthropology*. Retrieved 7 August 2021 from https://oxfordre.com/anthropology/view/10.1093/acrefore/9780190854584.001.0001/acrefore-9780190854584-e-228.

Samec, Tomas. 2018. "Performing Housing Debt Attachments: Forming Semi-Financialised Subjects." *Journal of Cultural Economy* 11(6): 549–64.

Shanker, Morris. 2003. "Will Mortgage Law Survive: A Commentary and Critique on Mortgage Law's Birth, Long Life, and Current Proposals for Its Demise." *54 Case W. Res. L. Rev.* 69 (2003–2004): 69–102.

Shang, Qiuyun, and Allison Price. 2018. "A Blockchain-Based Land Titling Project in the Republic of Georgia." *Innovations: Blockchain for Global Development II* 12(3–4): 72–78.

Shipton, Parker. 2009. *Mortgaging the Ancestors: Ideologies of Attachment in Africa*. New Haven, CT: Yale University Press.

Shipton, Parker, and Daivi Rodima-Taylor. 2015. "Land Tenure." In *International Encyclopedia of the Social and Behavioral Sciences*, 2nd edition, ed. James D. Wright, 231–37. Amsterdam: Elsevier.

Sikor, Thomas. 2006. "Politics of Rural Land Registration in Post-Socialist Societies: Contested Titling in Villages of Northwest Vietnam." *Land Use Policy* 23: 617–28.

Stout, Noelle. 2019a. *Dispossessed: How Predatory Bureaucracy Foreclosed on the American Middle Class*. Oakland: University of California Press.

———. 2019b. "Automated Expulsion in the U.S. Foreclosure Epidemic." In *Life by Algorithms: How Roboprocesses Are Remaking Our World*, ed. Catherine Besteman and Hugh Gusterson, 31–43. Chicago: The University of Chicago Press.

Van Erp, Sjef. 2013. *Contract and Property Law: Distinct, But Not Separate*. Maastricht European Private Law Institute Working Paper No. 2013/14. 18 pp.

———. 2016. "Ownership of Digital Assets?" *European Property Law Journal* 5(2): 73–76.

Velasquez, Sharon. 2020. "FinTech: Means to Inclusive Economic Development?" *Harvard Kennedy School Journal of Hispanic Policy* 32: 32–40.

Verdery, Katherine. 2003. *The Vanishing Hectare: Property and Value in Postsocialist Transylvania*. Ithaca, NY: Cornell University Press.

Vidal, Lorenzo. 2018. "The Politics of Creditor–Debtor Relations and Mortgage Payment Strikes: The Case of the Uruguayan Federation of Mutual-Aid Housing Cooperatives." *Environment and Planning A: Economy and Space* 50(6): 1189–1208.

Vos, Jacques. 2017. "Blockchain and Land Administration: A Happy Marriage?" *European Property Law Journal* 6(3): 293–95.

Waddilove, David. 2018. "Why the Equity of Redemption?" In *Land and Credit: Mortgages in the Medieval and Early Modern European Countryside*, ed. Chris Briggs and Jaco Zuiderduijn, 117–48. London: Palgrave Macmillan.

Wallace, Jude, and Ian Williamson. 2006. "Building Land Markets." *Land Use Policy* 23(2): 123–35.

Part I

Situating Land Mortgage in Time and Space

CHAPTER 1

 # The Glittering Mortgage, the Vanishing Farm
Enticement, Entrustment, Entrapment

PARKER SHIPTON

This chapter is about the mortgaging of farmland and about ways people understand it. It is also about how we do not: how we often misunderstand, miscommunicate, and mis-predict its outcomes, sometimes to our gain but often to our peril and that of others involved.

After a brief word about origins of the custom, as also discussed elsewhere in this volume, we look here into how we tend to think and speak about it. In the English language, as in other tongues, we use metaphor and stretch it in attempts to get our minds around it. These metaphors take many forms, as I shall show. The chapter turns next to some of the eventual outcomes in places where land titling and mortgaging have been tried, particularly in places where farming depends upon rain. Next it offers, partly on this retrospective basis, some observations and surmises about likely outcomes in places where land has not yet been titled as private property and mortgaging attempted. These include many parts of the tropics – more places than can be mentioned herein – where measures to get land titling and the mortgage process going are being hotly debated in policy circles. In some of these, they are being tried out in bold initiatives by legislators and program planners; but these have brought unpredicted, sometimes even perverse results. In others, as shown elsewhere in this volume, people engaged in farming are trying out mortgaging on their own, without following governmental or aid agency directives, sometimes to their own benefit and sometimes not. Finally, by way of caveat, this chapter connects to yet another, of my own, in this volume, suggesting how these effects can ramify and whom, beyond borrowers and lenders, they might affect.

A Very Human Contrivance

Mortgaging would seem as human as any act that humans have devised – a characteristic part of human economy – if its absence among other real creatures is any measure. It is uniquely human, but not universally human – far from it. Nor is it easy for all humans, maybe even for any human, fully to comprehend or to have yet explained, in its history, workings, variants, and outcomes. This human invention is evidently too complex and subtle, moreover, and its implications too wide ranging, to be explained by reference to one discipline's terms, or to any one locality or ethnic group. It takes some standing back to start to see it clearly.

The reflections here are made from a distance and meant to be general and comparative. But they are also based on field study, as well as on library and archival research, where the institution of mortgaging is a new idea, just recently being tried out. The field study has been conducted mainly in East Africa, with comparisons in West Africa and elsewhere.[1] In parts of western Kenya I came to know in repeated visits in the early 1980s and early 1990s, people in rural areas have been attempting to adjust to ideas like individual land titles and mortgaging. In that country (as in South Africa and a few other parts of the continent), ambitious programs and policies for bringing about these outcomes, in the name of market development and in hopes of economic growth, have been tried now for several decades.

In Kenya's case, these have been the first such nationwide attempt in Africa (unrolling since before the time of independence from Britain in 1963). There the presence of ancestral graves in family homesteads, for instance in western Kenya, has made land mortgaging a major issue of contention, as it has also in other parts of the continent where these graves are also associated with the supposed presence of the ancestors' spirits and are key markers of belonging.

Private titling and mortgaging of farmland or grazing land are still relatively new or untried attempts over most of the continent's countryside, as in rural Gambia and adjacent Senegal where I lived and conducted further research intermittently in the late 1980s and 1990s. There the governments have not made concerted moves toward privatizing farmland as individual (or taxable) private property, and such initiatives have remained under debate. But here too, as suggested in another chapter (Kristine Juul's) in this collection, mortgaging has lately begun to be tried in rural settings anyway, largely outside of government control or regulation.

In places elsewhere on the African continent, a few of which I have briefly visited as a researcher, programs for rural titling and mortgage facilitation are being resisted, rejected, or called intermittently to halt. Trying to understand the problems of programs and projects being carried out in varied parts of Africa by international aid agencies, parastatal lending agencies, and banks has meant interviewing there too, in their offices and out on farms, as in insider-outsider. Interviewing and reading into the history of land titling and mortgaging in Africa has led me to do some of the same on other parts of the world, especially in North America and among Native American or First Peoples there (some of whom I have known too and visited on their reservations intermittently for short periods over decades).[2] Struggles between larger and smaller-scale landholders and over wide inequalities, sometimes in forms as racialized as anywhere, have been playing out too at times in Kenya, sometimes violently, since early colonial times, much as in large parts of southern Africa too. Some of these are alluded to briefly herein.

Mortgaging takes time to understand. Nor are our understandings ever complete. The partitioning of the topic into disciplines and blinkered, inward-looking journals has been part of the problem, as many have noted – not least after revolutions, market crashes, or food riots. Nor would it make much sense to try to single out just one profession or discipline to challenge, each being a moving target anyhow with its own critics within. The connective reflection I offer in these pages is meant instead as a cautious caveat. It is meant especially for readers concerned with parts of the world where rain-fed farming has hitherto been the norm – and where mortgaging is being considered, debated, or tried out in rural areas as part of an ostensibly modern and future-oriented way of life. But let us first back up.

An Unnatural Combination?

"Possibly the weirdest of all undertakings" of humankind, wrote Karl Polanyi, has been to try to make a market out of land ([1944] 1957: 178). The mortgage is an integral part of that, maybe not our best invention. Is Polanyi untrustworthy? Let us see how Herman Melville, writing in the 1840s, described the semi-fictional near-paradise of Typee in the Marquesas where he had sojourned as his narrator was coming to understand it halfway through his story: "There were none of those thousand sources of irritation that the ingenuity of civilised man has created to mar his own felicity. There were no foreclosures of mortgages, no protested notes, no bills payable, no debts of honour, in Typee . . . or, to sum up all in one word – no Money! That 'root of all evil' was not to be found in the valley"

(Melville [1848] 1994: 101).[3] The list is a much longer paragraph; but there is the mortgage foreclosure, in the view of one of the United States' favorite novelists: first of the "thousand" human economic wrongs and sins of "civilisation" reflected from that distant mirror.

Nor may we be the only kind whose members can conceive of territory as exclusive property (as a kingfisher chases others from above a pond). But even if not, we are quite likely the only one that practices anything like the mortgage.[4] In the broader context of living beings, then, that practice, with its powerful but dangerous combination of loan, deadline setting, and legal seizure, may be considered a kind of act outside of nature's normal course. Here we must draw from the perspectives of several disciplines on that practice and the institutions, sometimes rather peculiar too, that have grown up around it.

The origins of pledging and mortgaging are obscure. Some archaeologists and others have suggested that some forms of land marking and subsequent mortgaging may have occurred in Greece or farther east in Mesopotamia over two millennia ago (as discussed in Michael Hudson's and Winifred Rothenberg's chapters in this volume). There is no reason, though, to assume the mortgage, as recurring form of thought and practice, began in any identifiable time or place. Nor do the forms found in the Mediterranean and Eurasia in some of the "classical" literature correspond precisely to modern-day definitions or to the forms of mortgaging most common around the world today.[5]

In many parts of the world, the idea of the land mortgage has never been accepted as normal or natural, let alone ethical – in most of Africa south of the Sahara Desert, for instance – until quite lately. (Part of Ghana offers one of very few exceptions, with a longer tradition of land pledging – sometimes with pledges "redeemable" later in the case of loan default – as Sara Berry's chapter in this volume discusses.) In some traditions, and for long periods, the pawning or mortgaging of land has been considered more objectionable than the pawning of humans or debt bondage or only taken over gradually from it.[6] In some places, for instance in Eastern Europe, land mortgaging has come and gone, sometimes enacted in tentative trials, sometimes banned in abrupt revolutions.[7]

Mortgaging never sits easily for long in human collective conscience or whatever may pass for it. This much we can tell by the fact that so many of the world's most popular religions, including Judaism, Christianity, and Islam, have seen millennia of debate over issues like lending at "interest." To some, in most versions of Islam for instance, the loan profiting described by this gently oblique English term is deemed a sin second only to murder.[8] The moral scruples and uncertainties we can tell, too, by the shifting of authority over its regulations in Britain, for instance, where this responsibility over it has slid back and forth between church and state institutions and between royal and chancery (or equity) courts. In the United States, we have novels and movies about threatened farm families and tragic news of farming people, gone into debt and suddenly rendered landless and homeless.[9]

In the longer, wider view, the truth becomes clear enough. Humans have trouble coming to terms in any lasting way with the human invention of mortgaging. What Keith Hart has written of borrowing and lending – "social relations entailed in credit/debt are fraught with difficulty" (2000: 200) – is as true of the mortgage as of any other form; maybe well the most, since it tangles up money with material property and emotional senses of home and belonging.[10]

Mortgaging has spread around through trade and empire, and through economic, legal, and other textbooks from industrialized countries and societies. It continues to be pushed from inside the largest aid agencies (not least, still, by voices within the World Bank), with speeches, projects, and programs touting notions of modernity and progress. The theories and justifications implicit in these initiatives are reminiscent of nineteenth-century social evolutionism and mid-twentieth-century modernization theories – even while hotly debated within aid agencies where not everyone believes in all this.[11] Titling and mortgaging are held out together as a carrot to farmers by lenders and their agents, eager to create new markets and enhance production.[12] For most of those farming or living on that land, though, that sweet, crunchy treat will not soon nor easily materialize. This is because lenders often turn out to demand forms of guarantee other than land in addition, for instance salaries or co-signatures, for what they consider their own security. For those who do manage to mortgage their land, the process has pitfalls hard to foresee, over the shorter term or longer. Just as farming is not an easy occupation, mortgaging is not easy idea.

Mortgage and Metaphor: The Reach and the Elusive Grasp

Wherever mortgaging occurs, it seems to come with mystery. People have to struggle to find idioms to frame it, and metaphors to help understand it.[13] Here are just a few used in English:

(1) *existential* metaphors like "lifelines" and "deadlines," or "realized" assets;

(2) *somatic* ones like credit as the "lifeblood" of an economic system;
(3) *culinary* ones like loan "tranches" (installments) or "slicing and dicing" of aggregated loans. But it does not end there. There are
(4) *pneumatic* ones like "inflation" rates and "balloon mortgages" (ones with continuing interest charges, followed by a single, big lump payment of principal required at the end); and
(5) *aquatic* ones like loan "pooling," "upstream and downstream" effects in food economy, or bank "bailouts." And if those seem like they may come from the weekend lives of suburban New Yorkers, well, let us add "hedge funds";
(6) *emotional* metaphors, with "interest" used as a euphemism referring to protracted, temporally calculated gain by lender and loss by borrower;
(7) *architectural* or other spatial metaphors, as with "passageway" to prosperity or "foreclosure" to indicate a cutoff (or, to get back to somatics, a yank-back, not to say blockage that asphyxiates a borrower);
(8) *faunal* or pastoral metaphor, as in chattel (originally meaning cattle), which means movable, thus also seize-able and removable, property, or contracts with "rider" clauses, or, to change nature of the beast in question, the lately increasing concern with "predatory lending";
(9) *botanical* or floral metaphor, with roots for belonging, uprooting, or deracination, for eviction and homelessness, and for disorientation that can be not just spatial but also emotional.

Finally,

(10) *religious* evocation, with "grace periods" as temporary forgiveness, and, if all goes well, "redemption" as repayment or recovery.

Now, some of these metaphors are recursive with vague implied antecedents, like "reclaiming" or "repossessing" (as in the dreaded "repo man"). As we proceed further into abstraction come light and dark, with their moral overtones, with "shadow banking."

Note a marked tendency of lending officials to slide into semi-abstract legalese, using words like "collateral," "foreclosure," or "distraint," likely to be unfamiliar to anyone just learning English. (This, even without the spiritual overtones of "grace" or "redemption.") But critics of the mortgage and mortgaging, especially looking back at the physical dispossessions, the impoverishment, and the emotional, psychological, and physical distresses involved in foreclosure crises and threats thereof, are not so easily taken along with this kind of lingo. No, they tend instead to turn back to a more bodily, animalistic idiom of pursuit and carnivorous consumption: the "predatory lender" or even, in a more depersonalized but still somatic idiom, "predatory bureaucracy."

Communicating about mortgaging can be a challenge, then, tugging right to the limits of human ability and the bounds of belief. We shift between the metaphors, trying one and then another. Nor are these all the ways we try to bring it down to size, make it more comprehensible — far from it. The sheer variety of the associated metaphors is one more clue to the difficulty we humans have in understanding, communicating about, or agreeing upon this invention — let alone collectively controlling this uniquely human contrivance.

But which terms and metaphors we choose matters. Language can be loaded. At the most basic, a term like "property" can make exclusive possession sound, well, proper. Lenders euphemize profits as "interest," or passivize borrowers of money and mortgagors of land as "loan*ees*."[14] Whereas money lenders may speak of loan foreclosure as "realizing assets" or "repossession" (as if they had ever owned these in the first place), mortgagors may speak of it terms of "seizure," "invasion," or even "raiding."[15] One who sympathizes with borrowers can call lenders predators like hyenas, or parasites like guinea worms. One who sympathizes with lenders can call borrowers behind on repayments "delinquents," like juvenile thugs. One who cares about questions of belonging, and about the potential loss of home and traumatic shakeup of habitual experience, is likely to choose a botanical metaphor: to speak of rootedness and uprooting.[16] This is a field not just for desk clerks, accountants, and auctioneers, but also for poets and playwrights. Most of its players are somewhere in between, wondering just where right and authority are found. It is hard to know whether, as for many lawyers, truth consists of signatures on contracts; whether, as for many rural Native Americans or Africans, still and always in spoken oaths, witness words, truth-testing ordeals, and divinatory dreams; or, as for many economists, in aggregated numbers.

Or in none of them. The signatures, often enough in rural Africa, take the form of thumbprints, leaving it open to doubt whether the verbiage of the contracts was ever fully communicated in the first place. The words need translations, and the translations of English and Indo-European terms like loan, income, interest, freehold title, contract, or foreclosure (or their near translations in other Indo-European tongues) turn out, culturally, to be ironically parochial. Most of them only half translate into regional or local tongues — or even not at all. (You find this out fast when you have one person translate a word and another translate it back. Back translation: a powerful tool of cross-cultural investigation.) The witnesses can move away or die, or their memories alter with alcohol or age. Or with "chai," (the Swahili euphemism of tea used for bribery or other incentives sometimes in English called sweeteners — for Anglophones do it too). The numbers are always subject to translational problems in survey interviews and counts. Not all peoples everywhere, for instance, use base ten for counting. (Some, as in many Nigerian societies, have traditionally used use base twenty instead; that is, a base of not just fingers but fingers and toes.) Stats are also subject to manipulation: sample-projecting from local onto national or wider screen; guesswork of approximation; official re-editing and politically motivated fiddling; and, just as with words, sometimes plain old lying. Facts and figures are two different things, though there is always hope for an overlap.

Land itself can also be quite a personal thing, or a familial thing, given time. Then, where the land is inherited, as noted, there are issues of burial and graves to be considered. This can mean issues of spiritual presence too, as perceived by mortgagors or their kin or neighbors. But even without these, there may be specific uses of land, for instance for medicinal plants, thatching, or seasonal grazing, unknown or of little concern to lenders at a distance. Or agricultural uses knowable only by sowing a crop or tasting the soil.

Even the numbers are never really culture free, value-neutral, or objective. Most in lending institutions are trained to think of "interest" in terms of a rate, calculated per unit of time. But many others, including among farming people in Africa, think of interest more as ratio of interest to principal, with time bracketed out. Many in lending institutions imagine interest as a constant line or parabolic curve, while many people in rural farming areas assume interest increments for crop loans ought to be suspended between harvest seasons (when few may have income outside remittances or subsidiary shop earnings) and thus occur only stepwise, when the crops provide something to repay with.[17] What seems normal and natural, that is, depends on who you are, where you come from, and whether some sort of schooling ignored it, conflicted with it, or overrode it.

But farming seldom follows these formulaic schemas for long. Droughts, floods, crop plagues, and epizootic diseases occur in their own time. Where heavy rains wash out roads or new countries afar take up growing the local cash crops, markets disappear as well. Prices that might, in limited local markets, equilibrate as inverse supply and demand need not continue to do so when trade and transport span longer distances;

and this can come as a surprise to farming people who have invested their land and labor in a crop and gone into debt for it to a bank or a parastatal (state-owned but partly independent) lender. All of this constant adjusting and recalculating that farming requires makes repayment schedules of mortgage lenders look more and more abstract and artificial.

Then time poses its own problems. Some assume a deal is a deal for good; others assume the terms of an agreement ought to be renegotiable as circumstances of borrowers and lenders change, as though by an unwritten statute of limitations (if not just common-sense morality). In a twenty- or thirty-year mortgage — spanning a whole generation — a lot can change in circumstances. Not least where families on bounded lands can shrink or grow very large. (In most of rural Africa, for instance, with some of the world's fastest-growing populations.[18]) Lots could happen between now and the deadline to remove from the picture the debt, the currency value (e.g., hyperinflation or soft/hard currency policy changes), or even the lenders or enforcers.

Not to be forgotten are the psychological concerns related to perspective and habituation. Human minds are not like calculating machines, or not just. For young people, a thirty-year loan may seem an eternity (a lifetime or more); for older ones with more historical perspective, not so long. Loans with repayment dates distant in time can anyway seem smaller, more conditional, than ones near-term — just as a tree can do in our vision — even perhaps with added interest charges. For most of us, where belonging is concerned, our emotions about gains and losses are asymmetrical, in the sense that gaining extra cash or ground can be less of an event than losing a place or a home.[19] Also asymmetrical, in comparison with each other, are the emotions of lenders and those of borrowers, when it comes to home loss.[20] This hardly needs pointing out.

Or so one would think. Few of us humans, if denied a mortgage, would dream of migrating to another planet just to gain such a loan deal's advantages. On the other hand, consider this popular song, by Dave and Phil Alvin, released in 2015: "World's in a Bad Condition." Two of its key lines are the refrain: "I declare this whole world's in a bad condition" and then the line "I guess I better move," that is, to another planet. The other key line in the whole song? "The banker's goin' to get my home." The asymmetric emotions, as often, gush out in the fantasy. Even then, as hard as poets, writers, and singers have tried over time, it is hard for a work of imagination to express all the things home can mean or how much.

Putting some of these principles together, we can say that at least three principles are likely to recur in sequences and stories of mortgage.

Enticement, Entrustment, and Entrapment: Violence in Slow Motion?

First is enticement, where the lure of loans with immediate payoffs tempts farming people to accept titling and fencing schemes in the first place. Or to accept cropping programs planned from far away. And to borrow when they should not or more than they should. A part of the attraction of mortgaging, for money borrowers, is the pleasure of anticipation: not just of receiving the loan, but also of eventually – if all goes as hoped – owning the property once paid off. This anticipation has a powerful psychological, and also physiological, effect (involving dopamine and other hormones). This latter sort of effect is only beginning to be understood: that is, the topic still remains mostly within the confines of specialized neuropsychology, even if it affects the topics of many other disciplines, from agronomy to economics to philosophy.[21]

Second, and central, is entrustment, with counter-entrustment: most often cash (sometimes with seeds, fertilizer, and other things) in one direction, a title to land entrusted in the opposite direction as a conditional pledge. Implicit in the requirement of the counter-entrustment (or collateral) is a kind of mistrust (or distrust) too. One is trusted, that is, to use the loan as somehow expected, but not necessarily to pay it back without added inducement. Trust has been a central topic to philosophy and related disciplines for millennia; and exchange, to anthropology for over a century. But the kinds of transfers that can connect serial links of entrustment from rural to urban (as in money loans) and from one generation to the next (as in land inheritance), have in many parts of the world only recently begun to attain the kind of cultural and social study they deserve. Meanwhile, the economic planning processes organized from international agencies and national capitals keep steamrolling outward, based mainly on theoretical speculations about incentives, market forces, and their effects.

Third is entrapment, whether willful on the part of a lender or just circumstantial, when any of a variety of things goes wrong for the borrower and any dependents, repayment delays stretch beyond agreed limits – and both livelihood and home come into jeopardy. Entrapment is not necessarily the result of cunning, malice, or blind greed. It can be, instead or in addition, the road to hell paved with good intentions. It is a road that stretches from city to countryside, even from international metropole to deep bush. Along this road stretch chains of bosses watching over their subordinates, who may be as mindful of losing their jobs as of satisfying the needs of their borrowing clients and their thus indebted families.

They may be toeing lines of permission and tolerance, lines shifting or obscure, when they make hard decisions about whether to extend a loan and forestall a mortgage, or when or whether to set up an auction to turn over the land to a new buyer – and to try to forget about the old borrower and kin evicted from their farm and home.[22]

Mortgaging farmland, then, is a gamble, and a big one. At best, it can bring development, new enterprises, or investments (say, school fees and a uniform for Junior), and postponed or avoided hardship (for instance, pills or a hospital trip for Grandma). At worst, it brings a demoralizing, energy-draining burden, a disincentive to work, achieve, or invest. This is so since once having gone into debt, one is working not just for one's own self, kith, or kin, but for a lender who may not be held so dear.[23] It can mean debt, dispossession, and displacement: a kind of violence – starting out in slow motion but then a sudden jerk changes the game of life. If, that is, once home, livelihood, and health are lost, it even allows life to continue.

The burden of debt and the stress of impending home loss can bring their own consequences. Drugs and gang formation for drugs and/or violence (a quicker way of paying off debts, or maybe just of intimidating collectors?) are two most evident in cities but not just there.[24] Along other lines, desperate religious attempts at escape or purification in "revitalization" or world-renewal movements are another possibility. So too, of course, are family bust-ups and suicides. These and other side effects lead beyond this chapter, but they are no less realistic for it.

Mortgaging is a process with some cybernetic looping, causing feedback loops that operate in iterative fashion. This is how. A promise of loans can make landholders want to have their land titled. Titling land can raise its cash value. (Tenure seems more secure to a buyer.) Raising its cash value can make the land more tempting to mortgage. (With more valuable land, a borrower can get a bigger loan.) The mortgaging tends to mean gambling the land away. The newly more active land market tempts more lenders to come offering loans. And so a circle is completed.

Property and Improperty, in Longer View

And now, let us loop back to look more closely at our own terms. "Property" can have a kind of "*im*property" about it, once its story is known. "Titling" need not suggest a moral or ethical entitlement; indeed, it might deny someone's claim or entitlement as a dependent or a future claimant. "Secure tenure," as an individual title deed, can make a landholding more *in*secure, tempting its owner, as it has so often done, to gamble it away in a mortgage without consent or even knowledge of dependents. Loan "security" for a lender can be *in*security, of a most personal kind for a borrower who mortgages a farm with a home.

North American history offers some sobering insight into what mortgaging can do to people dependent on small-scale farming and living on the land they farm. We might begin, for instance, by noting that mortgaging played a major role in the losses of lands that Native American people experienced in colonial times. This has not yet been fully documented, but the role of mortgage lending in evicting Native American residents from their homes and land in what are now called New England and New York, for instance, has become strikingly clear, as it was occurring already by about the 1610s in Virginia and was rapidly underway the 1670s in Massachusetts, in what would later become New York, and elsewhere in the East Coast colonies. Often the dealings were mixed with alcohol sale and consumption, as well as new, unaccustomed currencies and paperwork (sometimes signed by borrowers with drawings of animals instead of names, raising for any historian questions about language, illiteracy, and comprehension of terms demanded and ostensibly agreed upon in contracts). All these factors made the calculations of hazard especially dangerous and risks of loss more severe for people becoming impoverished and at risk of over-borrowing, becoming indebted, and losing their land anyway in foreclosure.[25] Farther west, after European settlement rolled on, it would be the General Allotment Act (also called the Dawes Severalty Act) of 1887 that proved the major watershed event for Native peoples. It was this that gave them the right to own individual land titles outside of trust lands; but also, by the same token, to lose them in sales and mortgage foreclosures.

A recurring theme in studies of Native American relations with outsiders of European descent is the frequency of misunderstandings about whether permissions and privileges of land use, once granted or otherwise transferred, were expected to be permanent or whether they could be reclaimed, or the former users could at least expect to be able to come back and use the land and its products and animal inhabitants too. The idea of land permanently alienable by purchase and sale, let alone by conditional transfers like pledges or (deadlined) mortgages, does not appear in any case to have been a widespread or broadly accepted one. In the legal terms of our times, it is rather as though contracts of transfer had within them implied statutes of limitations – limitations in duration, if not also in kinds of use allowable by the recipients in the interim. And some deals, we can be sure, differed between their oral and verbal renderings, most often to the disadvantage of parties more accustomed to placing trust in spoken word or even in nonverbal communication.

These recountings can of course be hard to interpret, and a simple statement like "Indians assumed their transfers reversible, their rights inalienable" probably would not suffice as blanket generalizations, since humans anywhere can in various measures absorb and accommodate discrepant understandings and compartmentalize them in their dealings with people from different backgrounds, cultures, and educative influences than their own. It is not inconceivable, or even unlikely, that some Native Americans did in fact accept that their land losses would be permanent once a deal was done. (Some, after all, had had long experience in schools, or as travelers, slaves, or interpreters.) But the very differences in shared, habituated understandings as so commonly reported and the very ambiguities in contractual agreements contain a message of their own: those who said yes did not always just mean yes. In all, we can safely suppose that most Native American people signatories or parties directly consenting to land transfers like mortgages or, depending on persons so involved, were agreeing in writing or verbiage to eventualities to which they did not agree in long-established custom or principle, or to which they agreed only under coercion in blind influence of intoxicants or bribes or otherwise in desperation.

To more than a few Native Americans, thus, the permanent barring from their and their forebears' accustomed homes, hunting and gathering lands, and garden and farmlands came as a shocking surprise in their eventual enforcement or threatened enforcement. It was one they did not deem fair, or (again now in loosely translated terms) moral, just, or civil. Such common misunderstanding, and seeming betrayal, sometimes involved different implicit assumptions about permanent transferability, sometimes also trickery or ambiguity in translation, and in governmental and legal paperwork not mutually understood by the parties involved.[26] These tendencies – the clashes of accustomed assumptions; the ambiguities, inconsistencies, and hidden clauses in agreements; the assumptions of options to plead, swap, or buy one's way back to redeeming land claims, and agreed belonging – have all become recurring themes in other parts of the world in more recent times and up to the present. Not least in Africa south of the Sahara, a topic to which we will return.

Nor were Native American people the only ones losing homes, gardens, and farmland to mortgage foreclosure in the central and western states by the late 1800s. Far from it. The new Euro-American occupants of the plains states subjected themselves to mortgages over both the shorter term (a year or two) and longer (up to seven years or more, but rarely the thirty-year mortgages so common in recent times). Farmers borrowed from many sources, including not just banks and specialized mortgage companies (some operating from Europe) and their agents but also railroads (which had been granted land by federal government and allotted it in turn to homesteaders) and eventually insurance companies. It was common, too, for farmers to take out more than one mortgage loan, sometimes from different sources, and often to use one as a way of paying off another.

Trust a Mortgage?

Settlers' and new farmers' hopes rose high, fueled in part by the promotional campaigns of railroads, state governments, and travel writers, as well as by the forerunners of today's chambers of commerce. But droughts, plagues of insects, and other misfortunes took their toll, as did new competition in the form of farm imports from abroad as the railroads became established. The periodic recessions and financial crises of the late 1800s and early 1900s came across the countryside like scythes. The wrenching farm family stories coming to light in histories like Osha Davidson's *Broken Heartland* (1996) and David Danbom's *Sod-Busting* (2014) make the hardships of foreclosure clear, with all the emotions so absent from most economic and legal studies. So, too, do those in Kathryn Dudley's *Debt and Dispossession* (2002) on the loss of more highly mechanized family farms a century later.[27] Feelings of anguished anxiety, betrayal, and humiliation, often with oscillating feelings of hope and helplessness, and often causing family recriminations and breakups, typify these histories of loss and deracination.

Accusations against mortgagees – that is, moneylenders – could be bitter. In farmers' eyes these moneylenders tended, especially in the harder times, to be deemed not just unproductive people (in the ways farmers produced food and milk), but as hard-hearted parasites. Closer examination shows that these lenders varied greatly in their characters and intents, some of them seeming to have been quite sympathetic and patient with their chosen borrowers, and willing to extend loan durations on occasion. Most seem not in fact to have been eager to see the loans defaulted upon. Land was not that easy for financiers to hold as an asset – it was dead capital, for a while, requiring upkeep and tax payments until re-sold. So foreclosure and auctioning were, for many of these moneylenders and temporary title holders, more of a last resort, as Danbom points out, and some therefore accepted crops instead of cash payments

(2014: 67). Nor must it be forgotten that many of these financiers indeed went out of business too, just as family farmers and small traders did, in the harder times. If farming is a hard task, involving both skill and luck in large measure, so is farming in chronic debt and under the threat of dispossession and eviction. And so, indeed, can operating as a loan broker or agent extending money into the countryside from cities and foreign nations where they know or care little about what the farmers in their debt and their farm family dependents in turn are experiencing.

Especially in farming areas where mortgaging is a new or revived idea, such cautions might make suitable material for early education. Elsewhere, such stories have sometimes served the purpose in summer camp dramas, or in the 1881 ballad by Will Carleton (1845–1912), "The Tramp's Story," taught in the author's native Michigan. It tells of a farm lost by an ambitious, land-expanding farmer to a mortgage foreclosure. It ends with alcohol, a family that scatters, and a wife, who had warned against the mortgage, dying under stress and with a broken heart. "Worm or beetle – drought or tempest – on a farmer's land may fall / But for first-class ruination, trust a mortgage 'gainst them all" (Carleton 1881: 132).

Experience is mounting, in the study of mortgaging; but big unknowns and debatable issues remain. One is what sorts of people – as distinguished, say, by age, sex, education, and religious tradition – are most likely to make the prudent decisions about farming and finance involving mortgages, or inversely, to make the most easily predictable mistakes. Some feminist scholars, for instance, have acknowledged that women's interests are threatened by land titling that favors men; and in this and further ways, we note these threatened by eventual farm mortgaging (on Kenya, for instance, see Englert and Daley 2008; Pala Okeyo 1980; and Shipton 2009). But others remain hopeful that women's gaining of their own land titles will give women (especially widows in patrilineal, virilocal societies – that is, ones with kinship traced through males and with women who move to live with husbands upon marriage) a stronger claim to belonging in a place and a steadier foothold in economic life. Will women who remain threatened by poverty, or beset with heavy family financial duties, be given access to loans on land collateral when in possession of their own land titles? Or will the promise prove elusive? If they do gain loans by mortgage, do women prove more prudent than men have done? Or might pressing personal and family needs for cash eclipse the longer-term duties of repayment, inclining them to take risks much the way men do? How the balance shakes out – whether land titling tends to advance or retard women's interests in general once mortgaging is involved – remains open for further research and consideration; and the answers may vary widely by context.

At the time of this writing, the law and politics of Native American nations are now entering a phase where land mortgaging, reminiscent of the hard times of colonial New England and the nineteenth century in the plains states farther west, is rising up again as an issue for debate and likely trial solutions. Many lending agencies have been reluctant in recent decades to lend money to Native American people because of tangled issues of sovereignty and jurisdiction (tribe or Native Nation, state, and federal government in some ways overlapping or only in ad hoc agreements), among other old reasons like racial and religious discrimination.[28] Voices are speaking out, however, for more access to credit for those who want it in hitherto underprivileged areas and populations, and this includes Native people on reserves and trust lands as well as in cities. The issue is being perceived, then, as one of fairness as well as of any risk and prudence. It is too early even to guess the reach and outcome of policies in formulation, for instance under Section 184 of the Indian Home Loan Guarantee Program of the Department of Housing and Urban Development (guaranteeing lenders, that is, not borrowers!).[29] Many of the loans will be for urban or other housing rather than for farms. It is clear, though, that issues of debate arise, just as there have been issues heating up for over half a century in Africa south of the Sahara and other formerly colonized parts of the world where international development agencies have tried to introduce land markets, including provisions for sale and mortgage.

A prudent planner of land tenure, finance, and mortgage policies in parts of the world that have not yet tried farm mortgaging – as is the case in much of the tropics – ought certainly to take into account the histories of farm mortgaging now becoming better known in Europe and North America, where it has been tried in generations and centuries past. Sorting out which lessons transfer and apply abroad will not, admittedly, be a simple or easy task. The kinds of soils, rains, crops, and animals will not be constant in comparisons between continents. Rain-fed farming and farm neighborhoods will usually differ in important respects from ones with irrigation, especially larger-scale irrigation – this latter kind typically involves far more centralized control. People living in settings where the dead are buried around homes (as in much of rural Kenya for instance and many other parts of Africa south of the Sahara) will be likely to offer stiffer resistance to mortgage foreclosure and auctioning than those in places where bodily remains are disposed of elsewhere. Those in areas where Islamic (or elsewhere, Mormon) faith predominates are likely to offer more resistance to mortgage lending and interest charging than those elsewhere. But now it is time to sum up.

Mortgage and the Trauma Track

Some aspects of mortgage finance are likely to be relevant in more contexts than not. These include:

(1) Temptations to title land as private property as land becomes more densely settled. (This appeals to farmers and others interested in clarifying and sorting out competing claims; and it appeals to tenants and land clients who see potential for solidifying their rights to belong on the land. It also appeals to those planners wishing to establish a tax base — less often to the landholders likely to be taxed on that land.)

(2) Likely inequalities arising between holding sizes as some families grow in size and others contract. Further inequalities appearing in financial experience, literacy, and numeracy between borrowers and lenders.

(3) Different modes and conventions of reckoning time — with emphasis on linear and constant forms of time, as by clocks or calendars, or on forms more seasonal, cyclical, and dependent on fluky vicissitudes of nature.

(4) Promises of future mortgage loans as incentives for rural people to agree to land titling.

(5) Pressures from politicians favoring some rural areas over others, when it comes time to allocate loans, to foreclose on mortgages and evict, or to declare moratoria on such actions.

(6) Incentives for lenders to "package" debts for sale and resale in bulk, removing the authority for deciding about foreclosures (and thus over consequent evictions) farther away from the farms, farmers, and animals concerned.

(7) Trauma for land and home losers, and for others threatened with such losses. Sufferings can include not just dispossession, eviction, and resultant disorientation, but also family and community division. Effects can also include re-evaluation of life achievement and of self-worth, in some cases leading not just to depression but also to attempts at suicide. While formal and informal educational systems may warn against the possible hazards and harms of mortgaging and foreclosure, these may take generations to appear in

curricula or in instructive dramatic showings. The progress of this sort of pre-emptive schooling for youth has been lagging almost everywhere mortgaging is being tried, auguring poorly for future farmer decisions.

(8) Tendencies for family farms, once auctioned and sold, to be bought by wealthier farmers and companies, sometimes in repeated sales in turn. This process, while not inevitable (and not always or everywhere irreversible), leads eventually to a concentration of holdings into fewer hands. In flatter, less rocky areas, it also lends farming to easier mechanization, threatening the livelihood of not just family farmers but also hired laborers.

In one way and another, then, the story is likely to keep looking familiar.

Enticement, entrustment, entrapment. Violence in slow motion, even over generations, but with an abrupt jerk and eviction, variously likely to ensue and hard to predict. The meaning of such words has gained a new dimension in recent years, and in events current at the time of this writing. Workers and families who have shifted in the movement from agricultural or mixed livelihoods into industrial and mining occupations have learned by bitter experience that these are not as reliable as many once seemed. (Mechanization and global trade have together seen to that.) The promise once offered by steady year-round salaries and continuing employment in industry has proved illusory, evanescent, for many, and the hardships then involved have proved deep — as voters in closed-factory towns and shut-down mining communities made clear.[30] Hopes of broader progress through cash cropping, industrialization, and the rise of financial markets have often turned to a reality of glaring inequalities, in which the mortgaging system, indebtedness, evictions, and impoverishment have played interrelated parts.[31]

The risks of farming, and of crop and market failure, are serious enough without the added hazards of land loss that a mortgage system can add through possibilities of foreclosure, distraint, and eviction; or if not eviction, then reduction to wage labor or tenancy. Whichever way, it is too easy for farming people in a mortgage system to lose land inadvertently, or to have to sell in debt and desperation. The episode of the coronavirus of 2019 and the years following, bringing all sorts of economic activity to a slowdown or a dead halt in town, country, and in between, once again threw mortgaging farmers and other rural property holders into panic and desperation, in a story still playing out at the time of this writing. Nothing guarantees that lenders will forgive or extend deadlines for repayments when circumstances make it impossible for farming people to repay their loans. Once indebtedness becomes widespread, it may be that nothing short of mass proclamations like the legendary jubilees by royal decree to annul debts, as practiced in ancient times in Mesopotamia, is likely to provide a general solution for catastrophes like these. And maybe not even that.

This past century's history, with the hindsight of a few generations, has made two things clear. One is that family farming, while seldom easy, looks to be not so bad a basis for livelihood.[32] Another is that it is precarious enough without compounded risks that a mortgage system can represent. And history has made anything that threatens farming – as banks and borrowers do with mortgaging – seem especially dangerous in retrospect. Borrower, beware. For farming people, especially in rain-fed regions like most of Africa, banks and parastatal financial institutions have turned out safer for saving than for borrowing – at least where land as loan "security" is concerned. And the rest of us now can know, if we did not already, that the impoverishing, punishing repercussions of foreclosure reach well beyond the farm.

Parker Shipton is Professor of Anthropology and African Studies, Boston University. Educated at Cornell, Oxford, and Cambridge, he has taught at Harvard and consulted for several international aid agencies. His books include *Bitter Money*, *The Nature of Entrustment*, *Mortgaging the Ancestors*, and *Credit between Cultures*. He has edited the book series *Peoples of Africa* and the *Blackwell Anthologies in Social and Cultural Anthropology* and co-edited *On the Human*, an online interdisciplinary forum of the National Humanities Center. A former President of the Association for Africanist Anthropology, he has received the Messenger-Chalmers Prize (Cornell), Curl Prize (Royal Anthropological Institute), and African Studies Association (Herskovits) Book Award.

NOTES

This chapter is revised from a shorter publication, "Mortgaging Farmland: Violence in Slow Motion?" In *Mortgage Across Cultures: Land, Finance, Epistemology*, ed. Daivi Rodima-Taylor and Parker Shipton, 11–18. Boston: Boston University African Studies Center, 2017. For thoughtful comments on drafts, I thank Daivi Rodima-Taylor, our other conference participants in the "Mortgage across Cultures" workshop at Boston University, Michael Whyte, and the anonymous reviewers. I am also grateful to my student assistants Rosie Carter and Devon Moehlenkamp.

1. When first introduced to farm mortgaging, as an anthropologist in training and guest of an officer of the Caja Agraria, a national land and agriculture

bank, and later on the Guambía reservation of the indigenous Misak people, in highland Colombia, I had hardly an inkling of the complex cultural, political, and ethical issues the topic involves. Doctoral studies in the late 1970s and early 1980s and later ethnographic research on credit and debt, entrustment and obligation, took me to live in rural western Kenya; and later research on the topics returned me there and to the Gambia. During the 1980s and early 1990s I also consulted on land and financial issues intermittently for aid agencies, especially the World Bank, on my own and later on Harvard University's behalf. Since then, briefer visits from my Boston University base back to Kenya and to Native North American reservations in the Pacific Northwest have helped keep me in touch with land issues – and accumulating more debts of gratitude to hosts and helpers at every stage.

2. A history of racial exploitation and discrimination over several centuries has divided northern Andeans in Colombia into types including large valley-based landholders (*latifundistas*), small-scale indigenous farming people (mostly *minifundistas*, living with animals on often steep mountainsides), descendants of formerly enslaved African-American people, and people intermittently fighting and killing over the differences (as well as over drug production and commerce, to which some have had to turn in desperation for a living).

3. *Typee*, an immediate sales success, remained Melville's most popular novel until the 1930s, when the long-sleeping *Moby-Dick*, written some eighty years earlier, rose to the surface of readers' interest and overtook it.

4. Please see my other chapter in this volume, "When Land Takes Wing," on human-animal connections involved.

5. On variants in ancient Mesopotamia, see Michael Hudson in this volume and Michael Hudson and Baruch Levine (1996, 1999). On forms of land mortgaging or its likeness in ancient Greece, see Moses Finley (1952) and other chapters in the present volume. See also Max Weber's sweeping comparative summary on the customs and political economy of farming in what he deemed the ancient world (1998). In each case, though, problems of language and area-specific convention, if not also of period context, render translation as "mortgaging" at least somewhat problematic.

6. On the long and widespread practice of human pawning in Africa, for instance, see Paul Lovejoy and Toyin Falola (2003). Often it has been elders pawning juniors, and males pawning females, for instance in marriage promises or pledges to wealthier, more senior males in hard times. While this can sometimes seem to outsiders callous or cruel, it is not always so clear whether it is more so than the pledging or mortgaging of land, whose occupants (of whatever age, gender, or state of dependency) may together stand to lose it for generations to come.

7. See Stefan Dorondel, Daivi Rodima-Taylor, and Marioara Rusu, in this volume, for discussion of East European and Asian socialist revolutions and post-socialist reforms and their bearing on mortgaging. For broader, longer-term discussions of property transitions – from public to private (or collective to individual) and vice versa – see Alain de Janvry, Gustavo Gordillo, Elizabeth Sadoulet, and Jean-Philippe Platteau (2001); Andro Linklater (2015). (Note: Of course, private need not mean individual only. It can also mean small or

medium-sized collectivities, as in land registration in the name of a family or neighborhood.) Many variously wide-ranging studies on mortgaging elsewhere focus mainly on housing and on town and city property, rather than on farmland. See, for instance, Danny Ben-Shahar, Charles Ka Yui Leung, and Seow Eng Ong (2008); Matthew Desmond (2016). And for recurrent "financial follies" (overborrowing, overlending, and related problems), such as came to light in the 2008 and 2020 financial meltdowns in North America and elsewhere, but over many centuries, see Cihan Bilginsoy (2015); Neil Harl (1991, on the 1980s); Reinhart and Rogoff (2011); and Brett Williams (2005).

8. Some of these historical and ethical issues are discussed in Parker Shipton (2009), especially in a comparative survey of literature in chapter 2, which serves as background for the book's more focused discussions on the Luo-speaking and other people of western Kenya and that nation's land titling and mortgaging. For some sweeping debates about the moral propriety of interest, usury, and the mortgage in some Christian traditions, see Benjamin Nelson (1969), especially on medieval and Renaissance ones; and Peter Selby (2009) on more modern ones. For cultural and social perspectives on contemporary Islamic schools and debates relating to mortgaging, interest, and risk logic, see, for instance, Bill Maurer (2006); Daromir Rudnyckyj (2014).

9. For cinematic treatments of mortgage foreclosure threats and their emotional and other effects, see, for instance, *Country* (1984), directed by Richard Pearce; *The River* (1984), directed by Mark Rydell; *Places in the Heart* (1984), directed by Roger Benton; and *Troublesome Creek: A Midwestern* (1995), directed by Jeanne Jordan and Steven Ascher. More recent treatments, as in the feature film titled *The Big Short* (2015), directed by Adam McKay, on the 2007–2008 mortgage market meltdown in the United States, underscore the recurring point about home loss, as differently felt from near and far, or as experienced in person versus on paper or cyber-screen. But it may be easy for viewers to confuse causes and effects of economic changes. At least one respected economist has suggested that the "subprime" mortgage "bubble," egregious predatory lending, ignored risk, unregulated derivatives, and mortgage defaults together made up a less important cause of the "global recession" in economy than commonly supposed by other economists. Instead, he argues that the "mortgage meltdown," while indeed real and extremely damaging to many, was more an effect of the broader recession and of resulting panic. He further suggests that that the "'Great' Recession" of 2007–2008 was less damaging than some previous ones (see Kotlikoff 2018). Evidence behind these latter claims cannot be judged here, but all can agree the mortgage made its downside widely felt in that historic episode.

10. Keith Hart's book also offers thought-provoking comments on trust in economic life more generally.

11. For critiques of social evolutionist theories as applied to land tenure in Africa, see Jean-Philippe Platteau (1996); Parker Shipton (2009). For a broader, philosophical critique of related ideas of property as evolutionary progress (reminiscent of countless other, anthropological critiques since the time when Lewis Henry Morgan wrote on savagery, barbarism, and civilization as a continuum in the 1870s), see David Schorr (2018). For an important cultural-

political critique of the notion of state and urban central government control of economic and other matters as "progress" (using southeastern Asian case material), see James Scott 2009.
12. It would not be fair or accurate to accuse all lenders in development projects of seeking interest profits for themselves or their institutions. Some of the loans, including ones from under the auspices of the World Bank (and especially the International Development Association [IDA] within it) and some from lenders operating as agents of grant programs of the US Agency for International Development, have occurred on concessionary terms. These include loans with no interest charges or with interest rates below rates of local or foreign currency inflation. This is not to deny that some loan and mortgage program supporters in the name of aid have held or hidden other economic self-interest at times, as in promoting particular crops, tools, or chemicals prescribed or, in the cases of some bank and government officials, potential interests in the land itself or profits from its sale. Or, at an extreme, keeping people content to stay put and not migrate abroad to donor or lender countries.
13. The roles of "framing" and metaphor in not just ordinary human communication – not just poetry and other self-conscious arts – but in thought more generally, including the large majority of it that occurs unconsciously, is a central theme in the influential work of George Lakoff and Mark Johnson (see for instance Lakoff and Johnson 1980; Lakoff 1990). They emphasize the groundedness of metaphor in personal experience, its cultural variation, and its importance for understanding and acting upon difficult or abstract concepts. Fauconnier and Turner (2002) elaborate further on conceptual framing and blending and their central functions in human thought. No one to my knowledge, however, has yet systematically studied the use of metaphors in communications about mortgages and mortgaging – or, a next step, done so across languages and cultures.
14. In these pages I follow convention in using the word "loan" and "lender" to refer to the money part of a mortgage transaction. Strictly speaking, though, the loan of a land title in compensation (often called "collateral") could be called a loan (or counter-loan) in itself.
15. This last one I have sometimes heard voiced in the country of the Luo ethnic group in Kenya. In these people's language, DhoLuo, a word they use for takeover after foreclosure is *peyo*, to raid. It is sometimes by listening to a people new to or only recently exposed to the idea of mortgaging and foreclosure, as to a people like Native North American people whose forebears suffered tragically by it soon after entering the tradition, that one can learn sentiments that sometimes get buried by office paper language or academic locution. (Imagery like the paper blizzard's blanketing, in Louise Erdrich's novel *Tracks,* about Native Ojibwe [Anishinaabe] land loss in the northern midwestern United States, comes to mind.) On the role of land titling (in the names of individuals) in the tragic loss of Native American lands from 1887 onward, see also Delos Sacket Otis and Francis Paul Prucha (1973); Francis Paul Prucha ([1984] 1986, 2000); Wilcomb Washburn (1986). Also, as everyone knows, feelings about troubling truths sometimes emerge through song, or

are voiced by fictional or mythic surrogates, when direct talk or written prose fails to convey them or seems too risky.

16. The terminology is not always stable over time, however. Evidence from a sample of fourteen California homeowners who lost their built places of residence upon foreclosure shows that they tended to refer to these, during that process, as their "home," but later only as the "house," and to start dissociating the lost property from their own personal identities, achievements, and failures – shifting idiom or focus, all as if to bury or trivialize the trauma or rationalize the loss (see Gross 2008).

17. The remarks here, and more generally in this chapter, apply more often to rain-fed than to irrigated farming, whose conditions may be more constant. Even in irrigated perimeters, though, problems like flooding and longer-term soil salinization – to say nothing of market price fluctuations caused from afar – can add hazards to mortgaging. And large-scale irrigation entails its own issues of centralized political control, sometimes becoming oppressive along gender lines as well. This is to say nothing of snail-borne and mosquito-borne diseases, which also can accompany irrigation flooding.

18. Book-length histories and ethnographies of mortgagor experience in Africa remain uncommon. One example, though, is a historical treatment (Murray 2002) on a rural South African neighborhood. Another is a historical ethnography (Shipton 2009) on land titling and mortgaging among Luo speakers and others in western Kenya. These are situated in comparison with colonial and aid agency policies, whose authors and implementers are also studied for their own perspectives. These sometimes prove radically different from, and often incommensurable with, those of their intended beneficiaries, as they often call them. Issues like the presence of ancestral graves, abandoned houses, and valued cattle enclosures on the land in question can be crucial points of contention when creditors attempt foreclosure and auction, as in the western Kenyan case. On the earlier history of the Kenyan land tenure "reform," with a focus on central Kenya, see Maurice P. K. Sorrenson (1967). For broader comparisons involving colonialism, racial discrimination (indeed, often racism), and land tenure variations as a combined topic, see the rather fiery historical critique in Brenna Bhandar (2018).

19. Dudley's study of farming people in Minnesota (2002) vividly examines the often devastating emotional and social effects of foreclosure and farm loss, even where ancestral graves and associated spirits are not involved (as they are often deemed to be in rural Africa). The "Heartland" in her subtitle suggests a double entendre, just as in Osha Gray Davidson's title *Broken Heartland*. See Noelle Stout's *Dispossessed* (2019) for a vivid, disturbing description and analysis of the effects of the housing foreclosure crisis in the Sacramento Valley of California in the early 2000s, an area hard hit where she had grown up and where she researched it for two years at the time. This source is unusual in its shifts in perspective, based upon interviews with both borrowers and lenders. Stout describes the emotional responses, rationalizations, and attempted concessions of lenders who sense themselves (or in some cases fear themselves) in relationships of trust and reciprocity with their borrow-

ers, when the handed-down algorithms of calculation used for determining "modification" (or forbearance) in collection and distraint tend to deny these. See also Allan Bogue (1955) and Danbom (2014) on home and farm mortgaging and foreclosures in the midwestern and western states in the nineteenth and early twentieth centuries, John Clarke (2001) on the western frontier of Canada, and Soederberg (2018). Many social workers and psychotherapists, of course, also have something to say on trauma associated with mortgaging, foreclosure, and eviction.

20. The asymmetry of human emotions about gain and loss, as a corrective to older theories of utility, has been an important theme in economic psychology (and experimental economics), famously brought to the fore since the late 1970s by research by Daniel Kahneman and Amos Tversky (see, for instance, Kahneman 2011). Experimental psychologists and economists continue to explore this and related topics of trust in lab experiments, and in game situations introduced in field settings (Cook, Levi, and Hardin 2009; Ostrom and Walker 2003). But much research remains to be done on the emotions, risk and reward predictions, temptations, and avoidances of mortgagors and mortgagees, not just as individuals but also as families, communities, and cultures. For evidence on how widely cultural ideas about mathematics (as presumptions and preferences) can vary, see Susan Ascher (1991).

21. See Robert Sapolsky (2017: 70–77) for a summary of recent findings on the endocrinal effects of anticipated rewards, particularly in dopamine release (the "hub of reward, anticipation, and motivation" [2017: 77]), from multiple brain regions (2017: 64), conditioned too by serotonin as another neurotransmitter. Genetic variation (though probably not just through any single gene) gives rise to varied human propensities to risk-taking and avoidance, socially conditioned and triggered in turn by individual experience. This subject relates to the addictive effects of gambling: not an irrelevant concern where farm yields are as risky as they often are in rain-fed settings. In its own way, undeniably, taking a mortgage in such a setting is gambling.

22. Some of the more instructive findings on these moral-practical dilemmas, doubts, and guilt feelings of lending and collecting agents – people under scrutiny from higher-ups in their organizations – are described in Stout's (2019) and other works based on the 2007–2008 economic "meltdown" in the United States. Even where loans and mortgages do not involve farms, graves, or ideas about related ancestral spirits (as they do, all of these, in much of rural Africa), these empathic and sympathetic feelings and emotional conflicts can be intense. See also Barbara Gross (2008) for cognitive-emotional adjustments, including about self-esteem and self-worth, made by borrowers interviewed after foreclosure and eviction.

23. For clarifying to me this important point I thank the late Momodou Sanyang, a Gambian small-scale farmer of long experience. Of course, debts to mortgage lenders are not the only ones that farming people must be concerned with, or necessarily the most meaningful or personally pressing. Elsewhere (Shipton 2007, 2009, 2010), for East Africans in western Kenya and others, I have sought to describe the role of loans and debts – with and without land involved – among wider entrustments and obligations, some lasting over generations.

24. Nor is it just at a small scale that principles like these can operate. Debt can relate directly to larger-scale violence and even war, as cause or effect. World War II, by one of many interpretations, was sparked in part by debts incurred by both winners and losers of World War I (temptations for either to plunder resources), and by punitive measures for the losers that further humiliated them. For discussions and conjectures about some other far-reaching effects of debt upon human lives, communities, and environments, see Peter Selby (2009: chapter 5) and David Graeber (2014); see also Graeber (2016) on bureaucracy.
25. On the many varieties of credit, debt, and barter, and also cash, in colonial-period Massachusetts, especially at the turn of the eighteenth century, see James Wadsworth 2017. On Native American land losses through mortgaging in colonial New England, see K-Sue Park (2016). On Mohican, Mohawk, Dutch settlers, and others in the period, across the Hudson in what would become present-day upstate New York, see Shirley Dunn (2000: 98–124; 1995); and on Native-colonist land struggles in the eastern colonies more generally, Daniel Richter (2013). On Virginia in the 1600s, see John Rolfe ([1616] 1951). On the move to private individual titling (here called allotment, as in the watershed General Allotment Act or "Dawes Severalty Act," 1887) that opened three decades of precipitous land loss for native people nationwide but especially the Midwest and West, much of it again via unaccustomed mortgages, debts, and foreclosures when not leases or outright sales, see Delos Sacket Otis and Francis Paul Prucha (1973); Francis Paul Prucha (1986, 2000); Wilcomb Washburn (1986). This followed the earlier mass shoving of most groups of indigenous people from east of the Mississippi westward in the "Trail of Tears" episode of the 1830s and then a series of treaties restricting their lands to reservations in the 1850s. Altogether it is a story with few happy episodes, fewer still involving mortgaging.
26. When Native American people speak of "repossession," they are as likely to be speaking of ending "barbed wire colonialism" and of regaining a respectful relationship with land and human ties to it, as they are of mortgage lenders' yanking their homes or their cars from around them. See, for instance, Badsalishheart. "Barbed Wired Colonialism." *Badsalishgirl*, 26 April 2018. Retrieved 26 June 2018 from https://badsalishgirl.wordpress.com/2018/04/26/barbed-wired-colonialism/.
27. A somewhat more sanguine view of farm mortgage history in the western United States, focusing on named companies, bank managers, and regulators, can be found in Michael Rosser and Diane Sanders (2017).
28. These are now matters of US law under the Equal Credit Opportunity Act, since 1976. New regulations have arisen too under the Consumer Financial Protection Bureau, created after the financial crisis of the 2000s decade under the Wall Street reform and Consumer Protection Act (the Dodd Frank Act).
29. For broad financial, managerial, and legal overviews of the new mortgaging issues and policies arising for Native American-held homes and lands, see David Listokin, Kenneth Temkin, Nancy Pindus, David Staneck, and the Urban Institute (2017) and Abby Hogan (2020). See also Sharlene Round Face (2016). Beyond lending under the HUD Section 184 Indian Home Loan Guarantee Program, other credit comes into question under the US Department of Agricul-

ture RHS Section 502 Direct Loan Program and the Veterans Administration Native American Veteran Direct Loan Program.
30. As is well known, in shut-down mining and industrial centers, as well as eviction-thinned farming communities, a promise and a widely shared, stretched reach for hope, which many would later learn were vain and illusory, occurred in the 2016 US presidential and related political elections.
31. For his famously broad and influential statistical pictures of the rise of financial and economic inequalities in twentieth- and twenty-first-century Europe, North America, and elsewhere, see Piketty ([2014] 2017, 2020).
32. Robert Netting (1993) provides a wide comparative survey of family farming on several continents, offering reasons for both its longevity and its distribution as a mode of human livelihood. Its lessons are to be taken seriously in an era of new land titling and mortgaging; of new waves of land requisition or land-grabbing, taking forms personal, political, and institutional; and of discontent among persons in town and country who have been left short of places to live and to farm. Much research remains to be done on the effects of mortgaging, foreclosure, and evictions of small-scale farmers on the establishment of larger-scale plantation agriculture, with all the worker subjugation and sometimes enslavement or lately more often quasi-enslavement that the latter can involve.

REFERENCES

Ascher, Susan. 1991. *Ethnomathematics: A Multicultural View of Mathematical Ideas*. Pacific Grove, CA: Brooks/Cole.
Ben-Shahar, Danny, Charles Ka Yui Leung, and Seow Eng Ong. 2008. *Mortgage Markets Worldwide*. Oxford: Blackwell.
Bhandar, Brenna. 2018. *Colonial Lives of Property: Law, Land, and Racial Regimes of Ownership*. Durham, NC: Duke University Press.
Bilginsoy, Cihan. 2015. *A History of Financial Crises: Dreams and Follies of Expectations*. New York: Routledge.
Bogue, Allan G. 1955. *Money at Interest: The Farm Mortgage on the Middle Border*. Lincoln: University of Nebraska Press.
Carleton, Will. 1881. "The Tramp's Story." In *Farm Festivals*, 127–32. Retrieved 3 March 2021 from http://name.umdl.umich.edu/BAE8956.0001.001.
Clarke, John. 2001. *Land, Power, and Economics on the Frontier of Upper Canada*. Montreal: McGill-Queen's University Press.
Cook, Karen S., Margaret Levi, and Russell Hardin, eds. 2009. *Whom Can We Trust?* New York: Russell Sage Foundation.
Danbom, David B. 2014. *Sod Busting: How Families Made Farms on the 19th-Century Plains*. Baltimore, MD: Johns Hopkins University Press.
Davidson, Osha Gray. 1996. *Broken Heartland: The Rise of America's Rural Ghetto*. Iowa City: University of Iowa Press.
de Janvry, Alain, Gustavo Gordillo, Elizabeth Sadoulet, and Jean-Philippe Platteau, eds. 2001. *Access to Land, Rural Poverty, and Public Action*. Oxford: Oxford University Press.

Desmond, Matthew. 2016. *Evicted: Poverty and Profit in the American City*. New York: Penguin Random House.
Dudley, Kathryn Marie. 2002. *Debt and Dispossession: Farm Loss in America's Heartland*. Chicago: University of Chicago Press.
Dunn, Shirley W. 1995. *The Mohicans and Their Land, 1609–1730*. Fleischmanns, NY: Purple Mountain Press.
———. 2000. *The Mohican World, 1680–1750*. Fleischmanns, NY: Purple Mountain Press.
Englert, Birgit, and Elizabeth H. Daley, eds. 2008. *Women's Land Rights & Privatization in Eastern Africa*. Woodbridge, Suffolk, UK: James Currey.
Erdrich, Louise. 1988. *Tracks*. New York: Henry Holt.
Fauconnier, Gilles, and Mark Turner. 2002. *The Way We Think: Conceptual Blending and the Mind's Hidden Complexities*. New York: Basic Books.
Finley, Moses. 1952. *Studies in Land and Credit in Ancient Athens, 500–200 B.C.: The Horos Inscriptions*. New Brunswick, NJ: Rutgers University Press.
Graeber, David. 2014. *Debt: The First 5,000 Years*. New York: Melville House.
———. 2016. *Utopia of Rules: On Technology, Stupidity, and the Secret Joys of Bureaucracy*. New York: Melville House.
Gross, Barbara. 2008. "The Experience of Home Foreclosure: Coping with Involuntary Loss of Home and Transition of Identity." In *European Advances in Consumer Research*, vol. 8, ed. Stefania Borghini, Mary Ann McGrath, and Cele Otnes, 87–93. Duluth, MN: Association for Consumer Research.
Harl, Neil E. 1991. *The Farm Debt Crisis of the 1980s*. Oxford: Wiley-Blackwell.
Hart, Keith. 2000. *Money in an Unequal World*. New York: Texere.
Hogan, Abby. 2020. "Mortgage Lending on Tribal Lands: Federal Fair Lending Protections, Public-Private Partnerships, and Tribal Solutions for Increasing Access to Mortgage Credit on Tribal Lands." *American Indian Law Journal* 9(1), article 3. http://digitalcommons.law.seattleu.edu/ailj/vol9/iss1/3.
Hudson, Michael, and Baruch Levine, eds. 1996. *Privatization in the Ancient Near East and Classical World*. Peabody Museum Bulletin 5. Cambridge, MA: Peabody Museum of Archaeology and Anthropology, Harvard University.
———. 1999. *Urbanization and Land Ownership in the Ancient Near East*. Peabody Museum Bulletin 7. Cambridge, MA: Peabody Museum of Archaeology and Anthropology, Harvard University.
Kahneman, Daniel. 2011. *Thinking, Fast and Slow*. New York: Farrar, Straus and Giroux.
Kotlikoff, Laurence J. 2018. "The Big Con: Reassessing the 'GREAT' Recession and its 'Fix.'" Boston, MA: Institute for Economic Development at Boston University, Discussion Paper 311.
Lakoff, George. 1990. *Women, Fire, and Dangerous Things: What Categories Reveal about the Mind*. Chicago: University of Chicago Press.
Lakoff, George, and Mark Johnson. 1980. *Metaphors We Live By*. Chicago: University of Chicago Press.
Linklater, Andro. [2013] 2015. *Owning the Earth: The Transforming History of Land Ownership*. New York: Bloomsbury.
Listokin, David, Kenneth Temkin, Nancy Pindus, David Staneck, and the Urban Institute. 2017. *Mortgage Lending on Tribal Land: A Report from the Assessment of*

American Indian, Alaska Native, and Native Hawaiian Housing Needs. Prepared for Department of Housing and Urban Development, Washington, DC.

Lovejoy, Paul, and Toyin Falola, eds. 2003. *Pawnship, Slavery, and Colonialism in Africa*. Trenton, NJ: Africa World Press.

Maurer, Bill. 2006. *Pious Property: Islamic Mortgages in the United States*. New York: Russell Sage Foundation.

Melville, Herman. [1848] 1994. *Typee* [Orig.: Typee: A Peep at Polynesian Life]. Ware, Hertfordshire, England: Wordsworth Editions Ltd.

Murray, Colin. 1992. *Black Mountain: Land, Class and Power in the Eastern Orange Free State*. Edinburgh: University of Edinburgh Press.

Nelson, Benjamin. 1969. *The Idea of Usury: From Tribal Brotherhood to Universal Otherhood*. Chicago: University of Chicago Press.

Netting, Robert McC. 1993. *Smallholders, Householders: Farm Families and the Ecology of Intensive, Sustainable Agriculture*. Stanford, CA: Stanford University Press.

Ostrom, Elinor, and James Walker, eds. 2003. *Trust and Reciprocity: Interdisciplinary Lessons from Experimental Research*. New York: Russell Sage Foundation.

Otis, Delos Sacket, and Francis Paul Prucha. 1973. *The Dawes Act and the Allotment of Indian Lands*. Norman: University of Oklahoma Press.

Pala Okeyo, Achola. 1980. "Daughters of the Lakes and Rivers: Colonization and the Land Rights of Luo Women." In *Women and Colonization: Anthropological Perspectives*, ed. Mona Etienne and Eleanor Leacock, 196–213. New York: Praeger.

Park, K-Sue. 2016. "Money, Mortgages, and the Conquest of America." *Law and Social Inquiry* 41(4): 1006–35.

Piketty, Thomas. [2014] 2017. *Capital in the Twenty-first Century*. Cambridge, MA: Belknap (Harvard University Press).

———. 2020. *Capital and Ideology*. Cambridge, MA: Belknap (Harvard University Press).

Platteau, Jean-Philippe. 1996. "The Evolutionary Theory of Land Rights as Applied to Sub-Saharan Africa: A Critical Assessment." *Development and Change* 27: 29–86.

Polanyi, Karl. [1944] 1957. *The Great Transformation: The Political and Economic Origins of Our Time*. Boston: Beacon.

Prucha, Francis Paul. [1984] 1986. *The Great Father: The United States Government and the American Indians*. Lincoln: University of Nebraska Press.

———. 2000. *Documents of United States Indian Policy*. Lincoln: University of Nebraska Press.

Reinhart, Carmen, and Kenneth S. Rogoff. 2011. *This Time is Different: Eight Centuries of Financial Folly*. Princeton, NJ: Princeton University Press.

Richter, Daniel K. 2013. *Trade, Land, Power: The Struggle for Eastern North America*. Philadelphia: University of Pennsylvania Press.

Rodima-Taylor, Daivi, and Parker Shipton, eds. 2017. *Mortgage across Cultures: Land, Finance, and Epistemology*. Boston: Boston University African Studies Center and Center for Finance, Law, and Policy.

Rolfe, John. [1616] 1951. *A True Relation of the State of Virginia Lefte by Sir Thomas Dale Knight in May Last 1616*. New Haven, CT: Yale University Press.

Rosser, E. Michael, and Diane M. Sanders. 2017. *A History of Mortgage Banking in the West: Financing America's Dream.* Boulder: University of Colorado Press.

Round Face, Sharlene M. 2016. "Leasing & Mortgages on Tribal Land: A General Overview Prepared for the 2016 CDIC." Bureau of Indian Affairs, U.S. Department of the Interior.

Rudnyckyj, Daromir. 2014. "Economy in Practice: Islamic Finance and the Problem of Market Reason." *American Ethnologist* 41(1): 110–27.

Sapolsky, Robert. 2017. *Behave: The Biology of Humans at Our Best and Worst.* New York: Penguin.

Schorr, David. 2018. "Savagery, Civilization, and Property: Theories of Societal Evolution and Commons Theory." *Theoretical Inquiries in Law* 19: 507–31.

Scott, James C. 2009. *The Art of Not Being Governed: An Anarchist History of Upland Southeast Asia.* New Haven, CT: Yale University Press.

Selby, Peter. 2009. *Grace and Mortgage: The Language of Faith and the Debt of the World.* London: Darton, Longman & Todd.

Shipton, Parker. 2007. *The Nature of Entrustment: Intimacy, Exchange, and the Sacred in Africa.* New Haven, CT: Yale University Press.

———. 2009. *Mortgaging the Ancestors: Ideologies of Attachment in Africa.* New Haven, CT: Yale University Press.

———. 2010. *Credit Between Cultures: Farmers, Financiers, and Misunderstanding in Africa.* New Haven, CT: Yale University Press.

Soederberg, Susanne. 2018. "Evictions: A Global Capitalist Phenomenon." *Development and Change* 49(2): 286–301. https://doi.org/10.1111/dech.12383.

Sorrenson, Maurice P. K. 1967. *Land Reform in the Kikuyu Country.* Nairobi: Oxford University Press.

Stout, Noelle. 2019. *Dispossessed: How Predatory Bureaucracy Foreclosed on the Middle Class.* Berkeley: University of California Press.

Wadsworth, James, ed. 2017. *The World of Credit in Colonial Massachusetts: James Richards and His Daybook, 1692–1711.* Amherst: University of Massachusetts Press.

Washburn, Wilcomb E. 1986. *The Assault on Indian Tribalism: The General Allotment Law (Dawes Act) of 1887.* Malabar, FL: R. E. Krieger.

Weber, Max. 1998. *The Agrarian Sociology of Ancient Civilizations.* London: Verso. Orig. pub. 1896, 1909 (parts), 1924 (complete).

Williams, Brett. 2005. *Debt for Sale: The Social History of the Credit Trap.* Philadelphia: University of Pennsylvania Press.

CHAPTER 2

 A Brief Legal and
Social History of Mortgage

DAVID J. SEIPP

Probably in every time and place where an individual current possessor of land has had the ability to sell that land – free of the claims of family members, social superiors, or others – the current possessor has had the power to borrow money by putting up the land itself as a pledge or security for repayment of the loan. In past centuries, such arrangements were extreme last resorts when all other resources and recourses had been exhausted, and even then were usually transacted with lenders already known personally to the borrowers. The characteristics that became much more common since the first half of the nineteenth century are the expectation that nearly every land-holding individual will use such an arrangement, the impersonality of the transaction, and its regular and ordinary use for the initial purchase of housing.

Jewish law, Roman law, and other early legal systems recognized arrangements that can be compared to the mortgage (Wigmore 1897). This brief account will skip to the first such arrangement to be given the name "mortgage" in England. Mortgage is the term used in English law and in legal systems derived from English law for the practice of pledging land as security for repayment of a loan (see Barton 1967: 237). The word was in use from at least the late twelfth century. It derives from *mort-* meaning dead and *-gage* meaning pledge (Littleton1903: 156–57). A mortgage or dead pledge was distinguished from a *vifgage* or living pledge (Blackstone 1766; Hazeltine 1904a: 552). In a living pledge, the produce of the land went to the lender in gradual repayment of the loan (Hazeltine 1904a: 552). In a mortgage, the produce of the land did not reduce the principal of the loan, the borrower usually stayed in possession, and the borrower was personally responsible for paying off the loan from whatever sources he or she could use (Hall 1965: 121). The mechanics of using land as security for repayment of a loan of money could take various forms. Three forms used at various times in England are worth mentioning.

First, in thirteenth-century England a mortgage could take the form of a lease (Hazeltine 1904a: 552–53, 556). The borrower would grant the lender possession of the borrower's land for a term of years, often seven years (Littleton 1903: 157). The lender would take the profits of the land for the period of years (see Barton 1967: 238). If the borrower did not repay the loan, the lender would take full, permanent ownership of the land (Hall 1965: 121). The lease therefore contained a condition that if the loan had not been repaid during the term of years, ownership of the land would transfer permanently to the lender.[1]

In this early lease form of mortgage, profits from the land that went to the lender provided an equivalent of interest on the loan, although taking interest (called "usury") was officially forbidden (Hazeltine 1904a: 552). Jewish moneylenders were permitted to receive interest from Christian borrowers. It was said that Jews in England were forbidden to own agricultural land, but the ban did not prevent the pledging of land as security for loans from Jews (see Richardson 1960: 83–85, 103). When Christian borrowers did not repay their loans, such land could be and was forfeit to Jewish moneylenders (Hazeltine 1904b: 46–50). It has been suggested that leases were categorized as an interest of lower status than "freehold," that is, life-long or inheritable ownership, because of their connection with moneylenders' security interests in land (see Richardson 1960: 84–86, 108). Jews were expelled from England in 1290 and did not return until the mid-seventeenth century.

A second form of mortgage became common in fourteenth-century England, remained the standard form of mortgages there until 1925 when comprehensive property legislation was enacted, and remains the form used in other countries deriving their law from England. In conjunction with a loan of money, the borrower would grant the lender the immediate, full, permanent ownership of land meant to secure the loan. This was a grant of land, as the lawyers said, "subject to a condition subsequent" (Hazeltine 1904a: 556–57). If the borrower repaid the loan by the day specified, then ownership of the land would automatically return to the borrower (Moreton 1990: 185). If the borrower did not repay the loan in full by the day specified, full ownership of the land remained with the lender. Typically, the borrower would remain in possession of the land, despite the fact that the lender had legal title to the land during the period of repayment of the loan (Sugarman and Warrington 1995: 113).

This was harsh. Under English common law, if the borrower's repayment of the loan was one day later than the date specified at the outset, or was one penny short of the full amount of the loan, the lender had full right to keep the land or sell it (Sugarman and Warrington 1995: 113). It made no difference that the value of the land was often far greater than the amount of the loan. English judges said that the common law would not protect fools who made bad bargains or were too optimistic about their ability to repay their loans. The fact that the conditional grant was and remained so long the most common form of mortgage shows how strong the positions of lenders and how weak the positions of borrowers have usually been.

A third form of mortgage was sometimes used in England from the sixteenth century onward. The borrower would transfer the legal title of land to trustees, who would hold it subject to the terms of a trust. The trust document would provide that, if the borrower did not repay the loan in full, the trustees would sell the land, would allow the lender to take repayment of the loan from the proceeds of the sale of the land, and the borrower would get any remainder of the sale price. If the borrower repaid the loan in full, the trustees would transfer ownership of the land back to the borrower (see Waddilove 2014: 152, 2018: 132).

When the amount of the loan was considerably less than the value of the land securing the loan, as was common, this trust form of mortgage barred the lender from receiving a windfall when the borrower failed to repay the debt in full. Probably for this reason, lenders preferred the second, simpler form of mortgage, the grant of land from borrower to lender with a condition subsequent returning the land to the borrower only after full and timely repayment, without the need for trustees.

In all three of these forms of mortgages, the borrower gives or grants an interest in land. This diverges from the modern colloquial understanding that a borrower "gets" or "takes out" a mortgage. It would be more correct to say that the borrower gets a loan and in return gives the lender a mortgage (Waddilove 2018: 120–21). For that reason, the borrower is called the "mortgagor" and the lender is called the "mortgagee."

Because the terms of most mortgages were so harsh, England's courts of Chancery, administering principles of equity, intervened to provide regular relief to borrowers who had failed to repay their loans. Although a court of common law would hold borrowers to the terms of their conditional grants of land (the second form of mortgage above), a court of equity would force the lender to receive repayment from the borrower after the date the borrower promised. Thereby, the borrower could redeem the land from the lender (Sugarman and Warrington 1995: 113–14). This became "the equity of redemption." At first this equitable relief was allowed only in exceptionally deserving circumstances. In the seventeenth century, it became available to every borrower who gave a mortgage.

With the equity of redemption, the mortgage was reconceived. The words of the mortgage document still typically granted the lender immediate ownership of the borrower's land, subject to a condition that transferred the land back to the borrower if the borrower repaid in full and on time. But in a court of equity, the borrower retained an "equitable" ownership of the land, an "equity." The lender's interest in the land was reduced from legal ownership to a mere security interest (Sugarman and Warrington 1995: 114). So while the mortgage document on its face appeared to provide for the same possibility that the full value of the land would forfeit to the lender, the equity of redemption greatly reduced this possibility of forfeiture.

It has been suggested that courts of equity gave effect to the interests of an aristocratic land-holding class who were far more often borrowers than lenders in mortgage arrangements (Sugarman and Warrington 1995: 119–30). Whatever the origins of the equity of redemption, it did not extend borrowers' opportunities to repay their loans indefinitely. After a borrower had received a reasonable amount of additional time to repay the loan and still had not repaid in full, the lender could ask the court of equity to "foreclose" the borrower's equity of redemption (Waddilove 2018: 13). Foreclosure would allow the lender to take possession and sell or lease the land. We speak colloquially today of foreclosure of a mortgage, but in fact, what gets foreclosed is the borrower's equity of redemption.

David Waddilove of Notre Dame Law School has sampled Chancery cases in England involving mortgages from 1580 to 1620. He generously provided me an advance draft of his observations about the typical or common types of mortgages that gave rise to cases in England's Court of Chancery between those years (Waddilove 2018: 119).

The purpose of most mortgages has changed from early modern England to the present. Today, mortgages are commonly used for the initial purchase of real estate. The same real estate the borrower wishes to purchase provides security to the lender for repayment of the loaned purchase price. This was not the case in early modern England. Borrowers mortgaged land that they had previously owned outright (Waddilove 2018: 121–22).

Records in Chancery suggest that borrowers were usually in extreme circumstances when they risked the property they owned by mortgaging it (Waddilove 2018: 123). Mortgages were often a last resort, when all other sources of credit had been exhausted (2018: 124). A statute set a maximum allowable interest rate of 10 percent, and the interest rate revealed in most mortgages that Waddilove surveyed was 10 percent, the maximum allowable (2018: 124). He concluded that mortgages were not generally an opportunity to obtain a lower interest rate (2018: 125).

Late medieval and early modern England depended on ordinary, everyday, ubiquitous extensions of credit between neighbors, friends, and relatives (see Clark 1981: 262). There were too few coins in circulation for ordinary trade and commerce to carry on entirely on a cash basis. Instead, neighbors lent when they had surplus and borrowed when they needed funds, usually by extension of personal credit, nearly always without putting up land as security (see Clark 1981: 247, 255–56).

Typically, the value of land mortgaged was higher, sometimes twice as high as the amount borrowed, or even higher. Failure to repay the loan in full thus resulted in forfeiture to the lender of land usually worth much more than the unpaid amount of the loan. In terms of the law of contract, this was a penalty, disfavored by courts of equity in other contexts (Waddilove 2018: 126–27).

In some cases, Chancery judges tried to give the children or heirs of a borrower an opportunity to redeem land that had been held in the borrower's family for many generations, a concern that may not have applied to land recently purchased by a borrower (Waddilove 2018: 128–30).

There were no banks, no lending institutions, and little in the way of a market for mortgage lending. Instead, borrowers and lenders were nearly always known to each other before the transaction. Assessments of credit-worthiness usually depended on individual personal acquaintance (Waddilove 2018: 133). It was very difficult for one in need of funds to find a lender he or she did not already know. For instance, the lawyer for a family might loan his clients money. A lawyer was well placed to know when his clients were desperate for a loan and willing to risk forfeiture of their land. There were certainly lenders who hoped that their borrowers would fail to repay the loans and would forfeit their land to the lenders (2018: 134–35).

Finally, Waddilove noted that mortgage documents set forth payment periods that were short, often one year or three years, but that borrowers and lenders could and often did agree mutually to roll over, renew, or continue their mortgage terms for additional periods of time, on payment of interest (2018: 136). It was unusual for a borrower to repay a loan in full as the original mortgage document required. Lenders would accept late repayment from borrowers, again with payment of interest, without requiring borrowers to go through the trouble and expense of applying to a Court of Chancery (2018: 138–39).

Waddilove's observations were directed at developing an historical account of why the equity of redemption developed when and how it did. I have adapted his conclusions for a very different purpose. Mine has been to show that the English law of mortgages developed for a type of transaction very different, in many aspects, from those to which that law has been applied in later centuries in England and in the many countries to which English law has spread.

In essence, a mortgage was a bet. The borrower wagered that he or she could repay the loan eventually and get back title to the land mortgaged. The lender bet that the borrower could not repay, and that the land would eventually be forfeited to the lender without possibility for the borrower to redeem it. This was a high-risk gamble in early modern England, not an ordinary means of acquiring land, not a transaction entered into by most young adults as they embark on independent lives.

A sense of moral disapproval seems to have attached to lenders who pressed their claims to take the land of borrowers mortgaged to them. In popular culture, lenders were often depicted as outsiders, social inferiors, or villains. Dante put usurers in the seventh circle of Hell. In Shakespeare's *The Merchant of Venice*, we are meant to root for the borrowers (Bassanio and his friend Antonio) against the lender (Shylock), as we disapprove of Dickens's Ebenezer Scrooge before the ghosts visit him, and of Mr. Potter in Frank Capra's movie *It's a Wonderful Life*. Profiting from the misfortune of another in such a direct and personal way appears to offend a strong and widely shared moral sensibility.

Two more recent developments seem relevant to the later history of the mortgage and deserve mention here. For centuries, the usual and expected pattern was for land, the principal form of wealth, to descend within families, inherited by children at their parents' death or given by parents to children upon marriage (Langbein 1988: 725–26). In the twentieth century, however, the pattern of intergenerational wealth transfer in many countries has changed (1988: 723). Parents now pay for higher education and professional qualifications for their children or set their children up in business for themselves (1988: 730–36). Sometimes it will be the parents who mortgage their land to make these investments in their children's lives.

Another recent development has been the intervention of government policies, particularly through the offer of income tax deductions, aimed at encouraging ownership of housing (see, e.g., Glaeser and Shapiro 2003: 38). The deductibility of home mortgage interest has helped spur a proliferation of lending institutions, of mortgage brokers, and of valuation appraisers. Now it is the experience of most young Americans from middle-class families to enter into mortgages to purchase their first homes independent of their parents' household. This is a dramatic change from the historical periods in which mortgages originated and in which the framework of legal and equitable doctrines underpinning mortgages in Anglo-American law developed.

It is not the job of historians, particularly medieval historians, to make policy recommendations, but I can point out a few lines for further inquiry. The word "mortgage" is almost a thousand years old, and the legal device it describes is much older. But some features of mortgages today in developed Western societies are very new. Four contrasts between the long history of mortgage and its present features come to mind:

(1) Mortgages were rare; they were extreme last resorts gambling to save family assets. Now they are typically the first major transaction that almost every young adult expects to undertake.
(2) Mortgages were designed for income-producing land. Now they are typical for a borrower's own housing.
(3) Mortgage borrowers nearly always knew their lenders personally. Now large, impersonal financial institutions have taken over mortgage lending.
(4) Mortgage lenders who pursued their legal rights were portrayed in literature and popular culture as villains. Now, a broad industry of lenders, brokers, insurance providers, and valuation experts have grown up to normalize the mortgage transaction; they make it seem ordinary and inevitable to subject almost every property-owner's personal finances to the uncertainties of global financial markets.

Most of these changes happened largely because governments strongly encouraged the shift from infrequent, last-resort mortgages of income-producing assets to universal, ordinary mortgages of housing. Interest rates have become lower, but the foreclosure mechanism developed in the seventeenth century still operates in roughly the same way when borrowers cannot repay. Now government legislators and regulators, as well as judges, are scrambling to find ways to protect homeowner borrowers from abusive foreclosure practices, or to make the impersonal financial institutions that perpetrate such abuses pay enormous monetary fines.

David J. Seipp is Professor of Law and Law Alumni Scholar at Boston University, where he teaches courses on trusts and estates and on legal history, and has taught property law. He works on medieval and early modern English legal history and has studied at Oxford, Cambridge, and Harvard. He has taken out mortgages twice in his life on home purchases and has paid off both mortgage loans early.

NOTE

1. Glanvill adds in G. D. G. Hall (1965: 121) that if there is no agreement and the debtor defaults, he must answer the creditor's writ in court.

REFERENCES

Barton, J. L. 1967. "The Common Law Mortgage." *Law Quarterly Review* 83(2): 229–39.
Blackstone, William. 1766. *Commentaries on the Laws of England* 2. Oxford: Clarendon.
Clark, Elaine. 1981. "Debt Litigation in a Late Medieval English Vill." In *Pathways to Medieval Peasants*, ed. J. A. Raftis, 247–79. Toronto: Pontifical Institute of Mediaeval Studies.
Glaeser, Edward L., and Jesse M. Shapiro. 2003. "The Benefits of the Home Mortgage Interest Deduction." *Tax Policy and the Economy* 17: 37–82.
Hall, G. D. G., ed. 1965. *The Treatise on the Laws and Customs of the Realm of England Commonly Called Glanvill*. Oxford: Oxford University Press.
Hazeltine, H. D. 1904a. "The Gage of Land in Medieval England." *Harvard Law Review* 17(8): 549–57.
———. 1904b. "The Gage of Land in Medieval England. II." *Harvard Law Review* 18(1): 36–50.
Langbein, John H. 1988. "The Twentieth-Century Revolution in Family Wealth Transmission." *Michigan Law Review* 86(4): 722–51.
Littleton, Thomas. 1903. *Littleton's Tenures in English*, ed. Eugene Wambaugh. Washington, DC: John Byrne & Co.
Moreton, Charles. 1990. "A 'Best Betrustyd Frende': A Late Medieval Lawyer and His Clients." *Journal of Legal History* 11(2): 183–90.
Richardson, H. G. 1960. *The English Jewry under Angevin Kings*. London: Methuen & Co.
Sugarman, David, and Ronnie Warrington. 1995. "Land Law, Citizenship, and the Invention of Englishness: The Strange World of the Equity of Redemption." In *Early Modern Conceptions of Property*, ed. John Brewer and Susan Staves, 111–43. Abingdon, Oxon: Routledge.
Waddilove, David P. 2014. "*Emmanuel College v. Evans* (1626) and the History of Mortgages." *Cambridge Law Journal* 73(1): 142–68.
———. 2018. "Why the Equity of Redemption?" In *Land and Credit: Mortgages in the Medieval and Early Modern European Countryside*, ed. Chris Briggs and Jaco Zuijderduijn, 117–48. London: Palgrave Macmillan.
Wigmore, John H. 1897. "The Pledge-Idea: A Study in Comparative Legal Ideas." *Harvard Law Review* 10(6): 321–350 (25 Jan.); 10(7): 389–417 (25 Feb.); 11(1): 8–39 (25 Apr.).

CHAPTER 3

 Land Tenure
From Fiscal Origins to Financialization

MICHAEL HUDSON

Exploring the fiscal origins of land financialization, this chapter takes us back to ancient Mesopotamia and Egypt for a look at the longest trends discernible in the histories of land control and finance. The earliest attested land tenure had evolved in that region as part of the palatial levy of corvée labor and military service. Self-supported land was allotted to citizens in exchange for these duties. However, the long historical trend has seen the net yield or rental value of land shift away from the community or palatial economy to creditors. Nominal landholders typically have served as intermediaries to pay the rental value initially to the tax collector and increasingly to mortgage lenders.

Early economies needed credit to bridge the gap between planting and harvesting. Debts incurred during the agricultural season were paid on the threshing floor. Fiscal problems were created as this credit passed into the hands of individuals acting on their own account. Debtors were obliged to pay interest in the form of crops or their personal labor – debt bondage to their creditors at the expense of palatial claims on their public service. By the second millennium BCE, Babylonian debtors began to pledge their land to creditors.

For many centuries, royal edicts kept such labor obligations and land transfers from disrupting traditional fiscal arrangements more than temporarily. New rulers restored the *status quo ante* when taking the throne, and when circumstances called for such Clean Slates. These acts prevented an independent oligarchy from emerging in the early Near East. But an inherent tension existed between the palace rulers and private creditors seeking to become large landowners. As classical Greece and Rome lacked the Near Eastern tradition of strong palatial authority, debt bondage became much harsher in this Aegean and Mediterranean periphery than was the case in the Near East, and an independent creditor oligarchy emerged. Land transfers to large estate holders and the subjugation of labor became irreversible. The result was an increasing polarization between large absentee landholders and smallholders.

The financialization of land tenure has intensified down to today's world. Nearly two-thirds of the US population own homes, and 85 percent of Scandinavians own homes. Taking on mortgage debt is a precondition for most homebuyers, and commercial real estate is even more highly debt-leveraged. The inflation of real estate prices on credit has enabled the financial sector to pry most of the land's economic rent away from the tax collector and also from private owners.

This chapter argues that since classical antiquity the "security of property ownership" has been subordinate to creditors holding mortgage claims. The nominal landholder's legal rights are less secure than those of creditors – this shift reflects long-standing political maneuvering between creditors and public authorities over who will end up with the land's rental value. The fight peaked in the nineteenth century when classical economists sought to recapture land rent for the nation by taxing it or outright nationalization of the land and other rent-yielding resources.

The Two Broad Approaches to the Origins of Land Tenure

Like the historiography of money's origins, there are two approaches to the origins of land tenure. Just as the individualistic approach imagines money to be a product of individuals bartering, it depicts property rights as being created primordially by individuals acting by themselves to clear land with their own labor. Such theorizing is a product of writers with ideological opposition to active government regulation and ownership. By contrast, the more historically grounded approach by archaeologists, Assyriologists, and Egyptologists finds the origin of money in the palatial economy, and land tenure to have taken form in the Late Neolithic or Early Bronze Age by communities assigning self-support land rights to families in proportion to their ability to provide corvée labor and serve in the military (for a general review, see Hudson 2019, 2004; Hudson and Levine 1996, 1999; Steinkeller and Hudson 2015).

The individualistic approach appears in Rome and is associated with personal greed ending a utopian Eden. As Seneca (4 BCE–CE 65) wrote (*Epistula* 90.34, cited in Lovejoy and Boas 1935: 272–73): "There was once a fortune-favored period when the boundaries of nature lay open to all, for men's indiscriminate use, before avarice and luxury had broken the bonds that held mortals together." Virgil (70–19 BCE) expressed this typical view in his *Georgics* (I.125–128):

> No ploughman tilled the soil, nor was it right,
> To portion off the boundaries of property.
> Men shared their gain, and earth more freely gave
> Her riches to her sons who sought them not.

But Rome's landlord class was predatory, and its landlordship was blamed on greed. As Pliny (CE 23–79) complained, "The latifundia have ruined Italy."

John Locke likewise viewed land tenure as personally carved out, but found this perfectly justified. His guiding axiom was that all men have a natural right to the fruits of their labor and viewed land as a product of this labor, not as a site provided by nature. No labor duties were acknowledged by Locke as being owed to the community or state, and in fact, no reference is made to the land's rental value, only a right to its yield:

> Though the earth and all inferior creatures be common to all men, yet every man has a property in his own person ... The labour of his body and the work of his hands, we may say, are properly his. Whatsoever then he removes out of the state that nature hath provided and left it in, he hath mixed his labour with, and joined to it something that is his own, and thereby makes it his property. ... For this labour being the unquestionable property of the laborer, no man but he can have a right to what that is once joined to, at least where there is enough and as good left in common for others. (Locke [1689] 1947: 134)

Locke wrote as if most rent derived from the landlords' own labor, not that of their tenants or the economy at large – and as if the landholder did not owe any labor to the community's governing body as a condition of his land rights. Absentee landownership does not appear in Locke's view, although an implicit corollary is that landlords have a right only to what they themselves produce, not to exploit and appropriate the labor of their tenants (or for that matter, what the community provides in support services). Locke did not distinguish between the original military conquerors, illicit land grabbers or foreclosing creditors and their heirs down through the generations, free of having to provide productive labor.

Since the nineteenth century, the rising price of land sites has occurred independently of effort by landlords. The rent they charge reflects the economy's prosperity and the value of public infrastructure investment increasing the rent-of-location, playing no role in the Roman or Lockean view of the origins of land tenure.

Fiscal Origins of Land Tenure

Early Mesopotamian languages had no word for "property." As part of a person's basic needs, land was viewed as an extension of its holder. "Although the term LUGAL (in Sumerian) and *bēlum* (in Akkadian) are habitually translated as proprietor, one does not find in the Sumerian and Akkadian vocabulary a term which designates 'property' in the abstract sense of law of property" (Szlechter 1958: 121; see also Cardascia 1959).

All landholders – and the population in general – were subordinate to a higher authority, headed by the palace ruler or pharaoh and their temples. These authorities allocated land tenure as part of the overall archaic fiscal system requiring the labor of citizens for large public projects and service in the military. To support the citizens subject to these duties, Mesopotamian and Egyptian land was divided into standardized lots. (The word "lot" derives from chance, as in drawing lots for sites calculated to produce a standardized crop yield under normal conditions.)

In contrast to Locke's view of labor creating land as an asset, land rights created labor obligations to the community, leading land tenure to be defined in fiscal terms. Land rights were linked to the holder's obligation to supply corvée labor to the palatial authority and serve in the army. "The man responsible for the tax was the 'owner' as far as the state was concerned" (Eyre 2004: 174; also 1999; discussed in Hudson 2015: 651–53).

Land tenure, debt, and monetary means of payment developed together in a symbiosis. Commercial "silver" loans financed foreign trade ventures. The agricultural cycle required credit for advances of seed or other agricultural inputs, as well as personal credit such as running up tabs at Babylonian ale houses c. 1800–1600 BCE. These agrarian debts were typically denominated in barley and were due at harvest time.

Money emerged as a means of paying these agrarian and commercial debts, above all to the palaces and temples. Silver and grain forming a bimonetary standard, with a *gur* "quart" of grain equivalent to a shekel of silver for denominating such debt payments.

Interest charges became the easiest way for creditors to obtain labor before a labor-for-hire market developed. Creditors extended loans in exchange for work (antichretic payment of interest), and ultimately obtained the debtor's land rights. That enabled creditors and large landholders to grow powerful enough to avoid their fiscal obligations by the second millennium BCE, especially in Mesopotamia's and Egypt's Intermediate Periods when central power waned relative to that of local chieftains and "big men."

Exemption from Agrarian Obligations in Cases of Drought or Flooding

The ability to repay agricultural credit was subject to the disruptions of weather and military fighting. A flood or drought prevented the expected crop yield and hence personal debts from being met. Rulers were pragmatic enough to recognize that debts (even to their palace) could not be paid without driving debtors to borrow from private creditors and hence owing their labor to them instead of to the palace. The Laws of Hammurabi (§48, c. 1750 BCE) specified that agrarian debts would not have to be paid in times of flood or drought – an archaic example of "acts of god" (in this case the storm god Adad) freeing rural debtors from liability. Near Eastern monarchies in the first millennium BCE still recognized that it would be self-defeating to permit much of the population to fall into bondage to enrich an independent oligarchy.

Land tenure preserved continuity of families on the land of their forefathers by giving hereditary preference to clan members. This practice was part of common law, attested mainly by attempts by creditors to circumvent restrictions on the sale or forfeiture of land to outsiders by the ploy of having debtors adopt them as sons (Stone 1987 and Stone and Owen 1991 provide many examples). The creditor-"son" taking the land into the creditor's own family might well be older than the debtor-"father."

Land Tenure for Large Institutions (Temples and Palaces) and the Military

From the earliest records down through the modern world, land owned by temples and other public institutions were set aside in the form of perpetual holdings with their own rules of taxation. Temple land provided food, wool, and other materials to supply their dependents who could not work in agriculture because of being widowed or orphaned, or because of illness, blindness, birth defects, or other infirmities. Many were employed in workshops to produce textiles and other handicrafts or beer to be sold.

Endowing temples with land, herds of animals and other assets enabled them to be self-supporting. That was the archaic alternative to taxation. Such endowments made their public holders the first documented permanent absentee landlords collecting a net usufruct from the land. Whereas private land transfers were limited in duration, sales to the large institutions were permanent, and temple land or that of the palace could not be alienated. These temple and palace lands thus represent history's first documented "permanent" property devoted to producing a regular rent-usufruct. Most of this land was let out on a sharecropping basis, usually via palace managers as middlemen, settling at a third of the crop by the end of the third millennium.

Rulers purchased lands from the communal groupings (as documented for instance in the Stele of Manishtushu in the Akkadian period c. 2250 BCE). Hammurabi turned hitherto clan-tenured land into inalienable royal property and leased it to soldiers, commissaries or feudatories subject to *biltum* and *ilkum* taxes for labor and military service or crop rents (Charpin 2003: 117; Roth 1997: 85–86). This land could not be sold or alienated for debt, as Hammurabi's laws (§37) invalidated any sale of rural fields, orchards, or houses belonging to soldiers, and §38 prevented them from being pledged as collateral (see also §48 and §§43–44). (Similar prohibitions of alienability of cropland held by the military and smallholders were imposed as late as the Byzantine period in the ninth and tenth centuries CE, discussed below.)

In sum, Bronze Age tenure for cropland had too many public obligations attached to it to be deemed "private" in the modern sense of being able to be freely sold or otherwise alienated without future recovery rights. What is called the "free market" for land tenure is essentially the "right" (actually, the liability) of its owners to pledge and forfeit land to creditors or sell it under duress to whomever they choose. Near Eastern rulers overrode this principle of alienation on more than a temporary basis in order to maintain a self-supporting citizen-army owing corvée labor. Modern "free alienability" would have to await Roman and subsequent law.

Freely Alienable Categories of Land and Other Real Estate

Merchants and other well-to-do citizens were able to freely buy or sell townhouses, including individual floors or rooms. These properties were not part of the subsistence sector, so there was no pressing need for rulers to redistribute them when they "proclaimed order." Ownership of such property was left intact, as were commercial silver-debts for mercantile activities.

The guiding logic was evidently that while merchants and other well-to-do might be obliged to sell or forfeit their townhouses, they still would have self-support land to provide for their basic needs as citizens. Only subsistence lands were protected from permanent alienation, so as to preserve a self-supporting rural population.

Clean Slates Restore the Status Quo Ante of Land Tenure

For thousands of years Near Eastern realms from Babylonia to the Levant (as in Judaism's Jubilee Year) recognized that society needed its citizens to survive by helping debtors recover their financial solvency. Without mutual aid, low-surplus economies suffered a flight of the population or civil warfare. To prevent this, rulers forgave personal debts.

There is no record of archaic ideological claims that economic growth would be maximized by letting individuals use their wealth to obtain the labor of debtors and monopolize the land for their own gain. There was general recognition that early economies could not afford to lose the corvée labor and military service of their citizens to creditors who used loans to obtain this labor. However, a proto-oligarchic class began to emerge, whose self-interest was to abolish the power of rulers to protect debtors from losing their liberty and finally their land as personal and agrarian debts mounted up faster than the ability to be paid. Defaults led to the concentration of land and wealth ownership in the hands of an oligarchy making itself into a hereditary aristocracy. That became the economic dynamic of classical antiquity.

Near Eastern rulers avoided this dynamic by asserting their authority and annulling agrarian "barley" debts, liberating bondservants to return to their families, and returning the land's crop rights to debtors who had pledged them as collateral. Self-support land could be alienated only until the next *misharum* proclamation. Hammurabi's laws insisted on the proper dating of contracts so that they could be rendered void in years when a *misharum* permitted debtors to reclaim their land.

Only after thousands of years of the Near Eastern economic and commercial takeoff did Greek and Italian oligarchies break "free" of the Clean Slates that cancelled debts and preserved land tenure for smallholders (see Hudson 1998, 2018). For these debtors a free market in land meant loss of their own self-support and liberty.

Classical Greek Revolutions Organize Formal Land Tenure

There are no economic records from the Greek Dark Age (1200–750 BCE). That is what makes this period "dark" to modern eyes. It seems to have been a period of warlord chieftains monopolizing the land and reducing much of the population to clientage. Throughout Greece these autocracies were overthrown by "tyrants" and other social reformers in the seventh and sixth centuries BCE, from mid-Greek Corinthian Isthmus region down to Sparta with its radical "Lycurgan" reforms, capped by Solon's reforms in Athens.

All these city-states reinvented their own land tenure arrangements on an ad hoc basis. The new, less anarchic systems allotted land to soldiers (the demos). This was easiest to achieve on land that was conquered or where new colonies could be established. But in due course the oligarchies that emerged grabbed the conquered public land and that of smallholders increasingly for themselves, especially in Italy.

According to legend, these seventh- and sixth-century revolts featured a combination of land redistribution and cancellation of the debts that obliged subjects to work the land of their creditors. Sparta's seventh-century reforms were the most radical. The local oligarchy retained its land monopoly in Sparta itself, but assigned the lands it conquered and their populations to serve as helots producing food for the rest of the citizenry (*homoioi*, "equals"), equal in their holdings of these conquered territories only.

In Corinth, the Cypselid family reorganized the city to make it a commercial center and put in place a self-supporting population by land redistribution and apparently debt cancellation. Athens experienced a series of crises that peaked in 594 when Solon was appointed archon ("dictator") to cope with the same problems of land monopolization and debt slavery that had brought tyrant-reformers to power in other cities.

Solon cancelled personal debts and banned outright debt slavery. He was widely expected to redistribute the land as reformers had done in other cities, but he only removed the *horoi* stones demarcating absentee land ownership (debtors still owed labor services, but remained free citizens, not slaves). He also banned land ownership by foreigners, thereby preventing foreign creditors from foreclosing.

Creditors in subsequent Greece and Rome were strong enough to prevent debt cancellations and land redistribution after the sixth century BCE. The size of one's landholding determined one's ranking for public office and the military, but the wealthiest families avoided fiscal obligations and any attempt by popular leaders to cancel debts and redistribute the land. Sparta's kings Agis IV and Cleomenes III sought to do this in the late third century BCE, but were defeated by neighboring oligarchies, which called on Rome to defeat Sparta. Within half a century, Rome would conquer, devastate, and loot all of Greece, finishing off the devastation in the Mithridatic Wars (88–63 BC).

A distinguishing feature of classical antiquity became its increasingly oligarchic character, blocking central authority to limit land appropriation and creditor claims by the most powerful families. This "individualistic" (in practice, oligarchic) breakaway is widely viewed as the essence of Western civilization.

The Roman Oligarchy's Fight to Avoid Tax Liability and Restrictions on Land Size

Roman land tenure was based increasingly on the appropriation of conquered territory, which was declared public land, the *ager publicus populi*. The normal practice was to settle war veterans on it, but the wealthiest and most aggressive families grabbed such land for themselves in violation of early law.

The die was cast in 486 BCE when Rome defeated the neighboring Hernici, a Latin tribe. After taking two-thirds of their land, the consul Spurius Cassius proposed Rome's first agrarian law. It called for giving half the conquered territory back to the Latins and half to needy Romans, who were also to receive public land that patricians had occupied (Dionysius of Halicarnassus, *Roman Antiquities* 8.77.2). The patricians accused Cassius of "building up a power dangerous to liberty" by seeking popular support and "endangering the security" of their land appropriation. After his annual term was over, he was charged with treason and killed. His house was burned to the ground to eradicate memory of his land proposal (Livy, *History of Rome* 2.41).

The fight over whether patricians or the needy poor would be the main recipients of public land dragged on for twelve years. In 474 the commoners' tribune, Gnaeus Genucius, sought to bring the previous year's consuls to trial for delaying the redistribution (Livy 2.54; Dionysius 9.37–38). He was blocked by that year's two consuls, Lucius Furius and Gaius Manlius, who said that decrees of the Senate were not permanent law "but measures designed to meet temporary needs and having validity for one year only." The Senate could renege on any decree that had been passed.

A century later, in 384, M. Manlius Capitolinus, a former consul (in 392) was murdered for defending debtors by trying to use tribute from the Gauls and to sell public land to redeem their debts, and for accusing senators of embezzlement and urging them to use their takings to redeem debtors. It took a generation of turmoil and poverty for Rome to resolve matters. In 367, the Licinio-Sextian law limited personal landholdings to only 500 *iugera* (125 hectares, under half a square mile; see Livy 6.35–36). Indebted landholders were permitted to deduct interest payments from the principal and pay off the balance over three years instead of all at once.

Most wealth throughout history has been obtained from the public domain, and that is what led to the creation of Rome's latifundia. The most fateful early land grab occurred after Carthage was defeated in 204. Two years earlier, when Rome's life and death struggle with Hannibal had depleted its treasury, the Senate had asked families to contribute their jewelry or other precious belongings to help the war effort. Their gold and silver was melted down in the temple of Juno Moneta to strike the coins used to hire mercenaries.

Upon the return to peace, the aristocrats depicted these contributions as having been loans and convinced the Senate to pay their claims in three installments. The first was paid in 204; the second in 202. As the third and final installment was coming due in 200, the former contributors pointed out that Rome needed to keep its money to continue fighting abroad, but had much public land available. In lieu of cash payment, they asked the Senate to offer them land located within fifty miles of Rome and to tax it at only a nominal rate. A precedent for such privatization had been set in 205 when Rome sold valuable land in the Campania to provide Scipio with money to invade Africa.

The recipients were promised that "when the people should become able to pay, if anyone chose to have his money rather than the land, he might restore the land to the state." Nobody did, of course. "The private creditors accepted the terms with joy; and that land was called *Trientabulum* because it was given in lieu of the third part of their money" (Livy 28.46).

Arnold Toynbee (1965: II, 250–51; see 341–73) describes this giveaway of Rome's *ager publicus* as the turning point polarizing its economy by deciding "at one stroke, the economic and social future of the Central Italian lowlands." Most of this land ended up as latifundia cultivated by slaves captured and imported en masse in the wars against Carthage and Macedonia after 198. This turned the region into "predominantly a country of underpopulated slave-plantations" as the formerly free population was driven off the land into overpopulated industrial towns. In 194 and again in 177, the Senate organized a program of colonization that sent about 100,000 peasants, women and children from central Italy to more than twenty colonies, mainly in the far south and north of Italy. Some settlers lost their Roman citizenship, and they must have remained quite poor as the average land allotment was small.

In 133, Tiberius Gracchus advocated distributing *ager publicus* to the poor, pointing out that this would "increase the number of property holders liable to serve in the army." He was killed by angry senators who wanted the public land for themselves. Nonetheless, a land commission was established in Italy in 128 "and apparently succeeded in distributing land to several thousand citizens" in a few colonies, but did not take it from Rome's own wealthy elite. The commission was abolished around 119 after Tiberius's brother Gaius Gracchus was killed (Hopkins 1978: 61–63).

Appian describes the ensuing century of civil war as being fought over the land and debt crisis.

> For the rich, getting possession of the greater part of the undistributed lands, and being emboldened by the lapse of time to believe that they would never be dispossessed, absorbing any adjacent strips and their poor neighbors' allotments, partly by purchase under persuasion and partly by force, came to cultivate vast tracts instead of single estates, using slaves as laborers and herdsmen, lest free laborers should be drawn from agriculture into the army. At the same time the ownership of slaves brought them great gain from the multitude of their progeny, who increased because they were exempt from military service. Thus certain powerful men became extremely rich and the race of slaves multiplied throughout the country, while the Italian people dwindled in number and strength, being oppressed by penury, taxes and military service. (*Civil Wars* 1.1.7)

Dispossession of free labor from the land transformed the character of Rome's army. Starting with Marius, landless soldiers became *soldati*, living on their pay and seeking the highest booty, loyal to the generals in charge of paying them. When Sulla brought his troops back to Italy from Asia Minor in 82 and proclaimed himself Dictator, he tore down the walls of towns that had opposed him and kept them in check by resettling twenty-three legions (some 80,000 to 100,000 men) in colonies on land confiscated from local populations in Italy.

Sulla drew up proscription lists of enemies who could be killed with impunity, their estates seized as booty. Their names were publicly posted throughout Italy in June 81, headed by the consuls for the years 83 and 82, and about 1,600 *equites*. Thousands of names followed. Anyone on these lists could be killed at will, with the executioner receiving a portion of the dead man's estate. The remainder was sold at public auctions, using the proceeds to rebuild the depleted treasury. Most land was sold cheaply, giving opportunists a motive to kill more than only those named by Sulla to seize their estates, but also their personal enemies. A major buyer of confiscated real estate was Crassus, who became one of the richest Romans through Sulla's proscriptions.

By giving his war veterans homesteads and funds from the proscriptions, Sulla won their support for his new oligarchic constitution, as a virtual army in reserve. But they were not farmers, and ran into debt, in danger of losing their land. For his more aristocratic supporters, Sulla distributed the estates of the rebels from the Italian upper classes especially in Campania, Etruria, and Umbria.

Caesar likewise promised to settle his army on land of their own. They followed him to Rome and enabled him to become Dictator in 49. After he was killed in 44, Brutus and Cassius vied with Octavian (later Augustus) promising their armies land and booty. As Appian (*Civil Wars* 5.2.12–13) summarized Octavian's success: "The chiefs depended on the soldiers for the continuance of their government, while, for the possession of what they had received, the soldiers depend on the permanence of the government of those who had given it. Believing that they could not keep a firm hold unless the givers had a strong government, they fought for them, from necessity, with good-will." Octavian gave his indigent soldiers "land, the cities, the money, and the houses, and as the object of denunciation on the part of the despoiled, and as one who bore this contumely for the army's sake."

The coming of Christianity did not attack the concentration of land ownership and tenure. Peter Brown (2012: 330, 366, and 327) notes that North Africa was the main source of Roman wealth from "the massive landholdings of the emperor and of the nobility of Rome." Its overseers kept the region's inhabitants "underdeveloped by Roman standards. Their villages were denied any form of corporate existence and were frequently named after the estates on which the villagers worked, held to the land by various forms of bonded labor."

A Christian from Gaul named Salvian (*De gubernatione Dei*, [The government of God] 5.9.45, paraphrased and discussed in Brown 2012: 433–50) described the poverty and insecurity confronting most of the population c. 440:

> Faced by the weight of taxes, poor farmers found that they did not have the means to emigrate to the barbarians. Instead, they did what little they could do: they handed themselves over to the rich as clients in return for protection. The rich took over title to their lands under the pretext of saving the farmers from the land tax. The patron registered the farmer's land on the tax rolls under his (the patron's) own name. Within a few years, the poor farmers found themselves without land, although they were still hounded for personal taxes. Such patronage by the great, so Salvian claimed, turned free men into slaves as surely as the magic of Circe had turned humans into pigs.

Church estates became islands in this sea of poverty. As deathbed confessions and donations of property to the Church became increasingly popular among wealthy Christians, the Church came to accept existing creditor and debtor relationships, land ownership, hereditary wealth, and the political status quo. What mattered was how the ruling elites used their wealth, regardless of how they obtained it as long as it was destined for the Church, whose priests were the paradigmatic "poor."

The Church sought to absorb local oligarchies into its leadership, along with their wealth. Testamentary disposition undercut local fiscal balance. Land given to the Church was tax-exempt, obliging communities to raise taxes on their secular property in order to maintain their flow of public revenue. (Many heirs found themselves disinherited by such bequests, leading to a flourishing legal practice of contesting deathbed wills.) The Church became the major corporate body, a sector alongside the state. Of course, its critique of personal wealth was nowhere near the socialist idea of public ownership of land, monopolies, and banking. In fact, the Crusades led to Church orders becoming Christendom's major bankers.

The Fight by Byzantine Emperors to Reverse Land Transfers to the *Dynatoi*

The archaic Babylonian tension between palace rulers and creditors who sought control of the labor and land of tax-paying smallholders was still being played out in the Byzantine Empire (effectively 330 to the sacking of Constantinople in 1204), coming to a head in the ninth and tenth centuries. Basil I (ruled 867–886) took the lead in limiting the alienability of tax-paying land. His successor Leo VI (886–891) supported demands by the aristocracy for a free market in land, letting it be sold to any purchaser (McGeer 2000: 35–36). But Romanos Lecapenus (920–944) saved the peasantry from being turned into landless clients by reviving the Law of Pre-emption that gave kinsmen and village neighbors the right of first refusal for land being alienated. *Dynatoi* (the powerful) who were not relatives were prevented from acquiring village land by adoption, gift, testamentary disposition, or foreclosure. (The law is translated in McGeer 2000: 46 and discussed by Ostrogorsky 1969: 275–76.)

The historically cold winter of 927/8, when the ground was frozen and crops failed, made this law urgent. Romanos wrote a prologue explaining that his ruling was "beneficial to the common good, acceptable to God, profitable to the treasury, and useful to the state." He nullified sales of land for less than its true value, expelling the purchasers without a refund.

Toynbee (1973: 175–76) describes the basic dynamic at work: "In protecting the small freeholders, civilian and military, against the designs of the large-scale landowners, the East Roman Government was not contending for the rights or for the independence of the small fry. The truth is that it was defending its own rights – its rights to the peasants' payments and services, which the feudal lords were trying to capture from the Government.... The small landowners were merely the object of that contest; their payments and services were the prize that was at stake." That judgment may be extended back through the entire course of recorded history. The fight was by oligarchy of creditors and large landowners to limit public power over themselves.

Constantine VII (945–959) moved to restore imperial control over military land and to recover the tax yield and services of its soldiers by preventing sales "below the fair price," defined at the remarkably high level of four pounds of gold for military land and two pounds for sailors' land (McGeer 2000: 105 and 18–19). His successor Romanos II (959–963) ruled that any land sold since Constantine had taken the throne in 945 was to be "restored without obligation to reimburse the buyers" (McGeer 2000: 81).

After a cold winter in 989 forced many peasants to sell out, Basil II (976–1025) moved against the leading oligarchic families, headed by the military aristocracy of Cappadocia and Anatolia that had gained dominance in the Byzantine court and church. But he was the last strong Byzantine emperor. The Byzantine *dynatoi* fought back by creating their own armies and using political stratagems to oppose royal control of land and natural resources. The Comneni Dynasty (1081–1184) disbanded military land tenure, shifting the army to professionals and foreign mercenaries paid out of tax revenues.

As was the case from Babylonia through Rome, most landed estates were assembled by foreclosing on subsistence lands pledged as collateral by debtors. Once these transfers were no longer reversed by royal fiat, the oligarchy took the surplus in the form of land rent for themselves and avoided paying taxes. The Byzantine Empire's fiscal ability to defend itself weakened to the point where it was easily conquered and sacked by Christian Crusaders in 1204.

Church Banking Orders Break Down
Local Constraints on Land Alienation

Medieval European sanctions against lands being sold, forfeited, or bequeathed to outsiders were eroded mainly by the Church bankers. Eager to gain endowments, especially from landlord-knights embarking on the Crusades, the Templars pressed for the land to be bequeathed freely – that is, to itself – instead of keeping its tenure in local communities. The churches catalyzed tolerance of such alienations. Once land could be forfeited to the Church's banking orders, thanks mainly to its dominant social status and the high status of its debtors, land could be transferred in due course to other outsiders by outright sale or to foreclosing creditors.

The Christian banning of interest had two major effects on land tenure. The first loophole was to charge money-changing fees (*agio*) for foreign exchange or payments among countries. This effectively re-invented the distinction that ancient Near Eastern practice had drawn between commercial silver loans and agrarian barley debts. The Church thus re-invented the distinction between productive and unproductive credit. And until the late nineteenth century, banks made most of their profits on international trade, not domestic mortgage lending.

Classical Rent Theory as a Rationale for Land Nationalization or Full Taxation

The nineteenth century saw classical political economy create a revolutionary logic for freeing society from the power of landlords. Unlike earlier times, the aim was not to protect smallholders or increase tax revenue. This time the beneficiaries of the land tax proposed by the French Physiocrats, Adam Smith, John Stuart Mill, and the "Radical Ricardians" were to be the industrial capitalists. Minimizing land rent by taxing landlords, instead of labor, commerce, or industry would minimize the price of food, the cost of living and hence the wages that industrial employers had to pay. That would free economies from the landlord class's extraction of rent.

A land tax also would increase foreign trade by making the economy more competitive internationally. This would benefit bankers, whose major market was trade financing and foreign exchange (with its *agio* charges). Bankers therefore no longer acted in alliance with landlords as in antiquity. Their leading spokesmen in England's Parliament was David Ricardo, whose 1817 *Principles of Political Economy and Taxation* refined the definition of land rent in terms of value and price theory. He defined rent as the excess of market price over real cost value. It therefore was unearned, not having any labor cost of production, because (contra Locke) land was provided by nature, not the landlord's efforts. In Ricardo's logic the rental overhead extracted by landlords was the major block to Britain's export trade in manufactures.

In addition to deciding who will end up with the rent (the landlord, the tax collector or the mortgage lender), the tax rate also determines what the price of rent-yielding land will be. The higher the tax rate, the lower the capitalized value of the after-tax rent. The question for nineteenth-century reformers was over whether to tax the full land rent as the basis of public revenue (instead of income or excise taxes on labor and capital), or to nationalize the land outright and set the rent rate for public purposes.

Seeing that parliaments throughout Europe were dominated by the upper house (such as Britain's House of Lords) controlled by the hereditary landlord class, the classical economists realized that land could not be taxed without far-reaching political reform. Land tenure, tax policy, and constitutional reform thus went together, rather as they had in classical Greece and Rome. In Britain, a parliamentary crisis arose in 1909/10 when the House of Commons passed a land tax but the Lords vetoed it. The situation was much like the fight between Rome's Senate and the plebeian assembly. But in Britain the crisis was resolved by ruling that the House of Lords could never again block a revenue act passed by the Commons. The Lords were deprived of the political monopoly that had enabled them to block progressive taxation and other democratic policies that threatened their *rentier* interests.

The logic for taxing the full land rent on economic productivity grounds was set back, ironically, by the most popular journalistic advocate of rent taxation, Henry George. He eloquently denounced American robber barons and England's absentee landlords in Ireland, but his muddled economic logic rejected classical value, price, and rent theory in an attempt to show how original he was. In the 1880s, he sought to create his own sectarian party, attacking socialists as rivals. His platform excluded all industrial labor reforms, consumer protection, and financial reforms as distractions from his Single Tax attack on landlords. To make matters worse, his libertarian opposition to strong government prompted socialists and other reformers to leave land tax advocacy to his followers, turning their focus to industrial labor problems, Wall Street's financial maneuvering and monopolies.

Today's FIRE Sector Backs the Financialization of Land Tenure

Landlords and allied *rentier* interests rejected the classical concept of land rent as unearned income. John Bates Clark's "value-free" economics, like subsequent free market doctrine down to the present day, denied that any form of income and wealth was unearned. The academic mainstream reverted to a Lockean assumption that the land's cost of production and rental income reflected the landlord's enterprise.

The banking and financial sector shifted its position to oppose rather than support land taxation. A middle class was emerging, home ownership was becoming popularly available, and bankers found real estate becoming their largest loan market. Today, some 80 percent of commercial bank lending in the United States, Britain, and other industrial economies occurs in mortgage loans. As savings grow exponentially at the top of the economic pyramid, they are recycled into the residential and commercial real estate market. The effect is to bid up prices for housing on credit, with a rising share of property values owed as debt (see Hudson 2012). As of 2018, less than half the value of US housing was homeowners' equity; most of the property value was owed to lenders.

Bankers understand that whatever rental income the tax collector relinquishes is available for new buyers to pay as debt service. As financial wealth and credit increase faster than the economy has grown, bankers have increased their lending terms from 80 percent of the purchase price to 100 percent (thereby requiring no down payments), while making interest-only mortgages instead of the formerly normal thirty-year self-amortizing mortgages.

The Financial, Insurance, and Real Estate (FIRE) sectors have joined together to try to persuade voters to blame the high cost of housing on property taxes, hoping to lower this tax further so as to increase the proportion of rent that can be paid out as interest. This is causing the rest of the economy to shrink. Rising defaults concentrate property in the hands of the financial class becoming an absentee owner class – a rental economy that reverses the democratization of land ownership and the nineteenth century's classical economic aim of freeing society from land rent (along with monopoly rent, including financial charges).

When it comes to land tenure, finance, and other economic structures, politics rules all. Oligarchies want no protection for mortgage debtors or renters. Called neoliberalism today, this idea of a "free market" and weak democratic policy means unfreedom for the population falling into dependency on wealthy *rentiers* for housing, credit, and other basic needs.

Michael Hudson is President of The Institute for the Study of Long-Term Economic Trends (ISLET), a Wall Street Financial Analyst, and Distinguished Research Professor of Economics at the University of Missouri, Kansas City. He has conducted research on the economic history of the ancient Near East as a research fellow at Harvard Peabody Museum.

REFERENCES

Brown, Peter. 2012. *Through the Eye of a Needle: Wealth, the Fall of Rome, and the Making of Christianity in the West, 350–550 AD*. Princeton. NJ: Princeton University Press.

Cardascia, George. 1959. "Le concept babylonien de la propriété." [The Babylonian concept of property]. *Revue Internationale des Droits de l'Antiquité* 6: 19–32.

Charpin, Dominique. 2003. *Hammurabi of Babylon*. London: I. B. Tauris.

Eyre, Christopher. 1999. "Village Economy in Pharaonic Egypt." In *Agriculture in Egypt from Pharaonic to Modern Times* (Proceedings of the British Academy 96), ed. Alan Bowman and Eugene Rogan, 33–60. Oxford: Oxford University Press.

———. 2004. "How Relevant was Personal Status to the Functioning of the Rural Economy in Pharaonic Egypt?" In *La dépendence rurale dans l'Antiquité égypienne et proche-orientale* [Rural dependency in Egyptian and near-eastern antiquity], ed. Bernadette Menu, 157–86. *Bibliotheque d'Etude*, vol. 140. Cairo: Institut Français d'Archéologie Orientale du Caire.

Hopkins, Keith. 1978. *Conquerors and Slaves*. Cambridge: Cambridge University Press.

Hudson, Michael. 1998. "Land Monopolization, Fiscal Crises and Clean Slate 'Jubilee' Proclamations in Antiquity." In *Property in Economic Context*, Monographs in Economic Anthropology 14, ed. Robert C. Hunt and Antonio Gilman, 139–69. Lanham, MD: University Press of America.

———. 2004. "The Archaeology of Money in Light of Mesopotamian Records." In *Credit and State Theories of Money: The Contributions of A. Mitchell Innes*, ed. L. Randall Wray, 99–127. Cheltenham: Edward Elgar.

———. 2012. *The Bubble and Beyond: Fictitious Capital, Debt Deflation and Global Crisis*. Dresden: ISLET.

———. 2015. "How the Organization of Labor Shaped Civilization's Takeoff." In *Labor in the Ancient World*, ed. Piotr Steinkeller and Michael Hudson, 649–64. Dresden: ISLET.

———. 2018. "*. . . And Forgive Them Their Debts*": *Credit and Redemption from Bronze Age Debt Remissions to the Jubilee Year*. Dresden: ISLET.

———. 2019. "Origins of Money and Interest: Palatial Credit, not Barter." In *Handbook of the History of Money and Currency*, ed. S. Battilossi, Y. Cassis, and K. Yago, 1–21. Singapore: Springer. https://doi.org/10.1007/978-981-10-0622-7_1-1.

Hudson, Michael, and Baruch Levine, eds. 1996. *Privatization in the Ancient Near East and Classical World*. Cambridge, MA: Peabody Museum, Harvard University.

———. 1999. *Urbanization and Land Ownership in the Ancient Near East*. Cambridge, MA: Peabody Museum, Harvard University.

Locke, John. [1689] 1947. "Of Property." In *The Second Treatise on Civil Government*. New York: Prometheus.

Lovejoy, Arthur O., and George Boas. 1935. *Documentary History of Primitivism and Related Ideas in Antiquity*. Baltimore, MD: Johns Hopkins.

McGeer, Eric. 2000. *The Land Legislation of the Macedonian Emperors*. Toronto: Pontifical Institute of Medieval Studies.

Ostrogorsky, George. 1969. *History of the Byzantine State*. Brunswick, NJ: Rutgers University Press.

Roth, Martha T. 1997. *Law Collections from Mesopotamia and Asia Minor*, 2nd ed. Atlanta, GA: Scholars Press.

Steinkeller, Piotr, and Michael Hudson. 2015. *Labor in the Ancient World*. Dresden: ISLET.

Stone, Elizabeth. 1987. *Nippur Neighborhoods*. Chicago: Oriental Institute, University of Chicago.

Stone, Elizabeth, and David I. Owen. 1991. *Adoption in Old Babylonian Nippur and the Archive of Mannum-meshu-lissur*. University Park, PA: Eisenbrauns (of Penn State University Press).

Szlechter, Emile. 1958. "De quelques considérations sur l'origine de la propriété foncière privée dans l'Ancien Droit Mesopotamien" [Some considerations on the origin of private land ownership in Old Mesopotamian law]. *Revue Internationale des Droits de l'Antiquité*, 3(5): 121–36.

Toynbee, Arnold. 1965. *Hannibal's Legacy*. Oxford: Oxford University Press.

———. 1973. *Constantine Porphyrogenitus and his World*. London: Oxford University Press.

Part II
Mortgage as Cultural Export
Land, Family, and the State

CHAPTER 4

 Inheriting Debt
Legal Pluralism, Family Politics, and
the Meaning of Wealth in Ghana

SARA BERRY

Building on Parker Shipton's ethnography of the socially constitutive character of debt in western Kenya and David Graeber's argument that debt creates and sustains social relationships, this chapter examines connections between debt, mortgaging and inheritance in Ghana. Land values increased in Ghana throughout the twentieth century under the combined influence of agricultural commercialization, urban growth, economic uncertainty and, in recent years, increased investment in large-scale agricultural and natural resource extraction ventures. As land values rose and competition over access to land intensified, land transactions – leases, loans, mortgages, and sales – have become increasingly commercialized and, in many cases, contested and insecure.

In the process, people have intensified efforts to reinforce land claims and to realize their commercial value by specifying more precisely both the spatial and temporal terms of land transactions. Land surveys are used to draw precise boundaries around parcels of land when land holders intend to sell, lease, mortgage, or build on them; witnesses are mobilized to confirm them; and transactions are frequently recorded in writing. In the case of transactions such as rentals or mortgages that are meant to be temporary, it is increasingly common for documents to specify a time when the loan must be repaid or the lessee's tenure ends.[1]

The pressures of commercialization and competition over land have also been reflected in changing practices of inheritance. In the past, before written wills had become common, kin groups took over the possessions of a family member who had died, appointing one of their members as "successor" to manage the estate and distribute its benefits among the group. And as land prices rose and competition over land increased, disputes over the inheritance of land-based assets multiplied, straining family relationships. In response, increasing numbers of Ghanaians wrote wills or gave away portions of their land while they were still alive, partly to gain control over the future disposition of their property, but also to forestall disputes among their survivors. As a shopkeeper in a suburb of Kumasi explained, he had written a will leaving his property to his wife "so that no one will bother her" after he had died.[2]

In the following pages, I discuss some of the implications of increasing land values and contestation over land for the transmission of land-based assets and obligations through inheritance and for economic and social relations among family members. The discussion focuses on Ghana in the late twentieth century, using court records and material gathered during several periods of field research in the Asante Region,[3] but also draws on historical studies of other West African societies to illustrate long-term changes in practices of borrowing, lending, and inheritance, and raise questions about their impact on family politics and the meaning of wealth.

Credit, Debt, and Inheritance

In his trilogy on the ethnography of debt and financial modernization in western Kenya, Parker Shipton describes precolonial Luo society as one in which social persons are crafted through lending and borrowing. Luo, he argues, did not acquire material goods (including livestock) in order to have them, but to build social relationships by lending (or giving) them to others. "Outstanding loans are not just a kind of wealth, but also a kind of power" (Shipton 2007: 208). What people lend, to whom and for how long both reflect and define their social personae and their relationships to others. Luo default on loans from development agencies, Shipton suggests, not because they do not understand the concept of repayment, but because they have other, more important debts to deal with (Shipton 2007: 101–2; cf. Bolt 2013).

Writing on a global scale, David Graeber generalizes the argument: an outstanding debt, he suggests, creates a relationship between borrower and lender that lasts until the debt is paid off. As long as a debt remains unpaid, debtor and creditor have a reason to keep track of one another, whether or not they often meet face to face. The obligation to repay may weigh heavily or lightly on the parties involved depending on the context, but the fact of an outstanding obligation establishes a relationship between them. Conversely, when a debt is repaid, "both parties can walk away and have nothing further to do with each other." Paying off a debt, he concludes, "destroys the very reason for having a relationship" (Graeber 2011: 122).

Graeber's point is logical but rests, it seems to me, on a foreshortened view of the temporality of credit and debt as forms of social interaction. When a debt is paid, the relationship associated with *that* transaction ends, but the borrower's access to additional loans (from that creditor and/or others) and the terms on which s/he can obtain them depends, in part, on whether the loan was paid off in a timely and/or socially acceptable manner. In a thoughtful review of the first volume of Shipton's trilogy, *The Nature of Entrustment*, Maxim Bolt points out that the social and economic repercussions of a loan include not only the obligations between debtor and creditor that persist while the loan is outstanding, but also what borrower and lender do with the things loaned and the collateral provided while they hold them (Bolt 2013; Graeber 2011; Shipton 2009; Weiner 1992). It also matters whether, when, and how debts are repaid, and how both creditor and debtor manage their relations in the process.[4] Like the assets left behind when a person dies, his/her debts form part of the legacy passed on to the heirs, drawing them into their predecessors' social obligations and shaping social relations among the survivors. In other words, the social repercussions of a debt carry forward in time: outstanding debts are socially generative while they remain incomplete, but a loan is not necessarily complete when the debt is paid off.[5]

Debt and Social Transformation in West Africa: *The Longue Durée*

While economic and political conditions have changed profoundly since the era of the transatlantic slave trade, credit and indebtedness continue to create and rework social relationships, as well as enabling and/or constraining economic activities. A number of insightful studies have documented the way credit and debt figured in social reproduction and the mobilization and exercise of power in pre-colonial African societies. The socially constitutive role of indebtedness was not limited to relatively decentralized societies such as those of western Kenya: rulers of pre-colonial states also wielded power by putting subordinates and rivals in their debt. Thomas McCaskie's masterful exegesis of the political marketplace at the center of Asante state power in the eighteenth and nineteenth centuries is a case in point. At the height of its power, Asante was ruled by kings who skillfully deployed state finances to reward loyal support and punish dissenters (McCaskie 1995: 56–58, 227–28).

Credit relations have also played a central role in enabling and expanding both local and long-distance trade. Ugo Nwokeji's study of the Aro slave trading diaspora in southeastern Nigeria (2010), Pierluigi Valsecchi's description of polities on the coasts of Ghana and Côte 'd'Ivoire as "a series of solar systems, with planets and satellites, some of which are engaged in different matriclan orbits at the same time" (2011: 176–77) and Ghislaine Lydon's detailed examination of trading networks in the western Sahara (2009) all illuminate the way traders used credit to accumulate followers as well as profits, building hierarchies that stretched across space without necessarily giving rise to centralized states or large bounded territories. In many cases, the accumulation of wealth and power was closely tied to religious beliefs and practices, centered on the authority of an oracle or powerful shrine (see also Allman and Parker 2005; Baum 1999; Ekejiuba and Dike 1990; Scheele 2012). In most of these histories, authority and obligation, credit and debt are portrayed as processes – continually performed, challenged, renegotiated, or broken as commercial, environmental, and security conditions changed.

Credit and debt also figured centrally in political economies of family life and social reproduction. African marriages were commonly legitimated by an exchange of gifts, although the donors, recipients, and amounts involved varied a great deal from one social context to another. In societies where acceptable amounts of bridewealth were substantial, payments were usually made in installments, spread over the lifetime of the couple or beyond. If a man died without completing bridewealth payments for his wife, responsibility for the unpaid balance might fall on his sons, whose status as full adult members of the lineage was only assured when their mothers' marriage(s) were fully legitimated (Comaroff 1980). Large outlays on funerals both honored the dead and demonstrated the achievements and social virtues of the living. As with marriage payments, families often incurred sizeable debts to provide honorable burials for their dead, and might spend years afterwards raising the funds to pay them off. In both cases, assembling the means to defray debts owed by a husband's kin or a parent's descendants is a socially generative process in itself. As a Ghanaian friend explained when I asked how his family had managed to cover the large difference between their outlays on a funeral and the donations they received during the ceremonies, "we contacted some of the brothers [who were living] abroad."

By inscribing material goods in celebrations of life cycle rituals, debts incurred for marriage gifts and funeral expenses underscore both the complexity and the social specificity of wealth. Widely cited as a distinctive feature of African social history, "wealth-in-people" was often generated or expressed through exchanges or transfers of wealth-in-things. Reflecting both the prevalence of "wealth-in-people" and the hierarchical character of many African societies, borrowers also sent people – dependent kin, clients, servants, slaves – as "pawns" to work for their creditors until their debts were repaid. In the event of non-repayment, pawns might remain permanently in a creditor's household, as did the children s/he produced there (see, e.g., Falola and Lovejoy 2003).[6] As Jane Guyer and Samuel Eno Belinga (1995) showed in their influential article "Wealth in People as Wealth in Knowledge," wealth-in-people is a multidimensional concept. In equatorial Africa, they argued, people were valued for their individual attributes – knowledge, skills, even non-conformity – as well as their role as units of labor or reproduction. Augmenting wealth-in-people should be understood as a process of composition rather than simple accumulation.

Building on their argument, I suggest that value is generated not only by compositional arrangements of individual attributes and skills, but also through patterns of interaction within and between families, polities, and other social groupings. Objects transferred or exchanged through marriage payments, funeral donations, contributions to naming ceremonies and other social rituals do not simply measure the "worth" of the bride, the baby, or the deceased. They create and nourish relationships among their families and with others who contribute to the rituals that celebrate and legitimate them. As illustrated in Shipton's portrayal of Luo identity as constituted through lending and borrowing (2007, 2009), Graeber's argument that loans create relationships (2011), John Comaroff's analysis of Tswana marriage as a process (1980), and Michelle Gilbert's account of "the sudden death of a [Ghanaian] millionaire" (1988), *actions* of giving and receiving, lending and borrowing, generate what might be called wealth-in-relationships – trajectories of social interaction whose value goes beyond the value of the things promised or exchanged, or the specialized knowledge and skills of the people involved.

The following pages seek to open a discussion on the usefulness of such a concept for thinking about the social consequences of commercialization, accumulation, and economic inequality in the twentieth century. To illustrate, I focus on inheritance – transfers of wealth-in-people through transfers of wealth-in-things that together build or attenuate social relationships. Before written wills became common in Ghana, individuals did not usually choose their own heirs. When a person died, whatever assets left behind were treated as a family legacy, to be used for the combined benefit of the deceased's surviving kin. Families met to choose a "successor" – not as the lucky recipient of the deceased person's estate, but to manage the estate on behalf of the family as a whole. Both the choice of a successor and the handling of the estate depended not only on available legal options, prevailing social practices, and possibilities of enforcing them, but also on relations among survivors. If disputes arose over the disposition of assets or who was entitled to share in their benefits, the successor was responsible for organizing a settlement. If that failed, the dispute might end up in court. Accumulated since the late nineteenth century, when colonial authorities began to keep written records of judicial rulings, court records provide a rich, though not representative, account of changing inheritance practices and a window into changing structures of family life.

The estate left behind by a person who has died includes the outstanding debts as well as assets. Whether named in the deceased person's will, or appointed by his/her family to manage the estate on behalf of the group, the executor(s) or successor(s) are legally and socially responsible for the debts left behind by the departed.

Kwame Kusi v. Andrews Abayie and Kwadwo Biewuo

The plaintiff in this case sued the executors of an estate over a loan of $25,000, which the plaintiff had made to the deceased on 30 September 1999. As collateral for the loan, the deceased had offered a house in an up-scale suburb of Kumasi. The plaintiff was now demanding that the executors pay him $25,000 plus accrued interest or the court would sell the house and use the proceeds to repay the debt. The executors (defendants) replied that since the deceased had left a will bequeathing the house "to named persons," they were not the ones to sue for recovery of the debt.

In rejecting the defendants' claim, the court spelled out the duties of an executor, citing Samuel Azu Crabbe, *The Law of Wills in Ghana* (1998: 274) and the Administration of Estates Act (Act 63, 1961).[7] Executors, the judge wrote, must (1) bury the deceased at their own expense (unless a spouse, children, or family of the deceased offer to contribute), (2) clear the estate of liabilities, including all outstanding debts, by selling the deceased's property, if necessary, and (3) distribute the estate according to the deceased's will or the rules of intestacy, whichever applies to the case in question. Until those duties are discharged, the executors hold the estate in trust for any designated beneficiaries. In this case, the executors' duties had not yet been fulfilled, and they were therefore the people whom the plaintiff should sue to recover his outstanding loan (High Court, Kumasi, CS 64/2003).

As this and the following cases illustrate, the responsibilities of the executor (or "successor") are not only financial, but include family governance. A number of the people I spoke with during fieldwork had thought a good deal about how their survivors would deal with one another, and how they could reduce the likelihood of future conflict. Successors could lease, mortgage, or even sell family property in order to clear debts left unpaid by the deceased, but were expected to consult with the beneficiaries before doing so. Several of my informants in a peri-urban neighborhood of Kumasi described such arrangements. K. M. succeeded his uncle whose estate included two houses (one old one new) at Kwadaso and an oil palm farm. Before he died, the uncle gave K. M. five rooms – one in the old house, four in the new – and left the rest to his family. When I interviewed him in 1993, K. M. was renting out his rooms in the new houses to teachers, in order to raise money to pay his uncle's medical bills. Once the bills were paid, K. M. said he planned to continue renting out the rooms. Since he lived in a house he had built for himself in Asokore-Mampong, he explained, he did not need to occupy the rooms gifted him by his uncle and could fulfill his responsibilities as successor by using them for the family. Rather than allocate them to individual family members, he planned to use the rental money to expand the family house or help relatives in need.

Inheritance: A Forum for Legal Pluralism

When families cannot agree, inheritance cases are likely to end up in court. As the following cases illustrate, Ghana's long history of interaction between custom and statutory law has both prompted and been shaped by processes of commercialization and changing relations and meanings of property.[8] From the early years of independence, both civilian and military regimes have worked to move beyond indirect rule, enacting numerous laws that abolish or redefine customary laws and chiefly prerogatives, but they have also relied on traditional authorities for political support, rewarding them with constitutional guarantees of their authority over "stool" land and, in the 1992 Constitution, denying Parliament the right to intervene in the selection or removal of any chief from traditional office (Constitution of the Republic of Ghana 1993: 164). These constitutional guarantees have, in turn, been reflected both in courts' recognition of customary rules that have not been specifically curtailed or abolished by statute, and in their willingness to entertain "traditional history" as evidence.

The plurality of both laws and rules of evidence are on display in court records of inheritance disputes. While inheritance laws have been rewritten to reflect both changing social practices and state agendas, reforms continue to recognize and accommodate customary practices, rather than replace them.[9] A case in point is the Intestate Law of Succession (Provisional National Defence Council Law 111), enacted in 1985 under the then military regime of Major General J. J. Rawlings.[10] A case in point is the Law on Intestate Succession (PNDCL 111), promulgated in 1985 by the military regime then in power, that fundamentally rewrote the custom that allocated a person's entire estate to his/her matrilineal kin to the exclusion of the surviving spouse and children. Rather than simply replace the traditional system with one that names the conjugal family as successor rather than the matrilineal kin, however, the law sought to compromise. Under PNDCL 111, the spouse (usually a wife) and children inherit the conjugal house and chattels, plus three quarters of the deceased person's self-acquired property.[11] The rest is divided among surviving parents and kin. Under this statute, families continue to appoint successors, not only to manage their (much reduced) shares of intestate estates but also, and perhaps more importantly, to take over the deceased person's duties as successor to relative(s) who died previously.[12]

While individual Ghanaians have made increasing use of wills and gifts *inter vivos* to take individual control of the property they leave behind, and the state has intervened to shift the intergenerational distribution of property from kin to conjugal families, both have steered clear of challenging the time-honored principle of "family property" – that is, assets inherited collectively by members of a family and subject henceforth to family governance rather than individual control. As I shall argue below, in the decades since independence, the accumulated weight of family property appears to have slowed the impact of commercialization on processes of inheritance and, to some extent, the erosion of family networks.[13]

The following court cases highlight some of the issues that have arisen in family debates over the management of debts left behind by the deceased. Collected through an unsystematic search of court records found at PRAAD (Public Records and Archives Department) in Accra and Kumasi, and the Library of the Council on Law Reporting in Accra, these cases are in no way representative of judicial rulings on these issues, much less of arrangements made by families in general, most of which do not reach the courts. Rather, I present them here to illustrate some of the points of contention that figure frequently in inheritance disputes.

"A Pledge Is Redeemable Forever"

Although legally certified mortgages have been in use in Ghana since the nineteeth century, pledging persists, in part because risks of default are high, leading banks and other formal lending institutions charge high rates of interest, or simply refuse to lend to borrowers who cannot guarantee timely repayment. For a good part of the twentieth century, agricultural capital played a dominant role in the expansion of credit in circulation. As assets that produce income for many years, cocoa (and other tree crop) farms are well suited to serve as collateral and have done so since the early years of cocoa growing in Ghana (Austin 2005; Hill 1963). In many cases, the actual work of harvesting and maintaining a pledged farm is done by hired laborers or sharecroppers who may include the person who has pledged the farm for a loan.[14] If a borrower failed to redeem pledged property during his/her lifetime, the debt passed to his or her successor(s), who might redeem it, or pass it on to the next generation, as they wished.

With unlimited time to repay a pledge, a borrower could forestall foreclosure indefinitely, although large or repeated defaults might limit his/her ability to borrow in the future. For a lender, the implications of a pledge were ambivalent. On one hand, if the borrower never redeemed the pledge, the collateral remained with the lender, becoming an additional asset. But the gain was uncertain. Because there was no time limit for repayment, in principle, the debtor's heirs – or their heirs – could come forward decades later and offer to redeem the pledge for the amount of the original loan. As the following cases illustrate, this could lead to a windfall gain for the "borrower" and a corresponding loss for the lender's descendants.

Oheneba Kofi Duo v. Kwame Manhyia

In 1996, a relative of the chief of Kenyase Kwabre filed a suit against a citizen of the stool for a 50-acre tract of land.[15] The trial court ruled in favor of the plaintiff, but the defendant appealed. Denying the defendant's claim that the land belonged to his family, the plaintiff told the Appeals Court that, at some point in the past, the then chief of Kenyase Kwabre had given the land to his wife, "as the custom invariably was," who was also an ancestress of the plaintiff. Sometime between 1883 and 1888, the husband of a descendant of the former chief's wife had pledged (some of?) the land to the defendant's predecessor for £4/13/-. Without mentioning this loan, the defendant claimed that his family had pledged land to the plaintiff in 1925, also for a loan of £4/13/-, and redeemed it for £12/-/- in 1949.

By failing to remind the pledgee of the earlier debt, the court admitted that the defendant's family had created "a false sense of ownership," but added that this did not override the legal principle that "a pledge is redeemable forever": it does not convert to a sale over time, no matter how much time has elapsed since the pledge was made.[16] By upholding the trial court's judgment in favor of the plaintiff, the Appeals Court ruled that a pledge made over a century ago was still a pledge, and could be redeemed by the successor(s) of the original debtor. The court record did not state whether the plaintiff was entitled to redeem the land for the original loan of £4/13/- (Court of Appeal 54/99. Judgment 20/11/2003).

If affirmed by the courts, a long-standing pledge may become a windfall for the debtor and a headache for the creditor. While the courts have attempted to place limits on such arbitrary gains and losses, they face challenges in navigating through competing versions of evidence drawn from "traditional history" and/or open-ended contracts. Established in 1976 to promote increased investment in agriculture by making credit available to farmers, Ghana's Rural Banks stopped lending to farmers when it proved difficult or impossible to recover the loans. (Farmers evaded repayment by, e.g., registering crop deliveries to the Cocoa Marketing Board in the names of their wives, relatives or friends; then reporting that they had not earned enough to cover their debts to the bank.) By the early 2000s, Rural Banks were limiting small loans to teachers and other civil servants whose salaries were paid through the banks, permitting the latter to deduct the amounts owed from the borrowers' accounts before disbursing the balance.[17]

Bonsu v. Manu and 3 Others

A cocoa farm was sold at public auction in 1946 because the plaintiff failed to pay court costs after losing a case to three of the defendants in the Asantehene's Court. At the time, the farm was pledged. The creditor complained but then agreed to the sale if the buyer (the fourth defendant) would repay his loan. The court records did not state whether the loan had been repaid, but noted that the buyer had been in undisturbed possession of the farm since 1946 and had enlarged and improved the farm in the interval.

In this case, the court ruled for the defendants, but did so on procedural – not substantive – grounds, arguing that the plaintiff had waited more than twenty-one days to challenge the sale of the farm at public auction, and had also taken the case to a Local Court rather than the

Asantehene's Court, which had authorized the sale in the first place. The contrast between this case and the preceding one underscores the difference between the legal latitude accorded to a debt between two individuals and that given to a debt between an individual and the state. In the former case, a farm pledged to an individual lender was treated as an open obligation, the court affirming that the right to redeem pledged property passes to the debtor's heirs in perpetuity. In the latter, a farm owner was given three weeks to challenge the court-sanctioned foreclosure of his farm on behalf of the stool (*Ghana Law Reports* 1961, Pt. 1).

Because of their temporal open-endedness, pledges have served as a source of both continuity and conflict in financial transactions and social relations among transactors. Deriving from the older practice of using people as collateral (see, e.g., Falola and Lovejoy 2003),[18] the principle that "a pledge is redeemable forever" continues to be reaffirmed in the courts, as well as in social practice – a pattern that illustrates David Graeber's argument that unpaid debts work to sustain social relationships over time. At the same time, however, the fact that a borrower's successor(s) can redeem mortgaged property even decades after the original loan means that they stand to benefit enormously from rising land values. By convincing the court that a piece of land, farm, or building was pledged, rather than sold, to its present possessor, the successor(s) of an erstwhile borrower are entitled to reclaim it for the amount of the original loan – a sum that may amount to a small fraction of its current market value. Not surprisingly, inheritance disputes often turn on the question of whether a bygone transfer of land was a sale or a pledge – as the following cases illustrate.

Kwame Mensah v. Abrokwa

In this case, the plaintiff (Kwame Mensah) sued for title to a cocoa farm that he had purchased from a man to whom the farm been mortgaged by the defendants, in 1939, for a loan of £4/11. After waiting years for the borrowers (defendants) to redeem the farm, the creditor sold it to Kwame Mensah, effectively foreclosing on the loan. The court agreed that the defendants had waited a long time to challenge the sale, but ruled that their challenge was still valid because the creditor did not give notice before foreclosing. Accordingly, the plaintiff's claim for title was dismissed.

This case had been wending its way through the judicial system for some time. In the original trial, the Kumasi West District Court ruled in favor of the original debtors (defendants), but the ruling was overturned in the Asantehene's Appeal Court. Undeterred, the debtors appealed to the Land Court, which ruled in their favor, and ended up in the West

African Court of Appeal, which upheld the Land Court's ruling. The court record contained no information about either the plaintiff's or the defendant's resources, but it must have cost a good deal of money, as well as access to knowledgeable lawyers, to take a case through four levels of adjudication. Like many other cases involving debts incurred many years in the past, it is likely that by the time the case was settled, the collateral was worth a great deal more than the amount of the original loan (*Ghana Law Reports* 1961, Pt. 1).

Nana Wireko Ababio (Kaasehene) v. Nana Kwabena Ofori (Chief of Nkontonko)

The gap between original and present value of a long-unredeemed pledge is even more vividly illustrated in a dispute between two senior Asante chiefs over a tract of land located in a site of industrial development on the southern edge of Kumasi. Because of its location, the land had become very valuable and, at first sight, the dispute appears to be a straightforward market-based clash over ownership of pricey real estate. That both litigants chose to base their claims on "traditional history" is a vivid illustration of the value of the past – and the judicial dilemmas posed thereby – in Ghana's political economy on the threshold of the twenty-first century.

The Kaasehene and his chiefly opponent both claimed that the disputed land had been granted to his stool by an Asantehene who ruled during the eighteenth or nineteenth century. (The Kaase stool traced its claim to a grant from Asantehene Opoku Ware I, who ruled from c. 1720 to 1750; the opposing chief of Nkontonko traced his to a grant from Asantehene Osei Yaw Akoto, 1824–33 [Wilks 1993].) In 1930, unbeknownst to the then Kaasehene, the first plaintiff had pledged a portion of this land to the defendant's predecessor for a sum of £8. Despite this deception, the Kaasehene and the descendant of his predecessor's transgressor had since joined hands, and were now suing jointly to redeem the land and permanently enjoin the defendant and his servants, agents, and others, from entering it.

The defendant denied the pledge, reiterating his claim that Osei Yaw Akoto had given the land to his ancestor. Moreover, he argued, the supposed creditor could not have pledged the land as the plaintiffs claimed. For one thing, he had been enstooled in 1934, not 1930 when the alleged pledge was made. In addition, his financial position in 1930 was abysmal. He did not have £8 to lend to anyone and had been obliged "to pledge two of his daughters in marriage to raise the necessary funds." To verify his predecessor's poverty, the defendant produced a marriage contract for one of the daughters, prompting the court to comment that "it is . . . interesting to note that the amount stated for the pledge was £8, no more no less – and [the marriage contract] also stated £8 no more no less."

Faced with opposing versions of "traditional history," the court decided on the basis of "incidents within living memory," plus the consistency of witnesses' testimony – pointing out, for example, that contrary to custom, the defendants' people had never settled on the land supposedly granted to them by the Asantehene and that the defendant admitted as much, but one of his witnesses contradicted him. Having concluded that the land was pledged, not given to the defendant, the court took the opportunity to reaffirm the law: "no matter how long property may have remained in pledge, the successor of the original pledgers or owners may exercise their right to redeem it whenever they decided to do so." Accordingly, the court ruled, the first plaintiff was entitled to re-possess the land for £8 – or what must have been a miniscule fraction of its value in 1999 (High Court, Kumasi, LS 23/323/91. Judgment 30/7/1999).

"Once a Family Property, Always a Family Property"

Just as debt serves to create or sustain a social relationship between lender and borrower, so inheritance raises questions of social entitlement and belonging. Both statutory and customary law distinguish between self-acquired property (which the owner may give, sell, or bequeath), and "family property" from which the successor may benefit, but does not own. Like pledges, family property carries the legacy of past transactions forward in time. By requiring that members of a family must consent to any transactions involving family assets, it also serves to sustain, as well as strain, family relationships.

Adwoa Mensah v. Afua Nkrumah and Another

The plaintiff in this case claimed a cocoa farm near Efiduase, a town east-northeast of Kumasi, stating that she had inherited it from her predecessor, and that the defendant was an *abunu* tenant who had stopped paying. The defendant counterclaimed that she was an *abunu* tenant on another farm; she had inherited the disputed farm from her father, who had held it as an *abunu* tenant. In an *abunu* tenancy, the tenant takes charge of a newly planted farm and takes care of it until the trees begin to yield enough fruit to cover annual costs of maintenance and harvesting. At that point, the farmer and the tenant divide the farm, and each takes half as their own property. Since an *abunu* contract results in permanent alienation of half the farm to the tenant, family property cannot be developed on this basis (See, e.g., Hill 1963).

To deny the defendant's claim, the plaintiff would have had to show that her ancestor (K.O.) had acquired the land before he died, and that it had become family property when it passed to his successor (B.). If that were so, the court pointed out, the defendant's father could not have acquired it as an *abunu* tenant or bequeathed his share of the mature farm to his daughter. Since the plaintiff had failed to prove that her predecessor held the farm as family property, she could not deny the defendant's claim (High Court, Kumasi, LS 1044/87. Judgment 6/4/2000).

"Self-acquired property" refers to assets that individuals acquire through their own efforts. Assets become family property when relatives make substantial contributions to developing them, or when they are inherited from a person who dies intestate. Despite the increasing use of written wills and/or gifts *inter vivos* in Ghana, intestacy remains widespread. Many people lack the means or do not bother to write a will; others prefer or feel obligated to leave it to their relatives and descendants to decide how to manage their estates. The extensive planning, expense, and drama that surround funeral celebrations in Ghana stem in part from their symbolic and practical importance in negotiations over the management of a deceased person's estate (de Witte 2001; Gilbert 1988; Mazzucato et al. 2006; van der Geest 1998, 2000). Family relationships continue to play an important role in such negotiations even if the deceased has written a will or given away his/her property while still alive. Written wills and gifts *inter vivos* are valid only for self-acquired goods. Assets left by a person who dies intestate, or who inherited family property, may not be gifted or bequeathed to recipient(s) of his/her choosing.

In re Krah (Deceased) Yankyeraah and Others v. Osei-Tutu and Another

In 1968, Krah purchased three square miles of virgin forest when he became head of his family. A wealthy man, he distributed much of this land to others – family members, strangers, and some of his laborers, on varied terms. He also made cocoa farms on his own account, one of which he gave to his wife. The family cultivated three of the cocoa farms "on a communal basis" until they began to yield in 1974.

In 1977, Krah wrote a will leaving some of his property to his ten children; the rest (excluding his wife's farm) to his family. In 1984, when Krah was very ill, a grandson produced a second will revoking the previous one and leaving the three cocoa farms to the grandson. Members of Krah's family sued, arguing that Krah had been too ill in 1984 to know what he was doing, and that the second will was invalid.

A majority of the court agreed, citing testimony that the farms had been cultivated jointly by members of the family as proof that they were family property Krah could not have bequeathed to his grandson. To buttress the judgment, the judges laid out their rationale: "Once a family property, always a family property. Therefore if a head of family mismanaged property, or treated it as his own, that would not change the family character of the property to become the head's own property. If it were so there would never be any family property" (*Ghana Law Report Digest*, 1989/90, Case #64. Judgment 22/3/89).

Once the family character of a property was established, it was up to the family head to manage it on behalf of the whole family, and that person should be given the authority to do so. Heads of families, the judges declared, must be able to allocate family land for farming or rent a room in a family house without calling a family meeting.

Without challenging the majority ruling in principle, two of the five presiding justices dissented. The deceased, they wrote, was "dealing with the land at Sukusuku as his own, carving portions for the family and retaining some for himself," adding that the plaintiffs should have provided more substantial evidence that "the Sukusuku land despite the acts of individual ownership retained a family character" (*Ghana Law Report Digest*, 1989/90, Case #64. Judgment 22/3/89).

I cite this case at some length not only because it illustrates the way questions of ownership intersect with issues of family governance when property is transmitted from one generation to another, but also because of their importance in the court's ruling. On the face of it, the case appears to be one of misconduct by an unscrupulous grandson, who tried to enrich himself by taking advantage of his grandfather's failing condition during his final illness. In ruling on the case, however, the judges paid no attention to the grandson's misdeeds, but focused instead on what might be described as constitutional principles of family governance and wealth. If the disputed farms were family property, Krah could not have bequeathed them to his grandson or anyone else, and the grandson's behavior, however deplorable, was irrelevant.

What did matter was Krah's behavior as family head, a position he held from 1968 until his death in 1984. Lacking documentary proof of title to the farms, the dissenting justices turned to the history of Krah's actions – specifically, his purchase, division, and use of the land. Because he "treated it as his own," they concluded, family ownership could not be established beyond a reasonable doubt. For the majority, on the other hand, the fact that Krah had cultivated the disputed farms "on a communal basis" with other family members was strong evidence of their "family character." In adding that a family head should not have to call a family meeting every time a specific form of land use would be authorized, the court implied that, in allocating parts of the land to relatives, laborers, and strangers for farming, Krah was only doing his job.

Yeboah and Others v. Kwakye

In this case, the court ruled that a house built by P. on land given to her by her father and a cocoa farm she established on land that her sister had acquired for the family, were family property. Sometime after the original house was built, P. mortgaged it in her son's name and used the loan to add on to the house. P. died before the loan was repaid: the family sold land to redeem the mortgage and named P.'s son as her successor. The son (defendant) then willed both the house and the farm to his wife and children, claiming his mother had gifted the cocoa farm to him, and he had purchased the building plot and taken out a loan to build the house.

In giving judgment for the plaintiffs, the court ruled that a farm on family land becomes family property on the planter's death. The planter may mortgage the farm while alive, but the family retains the right to redeem it. Finding that the son had not proved his claim to have bought the building plot or financed the house, the court ruled that the house and plot were also family property that would pass to the son's successor when he died. Because the house was family, rather than self-acquired, property, the son's wife and children had no right to live there except by permission of the family, and the family could enjoin them from entering the house if they wished to do so (*Ghana Law Reports Digest*, 1987/8. Case #63. Judgment 5/6/86).

Decided a few years after Ghana passed the 1985 Law on Intestate Succession (PNDCL 111), this case illustrates the kind of injustice associated with family property – here the dispossession of a widow and her children from their conjugal home – that the law was intended to prevent. In other cases, "family property" could work to protect people from exploitation by their kin.

Nana Baffoe Ababio and Adansi Boye v.
Kwabena Num, Kwaku Asiedu, and Yaa Akyaa

Two brothers applied to the court to sue two other brothers (Num and Asiedu) and a woman (Yaa Akyaa) over a house in a quarter of Kumasi known as New Suame. In 1948, Kwabena Num left their hometown and traveled to Kumasi "to seek his fortune." A blacksmith by trade, he settled in Suame (the center of metal-working and auto repair in Kumasi at the time), bought a welding machine and prospered, employing his brothers in his shop. With profits from the business and a loan taken out by the eldest brother, Nana Ababio, they built a two-story house with servants' quarters in New Suame, an extension of the rapidly expanding mechanics' district in Kumasi. The brothers built the house "together" but registered it in the name of the eldest, Nana Ababio, "to keep it as a family property." As of 1972, the buildings were occupied primarily by members of the brothers' family. "Only four rooms" were let to tenants, the court observed, so the house "was truly a family property."

Sometime later, Num opened a bank account in Asiedu's name and mortgaged the house, without informing Asiedu or his other brothers. In 1974, he bought a house in another Kumasi suburb and, in 1979, sold the house in New Suame to the third defendant, Yaa Akyaa to pay his debts. Although Num testified that he had told his brothers about these transactions, the court disbelieved him and ruled that, as head of the family, Nana Ababio was entitled to sue Num for damages. The sale to Yaa Akyaa was also declared null and void, allowing the brothers and their tenants to remain in possession pending the outcome of the suit (High Court, Kumasi, case found at the Council for Law Reporting, 1993/4).

To conclude this discussion of inheritance as a venue for family politics, I present a case in which the financial repercussions of an open-ended pledge intersected with a disputed claim to family property.

Madam Abena Adwapa v. John Amoah

The plaintiff claimed ownership of a cocoa farm that her late husband, K.T., had purchased from one K.D. and gifted to her sometime before he died in 1984. In 1994, the defendants sued the widow, claiming that the farm had been pledged, not sold, to the plaintiff's late husband by their relative (now deceased) for a loan of ¢4000 (4000 cedis). Implying that their relative K.D. had died intestate, they declared that the farm had thereby become family property and they now wished to redeem it on behalf of their relative's successor. A lower court had evidently ruled against the defendants, but they pursued the case to the Court of Appeals in Accra.

At the trial, K.T.'s successor testified that, in 1998, a relative of the defendants had offered him ¢4000 in repayment of a loan that K.T. had made to the defendants while he was still alive. By 1998, the value of the cedi had declined sharply from its level before 1984, and K.T.'s successor said he was surprised that anyone would bother with such a small amount, but he accepted it on behalf of K.T.'s estate. Later, however, when he heard that the ¢4000 payment was to redeem the pledged cocoa farm, he returned the money. During the trial, witnesses confirmed that the farm had been transferred to K.T. – though they did not know the terms – and that he had gifted it to his wife. K.T.'s successor added that he had not claimed the farm at K.T.'s funeral because it had been gifted to K.T.'s wife and was therefore not part of his estate. Under questioning, the defendants admitted that K.T. had felled timber and planted cocoa on the land, and they had not tried to reclaim it until long after K.T.'s death.

In ruling on the case, the Appeals Court declared that the defendants had not proved that K.D. had held the land as family property. (If he had, he could have mortgaged the land to defray the debts of the deceased or raise money for the family. The fact that he had not done so was deemed to weaken his claim.) Furthermore, the court noted, the widow did not claim the farm "in the name of the pledgee" – thereby "becoming a stranger" – and the defendants had allowed her to remain on the farm and develop it "in the honest belief that she is the bona fide owner." Having allowed her to remain in this position for ten years, the defendants cannot now "perpetuate fraud on a stranger who has taken possession of his [sic] land without asserting his [sic] right."

The fraud in this case was the defendants' attempt to pass off the sale of the farm as a pledge, thus claiming the right to "redeem" it many years later for a fraction of its present value. But the court appears to have gone further, although the rather convoluted language of the ruling leaves room for debate. By declaring the widow a "stranger," the court was, in effect, upholding her "good faith" ownership of the farm by invoking the customary distinction between agnatic and conjugal families. If her husband had held the farm as a pledge, the court implied, he and his successor(s) would have been obliged to return it if the debtor (or the debtor's successors) had repaid the loan, no matter how long the debt had remained unpaid.

That K.T. had given the farm to his wife (a "stranger" in relation to his matrilineage) and she accepted it "in good faith" proved that he had purchased the farm out of his own resources, it was his to give away, and the defendants' claim to the farm as "family property" was fallacious (Court of Appeal 22/2003. Judgment 26/3/04).

Conclusion

While the cases cited here are too few and far between to warrant any firm conclusions, they raise questions about the way practices of inheritance have changed in Ghana in the context of commercialization and growing competition over land. Recognized in both statutory law and custom, and reaffirmed by both court rulings and social practice, the institution of family property has, to some extent, prolonged the significance of family as a micropolity in which people fight and/or forge agreements over claims on wealth and belonging. Like wealth-in-things and people, wealth-in-relationships gain or lose value as circumstances change. The value of family property often varies from one family member to another, but individual gains and losses are linked to their relations with other family members, as well as their own conduct and their ties to authorities, witnesses, and others outside of their family networks.

The cases presented here, and the process of inheritance in general, also underscore the extent to which wealth and value are matters of time. I have written elsewhere about the many ways history adds value to objects and services that are exchanged in the market (Berry 2017). Focusing on inheritance – the transmission of wealth from one generation to another – also draws attention to the temporality of wealth, but in somewhat different ways. On one hand, disputes over pledging show how the passage of time can alter the balance of power between borrower and lender – turning a borrower's sacrifice of the use of collateral at the time of the loan to a windfall gain later on when the collateral is worth a great deal more than it was then. On the other, the irreversibility of group ownership in the case of "family property" means that the value of whatever assets are included is linked – in principle, "forever" – to family governance and relations among family members who participate in it.

Both the value and the political implications of a debt are products of time. As John Maynard Keynes famously observed many years ago, the amount of a debt may influence the relative power of the transactors – and not necessarily to the benefit of the lender. An analogous point may be made about time. As Graeber has pointed out, a loan creates a relationship between borrower and lender: the longer the debt goes unpaid, the longer the relationship lasts. Stories of inheritance in Ghana add to these observations in two ways. As illustrated by the cases of pledged property cited above, the longer a debt goes unpaid, the more the borrower stands to gain, especially if the items used as collateral consist of land or landed assets. In addition, the sociality of ownership embedded in family property complicates the common argument that commercialization *produces* conditions of atomistic competition, rather than vice versa. Families may not get along, but their shared interests in family property tend to prolong their relationships with one another. The question is not whether family ties are "breaking down" under the pressures of capitalist expansion, but how they are being reconfigured.

Sara Berry is a retired Professor of History at Johns Hopkins University. She has done research on land, development, agrarian change, political economy, and socio-economic history in sub-Saharan Africa, with primary emphasis on Nigeria and Ghana. Principal publications include *Fathers Work for Their Sons: Accumulation, Mobility and Class Formation in an Extended Yoruba Community* (University of California Press, 1985), *No Condition Is Permanent: The Social Dynamics of Agrarian Change in Sub-Saharan Africa* (University of Wisconsin Press, 1993), and *Chiefs Know Their Boundaries: Essays on Property, Power and the Past in Asante, 1896–1996* (Heinemann, 2001).

NOTES

1. The increasing use of spatial and temporal boundaries in land transactions is by no means limited to Ghana (see, e.g., Mathieu 2003; Chauveau 2006).
2. Several people with whom I discussed inheritance made similar comments.
3. Between 1993 and 2009, I carried out research on land claims and contests in urban neighborhoods in Kumasi, a sizeable rural town, and several smaller towns in peri-urban areas around Kumasi. Periods of research varied from one to six months.
4. Guyer's account of a day spent at a petrol station in southwestern Nigeria during a nationwide oil crisis provides a vivid ethnographic example of the knowledge and social dynamics involved in market transactions. In this case, negotiations dealt not with a loan, but with the distribution of a limited supply of a much sought-after commodity. Faced with the task of rationing her limited day's supply of petrol among the throng of increasingly restive customers, the proprietress navigated skillfully through multiple registers of entitlement among them, demonstrating her evident knowledge of the people she was dealing with, as well as her own diplomatic and performative skills. At the end of the day, many customers left dissatisfied, but conceding that distribution of the inadequate supply had been fair (Guyer 2007: 107–10). For other insightful examples of the cultural politics of contemporary exchange in Africa, see, e.g., Michael Degani (2015); Kristin Peterson (2014); Judith Scheele (2012); Kristov Titeca (2010); Kristov Titeca and Tom de Herdt (2012).
5. Much the same may be said of today's highly impersonal electronic "credit records" that may make or break a person's or an institution's ability to borrow in order to buy property, finance a business venture, obtain education or health care, or meet basic costs of living in times of need. Technologies of finance have changed dramatically, but the social logics have not. Whether orally transmitted, committed to paper, or preserved in a digital archive, past transactions affect future prospects – giving rise to the familiar paradox that going into debt may increase one's ability to borrow. What matters is knowledge of the conduct of the borrower and lender and the social context of their exchange. If a borrower is a client or relative, for example, a lender may confront social pressure to accept delayed repayment or even forgive a loan

that would not be forgiven if the borrower were a stranger. Of course, a loan to a stranger is risky too, unless one can rely on a third party to vouch for the stranger's reliability. Transfers of collateral, whether human or material, attest to the uncertainty that attaches to any exchange that remains to be completed in the future.

6. Although pawning became illegal under colonial and postcolonial rule, clandestine human collateral in the form of bonded servitude continues, in some instances, today.
7. Retrieved 25 July 2021 from https://acts.ghanajustice.com/actsofparliament/administration-of-estates-act-1961-act-63/.
8. The history of legal practice in Ghana involves an on-going process of adaptation among several legal traditions – state or "received common" law derived from the period of British colonial rule, laws passed by the Ghanaian state since independence, customary law, and "the living laws of the people" (Kasanga and Woodman 2004: 211). While the multiplicity of applicable legal orders can complicate the adjudication of particular cases, in practice families have considerable leeway to work out their own governing arrangements (Kasanga and Woodman 2004: 197–99).
9. Notoriously so in the case of chiefly authority over land, which was reaffirmed in the 1992 Constitution and strengthened under the Land Administration Reform Program, 2003–2011. This has become the subject of a substantial literature that I will not attempt to review here, beyond noting that a number of studies argue that chiefs have profited handsomely from negotiating large-scale land deals with foreign investors during the boom in "land grabs" since c. 2007 (Amanor and Moyo 2008; Cotula 2009).
10. Retrieved 7 December 2021 from https://ghanalegal.com/laws_subdomain/acts/group/9/PNDC-Law/.
11. As the term implies, self-acquired property refers to assets the deceased acquired through his or her own efforts. Property from which the successor benefits as a member of the inheriting family or that was acquired with the help of others is considered "family property," subject to management by "the family" rather than the deceased or other individual(s) who have been designated as heir.
12. The law entitles all children and spouses of the deceased to share in the estate, a stipulation that could oblige a surviving spouse to share the conjugal house with co-wives and/or children s/he did not recognize or get along with (Frempong 2004; Woodman 1996).
13. The courts' treatments of both pledges and family property are discussed at length by Gordon Woodman (1996).
14. The use of sharecroppers and/or hired labor in cocoa farming dates to the early years of the twentieth century in Ghana and in other West African economies (see, e.g., Austin 2005; Berry 1975; Galletti et al. 1956; Hill 1963; Takane 2002).
15. In incorporating "customary" structures of authority into the administrative apparatus of the colonial state, British officials referred to Ghanaians as "subjects" of both the colonial state and one or another chiefly office or stool. While this terminology fell out of favor after independence, the principle of

political duality did not. Hence, it has become common practice to refer both to citizens of Ghana and to "citizens" of the stool (Berry 2009).
16. To bolster his opinion, the Appeals Court judge cited Gordon Woodman's authoritative study *Customary Land Law in the Courts of Ghana* (1996: 150).
17. Interviews with the manager of the Kumawuman Rural Bank and residents of Kumawu and Juaben, 1994 and 2002.
18. I plan to discuss the legacy of pawning and its significance for family relations in the twentieth century separately.

REFERENCES

Allman, Jean, and John Parker. 2005. *Tongnaab: The History of a West African God*. Bloomington: Indiana University Press.
Amanor, Kojo, and Sam Moyo, eds. 2008. *Land and Sustainable Development in Africa*. London: Zed.
Austin, Gareth. 2005. *Land, Labour and Capital in Ghana: From Slavery to Free Labour in Asante, 1807–1956*. Rochester, NY: Rochester University Press.
Azu Crabbe, Samuel. 1998. *The Law of Wills in Ghana*. Accra: Vieso Universal (Ghana) Limited.
Baum, Robert. 1999. *Shrines of the Slave Trade: Diola Religion and Society in Precolonial Senegambia*. Oxford: Oxford University Press.
Berry, Sara. 2009. "Property, Authority and Citizenship: Land Claims, Politics and the Dynamics of Social Division in West Africa." In "Property and Authority: Fuzzy Relations, Fuzzy Realities," special issue ed. Christian Lund and Thomas Sikor of *Development and Change*, 40 (1): 23–45.
———. 2017. "History as Value Added: Valuing the Past in Africa." In *The Political Economy of Everyday Life in Africa. Beyond the Margins*, ed. Wale Adebanwi. Oxford: James Currey.
Bolt, Maxim. 2013. "The Loan Economy." *Anthropology of this Century* 7. http://aotcpress.com/articles/loan-economy/.
Chauveau, Jean-Pierre. 2006. "How Does an Institution Evolve? Land, Politics, Intergenerational Relations and the Institution of the *Tutorat* amongst Autochthones and Immigrants (Gban Region, Côte d'Ivoire)." In *Land and the Politics of Belonging in West Africa*, ed. Richard Kuba and Carola Lentz, 213–40. Leiden: Brill Academic Publishers.
Comaroff, John, ed. 1980. *The Meaning of Marriage Payments*. London: Academic Press.
Constitution of the Republic of Ghana [Ghana]. 1993. Retrieved 25 July 2021from https://www.refworld.org/docid/3ae6b5850.html.
Cotula, Lorenzo. 2009. *Land Grab or Development Opportunity: Agricultural Investment and International Land Deals in Africa*. London: IIED.
Degani, Michael. 2015. "The City Electric: Infrastructure and Ingenuity in Postsocialist Tanzania." PhD dissertation. New Haven, CT: Yale University.
de Witte, Marleen. 2001. *Long Live the Dead! Changing Funeral Celebrations in Asante, Ghana*. Amsterdam: Aksant Academic Publishers.
Ekejiuba, Felicia, and K. O. Dike. 1990. *The Aro of South-Eastern Nigeria, 1650–1980: A Study of Socio-Economic Formation and Transformation in Nigeria*. Ibadan: Ibadan University Press.

Falola, Toyin, and Paul Lovejoy, eds. 2003. *Pawnship, Slavery, & Colonialism in Africa.* Trenton, NJ: New World Press.

Frempong, Seth. 2004. "Application of the Law of Intestate Succession and Its Effects on Family Relationships in Asante." MPhil dissertation. Legon: Institute of African Studies.

Galletti, R. O., Kenneth David Sutherland Baldwin, and I. O. Dina. 1956. *Nigerian Cocoa Farmers.* Oxford: Oxford University Press.

Ghana Law Reports. 1961. Parts 1 and 2. Edited by N. Y. B. Adade: Accra, 1968.

Gilbert, Michelle. 1988. "The Sudden Death of a Millionaire: Conversion and Consensus in a Ghanaian Kingdom." *Africa* 58(3): 291–314.

Graeber, David. 2011. *Debt: The First 5000 Years.* New York: Melville House.

Guyer, Jane. 2007. *Marginal Gains: Monetary Transactions in Atlantic Africa.* Chicago: University of Chicago Press.

Guyer, Jane, and Samuel Eno Belinga. 1995. "Wealth in People as Wealth in Knowledge: Accumulation and Composition in Equatorial Africa." *Journal of African History* 36(1): 91–120.

Hill, Polly. 1963. *Migrant Cocoa Farmers of Southern Ghana.* Cambridge: Cambridge University Press.

Kasanga, Kasim, and Gordon Woodman. 2004. "Ghana: Local Law Making and Land Conversion in Kumasi, Asante." In *Local Land Law and Globalization: A Comparative Study of Peri-Urban Areas in Benin, Ghana and Tanzania,* ed. Gordon Woodman, Ulrike Wanizek, and H. Zippel. Munich: LIT Verlag.

Lydon, Ghislaine. 2009. *On Trans-Saharan Trails: Islamic Law, Trade Networks and Cross Cultural Exchange in 19th-Century Western Africa.* Cambridge: Cambridge University Press.

Mazzucato, Valentina, Miriam Kabke, and Lothar Smith. 2006. "A Transnational Funeral: Remittances, Decisions and Practices across National Borders." *Development and Change* 37(5): 1047–72.

McCaskie, Thomas. 1995. *State and Society in Precolonial Asante.* Cambridge: Cambridge University Press.

Mathieu, Paul, ed. 2003. *Making Land Transactions More Secure in the West of Burkina Faso.* London: IIED.

Nwokeji, Ugo. 2010. *The Slave Trade and Culture in the Bight of Biafra: An African Society in the Atlantic World.* Cambridge: Cambridge University Press.

Peterson, Kristin. 2014. *Speculative Markets: Drug Circuits and Derivative Life in Nigeria.* Durham, NC: Duke University Press.

Scheele, Judith. 2012. *Smugglers and Saints of the Sahara.* Cambridge: Cambridge University Press.

Shipton, Parker. 2007. *The Nature of Entrustment: Intimacy, Exchange and the Sacred in Africa.* New Haven, CT: Yale University Press.

———. 2009. *Mortgaging the Ancestors: Ideologies of Attachment in Africa.* New Haven, CT: Yale University Press.

Takane, Tsutomu. 2002. *The Cocoa Farmers of Southern Ghana: Incentives, Institutions and Change in Rural West Africa.* Chiba: Institute of Developing Economies Japan External Trade Organization.

Titeca, Kristov. 2012. "Tycoons and Contraband: Informal Cross-Border Trade in West Nile, Northwestern Uganda," *Journal of Eastern African Studies* 6(1): 47–63.

Titeca, Kristov, and Tom de Herdt. 2010. "Regulation, Cross-Border Trade and Practical Norms in West Nile District, North-Western Uganda," *Africa* 80(4): 573–94.

Valsecchi, Pierluigi. 2011. *Power and State Formation in West Africa: Appolonia from the 16th to the 18th Centuries.* New York: Palgrave Macmillan.

Van der Geest, Sjaak. 1998. "*Yebisa wo fie*: Growing Old and Building a House in the Akan Culture of Ghana." *Journal of Cross-cultural Gerontology* 13: 333–59.

———. 2000. "Funerals for the Living: Conversations with Elderly People in Kwahu, Ghana." *African Studies Review* 43(3): 103–29.

Weiner, Annette. 1992. *Inalienable Possessions: The Paradox of Keeping-While-Giving.* Berkeley: University of California Press.

Wilks, Ivor. 1993. *Forests of Gold: Essays on the Akan and the Kingdom of Asante.* Athens: Ohio University Press.

Woodman, Gordon. 1996. *Customary Land Law in the Ghanaian Courts.* Accra: Ghana Universities Press.

CHAPTER 5

 Tales of Mortgage, Risk, and Taxation in Rural Senegal

KRISTINE JUUL

This chapter explores two different ways of accessing capital in the rural countryside: mortgaging and taxation. The goals and intentions of these two modes of capital formation are clearly different, as one targets individuals aiming to raise capital for personal development objectives or to cover losses and unforeseen expenditures, while the other is concerned with revenue collection for the state or for local government with the goal of improving public services. Nonetheless, both are linked profoundly to issues such as debt, property rights, titling, market integration, and economic growth.

Despite these overlaps, the topics are seldom brought together in discussion. The dominant argument, propagated by World Bank economists such as Hernando de Soto, regards the establishment of clear definitions and defense of property rights as necessary prerequisites for improving poor people's access to credit institutions. Through the formation of so-called "meta" property (i.e., the paper trail of title and mortgage), the surplus value of assets can be freed up to provide the necessary capital for economic growth and development. Without this legal framework, people can do business only with their family or with those whom they know (de Soto in Joireman 2008: 1234).

Another approach is provided by scholars engaged in the relationship between taxation and development. In their view, improved taxation may also lead to economic development and growth, as strengthened revenue mobilization is likely to increase the ability of states or local government to provide security, meet basic needs, and ensure the development of infrastructure. Apart from providing state revenues, taxation creates important links between citizens and the state, developing accountability to citizens over tax policy and public spending. This enhances the motivation of states to promote prosperity among citizen-taxpayers, which, in turn, extends their tax revenue base (Bräutigam, Fjeldstad, and Moore 2008; Moore 2015).

Over the last thirty years, the credit argument has gained considerable influence. Financial inclusion through provision of credit to the poor has emerged as a high-profile policy for tackling poverty in the Global South and has benefited from widespread recognition from both public and private stakeholders. As early as 2011, it was estimated that over 200 million people had benefited from microfinance services, some, but not all, involving collateral (Guérin, Morvant-Roux, and Villareal 2014: 3).

Since then, more problematic aspects of this widespread credit business have surfaced. Critical accounts have highlighted how increasing financialization and global recession have amplified the existing dangers of downward social mobility, over-indebtedness, and pauperization among households who engage in debt to compensate for weakness in labor income and inadequate social protection mechanisms. At the same time, it has become evident that the microfinance model suffers from considerable institutional weakness, as few services have been able to exist without subsidy. One common challenge is the weak collateral situation of most borrowers: their lack of credit history and the no-growth nature of their income-generating activities, which consist mainly of small-scale buy-and-sell transactions in the informal economy. This combination of high risk and elevated administrative costs generally contributes to high interest rates.

In itself, debt is not a problem. On the contrary, it is central to the circulation of capital. It is a truism that borrowing is good if it helps you to gain financially and bad if it becomes a "financial burden." Whether borrowing contributes to "freeing" the assets of the poor, and thereby increasing their well-being or serves to worsen the conditions of the debtor depends on the local environment and the context-specific, nuanced processes that shape the nature of the credit demand and how microfinance services are implemented. As noted by Guérin et al. (2014: 14), discerning whether microcredit customers are potential entrepreneurs or simply desperately in need of cash is difficult in many environments, where both roles may be represented in one individual; entrepreneurs may fail if their investments turn out not to be profitable, but just as often they fail because of acute temporary cash demands due to unforeseen circumstances, such as accidents and illness. Because insufficient taxation and lack of revenue weaken the security net provided by the state, an unfortunate relationship exists between the proliferation of microcredit and the lack of public services. In this way, as Safiétou Kane notes, "microcredit has become a response to the failure of the Senegalese state to provide adequate basic services such as education and health to its citizens" (2013: 60).

Taxation, on the other hand, is often perceived as an unappealing necessity and has until recently received little attention in the development literature. This changed with the spread of what Keen has called the new fiscal sociology (Bräutigam et al. 2008; Keen 2013; Meagher 2018). This school of thought, which brings together sociology, economy, history, and political science, seeks to use taxation as a lens through which to explore changes in the social contract that links state and society, in contrast to the view of earlier economists that taxation undermines growth and exacerbates informality. As noted by Bräutigam, donors, policymakers, businesspeople, and civil society activists increasingly recognize the field of taxation as a new frontier for those concerned with state building in developing countries (2008). This relates primarily to its potential, when implemented progressively, to reduce inequality. Taxation is therefore, as Thomas Piketty has shown, not just a technical matter: "It is preeminently a political and philosophical issue, perhaps the most important of all political issues. Without taxes, society has no common destiny and collective action is impossible" (Piketty 2014: 493).

As discussed above, one quality of taxation particularly highlighted by tax propagators lies in the institution-building stimulus provided by revenue imperatives. If a state is dependent on broad general taxation, rather than on natural resource extraction or flows of development aid, then it will be more willing to make deals with its citizens and hence more motivated to help promote prosperity among its citizen-taxpayers. To strengthen tax collection, governments will be forced to build more effective public sector organizations. At the same time, expansion of taxation may prompt taxpayers to demand more control over how taxes are used, which, again, will make them more willing to pay. Through such processes of "tax bargaining," more reciprocity and constructive interactions may develop between governments and citizens. A "fiscal social contract" may emerge as taxpayers discover that payment of taxes gives them the right not only to services but also to representation. In this way, accountable and democratic governance structures that are beneficial for economic growth are likely to appear (Bräutigam 2008: 12; Moore, Prichard, and Fjeldstad 2018: 13).

A final, but so far neglected, issue is the spatial or territorial dimension of taxation and its relation to property. Through so-called internal territorialization, taxation creates and bolsters sanctioned authority in the countryside through homogeneous institutions and local representation that can ensure compliance with state regulation (see Peluso and Vandergeest 2001: 177). In this way, implementation of taxation provides an opportunity for states and local government to demarcate spatial fields in which they can exercise control.

On the individual level, payment of taxes may expand the rights of citizenship, underscoring membership of a certain group and compliance with the state or other authorities, which is likely to encourage protection of the rights and properties of the citizen. Taxation is therefore one of the strategies used by individuals and companies to make or improve their claims on land and resources or their claims of belonging (Juul 2006).

To a certain degree, the spatial dimension of taxation is therefore dependent on the existence of a land market. Where land markets are poorly developed and conventional land registration systems nonexistent, taxation and mortgaging become challenging endeavors. If no secure procedures exist for estimating the market value of assets used as collateral, the "debt capacity" of individual households is difficult to evaluate. Consequently, the presence or absence of a land market plays a role in what types of taxes are likely to be collected. In rural Senegal, where most land is supposed to be inalienable and is ultimately under the control of the state, neither clear property rights nor property taxation are well developed. As will be shown below, taxation under other forms still influences security of tenure, in ways that may turn out to be significant for capital formation (albeit slightly different from those involving mortgages).

The goal of this chapter is not to evaluate whether credit and lending represent a step forward for local populations or, conversely, if mortgaging practices contribute to an increase in their financial uncertainty. Nor is the ambition to assess whether poorly defined property rights are a barrier to individual and societal growth. Instead, the chapter seeks to understand how individual credit and local taxation practices in rural Senegal have influenced perceptions of property, mortgage, and public service provision. In this way, this chapter places mortgage debt and property in a broader framework that connects both the social practices of long-term conditionalities of debt as well as the role of the state.

To identify the issues at stake, two cases from Senegal are presented. First, the introduction of mortgages and the proliferation of individual formal credit institutions is discussed in the context of the livestock-dominated economy of the northern town of Dahra. In the second part, the role of taxation as a collective means to enhance the development of a local business environment is explored, along with the challenges and potential benefits of improved (property) taxation. By bringing together empirical evidence regarding local practices of taxation and mortgaging as they unfold in the pastoral economy in and around Dahra, a confusing and contradictory picture emerges that is likely to shed doubt on the underlying assumptions and normativities of the perspectives presented above.

A Tale of Mortgaging and Borrowing

To prepare for this chapter, I called M., my friend and former research assistant, to find out whether mortgaging had become an issue in the northern cattle-trading town of Dahra, where he lives. My preliminary impression had been that banking based on collateral and mortgaging was of limited importance in rural Senegal. Here, as elsewhere in the rural regions of the Sahel, land is in principle allocated free of charge by local government or village chiefs. Monetary transactions, although both frequent and wide-ranging, are handled primarily through kin-based informal credit arrangements based on trust. However, M. informed me otherwise. Not only was mortgaging common, but he had himself been very close to being evicted from his home. Indeed, credit institutions were now encouraging herders to take out loans, using not only their houses but also their animals and other goods as collateral. According to M., local engagement in credit and mortgages started in 2004, when various credit institutions opened branches in the town, providing people who were short of funds with an alternative to soliciting money from family and friends. He knew of several people who were in serious difficulties because of these credit schemes.

M.'s own case had developed as follows. Having been out of work for long periods of time, he had started a small business as a car insurance agent. Using all his savings, he was able to contract a number of insurance policies for vehicles that he would resell to transporters and other customers in town. Although the enterprise was successful, it did not take long before he was short of money and unable to pay his premiums to the insurance company. As most of his customers disposed of very little cash, their concern was to get as much as possible of the insurance license on credit. Once their mandatory car insurance expired, they put pressure on M. to renew the insurance and to let them reimburse him once cash was in hand. In order to be able to take out new insurance policies, M. took out a loan of CFA 500,000 (USD 834) with a credit institution, using his house, valued at CFA one million (USD 1,680)[1] including all fixtures, as collateral. His niece, who worked in the mayor's office, acted as guarantor. With this loan, he was able to service his debts and finance new insurance contracts.

Soon, however, M. found himself in trouble again. Because he had proved able to repay the previous loan on time, the credit institution encouraged him to borrow a larger amount, one million CFA, equivalent to the entire value of the mortgaged house. Unfortunately, M. was then ill for a long period. Unable to service his debt, he stood to lose the results of all his work, not to mention putting his niece into great difficulties, had it not been for his extended and international social network.

Like M., few Senegalese hold the formal title to their land. The frequency of lending based on mortgages on private property is therefore surprising. Outside the larger cities, land ultimately belongs to the state, making it difficult to claim extended ownership rights. Even in Dahra, with its approximately 40,000 inhabitants, plots are not privately owned but allocated through the municipality, where applicants pay a fee of CFA 1000 per square meter for the right of residency. If M. had defaulted on his mortgage payments, he would have lost not only his house but also the plot and the three huts that members of his extended family had erected there. M.'s case showed that the value of his homestead was highly unstable and that, even though he was not the owner of the land, he was still liable to lose it. From having acquired access to land as a function of membership and belonging, M. was transformed into a simple tenant, at risk of losing the right of occupancy if certain economic obligations were not met. Furthermore, his attempts to resolve a perpetual shortage of cash, characteristic of many rural households, by formal mortgaging of his house did not contribute to capital formation. Instead, access to a bank loan caused his debtors to repay even more slowly.

Credit in Transition

Loans and credit are obviously nothing new to the inhabitants of Dahra. Particularly among livestock traders, credit and informal lending agreements are well-integrated practices. Even in cases when sellers and buyers do not know each other, very large transactions are carried out on the basis of a combination of cash payment and credit (Diaw 1995: 63). Handling debts of this size and significance is a matter of interpersonal skills of networking, trust, and reputation. This negotiability is, however, not without social or financial cost. The risk of losing not only money but also reputation if obligations are not met is omnipresent for both lender and borrower (Guérin et al. 2014: 8).

Informal lending and credit is, of course, not limited to the livestock sector. As elsewhere in Senegal, myriad informal financial tools enable people to cope with everyday financial risks. The best known of these are the so-called *tontines*, saving groups where members contribute a weekly or monthly amount and take turns to receive the pooled sum. Often this money is invested in small-scale trading activities, livestock-fattening projects, or social networks through "ceremonial activities" (Baumann and Fall 2015: 187).

Even with the arrival of formal credit institutions, these borrowing patterns have not been abandoned. People combine multiple financial tools in ongoing circuits of borrowing, repayment, and reborrowing, in what Guérin et al. (2015) have termed *juggling practices*; money borrowed from one creditor is used to repay another creditor. Interestingly, the proximity of lender and borrower or between members of a *tontine* contributes to these juggling practices and increases lending with microfinance institutions (MFIs). Out of fear of falling behind with their trusted *tontine* or informal creditor, which would lead to dishonor, many people are willing to engage in formal borrowing to service their obligations in the informal sector. This intertwinement leads to a constant swapping of roles between debtors and creditors, as illustrated by the story of M., who as an insurance agent was under constant pressure to lend, as it was precisely the trust and reputation he had gained through these lending activities that made his business thrive. In this way, even the poorest and most indebted are likely to become creditors (Guérin et al. 2015: 12).

Likewise, easier access to formal credit over the last twenty years has changed conditions in livestock transactions by raising the proportion of cash payments. As will be shown below, this is reflected in profits, as sales based on high levels of trust-based informal credit have become less profitable. Despite (or rather because of) these complications, the success of microcredit in rural Senegal is widespread. On the busy main road that serves as the business center of Dahra, at least six different savings and credit institutions advertise their services with colorful signs on the modest houses lining the road. While some are state-controlled agencies, others are private mutual savings and credit institutions, often referred to using the umbrella term MFI.

Over the years, MFI portfolios have been growing steadily throughout Senegal as part of a general campaign for "financial inclusion." From 1998 to 2013, MFI client numbers increased more than tenfold, at an annual rate of almost 17 percent. Although this rate of increase has since slowed, there are no signs of any significant loan portfolio slowdown (Baumann, Fall, and Godfroid 2015: 133). On the contrary, the general "sanitation and professionalization" process of 2004 compelled MFIs to move beyond a preoccupation with social welfare to become nationwide institutions with a primarily commercial objective. In this process, dynamic market towns such as Dahra became interesting targets for a broadening of banking activities. The official MFI business model is a credit and savings model. Customers are encouraged to open a savings account, on the basis of which they can borrow. Among clients, savings tend to be understood mainly as a prerequisite for lending, as loans can be obtained only if applicants have the resources to pay a membership fee, bring a warranty share of 10 percent of the loan requested (the "savings"), and pay for an insurance policy to cover the debt in case of death. As described in M.'s case, a client who has proved responsible and creditworthy by servicing and repaying one loan is then allowed to take out a larger loan.

The loans are generally modest. In Dahra, the amounts mentioned during interviews ranged from CFA 50,000 to 3 million.[2] Interest rates are approximately 10 percent for a loan reimbursable over a period of six to eight months (i.e., 18 to 20 percent annually). Despite high costs and elevated interest rates, many loan-takers seemed to appreciate the opportunity to borrow money from formal credit institutions. Among the

Figure 5.1. Many loans are used for fattening rams for the annual Eid el Kabir celebration. © Kristine Juul.

reasons given by respondents was that taking individual loans freed them from the obligations of covering for defaulters in mutual savings groups.

The adequacy of the loans seemed to differ, just as tracing the actual uses of loans was complicated by the frequency of loan-juggling. Among the women interviewed, loans mainly provided cash for very small-scale trading or animal-fattening activities. In that sense, the small size of the loans obtainable seemed appropriate. Nonetheless, the individualization and the automatic upscaling of well-serviced loans presents challenges as well as opportunities, not least due to the MFI structure, which incentivizes credit agents to encourage clients to renew and increase their loans once the previous loan has been reimbursed.[3] In a cash-poor environment, such credit opportunities can be hard to decline, as a woman may also be under pressure from other family members to take up new loans. As observed by Donna Perry (2002) and Guérin et al. (2014: 14), this has transformed some women into informal moneylenders; as they proceed through the cycle of loans, the amounts involved become larger and larger, and some women simply do not know what to do with the money (Perry 2002: 35). In such a situation, money-lending makes perfect sense. Whether it enhances financial inclusion remains to be seen.

Of frequent concern, particularly among male respondents, were the short cycles and limited loan sizes:

> Usually it's around 50,000 CFA. That enables you to buy one animal for fattening. It does not really lead anywhere and at the same time it's too risky. With 50 to 500,000 CFA, you cannot buy things that would enable you to really change things in your life. The animals are expensive, fodder, medication, and vaccination are expensive. Within three months, you haven't made any savings but you risk losing your house. If you could take loans of 1 to 1.5 million, reimbursable within one year, then you could make a good fattening business of around 4 million. You pay the loan and you keep the rest. But the bank wants people to pay in sequences, and if they can't pay, then they are in trouble. Using your house as collateral would enable longer delays, and then it would work. Then the house would be useful. (Chef de quartier, Dahra, August 2019)

Assessing Creditworthiness in a Risk-Prone Environment

The raison d'être of MFIs lies in their acceptance that few clients dispose of assets suitable for seizure in the event of a loan default. As explained to me in an interview by the agent from Crédits Agricoles:[4] "It isn't really possible here. Instead, we check the status and reputation of the herders. We often go to the markets to check the necessary information. We inquire about their abilities to make a good fattening operation, how much cattle they possess, etc. The herding sector is known to be a risky one." Nonetheless, the use of collateral is often mentioned, even among cattle-poor clients, although the actual handling of collateral remains imprecise at best. Indeed, the meticulous assessment procedure described above was not reflected in the experiences recounted by the debtors interviewed, for whom borrowing money was something that took place within the confines of the credit and savings associations. Assessments of the economic potential of the lender on the ground became relevant only when loans were not serviced according to the modalities agreed.

Furthermore, the difference between formal mortgaging and "voluntary sales" often became irrelevant to debtors, as the methods used by credit agents forced debtors to sell vital assets or property in order to meet reimbursement conditions. This was the case of a small shopkeeper who felt obliged to sell his house to avoid the shameful and counterproductive situation of having credit agents appearing at his shop "every other day" when he was unable to service his CFA 3 million loan due to an unexpected rent increase.

Evidence from fieldwork shows that loans based on mortgage and personal guarantees not only exist but are widespread. This is in line with Elizabeth Holmes and Jules Ndambu (2011: 37), who found that 32.8 percent of their sample had taken loans involving some kind of guarantee, either in the form of a mortgage or based on individual or group bail. The most common forms were personal or group bail (32.8 percent and 12.1 percent, respectively), but third-party endorsements were also frequent (11.6 percent). In 18.1 percent of cases, security was taken in the form of stock or equipment (17.8 percent), houses (12.7 percent), or fields (6.8 percent). Only a small minority (3 percent) identified their pay slip as the basis of a guarantee, reflecting the limited number of salaried workers among MFI clients. The perils of such mortgaging practices can be seen in the case study below.

Case Study 1

A cattle trader, A., had taken several consecutive loans to finance his activities, using his house and the plot as security. At a certain point, more cash was needed. As A.'s experience told him that MFIs were partial to female borrowers, he persuaded his wife to take out a loan using fifty head of cattle allegedly in their possession as collateral. For a number of years, the couple made the loan repayments on time, enabling them to finance a flourishing cattle trade between Dahra and Dakar. In 2013–14, however, rain was scarce and two-thirds of the animals purchased died, inflicting a considerable loss. At this stage, the couple's total loans amounted to CFA 4 million each, a large but not unusual amount. Despite their huge efforts, they were unable to fully service the debt.

Credit agents then made several visits to the house, in some cases accompanied by police. Like many other defaulters, A.'s wife chose to travel to where the credit agents would not find her, but shortly after, A. was rounded up and jailed for a month.

When his wife, too, was arrested by the police, agitated neighbors summoned the *chef de quartier* to her defense. In a joint effort by relatives and neighbors, she was released after one night in prison, and sufficient money was mobilized to renegotiate the credit conditions and secure the house. When the case was finally taken to court, the judge ruled that a further CFA 350,000 should be reimbursed to the bank at a pace manageable for the borrower.

Although marked by the humiliation of the situation, the couple have not stopped borrowing from banks. At the time of the interview, A. was already taking loans from another MFI to continue his previous trading activities. Asked why he could not return to the old ways of trading cattle on credit, he explained that this is still possible, but that with easier access to formal lending, more cash is now circulating on the markets. Therefore, the prices obtained in trading arrangements involving high levels of informal credit are too low to ensure a decent profit margin.

The case described above shows how engaging with formal banks and MFIs involves new and more impersonal forms of interaction between credit agents and defaulting citizens. As borrower and lender are transformed into creditor and debtor, norms of courtesy and rules of confidentiality are easily breached, as are barriers of age, sex, and class (Shipton 2010: 2). In Dahra, many respondents criticized credit agents for not respecting common rules of confidentiality or the dignity and sense of honor of the individual when approaching a debtor. Very public visits by credit agents and police, and repeated threats of imprisonment, were seen as intolerable harassment. Respondents generally expressed understanding rather than disapproval of those who had failed to repay loans, and in many cases, neighbors intervened on behalf of debtors to force the bank to alter the repayment conditions. This was particularly the case when the new and individualized approaches to lending had repercussions on family members, for whom the mortgaging of mutual assets came as a surprise, revealed only at the moment of potential seizure.

However, a notable aspect of A.'s story is the court verdict that short-circuited the reimbursement procedures put forward by the MFI, abolishing the punitive interest rates imposed on the defaulter and allowing more gradual reimbursement. This underscores the nebulousness of the legal framework for micro-lending. A similar ambiguity was revealed in another case, where a family was expelled from two houses they had owned because a brother had (secretly) mortgaged the family inheritance when he needed cash for his cattle-trading business. Following the losses incurred by the brother in a road accident and the theft of animals by the butcher to whom they had been entrusted during his recovery, the bank seized the houses and evicted the family. Now, eight years later, the credit institution has still not made any move to auction off the confiscated assets, presumably because of the unclear legal situation of the plots and buildings seized.

Unfortunately, the empirical data available on these issues are too fragmented to allow substantial conclusions to be drawn concerning the legality of existing mortgaging practices. Nevertheless, the indications are that most of the population of Dahra is adopting an increasingly loan-driven financial culture, where juggling between different types of formal and informal credit institutions is widespread. Whether this will lead to increased capital formation in the longer run remains an open question. Meanwhile, the cases described help deepen our understanding of the considerable risks involved in activities of financial inclusion, for both lenders and borrowers.

For credit institutions, Dahra represents a market where financial flows are substantial and the potential for profit is considerable. Nonetheless, operations there are also risky, as land titles are infrequent and buildings usually represent a limited value that is difficult to activate. Considerable ambiguity prevails with regard to mortgaging, which takes as its point of departure the creditor having full and inalienable rights to land forfeited in case of foreclosure. However, this is the case for very few buildings outside the bigger cities; as a result, cases of seizure are limited, and incidences of foreclosure auctions even fewer. Moreover, the legality of such actions remains obscure, not only to creditor and debtor but also to the authorities. This is clear from the rulings given in the few court cases to date, which have sided with the debtor by allowing more flexible repayment.

Debtors seldom seem aware of the real costs involved in loan-taking. They seem confused, for instance, by hikes in interest rates in case of default and by the consequences of mortgaging. People generally complain that the loans available to them are small, and the repayment cycle so short that no real profits can be made. Even worse is the unhelpful attitudes of credit agents who, unlike informal lenders, refuse to renegotiate conditions. Finally, a significant difference exists between the individual approach to loan-taking exercised by the MFIs and the collective nature of the assets used as collateral. This can put family members at risk if the loan-taker faces foreclosure. As shown above, microcredit does not diminish the risks faced by producers. Illness, accidents, and climatic hazards all too often put a halt to entrepreneurial activities. Often the services provided by the state or local authorities are characterized by insufficient coverage and high user fees, which forces debtors to use the cash made available to them through credit in order to meet their immediate needs. This issue, nonetheless, receives little attention when titling and mortgaging are being praised by their proponents. This leads us to the issue of taxation.

Financial or Fiscal Inclusion?
Levies, Fees, and Decentralized Taxation

According to the proponents of the new fiscal sociology, citizens may be willing to pay more taxes if taxation leads to increased provision of goods that they value. This concerns services within health, infrastructure, education, as well as political voice. Whether and how these benefits materialize depends on the forms of taxation used. Compared to the readiness with which citizens in and around Dahra engage in debt relations with credit institutions, popular interest in increased taxation so far remains low, to say the least.

When people in northern Senegal talk of taxes, they are usually referring to the *impôt du minimum fiscal*, a flat-rate poll tax intended to finance the budgets of rural or municipal councils, the locally elected bodies installed in every village or municipality of the Senegalese territory since 1972. In 1996, further efforts to strengthen decentralization and fiscal autonomy devolved the responsibility for collecting local taxes from the representative of the state, the *sous-préfet*, to locally elected councilors. Despite moderate charges (CFA 900, i.e., USD 1.50, for each adult aged between fourteen and sixty),[5] this opportunity for taxpayers to control the use of locally collected funds did not translate into any observable zest for paying taxes. In 2001, there was a dramatic drop in tax receipts where many rural communities around Dahra reached down to 0.5 percent of the projected totals (Juul 2006: 823). A similar trend was found across rural Senegal, leaving local councils paralyzed by a lack of funding

(Echos 2001: 10–12). Far from bringing growth, development, and political accountability to rural communities, the budgetary reform had increased divisions between villages and political rivalry in these highly politicized communities, where councilors, according to the local electorate, "entertained themselves by levying taxes with their opponents, while others where not disturbed" (Echos 2001: 10). Although political cleavages have proven decisive for tax recovery rates, these are seldom considered in discussions of the merits of taxation.

According to civil servants interviewed in 2019, tax recovery in Dahra is improving slowly. In 2017 and 2018, the proportion collected had risen considerably, providing the municipality with a revenue of CFA 65 million out of a potential CFA 120 million. This still leaves a huge number of tax evaders. According to the Technical Director of Dahra Municipality, reasons for non-compliance revolve around the lack of service provision and fear that councilors will "eat" the money: "People do not understand that the taxes will be returned and used for improving local conditions. People are generally suspicious. They say they will not pay, because it makes no difference" (Dahra, August 2019). To explain these improvements, the Director pointed to increased local involvement from the respective *chefs de quartier* and to the experience of participatory budgeting, introduced by a local NGO over the last few years (for more on participatory budgeting, see Moore et al. 2018: 203). In line with the idea of tax bargaining to increase people's willingness to pay taxes through improved transparency and voice, the program of participatory budgeting aims to involve local populations in prioritizing the most significant problems to be resolved in the coming budget year. In Dahra, top priorities have so far been an extension of the electricity grid, improved access to tap water, better waste management, and installation of public lighting in all neighborhoods. Unfortunately, these wishes are, according to the Director, unachievable on a budget of only CFA 32 million. Unable to meet these expectations, higher tax compliance is, he regrets, more likely to result from a new municipal measure whereby the distribution of government-subsidized seeds and foodstuffs is limited to those who can produce a tax receipt.

The low level of public services is easily ascertained from the town's development plan; large parts of Dahra are still outside the electricity grid, and certain areas of town remain unconnected to the public water supply because of its limited capacity. Of the ten neighborhoods in Dahra, waste collection is carried out in only one (the center), and plastic bags and other garbage can be seen all over town (Municipalité de Dahra 2016).

Although the main road has been improved, financed through Chinese loans, people generally feel that significant improvements in the busi-

Figures 5.2. and 5.3. Despite taxation, public waste management is lacking and infrastructure and sanitation at the weekly livestock market remain very poor. © Kristine Juul.

ness environment have yet to be delivered. Traders on the cattle market, for example, complain of poor and insecure facilities without access to electricity or sanitary equipment, and with no medical facilities to cater for the frequent emergencies that occur when large crowds of people and animals are present.

If tax burdens do not result in improvements, the perceived fairness and equity of taxation will be affected. Even with the current increases, direct taxes (notably the *impôt du minimum fiscal*) constitute only 15 percent of municipal tax revenues, and it is therefore questionable whether participatory budgeting will produce results good enough to persuade people to comply with their tax obligations. As matters stand, revenues for infrastructure investments and other forms of public maintenance are provided either through subsidies received from central government or through so-called small taxes, which are far more difficult for local people to control.

Small Taxes and Property Taxes

The limited revenues provided through poll taxes do not imply that taxes do not play a role in the local economy. On the contrary, myriad small taxes and fees are imposed on ordinary people daily. In Dahra, significant taxes are levied on animals traded on the market, on vehicles or horse carts moving people around town, and on all sorts of commercial activities from market stalls to shops and retailers. Fees are levied on permissions to extract natural resources, just as fees are imposed on the use of schools, health clinics, and hospitals. Together with fees for marriage or birth certificates and for the distribution of plots, these taxes contribute substantially to the running costs and investments of the municipality.

Closer inspection reveals that such taxes are paid mainly by people in the informal sector and often account for quite a high proportion of their incomes. Because they are considered fees rather than taxes, these indirect flat-rate charges provide little opportunity for tax bargaining with local authorities, as they are less visible and are based on consumption rather than on wealth. In this way, the burden of such taxation tends to fall hardest on the weakest groups, notably women, migrants, and poor people engaged in the informal sector; in other words, on those who are least likely to be in a position to hold the local authorities to account (Meagher 2018: 6). In order to redress this situation, it may be fruitful to look more closely at taxation of property.

From being almost entirely ignored, taxes on real estate (land and buildings) have recently been taken more seriously. According to Odd-Helge Fjeldstad (2015: 152), few taxes are more appropriate than property taxes. Property is a visible and immobile indicator of personal wealth, which makes its taxation difficult to avoid. Although property taxes indisputably represent a non-distortional and highly efficient fiscal tax, in many African countries revenues from property taxes remain small, even nonexistent.

The property tax legislation currently in place in Senegal is relatively comprehensive (Monkam 2011: 48). As with taxation elsewhere in Francophone West Africa, it is designed and administered by the central government but involves some revenue-sharing arrangements with local government. Nonetheless, coverage remains almost nonexistent, even in the capital, and the legislation has been extended to rural areas to only a very limited degree (Monkam 2011: 54). As emphasized by Nara Monkam, reasons for the limited development of these institutions are to be found in the political more than in the administrative realm. Although titling and mortgages have become popular in many countries, taxation of property has powerful political enemies; taxing land directly affects people with considerable property wealth, and such people usually also have considerable political power. The limited use of property and land taxation does indeed "reflect the success of resistance of the rich and powerful to measures which harm their interests" (Fjeldstad 2015: 152).

Figure 5.4. Registration and issuing a birth or marriage certificate requires payment of a fee to the municipality. © Kristine Juul.

The sharp rises in property prices that most African cities have experienced during the last decades call for a greater emphasis on taxation of this sector. In the case of Dakar, property prices rose 256 percent between 1994 and 2010, and investors continue to enjoy double-digit rises in property prices.[6] In principle, net income from the leasing of property is subject to a 20 percent tax. In practice, the blunt advice on the homepage of the private company Global Property Guide gives reason for concern. Under the heading "Income tax is moderate in Senegal, but can be avoided," foreign investors are enjoined to invest in Senegalese real estate and reassured in the following terms: "Income tax [on property] is only selectively enforced, and tax officials are open to persuasion. As a local says: I suggest that you declare a part – perhaps 30 percent of the rental received. Never declare too much, it draws attention to you."[7] Thus, although legislation is in place, capacity remains weak, just as will and commitment among entrepreneurs and investors to adhere to existing legislation may be lacking.

This attitude may, however, turn out to be relatively short-sighted, as new winds seem to be blowing regarding property taxation. Interesting work by Diane de Gramont (2015) shows how taxation has transformed Lagos from a symbol of urban disorder to a widely cited example of effective African governance. After many years of relying solely on wealth from oil, the Lagos state government has, over a period of less than fifteen years, succeeded in multiplying its tax revenues. Using these resources to restore basic infrastructure and expand public services and law enforcement, the local government has managed to limit its fiscal dependency on central government. These major gains were achieved not only through collection of income taxes but also by the introduction of an efficient system for property tax administration and a simple but predictable arrangement for property valuation. What is most surprising in de Gramont's research is that reform commitment in Lagos was driven mainly by electoral pressure, including elite ambitions to construct an orderly and prosperous megacity. The case of Lagos shows that improved property tax collection can be achieved if there is high-level political commitment to the project and if the idea of a social contract between tax-paying citizens and a state providing infrastructure and services is promoted (see also Moore et al. 2018: 168).

In the case of northern Senegal, increased taxation could be a way to promote a more reliable and predictable business environment. Indeed, property taxation is closely associated with municipal government revenues because of the immediate connections between property values and services funded at the local level. Once services such as provision of water, sewerage, refuse collection, and policing are in place, property values are likely to increase. Furthermore, property taxation is regarded as progressive and equitable, because the taxes depend on wealth rather than being a levy on transactions (Monkam and Moore 2015: 4). Despite these obvious virtues, only twenty-six houses in Dahra are currently titled and hence taxable (according to an interview with municipal staff). These are, to our knowledge, also the only properties to serve as collateral for large-scale loan-taking with the big commercial banks.

With a housing stock mainly characterized by rights of residency to state-owned lands, and with a lack of formal structures through which private investors can pay tax, the business environment in Dahra remains underdeveloped and too insecure for larger companies to invest in. The two cases discussed below, which concern pastoralists and foreign investors trying to establish themselves in the pasturelands outside Dahra, highlight some of the territorial attributes of taxation and some of the difficulties in gaining legitimacy in a generally non-tax-paying environment (for an extended treatment of this conflict, see Juul 2006).

Two Tales of Taxation, Property, and Private Entrepreneurs

As mentioned earlier in this chapter, a benefit often invoked in relation to credit, mortgaging, and taxation is the potential for boosting economic growth and for creating a dynamic business environment capable of attracting private investors. At present, both systems are lacking. The following account explores the paradoxical situation in which gaining access to the payment of taxes also turns out to be a problem.

Particularly in pastoral areas characterized by high levels of mobility, taxes may act as a token of belonging (for an explanation of the role of taxation in pre-colonial times, see Tano 2000). For newcomers seeking rights of access and recognition of settlement as citizens, with the corresponding rights and obligations, tax payment has proven an efficient means of validating and strengthening territorial claims. The utility of tax payment in this regard is illustrated by the forceful attempts some years ago by local politicians to stop "foreign herders" from paying taxes in a rural community located not far from Dahra.

Since the late 1990s, the area was occupied by herders who had fled the drought-ridden Senegal River Valley in the late 1990s. Having set up an extremely efficient but also highly mobile herd management system (see Juul 2006), these, now quite wealthy, newcomers decided to settle more permanently and form their own village. This was authorized by the *sous-préfet* but local leaders protested against the decision claiming that the newcomers had never paid poll taxes locally, but only claimed to do so in their villages of origin. They could therefore not be recognized as local citizens. The newcomers insisted that they had previously paid the local leaders, but that the latter had recently been refusing to receive the tax payments. In the end, only one village among several was recognized and that at a high prize for the *sous-préfet*, as dissatisfaction among the politically well-connected autochthonous chiefs ultimately led to his removal. As the chief of the new village explained: "The reason that we were recognized was that we could show the receipts. It was fortunate that I had kept them, because the members of the rural council had hidden away the book in which tax payments were registered."[8] Payment of poll taxes, in this case, acted as a territorial strategy to make newcomers' presence official and legitimate. Obviously, it was precisely because of these attributes that certain autochthonous political leaders found it necessary to avoid their proliferation. Another group encountering problems with tax payment were private companies and entrepreneurs who wished to start business ventures in the area. As matters stand, rural councils often find themselves in something of a dilemma when it comes to resource mobilization and to attracting productive enterprises and private entrepreneurs to their constituencies. Many municipal services, such as allocation of land and the right to dig a well, are either free of charge or require a purely symbolic payment. According to legislation, companies are not subject to any form of taxation until their investments bear fruit and become taxable. Investors, therefore, enjoy obvious advantages, as they obtain land almost free of charge (which is why land is often abandoned when an investment turns out to be unrealistic).[9] An often-overlooked problem is that this leaves investors with a problem of recognition.

Gaining legitimacy in a non-tax-paying environment turned into a problem for the Saudi Arabian company Asylia Gum Sarl, which had ambitions to become the world's largest producer of gum Arabic.[10] Around 2005, this company started a plantation on 12,000 hectares in the pastoral zone, where the gum-producing *acacia senegal* trees can be cultivated (Juul 2006; Mbow 2010; Mujawamariya 2012). Negotiations had already started in 1999, during which large tracts of land were allocated by the rural council. Meetings were held with councilors, who were even invited on trips to Mecca. Local herders, however, did not readily accept the allocations, which they had learned about only when they questioned the hired laborers in charge of marking out the prospected clearings. In response, they simply continued to graze their animals within the confines of the allocated land, disturbing the growth of the newly planted trees. Although the plantation is now up and running, the original target of cultivating 50,000 hectares is far from being met.

The case shows that when land rights are given free of charge, the level of implied formal recognition is diluted, leaving an opening for the local population to question its validity. As no legitimate tools existed for the private investors to gain recognition and validate their claims, they instead tried to gain legitimacy through illicit means, such as personalized or collective tributes for schooling and health facilities. This "informal taxation" proved to be less secure than validation acquired through formal channels, but, in this case, it was the only option available.

Conclusion

The goal of this chapter was to investigate how individual credit and local taxation practices have influenced perceptions of debt, mortgage, property, and public service provision in the cash-poor environment of Dahra in northern Senegal. The chapter shows that links exist among taxation, credit, and debt, although these are seldom considered together. Since colonial times, the imposition of taxes payable in cash has worked as a means of integration into the market economy, as the financial requirements of taxation forced people to sell their products on the market. As a result, payment of taxes has also figured among the reasons for people falling into debt. Links were also identified between the widespread lack of social protection and shortage of public services from the state and local government and the need for borrowing through MFIs. On the one hand, people use microcredit to pay for services not provided by the state. On the other hand, illness and accidents, for which little public help is available, are common reasons for not being able to repay loans. Finally, taxation in certain cases acted to protect rights of residence, something which might positively affect local investment and mortgaging practices.

Contrary to the assumptions of de Soto, quoted at the beginning of this chapter, doing business with people other than family members has been common practice, even before mortgaging became a possibility. Nonetheless, the microcredit lending market has been widely embraced by local entrepreneurs, with or without title deeds. Credit practices are therefore not limited to formal institutions but coexist and interact with informal lending practices, often in ways that reinforce existing social hierarchies. That people engage in credit arrangements based on mortgaging does not imply, however, that people do not resist it or try to bend it in their favor.

For households with limited assets and unstable incomes, improved access to microcredit often widens the array of formal and informal credit options they can juggle. The widespread practice of recycling microcredit loans into informal loans, or taking informal loans to repay micro-loans, may solve certain immediate problems but does not alter the fact that formal social protection is in most cases ineffective or nonexistent. Too often, default and foreclosure are prompted by illness or accidents besetting the debtor, his or her livestock, or family members who are obliged to help. In such cases, foreclosure can turn out to be a very expensive solution, not only for the debtor but also for the credit institutions involved, given that they are unlikely to be able to recover their outstanding claims.

The case of Dahra clarifies an interesting aspect regarding the rules and practices of foreclosure among debtors characterized by weak collateral positions. Although plots are owned by the state and the buildings seldom represent a value equivalent to the loans taken, they are still perceived by both lenders and debtors as collateral. Nonetheless, a lack of formal titling makes it difficult, if not impossible, for creditors to carry out a forced sale. As shown above, little help is provided by the courts, who are hampered by the imprecise and hazy legal framework. To compensate for this high risk, credit institutions tend to use extremely visible recovery methods to compel the debtor to comply, and to impose high interest rates to recover their losses.

A more collective pathway for dynamizing the local economy and enhancing growth and development may therefore be found in the provision of infrastructure and services financed through taxation. For example, robust public health care provision or other forms of social security may turn out as a relatively cost-efficient way to increase the ability of clients to service their debts, limit foreclosures, and improve the turnovers of credit institutions. So far, the contributions of state and local government to the development of public services have been found wanting. In Dahra, basic services such as access to electricity, tap water, and refuse collection are limited to certain parts of town, which are not those parts where the people who pay most taxes live. Unfortunately, this has done nothing to encourage the population to demand greater public accountability.

Experimentation with participatory budgeting has proved interesting and promising. The impact will nonetheless remain too narrow if local decision-making is restricted to the small share of public revenues collected through the *impôt du minimum fiscal*. If fiscal dynamics and tax bargaining are to develop, a more progressive taxation system involving systematic taxation of property must be adopted. In this way, newcomers and private entrepreneurs can pay taxes and contribute to local development while gaining more secure rights over their landed assets and thereby to mortgaging. Clearly, more research is needed to clarify these territorial aspects of taxation, just as more time is needed to follow up on the experiences of participatory budgeting.

Acknowledgments

Many thanks to Daivi Rodima-Taylor and Parker Shipton for insightful comments and valuable suggestions.

Kristine Juul is Associate Professor of Geography at Roskilde University, Denmark. She has done research on land tenure, natural resource management, micro-politics, and mobility in pastoral societies in West Africa. Recently her work has diversified to include national parks, heritage, identity politics, and migration trajectories notably circular, onward mobility, and homelessness among migrants of West African origin in Denmark. She is currently co-editing a book on place.

NOTES

1. CFA 100 was at that time equivalent to USD 1.68.
2. Mean loan size has been roughly stable since 2006, at CFA 510,000 (USD 1,040) (Baumann et al. 2015: 139).
3. According to focus groups carried out by Elizabeth Holmes and Jules Ndambu, it is not uncommon for an agent to refuse or even propose a doubling of the loan if a client wants to withdraw (2011: 43).
4. Author's interview with credit agent Crédits Agricoles, Dahra, August 2019.
5. The *impôt du minimum fiscal* has six levels, starting at CFA 900 for persons with an annual income under CFA 599,000 and progressing to CFA 36,000 for those whose annual income exceeds CFA 12,000,000; see Worldwide Tax Summaries, "Senegal: Individual – Taxes on Personal Income." *Worldwide Tax Summaries*, 15 January 2021. Retrieved 9 July 2021 from http://taxsummaries.pwc.com/ID/Senegal-Individual-Taxes-on-personal-income. In Dahra, and other rural settings visited, there is a flat rate (interview, Directeur Technique, Municipalité de Dahra).
6. Global Property Guide, "Senegal's Property Boom Continues." *Global Property Guide*, 27 December 2014. Retrieved 28 February 2021 from https://www.globalpropertyguide.com/Africa/Senegal, citing National Statistics.
7. Ibid.
8. Interview, Thiargny, 1993, quoted from Juul 2006: 838.
9. John (2015) discusses some interesting cases from Rufiji, Tanzania, where investors received free land for cultivation of crops for biofuel but then sold the land on to others when the operations turned out to be unsuccessful.
10. Gum Arabic is the hardened sap of the *acacia senegal* tree, which is used in the food industry as a stabilizer, emulsifier and thickening agent.

REFERENCES

Baumann, Eveline, and M. Abdoulaye Fall. 2015. "Perceptions of Debt and Microcredit in Senegal." In *An Anthropological Economy of Debt*, ed. Bernard Hours and Pepita ould Ahmed, 181–99. London: Routledge.
Baumann, Eveline, M. Abdoulaye Fall, and Cécile Godfroid. 2015. "Malaise in the Senegalese Microfinance Landscape." In *The Crises of Microcredit*, ed. Isabelle Guérin, M. Labie, and J.-M. Servet, 133–51. London: Zed Books.
Bräutigam, Deborah. 2008. "Introduction." In *Taxation and State Building in Developing Countries: Capacity and Consent*, ed. Deborah Bräutigam, Odd-Helge Fjeldstad, and Mick Moore, 1–33. Cambridge: Cambridge University Press.
Bräutigam, Deborah, Odd Helge Fjeldstad, and Mick Moore. 2008: *Taxation and State Building in Developing Countries: Capacity and Consent*: Cambridge: Cambridge University Press.
De Gramont, Diane. 2015. *Governing Lagos: Unlocking the Politics of Reform*. Washington, DC: Carnegie Endowment for International Peace.
Diaw, Alioune. 1995. "Commercialisation des petits ruminants au Sénégal, le cas de l'axe Nord-Dakar" [Marketing of small stock in Senegal, the case of the North-Dakar axis]. Thèse. Dakar: Ecole Inter-Etats de Sciences et Medicines Vétérinaires (EISMV).
Echos des Collectivités Locales. 2001. *Taxes rurales: Le goulot d'étranglement 10–11* [Rural taxes: The 10–11 bottleneck]. Dakar: DGL-Felo/USAID.
Fjeldstad, Odd-Helge. 2015. "When the Terrain Does Not Fit the Map: Local Government Taxation in Africa." In *Perspectives on Politics, Production and Public Administration in Africa, Essays in Honour of Ole Therkildsen*, ed. Anne Metter Kjær, Lars Engberg-Pedersen, and Lars Buur, 147–15. Copenhagen: DIIS.
Guérin, Isabelle, Solène Morvant-Roux, and Magdalena Villareal. 2014. "Introduction." In *Microfinance, Debt and Over-Indebtedness; Juggling with Money*, ed. Isabelle Guérin, Solène Morvant-Roux, and Magdalena Villareal, 1–24. London: Routledge.
Holmes, Elizabeth, and Jules Ndambu. 2011. *Diagnostic sur la protection des consommateurs des services de microfinance au Sénégal: enquête auprès de clients* [Assessment of protection of consumers of microfinance services in Senegal: Survey among users]. Frankfurt: Frankfurt School of Management.
John, William. 2015. "Climate Change Discourse and the Intensification of Land and Water conflicts in Tanzania." PhD dissertation. Dar es Salaam: University of Dar es Salaam.
Joireman, Sandra. 2008. "The Mystery of Capital Formation in Sub-Saharan Africa: Women, Property Rights and Customary Law." *World Development* 36(7): 1233–46.
Juul, Kristine. 2006. "Decentralization, Land Taxation and Citizenship in Senegal." *Development and Change* 37(4): 821–46.
Kane, Safiétou. 2013. "Women and Development in Urban Senegal: Microcredit and Social Capital." *African Sociological Review* 17(1): 45–64.
Keen, Michael. 2013. "Taxation and Development – Again." *IMF Working Paper WP/12/220*. Washington, DC: International Monetary Fund.
Mbow, Cheick. 2010. "Africa's Risky Gamble." *Global Change* 75: 20–23.

Meagher, Kate. 2018. "Taxing Time: Taxation, Divided Societies and the Informal Economy in Northern Nigeria." *Journal of Development Studies* 54(1): 1–17.

Monkam, Nara F. 2011. "Property Taxation in Africa; Legislation in Practice." *Journal of Property Tax Assessment and Administration* 8(3): 41–60.

Monkam, Nara F., and Mick Moore. 2015. *How Property Tax Would Benefit Africa*. London: African Research Institute.

Moore, Mick. 2015. "Tax and the Governance Dividend." In *Perspectives on Politics, Production and Public Administration in Africa, Essays in Honour of Ole Therkildsen*, ed. Anne Metter Kjær, Lars Engberg-Pedersen, and Lars Buur, 159–71. Copenhagen: DIIS.

Moore, Mick, Wilson Prichard, and Odd-Helge Fjeldstad. 2018. *Taxing Africa: Coercion, Reform and Development*. London: Zed Books

Mujawamariya, Gaudiose. 2012. "Economics of the Gum Arabic Value Chain in Senegal." PhD dissertation. Wageningen: Wageningen School of Social Sciences.

Municipalité de Dahra. 2016. "Plan de développement communal de Dahra, Horizon 2016–2021" [Dahra communal development plan, Horizon 2016–2021]. République du Sénégal, Region de Louga.

Peluso, Nancy, and Peter Vandergeest. 2001. "Genealogies of the Political Forest and Customary Rights in Indonesia, Malaysia, and Thailand." *The Journal of Asian Studies* 60(3): 761–812.

Perry, Donna. 2002. "Microcredit and Women Moneylenders: The Shifting Terrain of Credit in Rural Senegal." *Human Organization* 61(1): 30–40.

Piketty, Thomas. 2014. *Capital in the Twenty-First Century*. Cambridge, MA: Belknap Press.

Shipton, Parker. 2010. *Credit between Cultures: Land, Finance, and Misunderstanding in Africa*. New Haven, CT: Yale University Press.

Tano, Felix. 2000. "Land Taxes and Charges in Senegal." In *Gérer le foncier rural en Afrique de l'ouest: Dynamique foncières et interventions publiques*, ed. Philippe Lavigne Delville, Camilla Toulmin, and Samba Traoré, 188–202. Paris: Karthala.

CHAPTER 6

 Signs of Trouble

Land, Loans, and Investments in Post-conflict Northern Uganda

METTE LIND KUSK AND LOTTE MEINERT

This chapter explores a number of recent cases from northern Uganda regarding land, loans, and investments. First, it provides a short introduction to the land tenure systems in postwar northern Uganda and gives a brief insight into ongoing land conflicts. After an overview of relevant literature evidence on land tenure security and loans in Uganda, we discuss the cases of our field study. We examine in detail a case from the Acholi region that deals with contested property relations and disputed land sales – expressed in the practice of putting up signs that say: "This land is not for sale." As it turns out, behind these signs were intriguing stories of trouble, disagreements, or conflicts of some sort. Then the discussion moves to the Karamoja region of northern Uganda, where people have little or no experience with formal credit and selling of land. Yet the fear of creating situations where people do not belong anywhere and become indebted to outsiders remains pronounced.

Property and Inheritance Patterns in Northern Uganda

The Land Act of Uganda, enacted in 1998, intended to enhance tenure security by recognizing different tenure forms and thereby rights to land. At the same time, the reform aimed to bring land to the market for sale (Sjögren 2014: 67), just as land tenure reforms in African contexts generally aim to pave the way for economic growth through the development of land markets (Colin and Woodhouse 2010: 1). For a number of reasons, the implementation of the reform in Uganda has been hesitant and slow.

Four Types of Land Tenure Are Recognized under the 1998 Land Act

1. *Customary tenure*, under which people have rights to land, but do not have formal titles; the land is vested in clan collectives and accessed through patrilineal inheritance and entrustment rather than through markets and money. Entrustment here is to be understood as conceptualized by Parker Shipton (2009) in his work in Western Kenya where it entails the keeping of something in care for further transmission in the future, the primary example being land. One receives land from previous generations, and one should preserve it for children and grandchildren to use in the future. Entrustment entails that rights to land are embedded in social relations, and thus makes the belonging or attachment of people and land intertwined. Land in this category has traditionally not been significant due to its economic value, but rather due to values of social identity, belonging, and generational succession.
2. *Freehold tenure*, which is individualized, titled, and registered land, accessed through the market, but also inherited as property. It can be contrasted with the notion of landholding through entrustment (Shipton 2009) as freehold tenure involves complete rights, including the right to alienate land for good.
3. *Leasehold tenure*, which provides for access to public land on a time bound contract.
4. *Mailo land*, which refers to land owned by the Buganda king and feudal landlords, rented by poorer tenants (Ravnborg et al. 2013).

In northern Uganda, like in sub-Saharan Africa in general, the vast majority of land in rural areas (around 90 to 95 percent) is held under customary tenure, and only a few people have land titles of freehold land or hold leased land (Atkinson and Hopwood 2013; Colin and Woodhouse 2010). This means that most people access land through kinship relations: sons inherit land from their fathers, and daughters access land through their husbands. As described above, transactions of land have traditionally been based on fiduciary culture and entrustment (Shipton 2009). Rights to use land were passed on from previous generations in the patriline based on an understanding of entrustment. Land was to be kept and cultivated only temporarily in care for further transmission to the next generations in the future. Traditionally, you could claim the amount of land you were able to use and cultivate: a principle that reflected a past when land shortage was not a problem and an approach to land-distribution based on labor – digging with a handheld hoe and herding cattle (Girling 1960).

The conflicts in northern Uganda, in particular with the Lord's Resistance Army (LRA) causing brutal war in the Acholi region from 1986–2006 and cattle raiding by armed groups in Karamoja, have meant that access to land has been limited and conflicts have been locked for decades. With the end of armed fighting since 2006 in the Acholi region, people have moved back to their original homes, and with disarmament in Karamoja, mobility as well as agricultural production have increased and some groups have moved into new territories.

After the twenty-year war in Acholi-land, people used to joke that "peace has broken out" due to the very high number of land conflicts in the region (Meinert 2015), where questions over who has rights to what land are prevalent. The social links connecting people to their land through kinship are missing for many, due to deaths (Whyte et al. 2012) as well as missing physical boundary markers, reflecting people's past belonging to a particular place that has often been destroyed or overgrown. In one subcounty in the region, 30 percent of the families reported to be involved in a land conflict (Meinert 2015). Land conflicts are of many different kinds and scales, including what people term "wrangles" between family members, neighbors, and clans; conflicts over district, county, and subcounty borders; conflicts between authorities (representing the army, the police, or the subcounty offices) or other institutions (schools, churches, health centers) and local inhabitants; and conflicts between large-scale investors, national or international, and local inhabitants.

In the Karamoja region, conflicts over territory are diverse, such as in-migration of cattle herders to agricultural areas (including Turkana from Kenya and Didinga from South Sudan), and conflicts between wildlife, wildlife authorities, and local people over territories alternatively referred to as game reserves, animal corridors, and indigenous land.

The recognition of different tenure forms in the 1998 Land Act aimed both to give legitimacy to various tenure forms and pave the way for a market in land. Several of the conflicts we have followed revolved around individuals who had managed to mortgage or sell off land that belonged to the broad category of "customary land," that is, land held collectively based on oral agreements and accessed through social relations – often kinship relations.

Credit, Customs, and Indebtedness

In Uganda, access to formalized credit, such as basic bank loans, varies greatly across regions. It seems quite limited in the Acholi region (Ravnborg et al. 2013), and it is certainly very limited in the Karamoja region. There are important regional and urban versus rural differences in access to formalized credit, and socio-economic and gender characteristics clearly matter too. Loans appear to be more common among urban men from southwest Uganda as many of them are educated and less poor (Ravnborg et al. 2013).

In their survey study of three districts in Uganda, including the Amuru in northern Uganda, Helle Munk Ravnborg and colleagues show how access to loans in Uganda is not primarily linked to titled land, as assumed by some scholars; loans are commonly collateralized with other forms of property or relations. Only one-third of the loans from formal credit institutions involved land used as collateral, and only one-fifth of these cases involved titled land (2013: 98). The degree to which the credit institutions demand land tenure documentation is described as "flexible" (2013: 98). According to Ravnborg and colleagues, the reason so few use the land as security for loans is not because the credit institutions are unwilling to accept land as collateral. The reason is rather people's hesitation to jeopardize their land, which is regarded as belonging to the family, clan, and community at large (2013: 98), and we would add, to the past and future generations.

A similar uncertainty was observed in the peri-urban areas of Gulu town, where a local politician facilitated savings groups, in the Acholi Lwo language called *bolicup*, to provide people with an alternative way of accessing credit without running the risk of losing their land in case of non-payment. In these groups, people save up collectively, members can take up small loans from the collective savings and repay with interest. The members were all aware of some people who had lost land due to loans taken from microfinance institutions, and they emphasized their unwillingness to jeopardize their land by entering into such loan agreements as well as the need to access credit once in a while.

Ravnborg and colleagues note: "Despite concerted efforts during the past decades to increase the supply of agricultural credit e.g., by providing subsidized capital funds to credit institutions, demand has not increased in practice as anticipated. Overall, only around a quarter of respondents had taken out a loan and the vast majority of those who had taken loans during the past five years had done so to finance non-productive investments, such as education for children, meeting health expenditures, repairing their houses, etc." (2013: 93). This indicates that the majority of these loans are what we might term "poverty loans," meaning loans used to cover immediate and urgent needs, rather than being part of a desired, long-term productive investment plan.

In the following section we consider empirical cases from our ongoing studies in the Acholi and Karamoja regions in northern Uganda that highlight some of the current issues related to land and loans.

Land Loans and Ramifications for Families and Neighbors: A Case from Acholi Subregion

After the LRA war in northern Uganda, people from one of the subcounties we worked in reported that an increasing number of residents have applied for bank loans against land and other forms of property as collateral. Yet many reported that they found it difficult to pay back the mortgage because their businesses were unstable. James, a local businessman, explained how people "take loans due to poverty and they want development, but business is [fluctuating] up and down. So, when the bank does not receive the money in time, they come and take the land." Sometimes family members are unaware that another family member has taken a loan against the same land and get an unpleasant surprise when they are evicted, which is what we saw in the case described below.

James, from a small rural trading center, borrowed money from Centenary Bank in Gulu town. He had paid back almost half of the sum, but unforeseen extra expenses – his first wife burned down part of his home when he wanted to divorce her – made him unable to raise the rest of the money in time. He had taken the loan with security in a house that he had constructed and three acres of land around it. His two neighbors, who had accounts in Centenary Bank, were standing in as guarantors. Now the bank had closed their accounts. One of them was a teacher and when the bank closed his account he could not receive his salary. James requested the bank to extend the deadline for his loan, but the bank declined. So he decided to sell a plot of the land to raise money to pay back the loan.

Figure 6.1. Borrowing money from the bank. Drawing by Mette Lind Kusk.

Figure 6.2. James sells off customary land to repay his bank loan. Drawing by Mette Lind Kusk.

James called a meeting to inform his brothers, parents, and paternal uncles about the decision. At the meeting, one of the uncles got extremely frustrated with the sale and he tried to grab some money from James (the land was sold for 1.4 million Ugandan Shillings, so he had almost 1 million Ugandan Shillings in addition to what he owed to the bank). The uncle was reprimanded at the meeting and told to accept the sale. The next evening, however, the intoxicated uncle went to the home of

James's parents. Only the mother was home, and the uncle attacked her with an axe. Luckily, one of her other sons came home and managed to stop the uncle before any serious harm was done. Both got minor injuries and the mother was very scared.

James interpreted the incident as caused by the land sale and thus, indirectly, by the loan. The land that was sold was part of ancestral land, and thus held under what can be termed customary tenure; but even though his parents had been consulted before the sale and had approved, the uncle had not been consulted. As ancestral land is generally viewed as an asset that cannot be exchanged for money but only shared among clan members based on how much of it they can use, bypassing a paternal uncle, to turn a collective asset into an individual one goes against the custom and the "rules." A peculiar aspect of the case is therefore that James's sale seemed to be accepted by most family members and was only explicitly opposed by one paternal uncle. We do not know the reason for this, but should also point out that we have only heard the story from James himself.

James described the uncle as being in need of land; he had many children, eleven of them sons who were expecting to inherit land from their father, and it was difficult for him to provide for them from the little land he had. The children were not in school and depended entirely on their ancestral land for subsistence farming. In the future, when the uncle's land is divided among them, each would get too little land to live from. While explaining the case, James seemed very understanding of his uncle's situation, even though he disapproved of the attack on his mother. James had never intended to sell part of their ancestral land. It had happened because his income was rather unsteady and unforeseen expenses kept turning up, making it difficult to keep up with loan repayment deadlines.

The mother, her husband, and the uncle went to the police where they presented the issue, but they were advised to solve the matter at home because they were so closely related. Our findings show that this is a common response from authorities when close kin wrangle over land matters. While it has been discussed in the literature how different actors attempt to establish themselves as authoritative when land matters are negotiated (see, for example, Lund 2008), we find it important to note that institutional reticence is also widespread in the Acholi region: people are told to handle their land issues by themselves, at home, without involving outside institutions. At home, James's mother, father, and uncle managed to reconcile, the uncle apologized and seemed sorry about what happened, and they had a small reconciliation ritual.

This case highlights some of the local social and economic ramifications of individual mortgaging of land in the contexts where land is mainly seen as a collective asset and often the only means of livelihood for families. What was initially an agreement between a man, his bank, and two neighbors became – when the deadline was not met – a conflict involving three other persons who were not part of the initial agreement but were related to the land, the uncle, mother, and brother. Their relationship to each other was put at risk as a consequence of the mortgage. In addition, the uncle's difficulties in providing for his children due to the lack of land seem to be of a more permanent kind now that the possibility of using some of the land designated to James was gone.

An individual mortgage in this context can be viewed as tying people to institutions and other people over time, just as it can disrupt and weaken local social relations. In James's case, the mortgage tied him to the bank as well as his immediate neighbors whose income served as collateral for the loan. Concurrently, the mortgage disrupted the social ties between close kin when the risk of losing land was actualized, just as an individual mortgage in shared land seemed to enhance power imbalances within the family. James's uncle was left in a weaker position, both economically and socially, due to James' inability to meet the bank requirements, and he faced an insecure future with fewer opportunities to improve his own and his children's livelihoods. James' position seems to be strengthened both socially, within the family, and economically through the earnings from the land sale. Yet many Acholi would argue that keeping land is a better way of securing yourself economically. Land is described as a "guarantor of life" by our interlocutors: "at least with land you can eat" whereas "paper money" disappears fast, leaving you without a stable basis for your future.

Contested Property Relations: "This Land Is Not For Sale" Signs

The conflict presented above revolves around a disputed land sale caused by the demand to pay back a loan. As in many other parts of Africa (Colin and Woodhouse 2010: 4, 9), such disputed land sales seem to be on the rise in the Acholi region – exemplified by a new element in the urban and peri-urban spaces, the not-for-sale sign. When moving around Gulu town, one can see signs saying: "This land is not for sale" or simply "not for sale." We are aware of the wider global phenomenon of not-for-sale signs (see, for example, Google Images for not-for-sale signs). Yet we are interested in what these signs may tell us about the land market and property relations in this particular place. At first glance it seems odd to advertise something that is not for sale. But by exploring the stories behind the signs, we get an entry-point into some of the core dilemmas connected to land tenure in northern Uganda: Is land, and should it be, an individual or collective asset; should it be vested in kinship relations and acquired through inheritance, or commodified and acquired through purchase?

The three cases of "not-for-sale" signs we explore here have several commonalities: all cases concern land where the owners do not live on the land and involve several actors who are intimately connected to each other making claims to the land. In two of the cases, a father has died and left behind land that his sons and wives have to share. Widespread polygynous marriages where men have children with more than one wife complicate these issues. Often an individual has the legal administration rights ("the paper") to a landholding to which several other actors view themselves as equally entitled and demand to be included in decisions to sell off even parts of the land. In one case, the son who had been given legal administration rights in a landholding, began to sell plots of land without consulting his brothers or sharing the money from the sales. In another case, a stepmother rented out a plot without sharing the income with her stepsons. Both cases involved disagreements and contested relational property rights. A young guy whose paternal uncle sold off a landholding explained why he opposed the sales: "To have plots in Gulu town is good, and it is good to keep them, because Gulu will soon gain city status, so they may become more valuable. You can secure an income by keeping the plots and renting them out. If you sell off the land, you will soon be left with nothing."

To sell land is to make its value relatively final, and a lot of people oppose land sales because they need land for the future, as the above quote reveals. Especially if the money is not shared in a family, land sales are frowned upon. But in a context where land markets are informal and the official judicial system does not function well, how do you make sure your land is not sold behind your back? Normally one's presence on the land would counter this, but when it concerns land where one does not live, it is less straightforward.

Formal registration and land titling are often presented as a solution to prevent land conflicts. Yet, as these and other cases show (see, for example, Colin and Woodhouse 2010), that assumption can be challenged. To have a landholding registered and titled does not change the complex property relations connected to that particular plot. Rather it might empower an individual to sell off the land by convincing the buyer of his or her ownership without the consent of the collectivity, causing more

Figures 6.3. and 6.4. Not-for-sale signs from Gulu town and the surrounding parishes. © Mette Lind Kusk.

conflict. Local leaders (LC1s – Local Council level 1), are often viewed as authorities who have to approve land sales. This is not always unproblematic. Some informants report having to pay high fees to the local leaders before they will approve of a sale, sometimes as much as 20 percent of the total cost of the land in question. Besides being an arbitrary fee, such "rules" also entice double sales, as it is good business for local leaders to approve land sales. At other times, sales are made without involving any local leaders. Even though such sales may not be legally binding, they may work in practice as taking such matters to formal courts can be an expensive, slow and unpredictable endeavor.

To put up "not-for-sale" signs on the plots proved to be an efficient strategy in all three cases to counter an individual's power to sell collectively owned land without the consent of the collective: the signs are a way of creating a physical presence and voicing claims without anyone physically being there. The aim is to scare away potential buyers by making them question the acclaimed owner's rightful ownership. In all cases, the signs seem to have worked; at least no more plots have been sold or rented out without collective consent. Behind the signs there turned out to be stories of trouble and disagreement, sometimes downright conflicts between family members. The signs may thus testify to a specific moral economy where property relations are contested and where social cohesion around land is up for discussion: Does the land belong to people or do people belong to the land?

Investments in Land: Wind Turbines in Karamoja

Another case from the Karamoja region illuminates the social and micropolitical processes involving the requests by newcomers, private investors, and missionaries to "develop" land. In Karamoja, people subsist from cattle herding and agriculture, and some areas are seminomadic. Access to land and grazing is based on the principle of sharing and entrustment. "Landowners" as such do not exist: people who use the land consider themselves to be custodians or caretakers of the land. In the local Ik language, a custodian is called *Amazeya jumui* meaning "leader of the soil," which clearly expresses a different relationship to land than property ownership.

In one of the cases we followed in the Kaabong district, a private foreign company requested to buy plots of land to build and test wind turbines for producing electric power. They bought land in seven different locations in Karamoja region. In the case we followed in Timu Parish this request created a historically novel situation, as no one recalled land ever being sold in the parish before, and no formal or informal institution was prepared for land sales or investments. Yet the private company needed owners to whom they could pay and sign a formal contract with, according to their standard purchasing procedures. The process of establishing the "original owners" of the land in this sharing and entrustment system, which has seen many different users of land over time, created a lot of social turmoil and raised many questions. A variety of formal and informal actors became involved, and diverse authorities were referred to or created in the process, including "owners" and "users" of land, clan elders, and subcounty chiefs (see also Lund 2008). People in that area have had very few experiences with investments in land, but they have heard stories from other parts of Uganda and Kenya about "land grabbing" and evictions of "squatters." There were stories how people had lost their land and forests due to "investments" by outsiders. The establishment of Kidepo National Park in 1959 in the northern part of the Kaabong district by the colonial authorities had forcefully displaced people and made hunting illegal. The memory of this displacement was still vivid for some Ik elders. When energy, oil, and mining companies, as well as large-scale agricultural enterprises purchase land in the region, people become worried for a good reason. They question the unfamiliar concept of "owning" land and discuss what it means in practice and over the course of time. Those who were established as the "original owners" of the wind turbine plot in Timu Parish were wondering, post-sale, if they should have insisted on renting out the land to the investors or selling it as a leasehold. Yet, according to the actors involved they were not given any options, merely presented with a certain amount of money. They did not receive any legal advice or guidance about the process of selling land and what an investment by a foreign company might entail. The idea that their ancestral land was now sold "forever" created profound uncertainties, with people asking questions such as: Where will our children live if people start selling more land?

Other community members who belonged to the local elite and were "development minded" were in favor of letting "outsiders" buy the land and make investments, which they hoped would benefit the local community in the long run. "They borrow our land and we will also benefit from it" is what the developmentalists in the community argued. They implied that the land still belongs to the community when they said that the company only borrows the land. Yet in legal terms the company owned the land permanently and could proceed to get land titles and other legal documents to prove freehold tenure.

Some of the interesting themes in this case are related to the historical introduction of ideas about ownership, investments, developmentalism, and cadastral logics in an area where land and belonging have been in flux and dominated by ideas about ancestral entrustment. As Jean-Pierre Chauveau and Jean-Philippe Colin (2010: 82) have suggested, we often assume a unilineal evolution from entrustment systems to cadastral sys-

Figure 6.5. The fenced plot bought by the foreign company for testing the feasibility of building wind turbines. © Lotte Meinert.

tems, but in reality, changes are far from unilineal. The values involved in transactions do not simply have to change from those based on trust and mutual understanding to those based on cash and contracts. Yet, many questions remain unanswered for the people on the ground: What is going to happen if the testing of the wind turbine pilot shows that it is feasible to build wind turbine parks that will require much larger areas of land? How will land transactions be conducted? What kind of values and moral economy will guide the transfers, and to the benefit of whom?

Implications of Our Study and More Questions to Explore

Our case material shows how the commodification of land has different ramifications for closely related kin and community members in northern Uganda. Some benefit from land sales and are able to generate new opportunities by engaging in social networks beyond immediate kinship – including neighbors, local leaders, finance institutions, and foreign investors – while others find themselves powerless when the land they considered an asset for their own and their children's future lives is sold off beyond their control. In other words, we see a connection between current processes of land mortgaging and sales in the region and enhanced power imbalances, potentially creating new kinds of poverty and inequality in these rural communities. Therefore, more research about these processes is needed, to understand how differently positioned actors navigate them in attempts to prevent extreme forms of dispossession.

More information is needed about the way loan agreements are made in practice from the perspectives of the borrowers as well as their relatives in the post-conflict communities in Africa. What are the conditions of the loans made against land as collateral, and how do people understand these conditions? What actors and institutions do people turn to and why? How do local opportunities and risks, dreams and fears play into people's willingness to borrow against land? If we consider that mortgaging land brings a future goal of generating income from the land into the present – what happens to the longer time horizons involving kin and younger generations? What measures can be taken to protect and safeguard those more at risk of not being able to pay back loans and keep assets? It is also important to consider that most of the loans are obtained for non-productive investments – reflecting a situation where people are forced to mortgage their land to pay for their children's school fees, medical costs, and other daily expenses. In areas where land sales, investments and borrowing are novel practices, what measures could be put in place to ensure that common people are able to get affordable legal assistance and advice?

Mette Lind Kusk is Assistant Professor at the School of Social Work of Aarhus University College, Denmark. Her research interests include land, conflict management, legal pluralism, and trust in institutions and in neighbors. Since 2012, she has conducted several periods of ethnographic fieldwork in and around Gulu town, northern Uganda.

Lotte Meinert is Professor at the Department of Anthropology of Aarhus University, Denmark. She has conducted anthropological fieldwork and worked in various parts of Uganda for more than seven years and done shorter periods of fieldwork in Indonesia and Kenya.

REFERENCES

Atkinson, Ron, and Julian Hopwood. 2013. *Land Conflict Monitoring and Mapping Tool for the Acholi Sub-Region*. Gulu: United Nations Peacebuilding Program in Uganda by Human Rights Focus.

Chauveau, Jean-Pierre, and Jean-Philippe Colin. 2010. "Customary Transfers and Land Sales in Côte d'Ivoire: Revisiting the Embeddedness Issue." *Africa* 80(1): 81–103.

Colin, Jean-Philippe, and Philip Woodhouse. 2010. "Interpreting Land Markets in Africa." *Africa* 80(1): 1–13.

Girling, F. K. 1960. *The Acholi of Uganda*. London: Her Majesty's Stationary Office.

Lund, Christian. 2008. *Local Politics and the Dynamics of Property in Africa*. New York: Cambridge University Press.

Meinert, Lotte. 2015. "Tricky Trust: Distrust as a Point of Departure and Trust as a Social Achievement in Uganda." In *Anthropology and Philosophy: Dialogues on Trust and Hope*, ed. Suune Liisberg, Esther Pedersen, and Anne Dalsgaard, 118–33. New York: Berghahn Books.

Ravnborg, Helle Munk, Bernard Bashaasha, Michael Kidoido, Rasmus Hundsbaek Pedersen, Rachel Spichiger, Alice Turinawe. 2013. "Land and Property Rights and Economic Behaviour in Uganda: Results from a Questionnaire Survey Conducted in Amuru, Masaka and Pallisa." *Journal for Peace and Security Studies* 1: 86–99.

Sjögren, Anders. 2014. "Scrambling for the Promised Land: Land Acquisitions and the Politics of Representation in Post-War Acholi, Northern Uganda." *African Identities* 12(1): 62–75.

Shipton, Parker. 2009. *Mortgaging the Ancestors: Ideologies of Attachment in Africa*. New Haven, CT: Yale University Press.

Whyte, Susan, Sulayman Babiiha, R. Mukyala, and Lotte Meinert. 2013. "Remaining Internally Displaced: Missing Links to Human Security in Northern Uganda." *Journal of Refugee Studies* 26(2): 283–301.

Part III

Old Rules and New Twists

Reinventing and Resisting Land Financialization

CHAPTER 7

 Reinventing Land Mortgage in Postsocialist Europe
The Romanian Case

STEFAN DORONDEL, DAIVI RODIMA-TAYLOR, AND MARIOARA RUSU

This chapter seeks to address an issue that has been barely examined in the scholarship of postsocialist land reform: the reinvention of land mortgage as a means of transforming agrarian relations in formerly socialist countries. After five decades of socialist organization of the agrarian economy, mortgage has returned as a tool to reshape and financialize the agriculture in Romania. During the socialist era when productive land was concentrated into state and collective farms, local agricultural communities saw an almost complete elimination of real property rights. The postsocialist land reform of the 1990s aimed to introduce profound changes and "modernize" the country by re-establishing private property in land. Property rights and land markets were expected to bring along social and economic restructuring of the agrarian communities, and land mortgage was viewed as the primary vehicle in rendering land a mobile asset, fueling rural investment, and improving economic productivity. The massive land restitution campaign was motivated by aspirations for justice but also economic efficiency.

Transition to the market economy began in the previously socialist countries of Eastern Europe in the late 1980s and early 1990s. Although legal frameworks for land mortgage currently exist in most of those areas, not many landholders are exercising their right to use land as a collateral for loans. In a vast majority of the new European Union member and accession countries,[1] land-based lending remains rather limited (Giovarelli and Bledsoe 2001). A mortgage is the transfer of a right in immovable property as security for repayment of a loan or the performance of an obligation (Giovarelli 2000). The reasons land mortgage has not become a viable tool for rural financing in postsocialist Europe are manifold. The market value of agricultural land is very low, exacerbated by excessive land fragmentation[2] after land restitution. Land privatization impacted each country differently, based on existing local patterns of land use and ownership, as well as state policies and political motivations. As many of these countries restored agricultural and forestlands to the former owners from the pre-World War II period, the restitution process has been fraught with challenges. These include unclear ownership records and conflicting claims, difficulties with establishing former owners who have deceased or moved away, ineffective reinforcement of foreclosure procedures, and incomplete legal frameworks. Overall farm yields have remained low compared to the European Union levels (Csaki and Zuschlag 2004). Land restitution processes have been slow and uncertain in many of the postsocialist countries, further reducing the confidence of banks in land-based lending.

In transitional and post-authoritarian settings, land property is frequently central in broader struggles over belonging and identity, and the formalization of land claims is a contested and political process (Shipton and Rodima-Taylor 2015). Decentralizing land tenure reforms have brought renewed attention to local forms of organization and authority and their contestation and redefinition (Geschiere 2009; Sikor et al. 2017). New norms and institutions for recording and transacting landholdings may arise locally, in parallel to the official ones of the state, while granting legitimacy to the parties mediating and conferring the property rights (Benjaminsen and Lund 2003; Sikor and Lund 2009).

Such intermingling of old and new authorities, normative templates, and collective and private forms of work characterizes also the landscape of postsocialist rural Romania. Land privatization reform in Romania was launched after the fall of the socialist regime in 1990 and aimed to radically change agrarian relations. Land restitution was motivated partly by the desire to bring about historical justice and partly to achieve economic efficiency in the agricultural sector (Swinnen 1997). Most of the agricultural land throughout the country's history had been held in large estates, while peasant farmers – those actually working on the land – had not had an opportunity to own the land they were cultivating.

Postsocialist central planners regarded land reform as a way to dismantle the collective organization of agriculture, improve land tenure system and increase rural productivity of a country once dubbed the "granary of Europe" (Dorondel 2016). As elsewhere in postsocialist Eastern Europe, land reform in Romania was an attempt to impose new meanings of property on local people and attach new values to land by utilizing novel economic language of efficiency, competition, and entrepreneurship. Postsocialist economic reforms were largely inspired by neoliberal agendas promoted and supported by international financial institutions such as the World Bank and International Monetary Fund (Schwengler 2008). The neoliberal economic model was the most prominent globally at the historical moment when the socialist regimes crumbled, and most East European countries adopted it (Ban 2016). Establishing private property rights, issuing land titles, and creating functional land markets were the principal goals of such land reforms, accompanied by a retreat of the state from the agricultural sector and the withdrawal of subsidies (Visser et al. 2019).

In our chapter we draw on academic literature and policy documents on postsocialist land reform in Eastern Europe comparatively and in Romania specifically, with a particular focus on land mortgage and rural finance. The analysis of scholarly and policy-oriented materials is complemented by data from primary ethnographic field research in Romania. That includes interviews with and participatory observation among Romanian policy makers and bank officers, but also surveys and informal interviews in the villages of southern Romania (Argeș and Teleorman Counties), with a particular focus on smallholder farmers who had recently applied for bank loans to expand their agricultural businesses.[3] We develop this chapter by focusing first on the pluralist dynamics of land formalization in Romania, while exploring the forms of rural production, property holding and authority in Romanian countryside throughout the recent history. We then present a short history of mortgage and bank loans in pre-socialist Romania, and proceed to examine the emergence of the legislative framework concerning mortgage after the fall of the Berlin Wall. We discuss the challenges of land-based lending in Romania as relating to incomplete cadastres, land fragmentation, and other issues that have accompanied postsocialist land restitution. We examine rural lending processes in Romania through the perspectives of lenders as well as borrowers – while striving for a multifaceted analysis of the still very scarcely explored issue of postsocialist land-based lending.

Understanding the Pluralist Dynamics of Land Formalization in Romania

Emerging from the need to dismantle the collective institutions imposed upon rural production in the socialist era, most of the mass-scale decollectivization efforts produced uneven and ambiguous results. While in some cases encouraging entrepreneurial initiative and small-scale farming, they have also led to legal and administrative challenges and proliferation of alternative institutional arrangements with their own specific histories (Shipton and Rodima-Taylor 2015). The effects of the privatization reforms on viable smallholder production have been unclear. While in Russia, for example, the rise of privately held family farms has been stalled and former collective farms have often transformed into privatized joint-stock operations (Lerman, Csaki, and Feder 2004; Miller and Heady 2003), novel market opportunities in postsocialist China have facilitated a co-existence of kin-based norms and networks with commercialized family farms (Brandstädter 2003).[4]

Postsocialisms therefore differ from each other — talking about a singular "postsocialist agrarian question" is a huge simplification, suggests Chris Hann et al. (2003). Differences lie in historical patterns of cultivation and practices of land use, property and market institutions, and local ecologies and cultures in which these institutions have been embedded. The study of the postsocialist agrarian property may thus be illuminative of particular property forms and productive technologies on the ways human groups live and work together, while questioning both Marxist and neoliberal narratives of property and belonging (2003: 4). The institutional and normative arrangements that ensued from socialist collectivitization were not just a product of ideological dogmas, but also "distinctive traditions of rural communities" (2003: 9), building on the collectivist traditions of the pre-socialist countryside. The socialist collective farms, in turn, were often characterized by hybridized arrangements of collective and private ownership and production. Stefan Dorondel and Stelu Şerban (2014) argue that the postsocialist agrarian question in Southeast Europe should be viewed within longitudinal social processes that have unfolded over more than a century, starting with the reforms of the nineteenth-century newly emerged nation states, and culminating with postsocialist decollectivization reforms (2014: 7). The authors point out that the issues that have historically characterized rural populations in those areas — including unequal distribution of income and high poverty — partly result from social differentiation that persists even in the current postsocialist era. Predatory land property (Bernstein 2011), often seen as a characteristic of the earlier peasant society, tends to endure in Romania after the breakup of collective farms and privatization of land and forests (Dorondel and Şerban 2014).

While the land reforms throughout the history of southeast European nation-states had striven to legitimize the central role of the state and transform peasants into "citizens," this process has not been straightforward. Dorondel and Șerban suggest that the socialist years saw the rise of a "hybrid" worker-peasant – a "semiskilled industrial worker forced by the communist regime to float between industry and farming" (2014: 20; see also Dorondel 2016; Kaneff 2002; Szelényi and Kostello 1996). Much of the income of the worker-peasant in Romania was derived from informal or side activities during the socialist as well as postsocialist period, therefore limiting the importance of market mechanisms in local livelihoods. Rural smallholdings remained intermeshed in broader work-exchange networks, constraining the preference toward larger plot sizes even in the postsocialist era: rural dwellers were not motivated to rent out landholdings or invest in larger plots, continuing their subsistence-oriented production patterns and remaining relatively independent of markets (Dorondel and Șerban 2014: 21). Decollectivization may thus have had an unexpected consequence of weakening rural production and property rights and exacerbating social differentiation. Former cooperative farm managers often emerged as new successful entrepreneurs, due to better access to resources and power hierarchies (Verdery 2003).

The co-existence of different landholding systems of varying degrees of formality may lead to the intermingling of older and newer kinds of entitlements and collectivities, and can render specific population groups increasingly vulnerable to manipulation by diverse actors and institutions (see Meinert and Rodima-Taylor 2017). In such situations of plural authority, contested cases may remain unsolved between the systems, with parties "forum-shopping" for a best possible outcome (Benda-Beckmann 2009). Evidence from transitional economies in other parts of the world, such as Africa, indicates that despite formal land titling reforms, traditional systems and arguments often serve to establish authority for the elites at the expense of the most vulnerable (Berry 2001; see also Berry, this volume). That also complicates land restitution processes. Land property can thus not only become an important part of forging new social identities and political alliances, but may inspire new kinds of competition and conflict.

The study of postsocialist landholding therefore forces us to question the socialist as well as neoliberal narratives about property rights and human collectivities. In order to expand the concept of property beyond the legal codes of private or collective rights, we need to embrace a "wider field of public claims and entitlements" (Hann et al. 2003: 26; 1993). The power to access and control resources may be of greater practical significance than legally sanctioned ownership. Such more expansive notions of property call on us to conceptualize it in terms of relations between persons, their claims and entitlements as members of communities (Hann et al. 2003).

The Romanian case serves as an illuminating example. In 1991, the Romanian Parliament passed the law to restore land to its former owners. Not all property is restored, however – the law applies only to the land in collective farms, not those in state farms. Furthermore, the ownership landscape of the farms that existed in 1959, prior to land collectivization, does not characterize the present moment, where many owners and their descendants have moved away or are otherwise not available to receive the landholding (Verdery 1996: 134). Cornel Micu (2014) points out that the disconnect between Western-inspired legalistic understandings of "land property" and the socio-cultural realities of the Romanian countryside has existed since the nineteenth century. Arguing that "land is culturally defined more as 'means of subsistence' and 'social connector' rather than as economic asset or means of production," Micu contends that the Western discourse of property rights that sees the property holder as inherently right-bearing, is at odds with Romanian cultural notion of landed property that makes it difficult to "differentiate between things and persons as separate entities" (2014: 133–34). The historically small size of plots and lack of alternative jobs in the Romanian countryside led people to see land as a family property, concerned with the livelihood of the whole family unit – and its sale therefore inconceivable. That embeddedness has had important implications to the development of land markets in the postsocialist era.

Frank von Benda-Beckmann (1999) has suggested that the property concept in the liberal legal and economic theory exaggerates the freedom of modern private ownership from legal and cultural restraints. To understand the true impact of changes in property rights, one needs to explore how these relate to changing power configurations and their contestation. The potentially conflicting property rules and norms of behavior, emanating from different ideological regimes and legislations, can be evaluated through their realization in social relations and social practices (Hann 2003: 25; 2007; see also Kusk and Meinert, this volume). The Romanian landholding has been historically diverse and governed by inequalities and social differentiation. While in some villages, Romanian families – usually those who had been among the first settlers of the village – owned strips of land for communal cultivation among their kin groups, in many others land was held by noblemen and the villagers acted as serfs who had to deliver taxes both to the nobleman and the king of the country (Dorondel 2016: 28–29). While some of these inequalities were addressed through the land reform of 1864 that granted some land to peasants based on their agricultural inventory such as oxen and cows, social and economic hierarchies remained as a pervasive feature in the Romanian countryside.

During the Soviet era, new forms of collective and individual entitlement were created – largely through informal practices. Katherine Verdery (1996) argues that the collectivization reforms in Romania resulted in making land movable, "elastic," by removing the grid of borders between landholdings. The postsocialist re-binding of that grid created spaces for contestation between individuals and for manipulation by village and commune elites (1996: 134–35). This elasticity incorporates and brings into contact new and old entitlements and social identities. While old socialist loyalties of communities and farm worker collectivities are disappearing, the ongoing "atomization" of identities may not be occurring on an individual basis, but rather at the level of family and extended familial networks within the emerging "ideology of kinship" (1996: 166). Verdery contends that the property regime under socialism could be characterized as "administrative" rather than juridical, as the norms of land access and use were determined by various layers of formal and informal administrative and power hierarchies in the collective farms and villages. Despite official ideology, socialist communes retained and developed a considerable degree of individual entrepreneurship and resource rights outside the formal juridical framework. Local power relations have continued to shape the rural landscape even in the postsocialist era. Local state bureaucrats have been able to assert their interests on the outcomes of land restitution reforms in many areas of the country, often replicating the pre-reform patterns of differentiation and inequality (Dorondel 2016).

A Short History of Land Mortgage and Land Reform in Romania

Romania has experienced several radical land reforms over the course of the twentieth century. The first reform that occurred after World War I in 1921 aimed at a shift in land ownership from large estates toward peasant smallholders – the actual cultivators of the land. In 1945, the newly appointed socialist government launched another land reform with similar aims to distribute land to poor rural inhabitants. The socialist regime nationalized and collectivized private farmland and forests in Romania, and established collective farming by 1962. The quasi-elimination of private property rights in land changed the agrarian structure of the country. Agricultural land was consolidated into large plots belonging to either state or collective farms. Subsequently, a large-scale mechanization of agriculture took place, in accordance with the socialist rhetoric of catching up with the industrialized Western countries.[5] This was followed by the third, postsocialist reform of land restitution and privatization of 1991, seeking once again to radically alter the country's agrarian structure.

Land mortgage in Romania was introduced in 1864, the date of the first Romanian land reform in modern times. The Civil Code passed in 1864 aimed to transform feudal agrarian relations into "modern" capitalist ones. At the end of the nineteenth century, Romanian agrarian property was polarised: a few wealthy families owned most of the agricultural land. At the turn of the century, 5,385 land properties (over 110 ha) representing 48.69 percent of the total of arable land were owned by 4,171 landowners (Creangă 1905: 3). Land properties between 10 and 100 ha represented 8.41 percent, whereas more than 1.3 million peasants had little to no land. Less than 0.5 percent of the population owned 47. 53 percent of the total arable land of Romania at that time. Agricultural productivity was extremely low, with machinery and technologies resembling those of the Middle Ages. Credit and mortgage were seen as the main tools for bringing capital into feudal agriculture. In the interwar period, both private farms and agricultural cooperatives borrowed and mortgaged their lands (Bulgaru 2003). Mortgage, however, was not very popular among the Romanian smallholders. Although there is not much data on mortgage loans from that historical period, existing evidence demonstrates borrowing both from agricultural and commercial banks, in case of a village called Dănești, as well as private money lenders, as in the case of the neighboring village, Cetățele (Șerban 2002). The interwar-era administrations created also the so-called Popular Banks, which offered advantageous credits to rural producers.[6]

Between 1948 and 1962, Romanian agriculture underwent a near complete collectivization: approximately 95 percent of the peasant families worked for collective or state farms, some of which comprised thousands of hectares (Cernea 1976). The collective agriculture was highly mechanized and utilized fertilizers and pesticides on a large scale. Between 1948 and 1989, land mortgage did not exist in Romania as private property had been abolished and the state subsidized agriculture.

Land Reform and Policy in Postsocialist Romania

After the fall of the socialist regime in 1989, a massive land reform was launched with the goal of introducing private property in the agricultural sector. Land seized by the socialist government was restored to former historical owners. That long and complicated process unfolded in three stages. The first restitution law (Law 18) was passed in Romanian Parliament in 1991 and stipulated that regardless of the size of the former land property, only up to 10 hectares of arable land was to be restituted per family. The second land restitution law, passed in 2000, stipulated that the size of the landholding to be restored to former owners was no larger than 50 hectares. The third law passed in 2005 specified "restitution *in integrum*," calling for the entire landholding seized by the socialist government be returned – prompting jokes among the administration that to put this law into practice, another country of the size of Romania might be needed.

Land reform was a long and arduous process aimed at a complete transformation of the rural property regime in Romania. In 1989, when the postsocialist reforms began, out of the 14,759 million ha of total agricultural land, 60 percent had been collectivized, 28 percent was state property, and only 12 percent constituted private property. By late 2015, the picture had changed drastically: 94 percent of all agricultural land was held as private property and only 6 percent remained in public ownership (INS 2016; Lup 2014). The neoliberal program of privatizing agriculture was complete.

These successive laws aiming at land restitution must be understood within a wider national context. A recent breakdown of the agricultural sector of Romania looks as follows: the country has 14.6 million ha of land under agricultural fields (arable fields constitute 64.3 percent of this), 32.9 percent pastures and meadows, and 2.8 percent vineyards and orchards (INS 2016). A population of 1.96 million persons work in the agricultural sector, representing 23 percent of the total work force – almost six times the average of the European Union (4.2 percent).[7] Despite the high number of people working in agriculture, productivity remains low, with the agricultural sector contributing only 4.7 percent to the country's GDP (INS 2016). These data are not surprising, considering that almost half of the population working in the agricultural sector is over fifty years of age, and over 60 percent of the people involved in agriculture have only primary education. Considering that only 7 percent of those employed in agriculture have a written contract, it is not surprising that Romanian villages have become deserted, with a high degree of rural migration to Western Europe (Anghel 2014; Popescu 2016).

Among other effects, land reform has produced an "atomized" agricultural structure with high farmland fragmentation and small holdings. Romania has 3.6 million farms that constitute 32.2 percent of the European Union total. The average surface area of a farm is 3.45 ha. The steep polarization of holdings by size contributes to the low productivity: while larger farms with surface area over 100 ha exploit 48.8 percent of total agricultural land, they represent only 0.3 percent of the total number of farms in the country. At the other extreme are small farms—those with less than 2 hectares—that represent 73.3 percent of total farms and work 13 percent of the arable land. In these subsistence-oriented farms, over 90 percent of the production is consumed within the household (50 to 52 percent in semi-subsistence farms) (Steriu and Otiman 2013). These farms make only sporadic use of modern technology and inputs. Most of them use seeds from the previous year and do not utilize pesticides or chemical fertilizers (Dorondel 2016). Thus, those farms are highly dependent on meteorological conditions, with production varying drastically from one year to another.

The assumptions of the decollectivization reforms that private land and resource ownership would lead to economic recovery and growth in the Romanian countryside have largely not materialized (Cartwright 2003: 171; 2014). Historically, experience with private smallholder farming had been limited in the country, with a prevalence of large estates and landholdings. Soon after the privatization reforms, persistent challenges with forming viable, medium-sized landholdings became evident (2003: 182). Many collective farm workers had lost their livelihoods, and informal labor pooling proliferated in local villages. A number of new landholdings, although formally privatized, continued to be governed by multiple entitlements and use practices. Elderly farmers who formed two-thirds of the owners of the newly privatized land found themselves encumbered by social and cultural constraints against the selling of land, with land seen as family patrimony (2003: 182). The lack of market infrastructures for small producers and the low profitability of agriculture combined to keep young people out of farming.

While undertaking radical reforms, the postsocialist state's budget for the agricultural sector has been bleak. This is combined with uneven and frequently changing institutional and legislative framework, and poor administrative and financial management. The funds spent by the Romanian government have often been aimed at correcting the effects rather than targeting the causes of the problems the agricultural sector was facing (FAO 2004). Countless changes in land laws created the impression that rights in land were not secure. Postsocialist land policies in Romania have not been consistent, and ironically, the land reform is still ongoing.

Agricultural Credit: The History of a Relationship of Mistrust

All these developments have contributed to a disinterest within the banking sector toward investing in Romanian agriculture. The financial sector in Romania is underdeveloped, and lenders and borrowers operate in an uncertain legal environment and within a taxation regime that is unfavorable for intermediaries (Chaves et al. 2001: 13). Most of the credit finance is intermediated by the banking sector, while the role of market-based intermediation provided through stock markets or other security markets is insignificant (2001: 14). The country remains underbanked, with the size and number of assets circulating in the banking system limited relative to the number of banks and personnel. A volatile macroeconomic environment, shortage of liquidity and non-performing loans have limited the performance of the banking sector (2001: 17).

The mistrust has been reciprocal as farmers have not found the loan terms favorable. Most of those looking to build an agribusiness have sought alternative ways to borrow money – from informal sector lenders to friends and family members. Most rural dwellers drew upon their existing financial resources such as pensions and off-farm jobs (Dorondel 2013; 2016). Only a few larger farms benefited from micro-credit from banks or international institutions.

The environment of mistrust toward formal finance fueled deceptive borrowing practices. There were instances of farmers, especially those who "knew someone" linked to politics, borrowing money from banks with no plans of paying back. In an interview that one of the article authors had with a farmer, the latter confessed that his father had borrowed money from a Romanian bank which, shortly after, went bankrupt. The father, a respected engineer, had borrowed money to buy machinery for his fictional agricultural association that he claimed to have founded with a group of friends on their restituted land. All the actors lived in nearby cities, however, and had zero agricultural knowledge.[8] This story was rather typical of the first postsocialist decade when several Romanian banks declared bankruptcy due to mismanagement and political corruption.

Land mortgage as an option to finance agricultural entrepreneurship was reintroduced by the land restitution law in 1991. This possibility was merely theoretical as until quite recently, banks had been reluctant to give loans to the agricultural sector. The unattractiveness of investing in agriculture has to do as much with the general conditions of postsocialist agriculture as with the evolution of the Romanian banking sector. Similar to other transition economies, the Romanian banking sector lacks reliable access to long-term funding and is limited in its ability to provide medium- and long-term loans (Chaves et al. 2001: 16). All that has adversely impacted rural lending.

During socialism, the country had only four commercial banks – needless to say all state owned – and the National Bank, which fulfilled also some of the functions of commercial banking. After the 1990s, the banking system underwent a rapid change. The National Bank of Romania separated its functions from commercial banking. New banks emerged, most of these as branches of foreign banks. The banking sector diversified its products and services and modernized its financial instruments (Pintea and Ruscanu 1995; Zapodeanu 2005). However, it also experienced corruption and mismanagement, and all Romanian commercial banks, except for one, were either sold to foreign banks or collapsed.

Commercial transactions involving restituted agricultural land were prohibited in Romania until 1998. High fragmentation of landholdings and incomplete titling have exacerbated the riskiness of land as collateral for the lenders, and land markets remain thin (Chaves et al. 2001: 41). The progress of titling has been hampered by inadequate bureaucracies – the registries of the Land Book offices are antiquated, poorly equipped and staffed, fueling disputes and delays. Due to deficient procedures and documentation, lenders have concerns about foreclosure reinforcement mechanisms and overlapping claims (2001: 41–42). The processes of land titling and transactions are also very costly in Romania.

Romanian farmers may have had some technical expertise based on their collective farm experience (Lampland 2002) or marginal knowledge about markets as in the case of non-collectivized shepherds (Dorondel 2016; Stewart 1998), but they were ignorant about the ways the banking sector functions. Many of them lacked basic financial literacy and were not able to financially plan or manage their farming and small business activities. This comes as no surprise when considering the age and education levels of those active in the country's smallholder agriculture. The largest group within this category is to be found over the age of sixty-five: 1.45 million people. The next largest group consists of people between the ages of fifty-five and sixty-four years (820,000 people). Together the two groups constitute 62.79 percent of the population active in the agricultural sector. Education levels of the farmers, regardless of age, are rather modest: only 0.23 percent of the older generation and 2.24 percent of the younger one possess specialized agricultural knowledge (Rusu 2016).

The country's banks, on the other hand, had minimal knowledge about agriculture until recently, and employed no personnel specialized in that sector, leading to a severely limited capacity of analysis of the creditworthiness of agribusinesses – especially those of smaller dimensions. The fuzziness of property rights, proliferating multiple claims and use rights for a single plot, and the lack of proper cadastral maps (Hann 1993; Dorondel 2016; Verdery 1996, 1998, 1999, 2003) added to the reluctance of banks to provide rural credit. The judicial system was not geared toward smallholders, while proving tolerant to large economic enterprises with huge private and public debts.⁹ Additionally, the rapid inflation of the early 1990s caused bank interest to skyrocket.

Land Titling and the Development of Land Markets in Romania

Challenges with land titling and the almost non-existent cadastral system emerged as major impediments to the development of viable land markets in postsocialist Romania.

Decollectivization of agricultural land had meant returning 11 million hectares to former landowners or their descendants, with 5 million requests to be fulfilled (Rusu 2002). This was an enormous challenge for Romanian authorities. The issuance of land titles was considerably delayed for a multitude of reasons: difficulties with identifying requested plots, family disputes and conflicting claims over landholdings, administrative bias and corruption in distributing available land, and poorly managed land registries (Dorondel 2016; Mungiu-Pippidi 2010; Verdery 2002). For example, in a village of 1,700 inhabitants in southern Romania, 30 percent of the issued land titles had serious flaws pertaining to landholding size, plot boundaries, or name of the title recipient, rendering the titles unusable. The worst thing, said the former mayor of the commune, is that the old generation or original titleholders has passed away. The young generation would have to generate the title info from scratch – very difficult for someone who does not know the history of a particular plot.¹⁰ The diverse array of documents testifying to land rights that the Romanian state had issued over time – including land vouchers, minutes allowing land possession, land title, and "legalized" land title documents – did not help matters. Each official paper had value for different purposes but only the legalized land title could authorize selling or mortgaging the landholding. One can understand why creditors refrained from taking seriously any loan requests that were not based on legalized land titles.

Land cadastres were another area causing headaches to the Romanian government over the past thirty years. The magnitude of agricultural land under cadastre in the country remains unclear. Some experts from the Ministry of Agriculture professed to the authors of this chapter that only 10 to 15 percent of the agricultural lands may be on cadastre. Completing the cadastre and including new landowners in the National Land Register has been a political promise of the government since the 1990s – one that has never fully materialized. The process has been further complicated by a lack of succession papers of the heirs of those who received the land in the early 1990s.¹¹ Many heirs of the entitled owners may have been working the land, but due to the lack of money they may have never closed the succession or registered it in the National Land Register. The lack of reliable cadastre also impedes an assessment of the size of the overall area under agricultural land in Romania and its quality. As one of the vice-presidents of the Academy of the Agricultural Sciences and Forestry (AASF) put it in a conference presentation: "Not identifying the land that we have is as if we do not have it."[12] The lack of cadastre makes the borders of the land ownership extremely fluid. Sometimes, as seen in Figure 7.1, the border mark between two plots is represented just by a wooden stick. As one of the authors witnessed during fieldwork, the dispute between the two neighbors meant that anytime one of the landowners was in the corn field, he was moving the border stick one meter toward the neighbor's property (Dorondel 2016). The moving borders of land continued until the anthropologist left the village, with the two owners ploughing and harvesting each other's field, accompanied by complaints to the local police and the mayor's office. The lack of secure cadastre also adversely impacts the willingness of lenders to accept land as mortgage collateral.[13] If the mortgaged land is not under cadastre, it has no value as it cannot be sold.

Figure 7.1. The moving border stick marking the land dispute between neighbors (June 2004). © Stefan Dorondel and Thomas Sikor.

The Romanian land market has been rather weak until recently. Strong social barriers still exist against selling land, due to its familial and kin group connotations (Verdery 2005). Land is seen as a form of social security for an uncertain future, and something to leave to one's grandchildren. The children's generation, however, seems more interested in working abroad than in agricultural activities in their village of origin. The hopes are therefore on the third generation who might turn to their roots: to the village, land, and agriculture.

Legally, selling land has become operational only since 1998, as the first land restitution law forbade selling the landholding that one had acquired through restitution. "Informal" land sales still took place – for instance, as "donations" of land to another person, for an unrecorded monetary payment. Unfortunately, we have no data about the magnitude of this informal land market. According to official records however, between 1998 and 2005, less than 1 percent of the total agricultural land of Romania was transacted. The situation has changed especially after Romania joined the European Union in 2007. That also marked the start of the acquisition of larger land tracts by foreign investors – a form of "land grabbing." Landholding prices started to increase, attracting the attention of the banking sector. Some observers consider that the European Union subventions played a significant role in rising land prices in the accession countries (Swinnen and Vranken 2010; van Herck et al. 2013).

Severe land fragmentation in the Romanian countryside was another factor not appealing to potential agricultural creditors. High levels of farmland fragmentation are a widespread challenge brought about by land restitution policies in many areas of postsocialist Europe. Extreme land fragmentation often involves large degrees of co-ownership, hampering the development of functioning land markets as well as shorter term land leasing. Persistently high costs of land registration and property transfer tax hamper land mobility and foster informal land transactions and hidden payments (Holst, Hartvigsen, and Lopez 2018). The lack of broader national frameworks for consolidation initiatives and uneven political support are frequent limiting factors (2018: 13).

Land fragmentation was blamed in the early 1990s for the widespread agricultural crisis in Romania that affected agricultural productivity (Riddell and Rembold 2000). The agricultural census of 2002 shows that there were 14.5 million plots of land, out of which individual households owned 14.3 million plots. Looking at the fragmentation pattern, one-third are compact agricultural holdings, one-third are moderately fragmented and one-third highly fragmented, consisting of more than four parcels (see Figure 7.2). The average size of the individual household is 1.73 ha,

Figure 7.2. Land fragmentation in a hilly village, Davideşti, Argeş County (2010). © Stefan Dorondel.

with each household holding three parcels on average with the average size of a parcel being 0.52 ha (Rusu and Pamfil 2005). These data show an extreme fragmentation of the agricultural land in Romania, consistent also with other postsocialist countries (see, for instance, Stahl 2010 for Albania). A slow process of land consolidation started only in the second half of the 2000s.[14] For instance, between 2002 and 2016 the number of farms decreased by 24 percent, which demonstrates land consolidation. However, small farms of less than 2 hectares comprise over 50 percent of the agricultural land at the national level.[15]

Recent Developments in Agricultural Credit

The involvement of commercial banks in the agricultural credit sector tends to be limited in the European Union accession countries in general. Land banks that act as intermediaries in the buying and selling processes and thereby make landholdings more mobile are lacking in those countries (Holst, Hartvigsen and Lopez 2018). The Guarantee Fund for Rural

Credit was established in Romania in 1994, with the participation of three commercial banks with equal quotas (BRD Groupe Société Generale, BCR, and Raiffeisen Bank) as well as the Romanian state through the Ministry of Agriculture and Development. The guarantees provided by the Fund were for loans issued by shareholder banks only and were meant for medium- and long-term loans to the private sector.

The winds of change started to blow after 2007 when Romania joined the European Union. EU subsidies became significant in Romanian agriculture, with the sum at the country's disposal for 2007–2013 being approximately 8 billion euro. Over the following five years, 2014–2020, around 20 billion euro was poured into Romanian agriculture. The EU subsidies require a financial effort from Romania as well, and the banks have started to notice business opportunities in the agricultural sector. The data we aggregated from the monthly releases of the National Bank of Romania clearly speak to this phenomenon.

Table 7.1. The evolution of bank credits for agriculture in Romania in 2005–2020. Source: Authors' aggregation based on monthly National Bank of Romania bulletins.

Year	Credits (Million Euro)	For agriculture, forestry, fishing (Million Euro)	Agricultural as percentage of total credit
2005	17,833.9	412.8	2.3
2006	31,129.6	819.1	2.6
2007	46,522.9	1,047.8	2.3
2008	57,408.6	1,404.2	2.4
2009	54,811.0	1,512.9	2.8
2010	60,493.6	1,672.2	2.8
2011	65,315.6	2,161.2	3.3
2012	64,046.7	2,336.4	3.6
2013	64,428.4	2,425.0	3.8
2014	65,371.5	2,630.6	4.0
2015	68,790.6	2,818.7	4.1
2016	77,229.0	3,082.0	4.0
2017	80,899.0	3,361.0	4.2
2018	84,729.0	3,479.0	4.1
2019	90,050.0	3,902.0	4.3
2020	93,163.0	4,219.0	4.5

This table shows at least two things. One is the low percentage of the agricultural credit of total credit in Romania (less than 5 percent). Second, for the last ten years, loans for agricultural purposes have steadily increased, indicating interest from both sides of this financial instrument. The cost of agricultural loans for the Romanian farmer is still prohibitively high – about three times the cost of loans to an average Western European farmer (Goșa, Nagy, and Otiman 2011). A farmer from southern Romania commented: "In France, banks offer farmers loans with a 2 percent annual interest, whereas in Romania, small farmers are simply forbidden from loans."[16] Another farmer lamented that to receive a loan from a large Romanian bank, he had to mortgage a brand new CLASS combine, which was valued by the bank at only 20,000 euro while he had paid 50,000 euro. This happened despite the fact that as he was already 60 percent funded through a grant of the EU, his solvency had been excellent.[17]

Until 2010, no bank in Romania accepted agricultural land as mortgage collateral. In order to finance one's small business of processing agricultural products or other similar venture, a farmer had to pledge real estate or agricultural machines as these were considered valuable assets that would be easy to sell in case of default. Additionally, such loans were given only to agricultural firms and not individual farmers – the latter were not considered reliable borrowers. Apart from a general uncertainty regarding the returns of the emerging smallholder production, the newly collectivized villages had acquired an image of chaos and lawlessness – a site of havoc wrecked by human looters and wild animals. Shortly after the fall of the socialist state in the early 1990s, villagers started to dismantle and steal pipes, engines, and other hardware of the Romanian irrigation system – one of the largest in all of southeast Europe – guided by the idea that everyone should gain something from the breakup of the collective farms (Dorondel 2005). Besides, most of the socialist agricultural infrastructure that remained in state ownership had fallen into decay due to the lack of investment and maintenance (see Figure 7.3). Wild animals such as boars ravaged corn farms in former floodplain areas. The emerging insurance sector was not helpful in mitigating such losses.[18]

The situation with rural financing in Romania has been improving slowly. In 2013, the government passed a law in an effort to support financial access to land by local farmers, stipulating that to obtain a landholding, the farmer needs to come up with 10 percent of the entire value of the chosen piece of property. For the remaining 90 percent, the state offers a 50 percent guarantee whereas the other half represents the value of the mortgaged land. While still not many banks are offering agricultural financing, efforts are made to understand the needs and challenges

Figure 7.3. A ruined pump station in Bistretu village, Dolj County (July 2014). © Stefan Dorondel

of smallholders. Interviews carried out with the representatives of two of such banks revealed that they employed agricultural engineers – people knowledgeable about smallholder economies – as heads of the agricultural credit departments. Farmers are provided assistance with compiling their business plans and restructuring loans. "That benefits both parties, as we do not want to transform our bank into a land selling firm," one banker assured us.[19] The rural mortgage process still has many challenges. The last soil analysis at the country level was carried out in the 1960s.

The irrigation system, where still in place, is not counted as an asset – meaning that the value of irrigated and non-irrigated land is virtually equal. In fact, as a bank official pointed out, the presence of the (still state-owned) irrigation infrastructure causes the costs of water and electricity to skyrocket, rendering the high-priced produce of that farm virtually unsellable.

Concluding Thoughts

This chapter explored the reinvention of an economic practice – land mortgage – after fifty years of interruption caused by the socialist regime.

While Romania has experienced some success recently with improving the situation with rural credit and expanding the range of eligible borrowers and forms of loan collateral, it is also clear that land reform in Romania is still very much an ongoing process. While the recent subsidies of the European Union have been helpful for creating new business opportunities for the agricultural sector, it is up to the Romanian authorities to facilitate an enabling economic environment for small and medium-sized farms and eliminate blockages present in the credit market.

This study is among the very first ones to explore the topic of postsocialist land mortgage. It is easier to find more in-depth studies of land mortgage in emerging economies in other parts of the world – such as Parker Shipton (2009) for Kenya – while postsocialist countries and southeast Europe are still conspicuously missing from the picture. The study of the re-emergence of private property in land in these societies can contribute important novel perspectives to our understanding of the role of pre-existing as well as new norms and organizational templates and the part of local communities as well as state actors.

In the postsocialist world, decollectivization reforms have added to the proliferation of normative practices and fueled conflicts and contestation around rural resource access and control. The new ideologies of market and private property are modified by older socio-cultural norms and templates, and re-shaped by traditional understandings of the "moral economy" – the ways to regulate economic relations through non-monetary forms (Hann 2003, 2006; Scott 1976). The cultural practices of mutuality and reciprocity that originate from the pre-socialist times affect the application of later state ideologies in local communities and impede the commoditization of certain resources and practices. Diverse collectivist ideas and templates of reciprocity thus endure and evolve through different formal regimes, affecting local forms and practices of property and belonging.

This chapter attempted to situate the reinvention of the land mortgage in the longitudinal processes of diverse tenure reforms in the Romanian countryside, and within the multiplicity of formal and informal actors and hierarchies that define the economic practices in local communities. At the same time, we contend that the "moral economy" explanation is not sufficient for understanding the reasons for the slow take-off of land mortgage in Romania. Equally, in these reforms we saw the evidence of the state trying to render legible and establish better control over local economic and political spaces, and forcefully govern by redrawing administrative boundaries and property rules (see also Scott 1998). It could be said that both collectivization and decollectivization reforms therefore entailed attempts of a radical modernist restructuring of the agrarian economy, with a goal to enhance economic and political control from above.

Our research also highlights the need to study the rural lending and borrowing relationship as a reciprocal, two-way arrangement, by including the perspectives of both farmers as well as the banking sector. Creating proper incentives for the lenders to participate in land mortgage is a factor still often overlooked both in the analysis as well as application of land privatization reforms. Even anthropological scholarship on land mortgage has rather been focused on one side of the coin – farmers and their alternatives to borrow against land. Our study foregrounds the importance of undertaking more systematic ethnographic and policy-oriented research into rural lending in postsocialist societies – an area of inquiry that still tends to remain in the shadows.

Stefan Dorondel is an anthropologist and environmental historian interested in the entangled history of rivers, wetlands, riparian population, and nation-states in Eastern Europe. His works also explore the intersections between built infrastructure and natural environment. His previous work was on land tenure, land reform, and forest restitution in postsocialist countries. He is the author of *Disrupted Landscapes: State, Peasants and the Politics of Land in Postsocialist Romania* (Berghahn Books, 2016) and co-author (with Thomas Sikor, Johannes Stahl, and Phuc Xuan To) of *When Things Become Property: Land Reform, Authority and Value in Postsocialist Europe and Asia* (Berghahn Books, 2017). He has co-edited (with Stelu Şerban) *A New Ecological Order: Development and the Transformation of Nature in Eastern Europe* (University of Pittsburgh Press, in print).

Daivi Rodima-Taylor is a social anthropologist, and researcher and lecturer at the African Studies Center of the Pardee School of Global Studies of Boston University. Her research explores the social meanings of property and finance, the morality and regulation of credit and debt, and the intersection of digital technologies with local economies in the Global South. She was educated at Tartu University and Brandeis University, and her work has been supported by the Wenner-Gren Foundation for Anthropological Research. She has been leading a Boston University interdisciplinary task force on migrant remittances and human security, and directs the BU ASC Diaspora Studies Initiative. She has conducted longitudinal field research in East Africa, co-edited special issues, and published articles in journals such as *Africa, African Studies Review, American Anthropologist, Global Networks, Social Analysis, American Ethnologist, Journal of*

International Relations and Development, Geoforum, Global Policy, and *Review of International Political Economy.*

Marioara Rusu is a senior researcher within The Institute of Agricultural Economics in Bucharest, Romania. She has more than thirty years of experience in the field of agricultural economics and rural development research, and as an expert and coordinator in projects with national and international funding (European Union, World Bank, FAO, IFAD, Ministry of Agriculture, Ministry of Education, Romanian Academy, etc.). She has experience in working with rural local actors and policy makers and using quantitative and qualitative research methods.

NOTES

1. Countries that had signed the treaty of accession to obtain the status of "acceding countries" of the European Union and were expected to become full member states on the date set out in the treaty.
2. We appreciate also Parker Shipton's comment that fragmentation has its pros and cons. It can mean it is hard to get from one field to another, and maybe some problems in mechanization – but it can also mean fairer distribution among offspring, and a more diverse set of soil conditions and microclimates to minimize risks of a holder's or family's farming.
3. This work was supported by a grant of the Ministry of National Education, CNCS – UEFISCDI, no. PN II-ID-PCE-2012-4-0587 (2013–2016).
4. For a more general view, see Oane Visser et al. (2019) and Stephen Wegren and David O'Brien (2018).
5. For more on collectivization, see Stefan Dorondel (2016); Gail Kligman and Katherine Verdery (2011); and Alina Mungiu Pippidi (2010).
6. For more details on policies, political programs, and institutions involved in transforming the Romanian agriculture at the end of the nineteenth century and the first half of the twentieth century, see Cornel Micu (2010).
7. Eurostat, "Farmers and the Agricultural Labour Force – Statistics." *Eurostat, Statistics Explained*, 22 June 2021. Retrieved 10 July 2021 from https://ec.eur opa.eu/eurostat/statistics-explained/index.php/Farmers_and_the_agricultural _labour_force_-_statistics#.
8. Interview with a 38-year-old farmer, in Bucharest, July 2016, by Stefan Dorondel.
9. About courts ruling unfavorably toward private initiatives, see Verdery (1999).
10. Interview by Stefan Dorondel and Stelu Serban with former mayor of Fântânele village, Teleorman County, August 2016.
11. Landholdings were returned to those considered legitimate owners – mostly old people who had died.
12. Public debate organized by the AASF, Bucharest, 17 of June 2016.
13. Interviews with three Romanian bank officers who are experts in agricultural credit, Bucharest May 2016 and August 2016. From the interviews with two

farmers, it also became clear that no bank would accept land as mortgage without a cadastre (Suhaia and Fântânele villages, Teleorman County, August 2016).
14. In this discussion, we do not want to overemphasize the value of the formal land title, sometimes presented as *the* mechanism of transforming inefficient agriculture into a capitalist, efficient rural economy (e.g., de Soto 2000). See Thomas Sikor et al. (2017) or Daniel Bromley (2005) for a critique of the assumption that private land property and clarity of tenure transforms agriculture into an economically productive machine.
15. Institutul Național de Statistică [National Institute of Statistics], 2017, Ancheta Structurală în Agricultură 2016 [The Structural Inquiry in Agriculture, 2016].
16. This is a quotation from a farmer's speech at the AASF, Bucharest, 17 June 2016.
17. Interview with the head of a 112 ha agricultural holding, Fântânele, Teleorman County, August 2016.
18. Interview with the owner of a 100 ha rural farm, Suhaia village, Teleorman County, August 2016.
19. Interview of Stefan Dorondel with the head of the agricultural credit department of a large Romanian Bank, Bucharest, May 2016.

REFERENCES

Anghel, Gabriel Remus. 2013. *Romanians in Western Europe: Migration, Status Dilemmas, and Transnational Connections*. Lanham, MD: Lexington Books.
Ban, Cornel. 2016. *Ruling Ideas: How Global Neoliberalism Goes Local*. New York: Oxford University Press.
Benda-Beckmann, Frank von, Keebet von Benda-Beckman, and Julia Eckert, eds. 2009. *Rules of Law and Laws of Ruling: On the Governance of Law*. Farnham, MD: Ashgate.
Benda-Beckmann, Frank von, and Keebet von Benda-Beckmann. 1999. "A Functional Analysis of Property Rights, with Special Reference to Indonesia." In *Property Rights and Economic Development*, ed. T. Van Meijl and F. Von Benda-Beckmann, 15–56. London: Kegan Paul.
Benjaminsen, Thor, and Christian Lund, eds. 2003. *Securing Land Rights in Africa*. London: Frank Cass.
Bernstein, Henri. 2011. "Is There an Agrarian Question in the 21st Century?" *Canadian Journal of Development Studies* 27(4): 449–60.
Berry, Sara. 2001. *Chiefs Know Their Boundaries: Essays on Property, Power, and the Past in Asante, 1896–1996*. Portsmouth: Heinemann, James Currey, David Philip.
Brandstädter, Susanne. 2003. "The Moral Economy of Kinship and Property in Southern China." In *The Postsocialist Agrarian Question*, ed. Chris Hann and the Property Relations Group, 419–40. Münster: LIT Verlag.
Bromley, Daniel. 2005. *The Empty Promises of Formal Titles: Creating Potemkin Villages in the Tropics*. Madison: University of Wisconsin, Department of Agricultural and Applied Economics.
Bulgaru, Valeriu. 2003. *Reforma agrară din 1921 – fundamente economice* [The economic basis of the agrarian reform from 1921]. Timișoara: Editura de Vest.

Cartwright, Andrew. 2003. "Private Farming in Romania, or, What Are the Old People Going to Do with Their Land?" In *The Postsocialist Agrarian Question*, ed. Chris Hann and the "Property Relations Group," 171–188. Münster: LIT Verlag.

———. 2014. "The Fall and Rise of the State in Rural Romania and Hungary." *MARTOR* 19: 63–74.

Cernea, Michael. 1976. "Co-operative Farming and Family Change in Romania." In *The Social Structure of Eastern Europe: Transition and Process in Czechoslovakia, Hungary, Poland, Romania, and Yugoslavia*, ed. B. L. Faber, 259–72. New York: Praeger Publishers.

Chaves, Rodrigo, Susana Sanchez, Saul Schor, and Emil Tesliuc. 2001. "Financial Markets, Credit Constraints, and Investment in Rural Romania." World Bank Technical Papers.

Creangă, George D. 1905. *Proprietatea rurală și chestiunea țărănească* [Rural landed property and the agrarian question]. Bucharest.

Csaki, Csaba, and Alan Zuschlag. 2004. *The Agrarian Economies of Central-Eastern Europe and the Commonwealth of Independent States*. ECSSD working paper no. 38. Washington, DC: World Bank.

de Soto, Hernando. 2000. *The Mystery of Capital: Why Capitalism Triumphs in the West and Fails Everywhere Else*. New York: Basic Books.

Dorondel, Stefan. 2005. "Land, Property, and Access in a Village from Postsocialist Romania." In *Between East and West: Studies in Anthropology and Social History*, ed. S. Dorondel and S. Șerban, 268–307. Bucarest: Editura Institutului Cultural Roma.

———. 2013. "Neoliberal Transformations of the Romanian Agrarian Landscape." In *Fields and Forests: Ethnographic Perspectives on Environmental Globalization*, A special issue of the RCC Perspectives 5: 13–22.

———. 2016. *Disrupted Landscapes: State, Peasants and the Politics of Land in Postsocialist Romania*. Oxford: Berghahn Books.

Dorondel, Stefan, and Ștelu Serban. 2014. "A Missing Link: The Agrarian Question in Southeast Europe." *MARTOR* 19: 7–30.

Food and Agriculture Organization (FAO). 2004. *Agriculture and Rural Development in Romania*. FAO Project, TCP/ROM 0167 – unpublished.

Geschiere, Peter. 2009. *The Perils of Belonging: Autochthony, Citizenship, and Exclusion in Africa and Europe*. Chicago: University of Chicago Press.

Giovarelli, Renee. 2000. *Mortgage in the Bulgarian Agricultural Sector*. RDI Reports on Foreign Aid and Development #104.

Giovarelli, Renee, and David Bledsoe. 2001. *Land Reform in Eastern Europe: Western CIS, Transcaucuses, Balkans, and EU Accession Countries*. Seattle, WA: FAO.

Goșa, Vasile, Andrea Nagy, and Paun Otiman. 2011. "Creditarea agriculturii românești. Sisteme de finanțare ale agriculture folosite în Uniunea Europeană și în România" [Lending to Romanian agriculture. Agriculture financing systems used in the European Union and in Romania]. In *Alternativele economiei rurale a României* [The alternatives of the Romanian rural economy], ed. Paun Otiman, 124–53. Bucharest: Editura Academiei Române.

Hann, Chris. 1993. "From Production to Property: Decollectivization and the Family-Land Relationship in Contemporary Hungary." *Man* (N.S) 28: 299–320.

———. 2006. *"Not the Horse We Wanted": Postsocialism, Neoliberalism, and Eurasia*. Munster: LIT Verlag.

———. 2007. "A New Double Movement? Anthropological Perspectives on Property in the Age of Neoliberalism." *Socio-Economic Review* 5: 287–318.

Hann, Chris, and the Property Relations Group. 2003. *The Postsocialist Agrarian Question*. Munster: LIT Verlag.

van Herck, Kristine, Johan Swinnen, Liesbet Vranken, P. Ciaian, and Dartis Kanc. 2013. *Possible Effects on EU Land Markets of New CAP Direct Payments*. Study for European Parliament. Brussels.

Holst, Frank van, Morten Hartvigsen and Francisco Onega Lopez. 2018. *Land Governance for Development in Central and Eastern Europe: Land Fragmentation and Land Consolidation as Part of Sustainable Development Goal*. Washington, DC: World Bank.

Institutul Național de Statistică (INS) [National Institute of Statistics]. 2016. Tempo Online Database. Retrieved July 2021 from http://statistici.insse.ro/shop/?lang=en.

Kaneff, Deema. 2002. "Work, Identity, and Rural-Urban Relations." In *Postsocialist Peasant? Rural and Urban Constructions of Identity in Eastern Europe, East Asia and the Former Soviet Union*, ed. Pamela Leonard and Deema Keneff, 180–99. London: Palgrave.

Kligman, Gail, and Katherine Verdery. 2011. *Peasants under Siege: The Collectivization of Romanian Agriculture, 1949–1962*. Princeton, NJ: Princeton University Press.

Lampland, Martha. 2002. "The Advantages of Being Collectivized: Co-operative Farm Managers in the Postsocialist Economy." In *Postsocialism: Ideals, Ideologies and Practices in Eurasia*, ed. Chris Hann, 31–56. London: Routledge.

Lerman, Zvi, Csaba Csaki, and Gershon Feder. 2004. *Agriculture in Transition: Land Policies and Evolving Farm Structures in Post-Soviet Countries*. Lanham, MD: Lexington Books.

Lup, Aurel. 2014. *Agricultura socialistă a României: Mit și realitate* [The socialist agriculture of Romania: Between myth and reality]. Constanța: Editura Ex Ponto.

Meinert, Lotte, and Daivi Rodima-Taylor. "ASR Forum: Land Disputes and Displacement in Postconflict Africa." *African Studies Review* 60(3): 7–17.

Micu, Cornel. 2010. *From Peasants to Farmers? Agrarian Reforms and Modernisation in Twentieth Century Romania. A Case Study: Bordei Verde Commune in Braila County*. Frankfurt am Main: Peter Lang.

———. 2014. "Social Structure and Land Property in Romanian Villages." *MARTOR* 19: 133–48.

Miller, Liesl, and Patrick Heady. 2003. "Cooperation, Power and Community: Economy and Ideology in the Russian Countryside." In *The Postsocialist Agrarian Question*, ed. Chris Hann and the Property Relations Group, 257–92. Munster: LIT Verlag.

Mungiu-Pippidi, Alina. 2010. *A Tale of Two Villages: Coerced Modernization in East European Countryside*. Budapest: CEU Press.

Pintea, Alexandru, and Gheorghi Ruscanu. 1995. *Băncile în economia românească* [Banks and the Romanian economy]. București: Editura Economică.

Popescu, Marin. 2016. *Agriculture Contribution to Economic Growth: A Prospective Study*. Bucharest: Editura Academiei Române.

Riddell, James, and Fritz Rembold. 2000. "Social and Economic Impact of Land Fragmentation in Rural Society in Selected EU Accession Countries." *Proceedings of the UDMS 2000*, 13–20. Delft University of Technology, The Netherlands, 11–15 September.
Rusu, Marioara. 2002. "Land Laws and Related Legal Institutions to Support Development of Land Markets and Farm Restructuring in Romania." In *Restructuring and Transition of Agrifood Sector and Rural Areas in Romania*, ed. Violeta Florian, Dinu Gavrilescu, Daniela Giurca, Mirela-Adriana Rusali, and Camelia Șerbănescu, 411–30. Bucharest: Expert.
———. 2016. "Rolul sistemului de informare și cunoaștere în agricultură în stabilizarea ofertei agricole" [The role of the information and knowledge systems in agriculture in stabilizing the agricultural supply]. In *Economie agroalimentară și dezvoltare rurală în țările din Sud-Estul Europei. Provocări pentru viitor*, ed. Cecila Alexandri, Camelia Gavrilescu, Mihaela Kruzlicika, and Marioara Rusu, 537–543. Bucharest: Editura Academiei Române.
Rusu, Marioara, and Virgil Pamfil. 2005. *Agricultural Land Reform and Land Consolidation in Romania*. Retrieved 28 June 2016 from http://www.fao.org/fileadmin/user_upload/Europe/documents/Events_2005/Land2005/Romania.pdf.
Scott, James. 1976. *The Moral Economy of the Peasant: Rebellion and Subsistence in Southeast Asia*. New Haven: Yale University Press.
———. 1998. *Seeing Like a State: How Certain Schemes to Improve the Human Condition Have Failed*. New Haven: Yale University Press.
Șerban, Stelu. 2002. "Strategii de reacție față de colectivizarea pământului în două sate din nordul României" [Reactions Strategies against Land Collectivization in Two Villagers from Northern Romania]. *Buletinul Institutului de Studii Sud-Est Europene* 9: 99–131.
Shipton, Parker. 2009. *Mortgaging the Ancestors: Ideologies of Attachment in Africa*. New Haven and London: Yale University Press.
Shipton, Parker, and Daivi Rodima-Taylor. 2015. "Land Tenure." In *International Encyclopedia of the Social and Behavioral Sciences*, 2nd edition, ed. James D. Wright, 231–37. Amsterdam: Elsevier.
Sikor, Thomas, Stefan Dorondel, Johannes Stahl, and Phuc Xuan To. 2017. *When Things Become Property: Land Reform, Authority and Value in Postsocialist Europe and Asia*. New York: Berghahn Books.
Sikor, Thomas, and Christian Lund, eds. 2009. *The Politics of Possession: Property, Authority, and Access to Natural Resources*. Oxford: Wiley-Blackwell.
Stahl, Johannes. 2010. *Rent from the Land: The Political Ecology of Postsocialist Rural Transformation*. London: Anthem Press.
Steriu, Valeriu, and Paun Ion Otiman, eds. 2013. *Cadrul național strategic pentru dezvoltare durabilă a sectorului agroalimentar și a spațiului rural în perioada 2014–2020–2030* [The national strategic framework for sustainable development of the agrifood business and of the rural areas for the period 2014–2020–2030]. Bucharest: Editura Academiei Române.
Stewart, Michael. 1998. "The Trauma of De-collectivization in Two Romanian Villages." In *Surviving Post-socialism: Local Strategies and Regional Responses in Eastern Europe and the Former Soviet Union*, ed. Sue Bridger and Frances Pine, 66–79. London: Routledge.

Swinnen, Johan. ed. 1997. *Political Economy of Agrarian Reform in Central and Eastern Europe*. Aldershot: Ashgate.

Swinnen, Johan, and Liesbet Vranken. 2010. *Review of the Transitional Restrictions Maintained by Bulgaria and Romania with Regard to the Acquisition of Agricultural Real Estate*. Report for the European Commission, CEPS. Brussels.

Szelényi, Ivan, and Eric Kostello. 1996. "The Market Transition Debate: Toward a Synthesis?" *American Journal of Sociology* 101(4): 1082–1096.

Verdery, Katherine. 1996. *What Was Socialism and What Comes Next?* Princeton, NJ: Princeton University Press.

———. 1998. "Property and Power in Transylvania's Decollectivization." In *Property Relations: Renewing the Anthropological Tradition*, ed. Chris M. Hann, 160–80. Cambridge: Cambridge University Press.

———. 1999. "Fuzzy Property: Rights, Power, and Identity in Transylvania's Decollectivization." In *Uncertain Transitions: Ethnographies of Change in the Postsocialist World*, ed. Michael Burawoy and Katherine Verdery, 53–81. Lanham, MD: Rowman & Littlefield Publishers.

———. 2002. "Seeing Like a Mayor, Or How Officials Obstructed Romanian Land Restitution." *Ethnography* 3(1): 5–33.

———. 2003. *The Vanishing Hectare: Property and Value in Postsocialist Transylvania*. Ithaca, NY: Cornell University Press.

———. 2005. "'Possessive Identities' in Postsocialist Transylvania." In *Between East and West: Studies in Anthropology and Social History*, ed. Stefan Dorondel and Stelu Şerban, 341–66. Bucharest: Editura Institutului Cultural Român.

Visser, Oane, Stefan Dorondel, Petr Jehlička, and Max Spoor. 2019. "Postsocialist Smallholders: Silence, Resistance and Alternatives." *Canadian Journal of Development Studies* 40(4): 499–599.

Wegren, Stephen, and David O'Brien, eds. 2018. "Symposium: Smallholders in Communist and Post-communist Societies." *Journal of Agrarian Change* 18(4): 869–925.

Zapodeanu, Daniela. 2005. "Restructurarea sectorului bancar românesc" [Restructuring the Romanian banking system]. *Analele Universității din Oradea*, 356–359. Științe economice series, vol. XIII. CD-ROM edition.

CHAPTER 8

 Distressed Publics
*Circumventing the Mortgage
from South Africa to Ireland*

NATE COBEN AND MELISSA K. WRAPP

As financial instruments of debt become more commonplace in once-unfamiliar domains — as mortgages enter into new spheres, new public housing projects, new fiscal endeavors — it can be easy to lose sight of their own provincialism. Even at the turn of the last century, the legal fiction of the mortgage was regarded as atavistically opaque: Frederic Maitland called the mortgage deed one long *suppressio veri* (suppression of truth) and one long *suggestio falsi* (false suggestion) (1909: 269). As contracts, mortgages masquerade as bilateral agreements made by two parties of equal capacity to come to mutually beneficial terms and be held responsible for those agreed terms. But the mortgage carries with it some deep imbalances: the creditor risks losing money on their investment, while the borrower risks losing something much less fungible: possession of the secured land, forever. In this chapter, we examine cases in South Africa and Ireland in which people recognize and work around those tacit imbalances.

Given the mundane mortgage's centrality to the complex derivative trading in the Global Financial Crisis, especially, "financialization" has become an increasingly common descriptive term in anthropology to explain the process by which new devices and instruments encourage different kinds of speculation, risk, and derivative thinking to rearrange preexisting economic methods of production, householding, and exchange (see Kalb 2013). It is a term that carries with it some implied ideas about both the movement of world history and the suggestive, if not determinative, power of instruments to bring about certain futures. In that formulation, a financial device like a mortgage is a kind of Trojan horse for a global process of abstracting everyday life, undoing the stability of the tangible and granular (i.e., making the home a security for a loan, "financializing" the home), and transcending toward an incorporeal universal, to the point that we see mortgage agreements themselves financialized and securitized.

The mortgage, despite its ubiquity in most contemporary property markets as a threshold for homeownership, and its strong association with the derivative trading that provided the conditions for the Global Financial Crisis, is a financial device with relatively weird medieval beginnings. There are debates about origins, but it seems largely to have come about as an English innovation on the Germanic *gage*, or pledge, of land. In English legal history the two common forms of the gage were the *vifgage*, the living gage, and the mortgage, the dead pledge. The former was "living" (according to Glanvill) in the sense that giving products of the land to the lender could reduce the principal sum of money loaned over time, while the latter was "dead" because those products of the land were just interest payments (i.e., "dead" to the principal) (see Seipp, this volume). The other difference was that the dead pledge tended toward "distraint" or "distress" of property, meaning the seizure of land to satisfy creditors, not just the products of the land, was a central risk of the mortgage form, in particular. Frederick Pollock and Frederic Maitland's story of the mortgage's rise in popularity over the *vifgage* details twelfth-century illiquid knights seeking out loans from Jewish lenders to finance their crusades (Pollock and Maitland [1898] 2010: 124).

In light of the long and varied history of the mortgage form, we might suggest that what is new about all this financial modernity is not the instrument, the derivative, or the speculation itself, as financialization might imply. Instead, what is new seems to be what kinds of problems the mortgage is expected to treat—global development, post-conflict transitional justice, unprecedented sovereign debt—and the shape of the failures that come about from mobilizing the mortgage in those projects. In the two case studies we present, in which people repudiate or avoid altogether the mortgage instrument in pursuit of homeownership, we ask why mortgages seem to be activating other reciprocities and debts that look more "traditional" and increasingly "clannish" (see Shipton 2009: 86) instead of ever-increasingly "contract-like" and bourgeois sensibilities. Research elsewhere has shown how the aftermath of financialization produced an increase in the reengineering and extension of reciprocities (Palomera 2014), and stoked the often-disappointed expectations of reciprocity between creditors and debtors (Stout 2016). Rather than begin from financialization, which presumes a relative lack of familiarity or literacy with financial instruments, we start from the over-familiarity that prompts the anti-mortgage, those methods by which people avoid the political and financial strings (and risk) attached to those larger projects that revolve around the extension of the mortgage to resolve novel problems. In the gap between what public institutions say mortgages will do politically and economically (e.g., give homeowners security, develop economies, teach financial responsibility) and what mortgages actually end up doing, there is a failure that nurtures new political imaginaries outside and around the mortgage (with varying degrees of success).

To be clear, we are not proposing that the presence of feudal forms in contemporary markets and political project are vestigial traces of the past holding back economic and political modernity. On this point, the political scientist Cedric Robinson proposes that the tensions between equality and inequality in feudal relations came to be articulated through new forms of rationality and calculation. In *Black Marxism*, Robinson demonstrates how racial order formed to structure relations between peoples within European societies. Capitalism, therefore, did not rationalize social relations, but expanded these racial distinctions. "Indeed, capitalism was less a catastrophic revolution (negation) of feudalist social orders than the extension of these social relations into the larger tapestry of the modern world's political and economic relations" (C. Robinson 1983: 10). Robinson's analytical approach calls into question the self-professed modernity of capitalism, a point that for us suggests that the veneer of balance implicit in capitalist financial instruments, the appearance of equilibrium between parties, hides a deeply uneven hierarchical relationship with very feudalist undertones.

We share two cases of government programs in very different contexts in which the mortgage is offered as a favored contemporary mode of political problem solving. In one scenario, the Financed Linked Individual Subsidy Programme (FLISP) initiative in South Africa, grants are extended to applicants to obtain loans for first-time home purchases. These would-be grantees make more than would qualify them for fully subsidized housing (known colloquially as "RDP"), but for them a mortgage from a commercial bank would be inaccessible. FLISP offers them a state-subsidized mortgage in lieu of directly subsidized social housing as a ticket into homeownership for a class of South Africans the government wants to recognize and shape as aspirational and upwardly mobile in its aim of advancing post-apartheid economic transformation. In another scenario, we look at the Abhaile scheme in Ireland, which provided already distressed mortgagors the opportunity to access legal assistance and personal insolvency professionals in the hope of encouraging "sustainable" mortgage remodifications in the longstanding mortgage arrears crisis that followed the 2008 financial crash. "Sustainability" was determined by lender/creditors and the alternative repayment arrangements

(ARAs) they offered were up to their discretion. In both scenarios we find a significant number of people wanting out of, not into, mortgages and the financial subjecthood and political modernity they supposedly offer.

We propose that the responses exemplify what we term "distressed publics," which refers not only to the contemporary conditions of economic precarity that these potential mortgagors teeter on, but to a seeming resurgence in clannishness to what we might call this "anti-mortgage" response. Instead of lining up to be newly minted financialized subjects, people in South Africa are responding to the initiative by working through networks of family, favors, and political patronage to access RDP projects. Rather than pursue a rehabilitated, and likely unrealistically penurious mortgage remodification, people in Ireland experimented with all kinds of ways to get out of a purgatorial path of "engagement" with their creditors. Again, we propose that the rise of distressed publics like the ones we introduce are not some sort of anti-modernist political formation, but rearrangements of the inchoate feudal-like character of the mortgage, with whatever materials are at hand. In this regard, we are in agreement with research, from South Africa in particular (James 2014), that sees innovations in government interventions into payments and debt not as a resolution of previously existing informal practices but as a new, dynamic force within a broader culture of credit.

To be "distressed" is to be in a financial jeopardy that stems from mortgage debt: distressed debtors are those who are behind in payments and are at risk of having the security underlying the mortgage agreement given (by a court order, in the terms of the contract, etc.) to their creditor. "Distressing" also refers to a process of making new forms look old. Think distressed furniture or distressed denim. What we propose here is a concept for appreciating novel financial and political formations, like mortgage avoidance, as something of a "distressed genre" (Stewart 1991) of response to the proliferation of liberal credit instruments as a method of remediation and governance. If the relations being taken up in efforts to avoid mortgages are styled in antiquarian, traditionalist, and feudal garb, then we should consider whether the algorithmic, technological, and modernist iterations of the contemporary mortgage form is not also a question of anachronistic fashion.

Evading Mortgages in South Africa

Cape Flats sand dusted the narrow asphalt road Zintle and Melissa Wrapp walked down as the sun began to dip behind Table Mountain, casting long shadows across rows of tightly packed subsidy houses. The scratching of boot soles accented breaks in conversation as the pair shuffled over the grit. Wrapp had come to Cape Town as an anthropologist studying the relationship between inequality and urban planning, specifically in reference to experimentation with new public housing interventions. Zintle was a young Xhosa woman, a bookkeeper involved with a nonprofit in the housing sector. After she became a friendly acquaintance, Zintle agreed to participate in an architectural walkthrough interview with Wrapp.

Starting at Zintle's home, the pair moved around the building, talking about its history, about how she came to own the property, its design, and a few irksome maintenance problems. Inside, they greeted her husband and four of his nephews, who lived in shacks at the back of the house, but were apparently permanently stationed in front of the living room TV playing cards. As soon as they were out of earshot, Zintle quietly mouthed "*All day* it's like this." Although she was strained by supporting the six of them, she was thrilled to soon be starting a position in a regional government office, which would mean a higher salary and greater job security.

As the two headed out of the sandy yard and down the street, Zintle reflected on her relationship with her neighbors, pointing out various houses and introducing Wrapp to friends along the way. They were close, and many people actually came from the same area of the Eastern Cape where she was born, including an aunt who lived down the road. As the two turned the corner, a massive house came into view. It had been converted into a two-story building and expanded to extend the full length of the lot, dwarfing the single-story structures surrounding it. "Wow," Wrapp remarked, "that one is huge." "It's very fancy," Zintle agreed, "You can't believe it. The owner of this house? She studied until standard 2. Standard 2! That's grade four. She didn't matriculate!" Wrapp asked the obvious question, "Then . . . how did she build that house?" Quickly glancing at a group of kids playing on the corner, Zintle, a diligent accountant scandalized, softly muttered, "She's scamming credit cards. *That's* how she got the money for it. And she owns about six *'maphela.*" Amaphela means cockroaches, or pests, in isiXhosa, and is slang for the informal taxis that are crawling, so to speak, all over the townships in Cape Town. The taxi industry is lucrative, but it is also considered something of a rough business; taxi bosses ruthlessly defend their routes, sometimes resulting in violent clashes over territory. She is a wealthy woman, Zintle was saying, but also dangerous. "So, how do the neighbors feel about her?" Wrapp asked, peering curiously at the mammoth building as they passed by. She shrugged slightly, "The thing is, she doesn't do it around here. She goes out to do it, somewhere else."

The irony, which Wrapp only realized on the drive home, was that Zintle had also acquired her home by illegal means. The house was built in 2006 as part of a public-private subsidized housing project, known colloquially as "RDP."[1] The original owner was an old man, "a pensioner," Zintle explained, who worked for the City of Cape Town. By the time he got off the housing waitlist and finally received his home, however, he was getting ready to retire in the Eastern Cape. Meanwhile, Zintle was living with her aunt on the other side of the road, finishing school and eager to establish her independence as she entered the working world. In 2012, Zintle bought the house, sort of. According to an amendment to the Housing Act (Act No. 107 of 1997, Amendment Act No. 4 of 2001), beneficiaries are restricted from selling (or renting) their homes within eight years of taking ownership.[2] "He's saying I'm his daughter to the Department of Housing. So it's something like that," Zintle said, laughing a little. To buy the house, she paid him directly in cash. Although she says she trusts him to give her the title deed, it technically did not exist yet. "They say the house must be ten years and older before they issue the title deeds. Even the owner doesn't have the title deed yet. I have plans to extend the house, but the thing is I'm waiting for the papers of the house before I do . . . in case he changes his mind."

We mention Zintle's profession, and the fact that both parties in this transaction worked (or would soon work) in government, not because it is scandalous, but as an indication of the fact that the illicit sale of RDP housing is so commonplace. Accurate statistics on the phenomenon are hard to come by, but in Dunoon (another township in Cape Town), for example, only an estimated four in ten RDP houses are occupied by the original beneficiary.[3] In 2018, the Gauteng MEC for housing Dikgang Moiloa reported the government was handling 30,000 cases of illicit RDP sales, with the number of cases reported escalating every year.[4] In 2006, the same year her house was built, the South African government introduced a new financing model to support people like Zintle — upwardly mobile, and earning too much to qualify for an RDP house, but too little to afford a commercial home loan on her own.

The Finance Linked Individual Subsidy Programme (FLISP) offers subsidies to first-time homebuyers who qualify for a mortgage; the subsidy is dispersed to the individual's bank, and helps put down a deposit on a house, or reduce their monthly payments. A little over ten years later, however, despite several policy revisions geared toward expanding access, FLISP is widely regarded as unsuccessful. The commonsensical explanation for why one might decline a mortgage in favor of a less secure, illegal means of acquiring housing is somewhat obvious: it is cheaper. But that does not fully explain what is going on here. We suggest that understanding the full complexity of stories like Zintle's is essential to understanding how programs like FLISP, which feature the mortgage as the nostrum for public policy woes like social housing, are unexpectedly generative in those failures. In the remainder of this section, we will unpack the purpose of FLISP, its shortcomings, and detail the alternative networks of obligation, indebtedness, and power that people are drawing on to circumvent institutional debt obligations.

Mind the Gap

Racial restrictions on residence, movement, and property ownership were foundational to architecting the system of apartheid, and creating a transient, black migrant labor force (J. Robinson 1996). But by the late 1970s, in the aftermath of the Soweto uprising and under mounting pressure from international sanctions, significant South African business interests began to advocate for the reversal of this position, instead framing the provision of housing as a means of preserving their economic position. At the time, legal housing options for black urban dwellers were largely restricted to single-sex dormitory blocks, known as "hostels," or a limited number of government-owned single-family homes. In 1977, billionaire businessmen Harry Oppenheimer (of the mining company Anglo American) and Anton Rupert (of the Rembrant Group conglomerate) set up the Urban Foundation (UF): a corporate-funded urban policy think tank. UF advanced a more classically liberal approach to managing South Africa's black labor force, arguing that black urbanization could be used as a means to "transform a discontented and threatening people into more compliant members of a mass-consumption society" (Smit 1992: 2, as cited in McDonald 2008: 63). One of the founders, Clive Menell of the Anglovaal mining conglomerate, put it quite candidly: "We became involved because we were scared. There was a concern for the country, of course, but there was also a selfish concern for our assets."[5]

Urban Foundation policies and practices have crucially shaped the South African housing landscape. In the late apartheid era, in keeping with policies advanced globally by the World Bank, UF facilitated the implementation of "site-and-service" housing projects throughout the country (Bond, Dor, and Ruiters 2000: 25). Also known as "self-help" housing (Smit 1992), these projects materially upgraded burgeoning informal settlements by offering beneficiaries "core" house structures with basic services, which were intended to be incrementally improved over time. Serviced sites were at the center of UF's "Housing for all" policy proposal (Urban Foundation 1990), which advocated for one-time "product-linked capital subsidies" dispersed to housing project developers ("the product" being "a standardized serviced site with freehold title"; Huchzermeyer 2003: 596). The thinking behind this approach was not only (again, self-interestedly) to create greater social stability and expand the number of middle-class consumers, but also to reduce the costs associated with urbanization. UF's policy approach, and its representatives themselves, exercised tremendous influence on South Africa's National Housing Forum (1992–94), widely criticized for the outsized role played by the private sector (Cirolia 2016). The negotiations in this forum resulted in the 1994 Housing White Paper, and the country's first democratic housing policy framework as a component of the Reconstruction and Development Programme (RDP).

With housing solidified as a central component of RDP, homeownership came to be seen as a vital element of restorative justice in South Africa (Marais and Cloete 2017). However, ten years in to the new dispensation, a problem emerged. Although 1.6 million new housing units were constructed by 2004, RDP homes were (and still are) reserved for low-income families – households earning less than R3,500 per month (approximately US$230, at today's conversion rates). This singular focus in government policy led to a gap, or a cohort of people Charlotte Lemanski terms "middle citizens" (2017) who do not qualify for government housing subsidies but also cannot afford a mortgage from a commercial bank. The Department of Human Settlements defines the gap as being comprised of households earning between R3,500 and R15,000 per month (roughly US$230 and US$1,000); Kecia Rust (2012) estimates some 25 percent of South Africans fall into this group. Liza Rose Cirolia has argued that the "gap market" is a nebulous category that does not actually correlate to a homogeneous or functional submarket (2016: 632). Nevertheless, the notion of this "gap" has been invoked to justify all manner of interventions into the housing market, including FLISP.

The Finance Linked Individual Subsidy Programme was introduced in 2006 to target the perceived gap housing problem. FLISP offers public grants (in amounts between R27,960 and R121,626; roughly US$1,850 and US$8,000) to qualified applicants to obtain loans for first-time home purchases. According to the State's Vision 2030 Strategy, "Gap housing is a policy that addresses the housing aspirations of people such as nurses, firefighters, teachers and members of the armed forces who ... do not qualify for RDP houses and do not earn enough to obtain home loans."[6]

FLISP fits within a broader range of practices of privatization perpetuated by the state in the name of individual responsibility and self-help, peddling a narrative in which the reduction of services ostensibly advances a "pro-poor" agenda. In Western Cape Provincial Minister of Human Settlements Bonginkosi Madikizela's words, "The reality is that we have to embark on a whole-of-society approach, instead of looking at the government as Father Christmas where people are just folding their arms and becoming passive recipients."[7] But after six years, participation in the program was sluggish at best, and government officials lamented that while they were well known for fully subsidized houses, "not enough [was] being done to provide housing" through FLISP (August 2013: 1). While at first the grant was only available for housing project developers to access, in 2012 it was extended to individual households as well. Similar to RDP housing, initially there were restrictions on selling FLISP properties within eight years of accessing the subsidy, and the government also retained the first right to purchase. In 2018, in another attempt to revamp the program, the government removed sales restrictions on properties purchased through FLISP, and increased the upper income threshold to R22,000.

Despite repeated efforts to expand access to FLISP, adoption remains poor. Property lawyers Wrapp interviewed in the Western Cape stated that every year funding for FLISP is "left over" in the provincial government budget (the organ that disperse the subsidy). In contrast, according to one lawyer, RDP subsidies (distributed each year by the first of April) are usually gone within a week. Similarly, senior banking officials have expressed that uptake has been "extremely low" (Lemanski 2017: 105). FLISP has been widely criticized by practitioners and academics alike; though manifold, these critiques generally cluster around two key issues: consumer education and technicalities of the policy.

Critiques of FLISP focused on consumer education assert that people either do not know about the program or, more fundamentally, do not understand home financing itself. Assertions of ignorance were commonplace among Wrapp's attorney interlocutors, with many laying the blame at the government's doorstep for not meaningfully engaging with low-income families to inform them about financing options. Efforts to redress this perceived ignorance generally take the form of promotional advertising and financial literacy workshops. In fact, in an effort to raise awareness about subsidy programs beyond RDP, banners advertising FLISP were literally plastered on the doorstep (outside provincial Department of Human Settlements offices) at the time of Wrapp's fieldwork.

In recent years, one Capetonian conveyancing attorney set up a website entirely devoted to promoting awareness of FLISP,[8] along with a

Figure 8.1. Exterior of the Western Cape Department of Human Settlements building. © Melissa K. Wrapp.

series of educational videos and a thirteen-part monthly workshop for homebuyers in the township of Khayelitsha. The same attorney also appeared in a local cable station's "All about Property" show in 2018, again seeking to reach more first-time homebuyers. The results of these nascent campaigns remain to be seen. However, regardless of awareness or financial literacy, others have raised questions around technical elements of policies governing FLISP, with many specifically taking aim at the income thresholds. Though many "gap" households may fall within the prescribed FLISP range, often these families' incomes are drawn from multiple, unstable sources (Lemanski 2017). Moreover, given South Africa's extreme levels of unemployment, oftentimes when people do have jobs and are upwardly mobile, they are obligated to financially support a wide family network. This social indebtedness (James 2014) means that a household's income on paper may not truly reflect how much of their paychecks they are taking home, or their ability to afford mortgage payments. And, even if they can, there are serious constraints on the supply of housing for the gap market (Cirolia 2016), no doubt a factor in the recent decision to remove restrictions on FLISP-purchased home sales.

Obligations Otherwise

These criticisms are focused on the supply side of the FLISP; that is, on the ability of applicants to access housing either based on cost, availability, understanding, or familiarity with the program. However, we wish to suggest that the low uptake is also due to demand. Many of Wrapp's interlocutors show little interest in acquiring a bond. This is not borne out of an ignorance of financing options, but rather an intimate knowledge of their violent effects. The South African Human Rights Commission has suggested that evictions through bond defaulting are "systemic" (2008: 44). In the same hearing, the South African Police Service stated, "in most eviction cases, occupants have never been to court, did not know the date of the hearing and had not been given a chance to state their side of the story" (2008: 39). Wrapp's fieldwork with grassroots community activists immersed her in hundreds of cases of disputed properties that they were involved in mediating, primarily in Cape Town's oldest black townships; this participant observation exposed Wrapp to countless cases in which "bond houses" (as her interlocutors termed them) were repossessed and auctioned off. To choose among myriad examples, in one particularly memorable case in Wrapp's neighborhood, a house had been sold to a woman named Thabisa. Thabisa's boyfriend moved in with her and took out loans to renovate the home. One day the couple split and the boyfriend, who moved out, stopped making payments on the loans. Eventually the bank sold the house to another family. But when the family arrived, Thabisa told them ominously, "You are not going to stay in this house. You will not wash in this house. You will not eat in this house!" The word around the neighborhood was that Thabisa used *muti* (traditional medicine) to perform a ritual in the home before leaving, a rumor seemingly confirmed when the new family started discovering snakes in the house. They fled, and the house still stands empty.

Though the otherworldly hazards in the case of Thabisa's house loom large, and are somewhat extraordinary, the financial risks are commonplace and commonly understood. The traumatically public theater of evictions – of a notice appearing on one's front gate, of sheriffs dragging prized possessions and furniture into the street, of clutches of neighbors gathering at a distance to watch, or in many more cases forcefully and defiantly dragging that furniture back inside – is painfully familiar. In weekly community meetings about housing issues that Wrapp attended in the township of Gugulethu, one activist in particular was in the habit of making speeches to explain elements of property law. "When you buy something in a store, you get a receipt," he would expound week in and week out, community members respectfully nodding along. "When you have a bond, the bank has the receipt for the house." His account hinged less on the technicalities of financing, and more on questions of power. "You can be sitting, comfortable in your house," he would say, miming someone sprawled in an armchair, "But it's not yours. The bank can come and take it, and then you have nothing! Because they have the receipt."

Instead of submitting to the rigid hierarchy of a mortgage, many favor other, more flexible relational dynamics; in other words, they would rather accept the vulnerabilities of interpersonal agreements, legal or otherwise, than be subjected to the vagaries of the market. The forms of mortgage avoidance in South Africa are as complex and idiosyncratic as the circumstances that precipitate them. They include gaining access to new RDP housing projects, either through informally purchasing properties once the development is completed, like Zintle did, or finding one's way onto a list of beneficiaries for new projects. In a sea of shifting policy prescriptions, government bureaucracies, and contractors, definitive proof of individuals buying their way onto beneficiary lists is hard to come by; allegations of the practice, however, are rife, and usually entail people making payments to officials or developers. In one interview Wrapp conducted with a community leader (the very person responsible for curating the list of eligible beneficiaries for the developers of a new project), the man, a "non-qualifier," talked openly about his daily prayers that he would not be caught for slipping his name (and the names of several family members) onto the list.

Others try their luck (*thath'ichance*) with vying for control of government rental houses built before 1994. These "family homes" were administratively passed down between family members during the apartheid era. In keeping with the global trend toward Thatcherite "right to buy" schemes, which similarly animated Urban Foundation ideas, the government has made an effort to transfer these properties to qualifying occupants. While officially known as the Discount Benefit Scheme, Wrapp's interlocutors refer to this process as the *nikezela* (hand over). However, several decades later, thousands of township properties are still without title deeds. Rather than qualifying for and paying down a bond, acquiring the title deed to one of these properties involves navigating complex familial, community, and state administrative dynamics; demonstrating a legitimate claim through Xhosa clan lineages; and negotiating grassroots community platforms for conflict mediation, like the one Wrapp ethnographically investigated. Though arduous, many would rather maneuver through these relations than be subjected to the strictures of a mortgage.

Still others seek to "fill in the gaps" a bit more literally. An increasing number of renters are turning to backyarding (or "infill" housing), living in informal dwellings built in between formal houses. Previously, backyarders were predominantly comprised of men living in the yards of their family's houses, where space inside is at a premium and it is seen as culturally inappropriate for adult Xhosa men to live in the family home. However, given the lack of affordable housing, the appealing blend of autonomy and communal living that backyarding offers (the primary draw for Wrapp, who lived as a backyarder during her fieldwork), and the promise of rental income for property owners, the practice is becoming increasingly common. According to Louis Lategan, "Backyard dwellings are one of the fastest growing housing sub-sectors, absorbing more households than informal settlements and delivering a major share of new accommodation" (2017: 5). Backyard rental agreements vary dramatically from house to house – some sign written contracts, others pay in food or favors, and some pay nothing at all. Some backyarders are simply renting temporarily to be close to a new job opportunity; for others, it is the home where they start and raise their families.

By GINI metrics, South Africa is widely regarded as one of the most unequal countries in the world. Though the country's unemployment levels are staggering, they are even higher in black townships. Proponents of FLISP posit homeownership as a means to radically transform conditions of economic inequality and redress the historical injustices of credit apartheid (James 2014) for would-be black bondholders. In each of these forms of mortgage avoidance, however, people turn instead to familial and clan networks, to other forms of payment, tenure, and obligation. In actuality, people are doing a lot to "fill in the gaps" themselves, not because they are uninterested in, or ignorant of, the promises liberal credit instruments, but perhaps precisely because they intimately understand how mortgages work, and choose to live otherwise.

The Distressed Irish Mortgage

Ciarán – clean-shaven, ruddy, and dressed in the gentle tweed coat of a retired *garda* (police officer) – did not shout, but spoke with a firm gravity in the hallway of a turn-of-the-century courthouse.[9] He raised an arm and pointed to a heavy courtroom door as he delivered a practiced but impassioned *j'accuse* about the economic struggles of rural Ireland after the unprecedented real estate crash of 2009, the ineffective and nonexistent support given to mortgagors after the crash, and the home repossession proceedings happening on the other side of that heavy door. He instructed Nate Coben, an American ethnographer researching these repossession hearings in rural Ireland, to observe the new stratification of a world organized around mortgage debt dating to before the crash: "There two worlds colliding in there: the common people's world, and the world of solicitors who go to luncheon together, or to brunches ... They *judge* everyone; there are two colliding worlds and one is seen to be better ... We are only peasants to them."

Ciarán's accusation of presumptuous, lordly behavior is a particularly cutting one in rural Ireland, especially in the context of home repossessions. In the late nineteenth century, the Land League, an anti-eviction movement that promised the "fall of feudalism" (Kane 2001), forged an Irish nationalism for which landownership would act as the political, economic, and moral basis of the nation in the twentieth century (see Lee 1989; Dooley 2004; Campbell and Varley 2013). Lay litigant activists like Ciarán (i.e., people who organized as non-represented litigants in mortgage debt cases) regularly invoked this history of eviction and land reform-based nationalism in rural Ireland – some used "land league" in their group's titles – but few reanimated that past with as much verve and pointed eloquence.

Yet Ciarán was also involved in the courtroom world "in there." At the outset of that day's court hearings in this rural midland county, Ciarán was introduced by the county registrar – a quasi-judicial public servant who acts as clerk to a judge, but who presides over the applications creditors make for repossession at the local county level. What was particularly surprising was that his presence and available assistance was announced alongside that of the Money Advice and Budgeting Service (MABS), an independent, state-funded credit counseling agency that had recently become the state-promoted intermediary for renegotiating distressed mortgage debt from those courts. Working in the same setting with the same public were two parties working at cross-purposes: MABS, who offered advice and support with the goal of rehabilitating distressed mortgage debt, and Ciarán, a former *garda* who convinced despondent distressed mortgagors to defeat their creditors, defend their freehold, and exit the irredeemable mortgage without further penalties. What about the social life of distressed mortgage debt in rural Ireland had brought these strange bedfellows together, while also feeding a budding antagonism between them? Why in the boom and bust cycles of real estate in the twenty-first century did concerns about new feudal relations seem to be percolating, not perishing?

What arose as a sort of rival to mortgage renegotiation were lay litigant groups like the one Ciarán belonged to that had three general tendencies, all of which were responses fostered by an absence of proactive state debt forgiveness or write-downs: first, they advertised assistance that would defeat banks and deliver the home on the mortgagor's terms back to them. Second, they at least partly relied on tactics that looked for legal loopholes, usually caused by very real contradictions and messiness of English and Irish common law legal history. Third, they drew on nationalist imagery from the nineteenth century evictions of tenant farmers by English and Anglo-Irish absentee landlords to suggest the state had betrayed the nationalist goal of a republic of freeholders. The state's calculated absence in protecting the homeowner soured an already fraught relationship with people who read in the news about financial institutions and developers being rehabilitated, but whose own debts were pursued for repossession.

It should be noted, however, that a significant amount of mortgage holders who joined in these "anti-eviction" groups were not necessarily owner-occupants of their mortgaged properties. Indeed, many took out mortgages to speculate on holiday and "buy-to-let" homes, hoping to become impressive landlords themselves, but getting left awash in mortgage debt. These distressed would-be big-timers were "too small" to be rehabilitated and too overextended to hope to repay their debts, and so turned toward repudiation of the mortgage alongside distressed owner-occupants.

In the rest of this section, we will describe the methods of remediating, renegotiating, and repudiating distressed mortgage debt that was left as the state, which owned or sold most of the mortgage debt underlying the homes being pursued for repossession in these courts, abdicated a central, proactive position among a republic of freeholders.

Remediation

In March 2018, the OECD's economic survey of Ireland paid particular attention to the "judicial inefficiencies" in repossessing (analogous to foreclosing) family homes and suggested that the slow speed of repossession proceedings (one and a half years, they estimated) was a key reason why Ireland's otherwise good economic prospects were "clouded with uncertainty." Because Ireland had taken out large loans to cover the costs of bailing out its financial institutions (buying their loan portfolios including most Irish mortgages), the international economic community had an interest in the fiscal strategies Ireland took toward regularizing the repossession of its homeowners. But what the OECD recognized as "judicial inefficiency" was not so much a lack of efficiency, as a long-term ambivalence among a variety of public actors about what should be done about the vast "non-performing" debt (e.g., mortgages in default) on the state's books.

The Abhaile (pronounced "ah-wahl-yeh") scheme was one such ambivalent half-measure. It was an Irish government-backed program to provide assistance to distressed mortgagors – borrowers who had defaulted on their mortgages and were falling deeper into arrears from consecutive missed monthly payments. The scheme's name comes from the Irish word for "homeward." As the name suggests, the scheme was not set up to offer protections or write-downs that would secure tenure of the home, but instead enlisted some state-funded agencies to guide distressed mortgagors on the uphill path of "engagement," as the long series of correspondence and negotiation was often called in the courtrooms where creditors sought the repossession of mortgaged homes.

The Abhaile scheme was largely aimed at outreach – giving distressed mortgagors, who often were absent from courtroom hearings because of fear or stress, enough hope of redemption to try to work toward a long-term solution. "Redeeming" here denotes the full repayment of the mortgage debt (although the moral and theological register it indexes is also intimately tied to the history of the mortgage). In concrete terms, the scheme enlisted the work of credit counselors from MABS, which was primarily set up to help people in danger of being deprived of heat, electricity, or shelter on the basis of personal debt.

Abhaile really only formalized the proactive experiments by a few key individuals. Several years before Abhaile, some MABS took it upon themselves to get in front of the anticipated avalanche of evictions by reaching out to distressed mortgagors by attending courtroom hearings. The first MABS representatives to take initiative did so in close dialogue with county registrars. While it was the job of county registrars to oversee repossession applications, few saw their job as rubberstamping large-scale dispossession in their counties. Those credit counselors began to provide free assistance to indebted mortgagors. They were especially helpful in regard to filling out Standard Financial Statements (SFS), the key item of paperwork that were snapshots of their income, assets, lines of credit, other debts, children, and so on. The SFS was also the key item from which a creditor could determine the "sustainability" of mortgage debts. In conjunction with the assistance and alibi that MABS provided, County registrars meted out discretionary forbearance, a kind of legal patience, not only for distressed mortgagors who were willing to entertain engaging with MABS but also for the many distressed mortgagors who were absent from the courtroom. The hope was that forbearance could lead them to have that "road to Damascus" moment (as one county registrar put it) and begin to engage. The hope was, for those county registrars, that even if voluntarily "surrendering" the home was the only realistic option suggested by the numbers, the help of MABS might "help them take that walk in their head" and come to terms with that loss in the most pragmatic way.

The Abhaile scheme formalized the initiative taken by concerned credit counselors and county registrars into what Elizabeth Dunn calls an "adhocracy," a form of power that generates the very uncertainty it ostensibly is created to stabilize (2012). It expanded the courtroom dialogue that MABS began to engage in and added a couple more tools to help delay repossession, but it guaranteed little more than what concerned public servants were already accomplishing.

The most evident change brought in along with the Abhaile scheme were "duty solicitors," attorneys who would be on hand in courtroom proceedings to speak for borrowers and explain, based on MABS's consultation with them shortly before the hearing, what the status of negotiations were with the creditor and the length of, and reason for, the adjournment they would seek that day. It was not legal aid, which implies actual legal representation. It only provided the semblance of legal aid without actually providing the same assurances (and incurring the same professional liability) as legal representation. Their presence encouraged disheartened borrowers to feel they had someone in their corner. Like the many distressed mortgagors who stayed out of the courts, distressed mortgagors who worked with duty solicitors often described their fear and unfamiliarity with courtroom dialogue as an obstacle to appearing: it was a vexing place to many of these borrowers and speaking in court brought up all the pent-up fears of losing their home they had been suppressing. Having their private shame aired in public court, borrowers often sidled up closely to the bench, whispering about their particular circumstances as much as they could until legal representatives of the creditors might complain that they could not hear. When people did appear and speak, it was not uncommon to see them physically shake, hands trembling as they clutched a piece of paper from a friend suggesting how they should argue their position; their voices would falter and crack as they offered whatever they could to stave off the permanent loss of their homes.

Part of the overall ambivalence in terms of resolving the mortgage arrears problem was also down to the banks themselves. The fact is repossession is often the last course creditors want to take, especially when the real estate market is down; banks want the legal machinery that enforces possession but prefer a steady stream of revenue from borrowers' monthly payments. Many distressed mortgagors Coben spoke with felt that being taken to court was simply a heavy-handed way for banks to scare up payments in the short-term without a good faith attempt to make the loan sustainable through a negotiation.

Renegotiation

The Abhaile scheme did not give borrowers any direct way to seek a write-down of debt or even force their creditor to engage with them in any substantial new way. Most importantly, creditors were still the ones whose prerogative it was to put forward any kind of loan modification proposal to a distressed mortgage whose debt they deemed, after reviewing their standard financial statement, "sustainable." It was also their prerogative to choose what that loan restructure type was – technically called an "Alternative Repayment Arrangement." As of June 2017, roughly when the fieldwork for this research concluded, 120,398 mortgages were classified as "restructured" out of a total of 732,439 residential mortgages, roughly 16 percent of the country's total mortgages (see McCann 2017).[10] Among the different "restructure" types the Central Bank of Ireland catalogued were split mortgage restructures (24.3 percent) and arrears capitalization (33.2 percent). The Central Bank of Ireland guidelines did not compel creditors in this situation to offer anything that was not in their direct interest. Creditors chose the renegotiation path and offered it to the borrower, who could refuse it, but that would exit them from the Central Bank of Ireland's Mortgage Arrears Resolution Process and increase the possibility of repossession.

These two creditor-preferred paths toward a remodified loan illustrate how the path of so-called "engagement" between borrowers and creditors frustrated so many distressed borrowers and muted their enthusiasm for restoring the mortgage:

"Capitalizing arrears" means the payments a borrower has missed are treated as part of the principal. So, if a borrower missed five months of payments at €1,000/month – forget interest for this hypothetical – on a loan that was originally for €100,000 but has been paid down to €80,000, when the arrears are capitalized, the remaining balance of the loan is now €85,000. That would seem similar to a term extension except the term is not extended. That means monthly payments – the ones that the distressed borrower was not paying in full, which is why they are a distressed borrower – now have to be increased for each month to pay off that higher sum over the same period of time. Because those original mortgage amounts were tethered to a valuation of the property that was dramatically inflated by a housing bubble prior to the Irish real estate's precipitous crash in 2009, even if the distressed borrower has found new employment after the worst part of the recession had past, the new monthly payments are out of whack with any notion of financial "sustainability." And yet, it is in the terms of "sustainability" that capitalization of arrears has been the most frequently (33.2 percent) offered type of mortgage restructure.

A "split mortgage," sometimes called a "warehouse loan," on the other hand, significantly reduces the monthly payment that the borrower has to make. It does that by "parking" a portion of the debt, now called the split balance, at the end of the loan term and then scaling monthly payments down to correspond to the lessened unparked amount, the main balance. So, if a borrower still owed €100,000 on their thirty-year mortgage, a split mortgage restructure might park €40,000 to be paid in fifteen years in one lump sum (the percentages and terms vary). The scheduled payment for the next fifteen years (again, ignoring interest rates) will be €333.33/month instead of €555.55/month. And then there is that €40,000. How can the borrower expect to pay off such a large sum at once? Dying is one way. Most of the split mortgage offers Coben came across required the borrower to have a life insurance policy and to use that as collateral in the new agreement. If the mortgagors are still alive, then the debt would be repaid by repossession: the creditor would repossess the home and sell it in order to get their compensation. There are ways that borrowers could make contributions to that parked debt that resembled something a little bit like credit card rewards, like offering to match 5 percent of the borrower's yearly repayments as a reduction to the parked split balance or incentivizing monthly overpays by matching an additional 20 percent of the overpayment toward the split sum.

Between capitalization of arrears and split mortgages, what was on the table for the majority of distressed borrowers only "kicked the can down the road," a frequently used vernacular phrase usually heard used by legal representation of creditors in reference to borrowers who were given adjournments when, the creditors claimed, full repayment of the loan was hopeless. Indeed, there was a significant correlative relationship between continued repayment on a remodified loan and previous default between 2008 and 2016, suggesting that the most frequently occurring restructure types for distressed mortgagors were insufficient (McCann 2017). After all, capitalizing arrears, one-third of loan restructures, told a person in arrears, "We will treat those missed payments as extra principal, so if you make pay a portion of that extra on top of your monthly payments for the rest of your loan period, that's fine." Given that these are people who by definition could not make previous payments, the hope is that they have since gotten a better paying job or a new source of wealth.

Even more provisional than the actual restructures, which seemed to only press pause on an eventual future default, creditors often asked borrowers to submit to a trial period to test their sustainability on a new loan repayment scheme. On a trial period, the creditor could for any number of reasons end the trial period and exit the mortgagor from the Mortgage Arrears Resolution Process outlined by guidelines from the Central Bank of Ireland. Creditors could justify that on the grounds of "non-cooperation," without documenting what that meant, or concluding that while repayments were being made in the trial period the loan was simply not sustainable in the long-term. The guidelines did call for some documentation, but it was a very unenforceable and unobserved part of a light-touch code of conduct. A trial period could encourage the borrower in arrears that their payments were in the service of a permanent solution and restart a stream of lowered revenue that had stopped. When exited from their trial period, the disheartened, stressed, and confused borrower would stop making payments, lose faith in the path of engaging with creditors altogether, and become a statistic of repeat default.

The terms of the new debt relationships that an ARA facilitated could only be offered unilaterally from the creditor to the borrower. In the case of the two most frequently offered kinds of restructures in the country, both made freehold possession that much more provisional and dependent on the financial institution's authority to estimation of the mortgagor. In the case of the split mortgage, comprising a quarter of the nation's loan restructures (especially among distressed mortgagors), this represented a new de facto form of the life estate, that feudal form of tenure in which possession of the land reverts to the lord on the tenant's death. But whereas it was a recognized form of tenure in feudal Europe, this new life estate was an effect of what financial institutions were given leeway by a deferential state to create.

Repudiation

As in the case of South Africa's public housing mortgage intervention, "financial literacy" was a popular, depersonalized way of assigning blame after the 2009 crash: too many people just did not understand how mortgages worked, or did not take care to get good legal advice.[11] But by not providing write-downs or substantial legal aid that might alleviate that purported lack of literacy, Irish governments left individual mortgagors to either accept repossession or seek out their own advice, as if to redouble the original lack of financial and legal literacy. There was a large gap in the years between the crash and when Abhaile was expanded from a few counties to the nation: many distressed mortgagors had already found people, other lay litigants, who offered legal advice to fill the void – people like Ciarán, the lay litigant activist and former *garda*, who would encourage them to defeat, not work with, banks.

Ciarán questioned MABS's motives as the favored source of advice in the Abhaile scheme. Echoing popular antipathies to the professional legal class, he said, "They're all scams, and solicitors are the first to profit off of [the implemented schemes]." It was nothing more than a way to enrich lawyers and MABS employees who would "convince you to live on nothing, go through various court processes, and then tell you after a year or more that [you] should hand in the keys," referring to a voluntary surrender of the home.

From the perspective of a rural county whose economy was once based on flax but had become based on dairy and mushrooms and thinking about an aging group of debtors like himself, Ciarán drew attention to the non-fungible future of the homeowner: "They, the MABS, the duty solicitor . . . will all say you can get a 'new start,' but you can't." He emphasized that in 2017, about nine years after the crash, most borrower-defendants were past their prime working years, so starting over was virtually impossible. "They keep telling us that the jobs are returning but the economy hasn't recovered down the country. All the jobs are coming to Dublin, none of the jobs are coming out here." A world without the security of tenure homeownership ostensibly provided and stuck with bad credit and little work prospects, renting was an unlikely option for most. For the tens of thousands of distressed mortgagors in rural Ireland, he insisted, there was no option but to fight, especially in a nation that had in the preceding decades transformed the public good of social housing into "unproductive capital," a matter better left to the market.

The lay litigant groups that offered support and advice to "fight" and "defeat" banks took different tactics, some more effective than others in a courtroom setting. One of the more notable, if not successful, methods that distressed debtors took to redress the unevenness of debt renegotiations was what I will call lay litigant trust (it was not put forward by legal professionals or recognized as a real trust).

These trusts were directed at lay litigants and promised distressed mortgagors that they had the power to defeat creditors by separating legal and "equitable" ownership (this is how trusts work) and then, by virtue of making it a so-called "private trust in private," disappearing the mortgage charge somewhere in that separation of powers (decidedly not how trusts usually work). This second, more fantastic, part was informed in part by a growing uptake in Ireland for North American right-wing

Sovereign Citizen rhetoric adapted to Irish nationalist concerns. During the summer of 2013, Coben witnessed people request certified copies of their title documents from the public country of the Irish Land Registry in an effort to join the most publicized of these lay litigant trusts, nicknamed the Kilkenny Trust, which claimed on the front page of national papers to have several billion euros worth of properties put under its trusteeship. In the following years, Coben met many people like Ciarán who had participated in the Kilkenny Trust but could not account for its present status. While no court ever recognized this as a legitimate and enforceable trust, let alone its capacity to effectively erase the mortgage, it did effect a new economic, legal, and political relationship between a borrower and the trustee. These were the main (purported) components of that trust:

1. The client purchases the certified copies of their title and mortgage instrument for properties they want to put in the trust.
2. The client pays €250 to the trust per property.
3. The trust associate introduces the client to a notary public, who witnesses the client sign over their legal rights to the properties.
4. Once ratified, the trust's properties are subject to the jurisdiction of the Universal Community Trust.
5. The client has a 999-year lease on the property with a ground rent of €100 per year. They are now a tenant of the trustee, who has "power of attorney" over the property.
6. The trustee now has the legal authority over the trust and removes the debt from it. Now entrusted, the mortgage charge is not in Ireland's legal jurisdiction anymore, so is unenforceable.

Who is this trustee that the distressed mortgagor has now ostensibly assigned "power of attorney" and legal possession of their home and to whom now they will pay rent? Likely a stranger who could at best establish themselves as a friend of a friend. They are people who came across as "common people" to people who are distressed in every sense of the word, and those have grown justifiably cynical toward a class of legal and financial professionals whose expectations of financial and legal literacy seem to only be there to exclude them and justify their eventual dispossession. These distressed mortgagors elected, with limited choices, to become beneficial tenants in the trust of a relative stranger, a new landlord. The annual ground rents might seem nominal – annual ground rents still exist as a bureaucratic anomaly in Ireland – but Coben spoke to people who put their property in the trust and said some of these trustees had indeed continued to collect rents from the original mortgagor. In return for the authority and wealth they at least provisionally transferred to the trustees, the distressed mortgagor received the promise of protection.

The country hotel bar was a popular place to deliver testimonials for the trust, and in the spring of 2016, Coben sat in one with a man, introduced by a mutual friend, who wore black who advertised a similar version of trust to the Kilkenny Trust. When Coben asked about the differences between his "private trust in private" and the seemingly unsuccessful Kilkenny Trust as a point of comparison, the man balked, but replied that Kilkenny had been sound, but the trustees were weak. They had no idea what they were doing or how to direct the trust and protect its beneficiaries. He insisted that if the trustee (he never explicitly said he was the one) knew his powers, "the trust cannot be penetrated by any man, beast or creature on Earth . . . He can do anything."

For the man dressed in black it was clearly not only like, but *was* a sovereign power, and that is how he advertised it to potential customers. He told potential clients that the provenance of the trust was as a device to hold land for knights who left on crusades. The history of the trust certainly has roots in the Crusades, as shown in the man in black's story (see also Thomas 1999), but more intriguingly in reverse: that story suggests that Franciscans, looking to hold property intergenerationally and collectively without owning material possession of that wealth in life, came into contact with Islamic *waqf* in their Crusades; they were inspired to adapt it to English land law (see Gaudiosi 1988). The man in black's version of the Crusades story gave his trust a millenarian, Christian genealogy and moral purpose, and indexed forms of righteous sovereign authority vested in a Christian morality prior to the modern nation-state. What is also so striking about his origin story is that it is, in fact, accepted by many as the origin story for the mortgage. The man in black's sales pitch for his confidence game was also a hypothesis about the deeply feudal entanglements of modern finance, the ineradicable appeal of status, and an abdicated protective authority those feudal forms encourage, all distressed and misrecognized in the flotsam of a crash.

Now, a decade after that crash there is relatively little change in the outlook for most distressed mortgagors. They go in and out of county registrars' courts either hoping to engage with their creditor toward a meaningful resolution or bringing a new friend into court to whisper in their ear some advice they hope will save them from the purgatorial stasis of defaulted debt. In either case, the mortgage, as the central object of attention or avoidance, radiates a neo-feudal unevenness. By leaving deferring resolution to the mortgage and the machinery of repossession, Irish governments provided the preconditions for new populist sensibilities and political arrangements. This was not an atavistic appeal to the past, but the shared making of a new, "distressed" public where the lingering irresolution of irredeemable debts would become part of the fabric of the political community.

Conclusion

In *Dead Pledges* (2017), Annie McClanahan argues debt is such a ubiquitous cultural phenomenon, and such an obtuse narrator in its own self-representation, it is best understood through the cultural activities and representations around it. In this chapter we have examined mortgage avoidance, cases where people have imagined and generated new sets of social relations and ideologies in response to, and abnegation of, the mortgage – in other words, political and social imaginaries that envision debt without mortgages. In the relations of reciprocity engendered in South Africa to avoid the mortgage solution to the "gap housing" problem and in the rebirth of the life estate and petty fiefdoms of banks and shadowy trustee figures in Ireland, there is an inclination toward something like a "living pledge": a debt that organizes activity around the extension, rather than foreclosure, of possibility. Here in response to systems offering what is ostensibly a modern alternative, we see a new impetus for the "gathering of people" (James 2014: 197).

We examined two large-scale public projects, the provision of post-apartheid social housing in South Africa and the fiscal resolution of an unprecedentedly large mortgage market crisis in Ireland, which pivoted on that morbid endpoint of the mortgage hanging over debt. For all their own creativity and novelty, the anti-mortgage techniques we encountered in our research often took on the garb of older arrangements, whether feudalist, traditionalist, or even primordialist in their styling.

What all this ethnographic observation adds up to is a conception of the public that is more in flux, more unsettled than in the ideal-typical category of bourgeois political morality, as theorized by Jürgen Habermas (1991). The mortgage's self-representation as a simple contract does align with the bourgeois political morality in the Habermasian notion of the public sphere. But in the cases examined here, we observed publics in which such principles were in contention with those implied by other political arrangements. In Ireland, public officials tasked with enforcing the morality of a contract on indebted homeowners collaborated to create a space to forestall the repossession of the mortgage, holding out hope for some future resolution. In their expansion of that space of deferred stasis, and in the ways people interpreted that space, nationalist and even religious moral orderings around land and redemption contended with the bourgeois imperative to enforce the contract. In South Africa, those in the "gap market," for whom mortgage contracts were long inaccessible, now look askance at public programs to expand access to home loan finance. Calling upon alternative forms of political morality and networks of accountability, those living in the gap between promised equality and persistent inequity instead choose to forge more flexible, provisional relationships with kith and kin. In these "gaps" we observed how unanticipated developments that were not so much "counterpublics" as publics anxious and unsettled about the self-representations of bourgeois political morality conveyed with the mortgage, and the erasure of status.

What we observed as stirrings for more self-evidently status-based relations, hierarchies, and asymmetries were not anti-mortgage in the sense that they rejected the inherent imbalances contained in the mortgage, but posited more explicit forms of unevenness in response to the failure of bourgeois morality. This is what we mean by "distressed publics": movements, activities, aesthetics that seem atavistic and backward-looking are contemporary imaginings of a prior mode of governance that critique not only the state failures, but the continual misrecognition of those failures as successes, of late feudal involutions and inequalities for modern innovation.

Nate Coben is a cultural anthropologist of property, finance, and Europe. His ethnographic research examines the political, moral, and socio-political ramifications of long-term mortgage debt in rural Ireland. His research was funded by the NSF Doctoral Dissertation Improvement Grant in Law and Social Sciences. He is currently a Junior Specialist at the University of California, Irvine.

Melissa K. Wrapp is a cultural anthropologist of property, design, and race. Her ethnographic research explores the relationship between practices of experimentation in South African housing design and broader shifts in racialized property relations and activist practice post-apartheid. Her dissertation fieldwork was funded by the National Science Foundation Cultural Anthropology and Law & Social Sciences DDRIG Programs. Wrapp is a PhD candidate in anthropology at the University of California, Irvine. She has an MPhil in social anthropology from the University of Cambridge and a BA in anthropology from the University of Notre Dame.

NOTES

1. RDP is an acronym for "Reconstruction and Development Programme," the democratic government's post-transition policy framework. Although this house was technically built in the "BNG" policy era ("Breaking New Ground"), which began in 2004, people still refer to any post-1994 subsidized housing as RDP.
2. And after eight years, the government is meant to have the first option in any sales.
3. Anél Lewis, "The RDP Houses for Sale Scandal." *IOL*, 13 March 2015. Retrieved 11 July 2021 from https://www.iol.co.za/news/the-rdp-houses-for-sale-scandal-1831598.
4. Thulebona Mhlanga, "RDP House Buyers Beware." *Mail & Guardian*, 3 August 2018. Retrieved 11 July 2021 from https://mg.co.za/article/2018-08-03-00-rdp-house-buyers-beware.
5. Saul Hansell, "Clive S. Menell, 65, Mining Executive in South Africa." *The New York Times*, 25 July 1996, sec. B. https://www.nytimes.com/1996/07/25/world/clive-s-menell-65-mining-executive-in-south-africa.html. This is not ancient history – Clive Menell supported South Africa's current president, Cyril Ramaphosa, as he completed his legal studies and recruited him to the Urban Foundation.
6. Pocket Guide to South Africa 2015/16, "Human Settlements." https://www.gcis.gov.za/sites/default/files/docs/resourcecentre/pocketguide/PocketGuide15-16SA_humansettlement.pdf.
7. Michael Morris, "Housing Policy Shake-up on Cards." IOL, 7 December 2016. Retrieved 7 July 2021 from http://www.iol.co.za/weekend-argus/housing-policy-shake-up-on-cards-2095844.
8. "Welcome to FLISP." FLISP. Retrieved 11 July 2021 from flisp.co.za.
9. "Ciarán" is a composite character of several similarly involved individuals Coben spoke with over the course of his research.
10. It is important to note that this could refer to multiple mortgages on the same home. Some critics of the statistical releases argued that some of these ARAs were too idiosyncratic and provisional to be "restructures" in the technical sense.
11. "Financial literacy" and "legal literacy" were terms directed at individual borrowers, not creditors, many of whom notoriously demonstrated little prudence or wisdom in boom years.

REFERENCES

August, Kahmiela. 2013. *Report Emanating from the Strategic FLISP Workshop Held on 15 August 2013 at Fountains Hotel, St Georges Mall, Cape Town*. Cape Town: Western Cape Government Human Settlements.

Bond, Patrick, George Dor, and Greg Ruiters. 2000. "Transformation in Infrastructure Policy from Apartheid to Democracy: Mandates for Change, Continuities in Ideology, Frictions in Delivery." In *Infrastructure Mandates for Change 1994–1999*, ed. by M. Khosa, 25–46. Pretoria: HSRC Press.

Campbell, Fergus, and Tony Varley, eds. 2013. *Land Questions in Modern Ireland*. Manchester: Manchester University Press.

Cirolia, Liza Rose. 2016. "Reframing the 'Gap Market': Lessons and Implications from Cape Town's Gap Market Housing Initiative." *Journal of Housing and the Built Environment* 31: 621–34.

Dooley, Terence. 2004. *"The Land for the People": The Land Question in Independent Ireland*. Dublin: University College Dublin Press.

Dunn, Elizabeth. 2012. "The Chaos of Humanitarian Aid: Adhocracy in the Republic of Georgia." *Humanity: An International Journal of Human Rights, Humanitarianism, and Development* 3(1): 1–23.

Gaudiosi, Monica. 1988. "The Influence of the Islamic Law of Waqf on the Development of the Trust in England: The Case of Merton College." *University of Pennsylvania Law Review* 136(4): 1231–61.

Habermas, Jürgen. 1991. *The Structural Transformation of the Public Sphere: An Inquiry into a Category of Bourgeois Society*. Cambridge, MA: MIT Press.

Huchzermeyer, Marie. 2003. "A Legacy of Control? The Capital Subsidy for Housing, and Informal Settlement Intervention in South Africa." *International Journal of Urban and Regional Research* 27(3): 591–612.

James, Deborah. 2014. *Money from Nothing: Indebtedness and Aspiration in South Africa*. Stanford, CA: Stanford University Press.

Kalb, Don. 2013. "Financialization and the Capitalist Moment: Marx versus Weber in the Anthropology of Global Systems." *American Ethnologist* 40(2): 258–66.

Kane, Anne. 2001. "'The Fall of Feudalism in Ireland': A Guide for Cultural Analysis of the Irish Land War." *New Hibernian Review* 5(1): 136–41.

Lategan, Louis. 2017. "Informality and Sustainability: Reflecting on South Africa's Informal Backyard Rental Sector from a Planning Perspective." PhD dissertation. Potchefstroom, South Africa: North-West University.

Lee, J. J. 1989. *Ireland, 1912–1985: Politics and Society*. Cambridge: Cambridge University Press.

Lemanski, Charlotte. 2017. "Citizens in the Middle Class: The Interstitial Policy Spaces of South Africa's Housing Gap." *Geoforum* 79: 101–10.

Maitland, Frederic. 1909. *Equity: A Course of Lectures*. Cambridge: Cambridge University Press.

Marais, Lochner, and Jan Cloete. 2017. "Housing Policy and Private Sector Housing Finance: Policy Intent and Market Directions in South Africa." *Habitat International* 61: 22–30.

McCann, Fergal. 2017. "Resolving a Non-Performing Loans Crisis: The Ongoing Case of the Irish Mortgage Market." 6 December 2017. Central Bank of Ireland Research Technical Paper.

McClanahan, Annie. 2017. *Dead Pledges: Debt, Crisis, and Twenty-First-Century Culture*. Stanford, CA: Stanford University Press.

McDonald, David A. 2008. *World City Syndrome: Neoliberalism and Inequality in Cape Town*. London: Routledge.

OECD. 2018. *OECD Economic Surveys, Ireland*. March 2018. https://www.oecd.org/eco/surveys/Ireland-2018-OECD-economic-survey-overview.pdf.

Palomera, Jaime. 2014. "Reciprocity, Commodification, and Poverty in the Era of Financialization." *Current Anthropology* 55(9): S105–S115.

Pollock, Frederick, and Frederic Maitland. (1898) 2010. *The History of English Law before the Time of Edward I, Vols. 1 and 2* (Reprint of 2nd edition). Indianapolis, IN: Liberty Fund.

Robinson, Cedric J. 1983. *Black Marxism: The Making of the Black Radical Tradition.* Chapel Hill: University of North Carolina Press.

Robinson, Jennifer. 1996. *The Power of Apartheid: State, Power, and Space in South African Cities.* Boston: Butterworth-Heinemann.

Rust, Kecia. 2012. *Housing Matters: The Importance of Housing Finance in Financial Sector Development in Africa.* Johannesburg: Centre for Affordable Housing Finance in Africa.

Shipton, Parker. 2009. *Mortgaging the Ancestors: Ideologies of Attachment in Africa.* New Haven: Yale University Press.

Smit, Dan. 1992. "The Urban Foundation: Transformation Possibilities." *Transformation* 18: 35–42.

South African Human Rights Commission. 2008. "Report on the Public Hearing on Housing, Evictions and Repossessions." Retrieved 11 July 2021 from https://www.sahrc.org.za/home/21/files/Reports/Housing%20Inquiry%20Report_2008%20web.pdf

Stewart, Susan. 1991. "Notes on Distressed Genres." *Journal of American Folklore* 104(411): 5–31.

Stout, Noelle. 2016. "Petitioning a Giant: Debt, Reciprocity, and Mortgage Modification in the Sacramento Valley." *American Ethnologist* 43(1): 158–71.

Thomas, David A. 1999. "Anglo-American Land Law: Diverging Developments from a Shared History: Part I: The Shared History." *Real Property, Probate and Trust Journal* 34(1): 143–203.

Urban Foundation. 1990. "Housing for All: Proposals for a National Housing Policy." Policies for a New Urban Future. Johannesburg: The Urban Foundation.

CHAPTER 9

 Governing the Old City
*Land Records, Digitization,
and Liquidity in Lahore*

TARIQ RAHMAN

Lahore is an ancient city. Lahore is a megacity. Though I can think of nothing more cliché to say about an Asian city than describing it as a "land of contrasts," I find the phrase to be a productive one to describe the tension between Lahore's past and present when it comes to the city's land records. In this chapter, I consider a state-led, World Bank-inspired effort to digitize Lahore's land revenue system. During ethnographic fieldwork conducted in what is generally called "old city" Lahore, I had the chance to speak with local *patwaris* (land revenue officials), real estate brokers, and residents. What I learned was that despite tens of millions of dollars, years of effort, and an assortment of global experts, land in the old city had stubbornly refused its invitation to the twenty-first century, instead clinging to Lahore's tumultuous, convoluted, and still very present past. Why has the state's project failed? How does the ancient city continue to haunt the megacity? What might all of this have to do with the particular qualities of land itself?

Central to digitization efforts in the old city is the desire to replace *patwaris* with a rational, orderly, and technical system. *Patwaris* were originally introduced to the broader Punjab region during the pre-colonial Mughal state, in which they served as village accountants for the purposes of revenue collection on agricultural land. As land in South Asia transitioned from state to privately owned property under British rule (Guha 1963), *patwaris* were accorded a more central place in land revenue administration (R. S. Smith 1996). Aiming to establish a greater degree of hierarchy and efficiency, British officials tasked *patwaris* with recording the ownership, location, measurement, and sale of land, a role that also extended to urban settings. Since independence, however, *patwaris* have acquired a reputation for corruption in Pakistan. Increasingly, they are framed by state officials as an outdated artifact of British rule, petty tyrants who use their colonial-era authority to extract bribes in exchange for services. For more than a decade, a campaign has been underway in Punjab to replace *patwaris* with a digital database capable of removing the human element from the land revenue system.

Throughout the different institutions and projects that digitization has entailed, the discourse of financial empowerment has been a common thread. From the view of key stakeholders, replacing *patwaris* with a digital database would remove a longstanding barrier to economic mobility. The idea of a land records database was first introduced in rural Punjab by the World Bank, which claimed that "the low mobility of land markets contributed to preserving the highly unequal distribution of land and, therefore, opportunities to improve people's livelihoods" (Gonzalez 2016). When the Government of Punjab decided to expand digitization to Lahore, officials aimed to improve access to urban land and housing markets, a change they believed would boost economic activity throughout the broader region (Adnan 2015). In each of these narratives, the welfare of Punjab's rural and urban poor rests on their ability to buy and sell land, the improvement of which can only be achieved through the digitization of land records.

Given the importance of record keeping during British colonial rule (Berman 1999; Cohn 1996; Feldman 2008), efforts to increase the liquidity of land through bureaucratic technologies are neither new nor unique to Pakistan. Alain Pottage (1994; 1995) has shown how land was removed from its local context in England through advancements in cartography and title registration, a process crucial to establishing the fungibility of landed property. Following the same strategies to Britain's imperial settings, scholars have linked bureaucratic standardization to the dispossession of small farmers in Kenya (Shipton 2009) and indigenous communities in South Australia (Bhandar 2018). Colonial-era approaches to land management have also influenced development organizations such as the United Nations, the World Bank, and the International Monetary Fund, whose implementation of similar policies throughout the Global South has led to widespread disenfranchisement (Keenan 2018).

In his illuminating ethnography of urban Pakistan, however, Matthew Hull (2012) reveals how the paper artifacts central to governance are used by local residents to thwart dispossession. As key documents such as maps and titles are stolen, forged, hidden, and otherwise appropriated, bureaucratic rule is undermined and urban governance becomes an all but participatory process. But if bureaucratic standardization is betrayed by paper artifacts in urban Pakistan, then digitization threatens to consolidate state power. Toward the end of his fieldwork, Hull follows the efforts of a foreign firm to acquire a large swath of land through the creation of a digital database. Hull observes that: "The capacities of the database for dispossession were magnified by its control by a couple of individuals. But the public systems in place in India and being developed in Pakistan might serve the same ends. And the broad participation required by paper infrastructures of land records might prove a much stronger protection against dispossession" (Hull 2012: 256). Among anthropologists of bureaucracy, Hull is not alone in his wariness of e-governance. Commenting on work such as Hull's, Kregg Hetherington has argued that "much of the work on the materiality of documents describes spaces that are fast becoming obsolete as bureaucracies digitize and adopt forms of storage that are only partly analogous to classic paper documents." "The ideology that accompanies these practices," Hetherington adds, "is that of a control revolution, first dreamed of in the 1940s, in which humans as well as documents disappear from the wrinkles of a perfect governmental machine" (2012: 246).

The struggle to digitize land records in old city Lahore suggests that concerns about e-governance's centralizing capacities may be premature. In Lahore, e-governance is a far cry from the purifying force that it claims to be. Though land records have been scanned and made accessible to the public at computerized service hubs, *patwaris* remain central to the city's land revenue system. Unable to fill the gaps between documents and local knowledge, the database relies on the expertise of *patwaris* to complete land transactions. As objects that hold together entangled histories and longstanding social networks, plots of land defy comprehension by digital interfaces alone. Shifting analysis away from paper, bureaucrats, and databases and toward land itself, this chapter shows that governing the old city remains a social and material practice.

What Is an Old City?

Lahore's origin story remains an unsettled one. Oral traditions trace the city to its founding by Prince Lava, the son of Hindu deity Rama and Rama's consort, Sita. Some historians date Lahore to its first appearance in archival records between the first and second centuries CE, while others view Lahore's history as beginning once the city began to gain political importance under the Caliphate in the mid-seventh century (Latif and Bahadur 1892). In either case, most scholars agree that Lahore's formative years occurred during the height of Mughal rule, at which time the city was designated as the capital of the sprawling South Asian empire. Indeed, it was toward the end of the sixteenth century under Mughal emperor Akbar that Lahore's famed walls and thirteen extravagant gates were originally constructed, forming a boundary between the city and its agricultural surroundings.

During the time of the Mughals, Lahore proper was considered to be the extensive network of *bazaars* (markets), *havelis* (mansions), and *mohallas* (neighborhoods) that existed within the city walls. Beyond the walls, however, long *bazaars* and thickly populated *mohallas* developed and gradually extended the city's perimeter (Chaudhry 2000). Through the nineteenth and twentieth centuries, Lahore's physical expansion continued under colonial rule. The city's boundary wall and gates were destroyed by the British following the Indian Rebellion of 1857. Finding themselves unable to penetrate the density of the inner-city (Glover 2008), colonial town planners opted instead to construct administrative, commercial, and residential centers in Lahore's outlying areas, further drawing the city toward its periphery.

Following Pakistani independence in 1947, the trend of horizontal growth has only intensified. Urban planning powers have been transferred to the Lahore Development Authority (LDA), an outgrowth of the colonial-era Lahore Improvement Trust. Reflective of a broader national commitment to modernist urban planning (Daechsel 2015; Harper 2015; Hull 2012), the LDA has prioritized the development of low-density, master planned residential settlements in the city's peri-urban areas. In step with postcolonial cities elsewhere that have viewed development as synonymous with modernism (Ghertner 2015; Harms 2011; Holston 1989), the LDA frames traditional forms of socio-spatial organization as belonging to Lahore's "backward" past, which the organization seeks to overcome through a rigid commitment to modern planning principles (Malik 2014). Since independence, the LDA has enacted a series of bylaws restricting new construction largely to housing schemes, or residential communities beholden to specific regulations with respect to plot size, building height, street width, and a number of other areas. More than three hundred such schemes had been established by the time Lahore's population surpassed 11 million in 2017, and the city's built area has expanded by nearly 20 percent within the past two decades alone (Javed 2017). Today, the area once known as Lahore proper and the center of the Mughal Empire has come to be called simply the "old city."

Making Land Liquid in the Absence of Mortgage

Lahore's rapid physical expansion has been aided by the city's lively real estate market. Real estate plays an integral role in Pakistan's economy; it is the country's second largest employer after agriculture and linked to 250 ancillary industries including steel, cement, and timber. Though the purchase of property is limited to Pakistani nationals, real estate has become the investment of choice for citizens living both in Pakistan and abroad, and national real estate stock is estimated to be worth $700 billion (Lamudi 2015). Lahore's particular conjuncture of a burgeoning population, widely available peri-urban land, and the LDA's urban planning policies has made it especially popular with investors, and today the city is known as one of only a handful in the world where real estate provides a return on investment of more than 100 percent.

However, relative to the significance of real estate to Lahore's economy, the city's mortgage market remains underdeveloped. Across Pakistan, only 14 percent of the population makes use of formal financial services. When it comes to real estate transactions, a mere 1 to 2 percent are processed through housing finance credit lines. Indeed, mortgage qualifications in Pakistan are extremely restrictive, and approximately two-thirds of the population are ineligible based upon income alone (Nenova 2010). Furthermore, usury is considered *haram* (forbidden) in Islam, and financial devices such as interest-bearing deposits and bank loans remain taboo in the Islamic Republic. Rather than a mortgage system designed to facilitate investment in high-cost housing assets, it is the individual trading of relatively inexpensive plots of land that largely fuels Lahore's booming real estate market.

Under the housing scheme model established by the LDA, cheap plots of land have become the most highly sought-after investment option in Lahore. After independence, the LDA was faced with the all but impossible task of developing a modern metropolis with little to no access to capital. Partition from India left the Pakistani state with only 17.5 percent of the financial assets and 10 percent of the industrial base of the former colony. Furthermore, a significant amount of the resources that remained were funneled to the armed forces due to rising enmity with the Indian government (Jalal 1990). Therefore, the LDA embraced an investment-led approach to fund their modernist aspirations. Housing schemes are master-planned residential communities in which individual plots are made available for residents to construct their own homes. However, low density housing requires large areas of land, and preparing the terrain for settlement entails leveling the soil, laying gas and water pipes, and constructing water tanks and electricity towers. As such, the LDA opted to raise capital for the construction of housing schemes through presales of plots. Thus, when the LDA launched a new project, this did not mean that land had been fully developed or even acquired, but rather that a map had been released in which the quantity, dimensions, and locations of future plots was announced. For many Lahoris, plots in housing schemes were an ideal investment opportunity. If an investor purchased a plot at a low rate early on, they could easily sell it for a higher price as the project progressed. For the LDA's part, housing schemes developed as funds from presales became available, a process that typically lasted four to five years. Under the LDA model, real estate investment came to center on low-cost assets that could be individually bought and sold rather than high-priced ones linked to loans and collateral. In other words, land's liquidity functioned much more like a stock market than a mortgage market.

In fact, in Lahore's real estate market, liquidity often ends when the construction of a house begins. The illiquidity of constructed property relates to not only the limited availability of mortgage, but also the central role of the extended family household in Pakistani society. In Islam, the inheritance of estates through predetermined shares is linked to distinct conceptions of family, property, and their interrelationship. This is particularly the case with the landed property on which extended family homes are built. The inheritance of the home according to a fixed distribution of shares is intended to reinforce Islamic understandings of responsibility between adult children and parents as well as siblings. Thus, the sale of a house is often in tension with prevailing social norms, the complications of which are magnified by the need for all shareholders to agree.

The distinct way that financialization has taken shape in Lahore has led to a particularly destructive pattern of urban development. The continuous expansion of the city into its agricultural hinterlands has depended upon the often-coerced displacement of small farmers, many of whom were previously providing urban residents with fresh and inexpensive produce (Hussain 2014). Widespread investment in Lahore's land by Pakistanis living both at home and abroad has exponentially increased the cost of land, and as a result, housing. House prices in Lahore have more than doubled since 2011 (Zameen 2019), and approximately 40 percent of the population live in informal settlements constructed throughout the city (Government of Pakistan 2015). Perhaps most egregiously, the majority of the plots developed in recent years remain vacant. The unlucky holders of these plots are unable to sell them to either other investors as prices have stopped increasing or local end-users for whom the price is nevertheless out of reach.

State efforts to bring old city Lahore's land into the financial asset class through digitization must be viewed within the broader context of the city's real estate market. Though land is indeed a robust financial investment in Lahore, the impact of financialization has been devastating for urban space and life. Moreover, all investors are not created equal. Digitization in the old city strives to create financial investments out of intergenerational land, which differentiates residents from investors who typically trade in a portfolio of freshly developed plots. In this scenario, it is old city residents alone who are expected to exchange the value of an extended family home for that of a financial asset, a far-reaching inequality that is obscured by institutional discourses of empowerment.

Land Records, Digitization, and the World Bank

Old city Lahore is home to many of the booming metropolis's working-class residents. In contrast to the housing schemes ballooning the city's ever-expanding perimeter, the old city is characterized by substandard construction materials, narrow and crumbling roads, and decaying infrastructure. One particularly important way the distinction between the old city and the rest of Lahore has borne out is the management of land records. While newer settlements produce clean titles overseen by the LDA or individual developers, the old city remains tethered to the land revenue system established by the Mughals, specifically the *patwar* system. As land revenue officials, *patwaris* are responsible for documenting land ownership in a given area. In order for land to be bought and sold, *patwaris* have to issue sellers a *fard*, or an official land record copy reflecting the rights of ownership of land. Much of a *patwari's* labor consists of establishing property rights for a given plot of land, which includes poring over centuries-old documents, tracing kinship lineages, and consulting with family, friends, and neighbors. In the old city, *patwaris* are equally known for their unparalleled local knowledge and their very human susceptibility to error, corruption, and bribes.

It was the double-edged reputation of *patwaris* that led the World Bank to launch the Land Records Management and Information Systems (LRMIS) project in 2007. LRMIS was a ten-year, $115 million effort to digitize rural land records across Pakistan's Punjab province. While land records in rural Punjab primarily pertain to agricultural plots, like old city Lahore they are controlled by *patwaris*. LRMIS discourse reflected economist Hernando de Soto's (2000) description of land in the Global South as "dead capital" whose awakening depended upon the establishment of modern property rights, and thus the aim was to bring reason, transparency, and order to a system considered opaque and, ultimately, subjective. At the heart of LRMIS was the belief that empowerment in rural Punjab hinged upon making land liquid, or an asset that could be quickly bought and sold. For the World Bank, whatever historical, social, or spiritual relationships to land that existed were worse than unimportant – they were hinderances. Land was an asset to be leveraged for future profit. Rural Punjabis were natural born stockbrokers who simply had not yet been given access to the market.

The LRMIS project focused first and foremost on the elimination of *patwaris*. For World Bank officials, *patwaris* played a traditional, but ultimately obstructive human role. World Bank reports are openly hostile toward *patwaris*, describing them as "predatory middlemen" and, most damningly, accusing them of "reducing the liquidity of family assets composed mostly or wholly of land" (The World Bank 2017: 1). In the eyes of the World Bank, liquidity would naturally follow from the replacement of the *patwari* with a digital system, as the value of long-held but inaccessible local assets would finally be unlocked.

Under the decade-long LRMIS project, 10 million pages of records were scanned and 144 computerized service hubs called Arazi Record Centers were opened throughout Punjab. The World Bank hails LRMIS as a resounding success. Its website champions the project as an example to developing countries in Africa, Latin America, South Asia, and Southeast Asia, and in 2017, the organization held an international conference in Bangkok, Thailand, where government officials and development experts gathered to learn from the LRMIS model.

And yet, the World Bank clarifies that it was unable to completely eliminate the role of *patwaris*. As one article explains:

> The software and the IT system, however, were unable to resolve the land records conundrum on their own unless a sustained and a clear social strategy to include and promote the participation of the ancestral Patwari system within the new and sophisticated computerized system was set in place. The incentives to foster the involvement and participation of the Patwaris to clean and update the records was and remains crucial. They continue to play a key role within the overall governance of the land records system, but in a regularized form with checks and balances. (Gonzalez 2016)

In this stunning admission, World Bank officials reveal that even with the establishment of a new digital database, *patwaris* continue to play a fundamental role in the land revenue process. In other words, the institution's sweeping efforts to modernize Punjab's land records system remained dependent upon the very source of local knowledge that they were intended to replace.

New Technologies, Old Habits

Though the World Bank project concluded at the end of 2016, the Government of Punjab formed the Punjab Land Records Authority (PLRA) the following year with the intention of extending the digitization process to old city Lahore. Similar to LRMIS, digitization in the old city was inseparable from liquidity. A central figure in LRMIS, chairman of the Punjab Information and Technology Board Umar Saif linked the digitization of urban land to the modernization of Pakistan's economy. Comparing Pakistan's housing market to that of the United States, Saif argued that: "The American economy moves by basically changing half a percent of the mortgage rate, up or down, since land being the basic asset is liquid. You can do business on it, you can borrow against it, you can lease a car, you can mortgage your house and so forth. However, in Pakistan, the basic land asset is illiquid" (Bukhari 2018). However, also like LRMIS, the process of implementing PLRA was not as straightforward as it seemed. Through conversations with *patwaris* in the old city, I learned more about the "land records conundrum" that plagued digitization efforts in Punjab.

As with LRMIS, under PLRA land documents in the old city had been scanned and made available at newly built Arazi Record Centers. However, the system was encumbered by the countless number of discrepancies that exist in *patwari* records. To be sure, *patwaris* are meticulous record keepers. *Patwari* offices are nothing if not well-organized, their walls lined with shelves displaying neatly arranged record books that often date to the eighteenth century. Moreover, contrary to the World Bank's description of *patwaris* as rogue bureaucrats peddling a private collection of land records, the *patwar* system functions through a rigorous network of checks and balances. *Patwaris* are only the innermost sphere of a multitiered bureaucratic structure. *Patwaris* are supervised by *qanoongos*, which report to *tehsildars*, who themselves bridge cities with district and provincial levels of governance. In the instance of property transfer, *patwari* records are checked against the district land registry and the transaction must be approved by the *qanoongo*. According to *patwaris*, the multiple layers of bureaucratic oversight characteristic of the *patwar* system make individual manipulation of records difficult if not impossible.

Nevertheless, history has not been kind to land records in the old city. First, though the *patwari* profession is an age-old one, landownership has changed dramatically from the Mughal through the colonial and postcolonial eras. Under British rule, rights in land transformed from a share in the agricultural produce of state-owned land to individual ownership of landed plots. Proprietorship brought land into the realm of inheritance law, which itself has changed according to customary, colonial, and religious interpretations. Thus, establishing the rightful ownership of land involves not just studying kinship lineages and documents but also contextualizing them within Lahore's intricate legal landscape. Second, the old city was particularly impacted by Pakistan's partition from India, which witnessed the displacement of thirteen million people across the subcontinent. As a major city located just beyond the newly created border, Lahore alone received approximately a million refugees, nearly doubling the city's population. Many refugees were resettled in abandoned homes in the old city on the basis of property previously owned in India. In order to receive a land title, however, refugees had to authenticate their stated assets, which a significant number failed to do. Even so, these properties continued to be inherited, subdivided, and sold over multiple generations, processes that remained undocumented in *patwari* records. When residents seek to legally transfer such properties, it can be an arduous task for *patwaris*, requiring days or even weeks of research.

In this context, the idea that *patwaris* could be replaced by a computer sounds all but absurd. Indeed, *patwaris* in the old city understood perfectly well why they still had jobs. In order to transition to a digital database, PLRA had to establish a blank slate for land records in the old city, or what the organization referred to as "zero zero." Achieving zero zero meant scanning only the most recent records and not the archives of earlier ownership and transfer, much less the other sources *patwaris* typically rely on such as kinship charts, field maps, and logs of previous errors. When Arazi Record Centers emerged in and around the area, it quickly became apparent that the database was critically flawed. Residents seeking a digital copy of their *fard* were not recognized by the system and told to go to the *patwari* to verify their ownership rights. For their part, *patwaris* continued to do the work that they have always done, sifting through records and cross-checking information with other residents. I asked one *patwari* why PLRA could not simply scan the remaining documents and fill the gaps in the records themselves. He replied:

> Brother! This system won't work until a *patwari* sits with the computer. I have been here doing this work for twenty-five years. The revenue system is full of complexities and even we still have to get help from our seniors. How will these new people do this work? It's very difficult. It's all practical work. And those kids who have a degree in computer science and work

there, in my opinion, they won't be able to figure it out. They won't be able to understand the problems. They don't have the experience.

As a result of their initial failure to establish zero zero, PLRA has ordered *patwaris* to resolve all existing discrepancies in the current records, a process that they insist can be completed within months but that *patwaris* claim will take a minimum of four to five years. Meanwhile, *patwaris* continue to play a fundamental role in the old city's land revenue system with the new digital database almost entirely dependent upon their labor. For now at least, land in the old city appears to be as tethered as ever to the manual work of bureaucracy. In considering the social and material qualities of land itself, perhaps this should come as no surprise. As objects that are both immovable and imbued with an immense amount of cultural value, intergenerational plots of land in the area are deeply imbricated with local knowledge. That is to say, land in old city Lahore is both physically and socially embedded in relations that exceed digital representation.

Toward an Ethnography of E-governance

Though digitization was intended to increase the liquidity of land, at present the process appears to have had the opposite effect. Rather than replacing *patwaris*, digitization has added yet another layer to the already tortuous process of buying and selling land in old city Lahore. When I asked a local real estate broker what had changed since the transition to the digital database, he responded that whereas previously he only had to pay a bribe to the *patwari*, now he has to also pay one to the *computer wallah* (computer guy). The broker's comment was consistent with broader complaints about Arazi Record Centers. A number of newspaper editorials have criticized the PLRA for long lines, rampant bribery, and the continued involvement of *patwaris* (Ahmad 2018; Omer 2019; Tariq 2019). Similarly, on the World Bank's own blog post celebrating LRMIS, one commenter writes: "This is to notify you that the new system is again under the shadow of bribery in all aspects. From hiring to service delivery. You can judge for yourself while visiting the service centers" (Gonzalez 2016).

Many blame the failure of PLRA and LRMIS on their surrender to colonial-era bureaucracy. In this view, the *patwari* system is simply too deeply entrenched and influential to ever be replaced. Criticizing the Government of Punjab's efforts, one journalist insists that "the patwaris and bosses are so powerful that they have practically defeated the PLRA system" (Ahmad 2018). But there is another explanation for why the state has been unable to remove lower-level bureaucrats who, after all, are government employees. *Patwaris* have managed land records in old city Lahore for more than a century. Though documents are crucial to *patwari* praxis, their knowledge cannot be reduced to paper. This has less to do with *patwaris* than the nature of land in the old city. Old city Lahore is composed of plots of land that are crisscrossed by Pakistan's tumultuous past. Meanwhile, the same parcels hold together relations between family members, neighbors, and residents and the state. A *patwari's* job consists not only of recording land sales but also mediating their historical and cultural vicissitudes. The failure to produce an orderly technical system for land records lies not so much with government corruption but rather digitization's inability to capture the social and material qualities of land. In an era where neoliberal discourses of transparency are ubiquitous (Ballestero 2012), the horizon of e-governance has been exposed.

With digital solutions becoming a normative policy prescription for governments in the Global South, anthropologists have observed that e-governance and its promise of purity increasingly forms the boundary of political action (Mazzarella 2006; Poggiali 2016; Rao 2018). Nevertheless, projects such as LRMIS and PLRA cast doubt on the all-powerful reach of digital bureaucratic infrastructures. Not attending to such slippages risks reproducing digitization's narrative of itself as the wedge between a formal computational world and the informality of everyday life. If old city Lahore reveals nothing else, it is that digital space is flush with extra-digital relations. The fate of digitization in the old city resonates with scholarship at the intersection of computer science and social science that has long problematized the idea of autonomous databases, including Brian Cantwell Smith's (1994) claim that digitality is a thoroughly human achievement and Paul Dourish's (2017) important observation that the materialities of databases themselves constrain, enable, limit, and shape digital representations. What these authors make clear is that digital interfaces reconfigure rather than expunge social and material worlds. In any study of e-governance, therefore, it is necessary to approach digitization less like a clean slate and more like a bureaucratic palimpsest. Moving forward, the task for anthropologists should not be one of identifying the practices that digitization is replacing, but rather following what becomes of states, citizens, and records when such projects inevitably fail.

Tariq Rahman is a PhD Candidate in the Department of Anthropology at the University of California, Irvine. He researches real estate in Lahore, Pakistan, conducting fieldwork with developers, investors, brokers, bureaucrats, and residents to understand how the social and material qualities of land entangle with processes of financialization in the city. His research has been supported by the National Science Foundation, the Social Science Research Council, the Wenner-Gren Foundation, the American Philosophical Society, the American Ethnological Society, the American Institute of Pakistan Studies, and the Center for Asian Studies and Center for Global Peace and Conflict Studies at UCI.

REFERENCES

Adnan, Imran. 2015. "Urban Governance: Urban Unit Set to Start Work on Land Record Automation." *The Express Tribune*. Retrieved 22 October 2018 from https://tribune.com.pk/story/943103/urban-governance-urban-unit-set-to-start-work-on-land-record-automation/.

Ahmad, Shahzad. 2018. "Patwari System May Get Fatal Blow This Time." *The Nation*, 3 December. Retrieved 30 August 2019 from https://nation.com.pk/03-Dec-2018/patwari-system-may-get-fatal-blow-this-time.

Ballestero, Andrea S. 2012. "Transparency in Triads." *PoLAR: Political and Legal Anthropology Review* 35(2): 160–66.

Berman, Bruce. 1999. *Control and Crisis in Colonial Kenya: The Dialectic of Domination*. Athens: Ohio University Press.

Bhandar, Brenna. 2018. *Colonial Lives of Property: Law, Land, and Racial Regimes of Ownership*. Durham, NC: Duke University Press Books.

Bukhari, Muhammad Faran. 2018. "Govt's Tax Collection Can Go through the Roof." *Profit by Pakistan Today*, 24 September. Retrieved 25 September 2018 from https://profit.pakistantoday.com.pk/2018/09/24/govts-tax-collection-can-go-through-the-roof/.

Chaudhry, Nazir Ahmad. 2000. *A Short History of Lahore and Some of Its Monuments*. Lahore: Sang-e-Meel Publications.

Cohn, Bernard S. 1996. *Colonialism and Its Forms of Knowledge*. Princeton, NJ: Princeton University Press.

Daechsel, Markus. 2015. *Islamabad and the Politics of International Development in Pakistan*. Cambridge: Cambridge University Press.

de Soto, Hernando. 2000. *The Mystery of Capital: Why Capitalism Triumphs in the West and Fails Everywhere Else*. New York: Basic Books.

Dourish, Paul. 2017. *The Stuff of Bits: An Essay on the Materialities of Information*. Cambridge: MIT Press.

Feldman, Ilana. 2008. *Governing Gaza: Bureaucracy, Authority, and the Work of Rule, 1917–1967*. Durham, NC: Duke University Press.

Ghertner, D. Asher. 2015. *Rule by Aesthetics: World-Class City Making in Delhi*. New York: Oxford University Press.

Glover, William J. 2008. *Making Lahore Modern: Constructing and Imagining a Colonial City*. Minneapolis: University of Minnesota Press.

Gonzalez, Mary Lisbeth. 2016. "Land Records Go Digital in Punjab, Pakistan." *End Poverty in South Asia*, 26 October. Retrieved 13 July 2018 from http://blogs.worldbank.org/endpovertyinsouthasia/land-records-go-digital-punjab-pakistan.

Government of Pakistan. 2015. "National Report of Pakistan for HABITAT III." *Government of Pakistan*. Retrieved 11 November 2017 from http://habitat3.org/wp-content/uploads/Pakistan-Final-in-English.pdf.

Guha, Ranajit. 1963. *A Rule of Property for Bengal: An Essay on the Idea of Permanent Settlement*. Paris: Mouton and Co.

Harms, Erik. 2011. *Saigon's Edge: On the Margins of Ho Chi Minh City*. Minneapolis: University of Minnesota Press.

Harper, Annie. 2015. "Islamabad and the Promise of Pakistan." In *Pakistan: From the Rhetoric of Democracy to the Rise of Militancy*, ed. Ravi Kalia, 64–84. New Delhi: Routledge.

Hetherington, Kregg. 2012. "Agency, Scale, and the Ethnography of Transparency." *PoLAR: Political and Legal Anthropology Review* 35(2): 242–47.

Holston, James. 1989. *The Modernist City: An Anthropological Critique of Brasília*. Chicago: University of Chicago Press.

Hull, Matthew S. 2012. *Government of Paper: The Materiality of Bureaucracy in Urban Pakistan*. Berkeley: University of California Press.

Hussain, Nadim. 2014. "Land Mafias and Housing Societies." *Express Tribune*, 2 May. Retrieved 3 January 2017 from https://tribune.com.pk/story/703320/land-mafias-and-housing-societies.

Jalal, Ayesha. 1990. *The State of Martial Rule: The Origins of Pakistan's Political Economy of Defence*. Cambridge: Cambridge University Press.

Javed, Umair. 2017. "Lahore's Bleak Future." *Dawn*, 23 October. Retrieved 14 August 2018 from https://www.dawn.com/news/1365556.

Keenan, Sarah. 2018. "Making Land Liquid: On Time and Title Registration." In *Law and Time*, ed. Sian Beynon-Jones and Emily Grabham, 145–61. Abingdon: Routledge.

Lamudi. 2015. "Lamudi Real Estate Market Report 2016." *Lamudi*. Retrieved 21 March 2018 from http://www.lamudi.pk/research/whitepaper-2015/.

Latif, Syad Muhammad, and Syad Khan Bahadur. 1892. *Lahore: Its History, Architectural Remains and Antiquities*. Lahore: New Imperial Press.

Malik, Hala Bashir. 2014. "Enabling and Inhibiting Urban Development: A Case Study of Lahore Improvement Trust as a Late Colonial Institution." Thesis. Boston: Massachusetts Institute of Technology. https://dspace.mit.edu/handle/1721.1/91409.

Mazzarella, William. 2006. "Internet X-Ray: E-Governance, Transparency, and the Politics of Immediation in India." *Public Culture* 18(3): 473–505. https://doi.org/10.1215/08992363-2006-016.

Nenova, Tatiana. 2010. "Expanding Housing Finance to the Underserved in South Asia: Market Review and Forward Agenda." *The World Bank*. Retrieved 2 January 2017 from http://documents.worldbank.org/curated/en/393181468114238340/Expanding-housing-finance-to-the-underserved-in-South-Asia-market-review-and-forward-agenda.

Omer, Shahab. 2019. "Punjab Punch: The Power of Patwari." *Pakistan Today*, 4 August. Retrieved 30 August 30. https://www.pakistantoday.com.pk/2019/08/03/punjab-punch-the-power-of-patwari/.

Poggiali, Lisa. 2016. "Seeing (from) Digital Peripheries: Technology and Transparency in Kenya's Silicon Savannah." *Cultural Anthropology* 31(3): 387–411.

Pottage, Alain. 1994. "The Measure of Land." *The Modern Law Review* 57(3): 361–84.
———. 1995. "The Originality of Registration." *Oxford Journal of Legal Studies* 15(3): 371–401.
Rao, Ursula. 2018. "Biometric Bodies, Or How to Make Electronic Fingerprinting Work in India." *Body & Society* 24(3): 68–94.
Shipton, Parker MacDonald. 2009. *Mortgaging the Ancestors: Ideologies of Attachment in Africa*. New Haven, CT: Yale University Press.
Smith, Brian Cantwell. 1994. "Coming Apart at the Seams: The Role of Computation in a Successor Metaphysics." Paper presented at Intersection of the Real and the Virtual, Stanford, California, 2–4 June.
Smith, Richard Saumerez. 1996. *Rule by Records: Land Registration and Village Custom in Early British Panjab*. Delhi: Oxford University Press.
Tariq, Waleed. 2019. "Understanding the Dying Patwari System." *The Express Tribune*, 4 June 2019. Retrieved 30 August 2019. https://tribune.com.pk/story/1986863/1-understanding-dying-patwari-culture/.
The World Bank. 2017. "Punjab Land Records Management and Information Systems Project." *The World Bank*. Retrieved 14 July 2018. http://documents.worldbank.org/curated/en/632241498842804246/Pakistan-Land-Records-Management-and-Information-Systems-Project.
Zameen. 2019. "Lahore House Price Index (Oct 2019)." Retrieved 9 November 2019 from https://www.zameen.com/index/buy/houses/lahore/.

Part IV
Coming Full Circle
Hopes, Ideologies, and Life on the Ground

CHAPTER 10

 Mortgage Credit as an Instrument of Economic Growth in Colonial Massachusetts, 1642–1777

WINIFRED B. ROTHENBERG

"A modern capital market and banking system did not exist in America from 1607 to 1790, and then, almost overnight, they did" (Sylla, Wilson, and Wright 1997: 16). The "almost overnight" is hyperbole, as everybody knows markets do not happen overnight; but its audacity pales beside Gordon Wood's stunning description of the 1780s as "the most critical moment in the entire history of America." "In the 1780s," Wood has written, "we can actually sense a shift from a pre-modern traditional society to a modern one . . . Something momentous was happening in the society and culture that released the aspirations and energies of common people as never before in American history, or perhaps in world history" (1994: 46).

Whatever that "something momentous" was, that is what one looks to in order explain the decisions of common people, "almost overnight," to divest from farm physical capital in favor of financial assets. Where probate inventories before 1780 had listed wooden plows, harrows, hay forks, axes, hoes, harnesses, grain cradles, cattle, oxen, and cleared plow-land, there appeared, after 1780, shares of stock in the Warren and Charles River Bridge companies, the Providence Turnpike, the Middlesex Canal Company, the Massachusetts Hospital Life Insurance Company, marine and fire insurance companies, Massachusetts and US government war bonds, and shares in the capital stock of nine private banks (see Rothenberg 1985). Further portfolio analysis discovered a five-fold increase in the wealth elasticity of demand for financial assets by all but the poorest wealth quartile; some flexibility of interest rates around the 6 percent usury ceiling; more readily negotiable debt instruments; longer and thicker credit networks linking more and more remote borrowers and lenders; and a negative sign on the coefficient of ACRES in the wealth regressions. Lastly and significantly, Chow tests found the inflection point for all these indicators in 1781 (Rothenberg 1985: 800, Figure 1; or 1992: 137, Figure 8). Taken together, these results testify to the capitalist transformation that will prove so consequential for the economic development of rural Massachusetts.

In addition to financial assets, there were mortgages, in some eyes a mainstay of the English and imperial market (Anderson 1969), which will prove to be the principal instrument to augment the private capital stock of both borrowers and lenders. By capitalizing the value of a collateralized asset, a mortgage captures the seminal power of capital to grow exponentially – like a living thing – from within. This is the endogenous growth process that Hernando de Soto has famously called "the mystery of capital" (1989, 2000).[1]

The point, however, has been hotly contested by those who argue that a mortgage so early in the development process was only a loan to smooth consumption over the "dying times." To wager the family farm against long odds has too much the odor of the "commodification" of land, which, like the "commodification" of labor,[2] must be made to wait upon the capitalist transformation of the countryside. "The connection of mortgages with an embryonic capital market," they argue, "can only be described as hypothetical; they were rarely raised explicitly for productive purposes, so that to all intents and purposes they differed hardly at all from other forms of borrowing primarily to finance consumption" (Holderness 1975: 112).[3]

So we begin this study with a question: what role did mortgages play in the economic history of colonial Massachusetts? Were they an investment? Or were they, like other forms of borrowing, "but a temporary and fortuitous adjustment of liquidity" (Holderness 1976: 97) to finance consumption?

In truth, a distinction between the two can be exaggerated. Consider the farming frontier where survival is severely constrained by imperfect capital markets and a severely limited family labor supply.[4] Current production for investment will of necessity compete for capital and labor with current production for consumption. If, because of a lack of credit, future investment can come only with the sacrifice of a sustainable level of present consumption, families may be driven to abandon farm-making altogether (Lewis 1999). When, as on the farming frontier, the household as unit of production is perfectly congruent with the household as unit of consumption, a distinction between investment and consumption is not only difficult to make in accounting terms; as a lived experience, it may be a distinction without a difference.

Even in the case of the "calamitous mortgage": "the charitable man who comes to the help of distress out of goodwill" (Holderness 1976: 97; Wilson [1572] 1965: 23) is clearly making a consumption-smoothing loan, but it too may have been "productive investment" in the degree to which it forestalled the borrower's descent into tenancy, landlessness, and the diminished productivity associated with them.[5] Mortgage credit that contributed to preserving a sturdy yeomanry in rural New England – be it consumption or investment – contributed thereby to the enduring political, institutional, and cultural correlates of widespread land ownership to which we give the honorable name "Jeffersonian democracy."[6]

Some Ecological Constraints: Population Growth, Climate, and Access to Markets

The following section will closely analyze a sample of 1,529 mortgage contracts to understand how farm mortgages provided credit to the rural economy of colonial Massachusetts. But first, in this section, acknowledgment will be made of three broadly ecological factors of particular relevance to the mortgage market: (1) rapid population growth; (2) climate change – unforeseen, uninsurable, and occasionally apocalyptic; and (3) what Donald McCloskey once called "the missing market in insurance," which left commodity markets the only hedge against risk (1991: 352).

(1) In colonial Massachusetts, despite starving times, bitterly long, cold winters, and wars against the indigenous population, birth rates were higher, mortality rates were lower, and life expectancy was longer than in the seventeenth- and eighteenth-century England from which the settlers had come. For the millennial volume of *Historical Statistics of the United States*, John McCusker estimated the population of colonial Massachusetts to have been growing at the rate of 2.8 percent per annum to increase 30-fold between 1640 and 1780 (2005).[7] In contrast, the population in England is estimated to have grown at the rate of only 0.26 percent per year between 1700 and 1750 (2009: 280).[8]

Compounding the effects of population pressure was the distinctive pattern of settlement in the Bay Colony, a pattern that created artificial "Malthusian frontiers" by distributing that population increase not randomly over limitless space, but channeled into surveyed, chartered, and well-bounded townships each of which, within two or three generations, would bump up against the density, scarcity, stinting, compaction, stratification, conflict, "hiving-off," and community collapse that Kenneth Lockridge has called "Europeanization" (1970; see also Park 2016).

To mitigate the press of a population (and its grazing livestock) that was more than doubling every fifty years, the proprietors of some town lands closed, divided, and privatized the commons, bequeathing the best lots to their own sons and replicating thereby a hierarchy consisting of inhabitant, sojourner, resident, commoner, voter, church member, freeholder, householder, townsman, tenant, taxpayer, shareholder, and finally proprietor, a hierarchy which would come to fix upon rural hinterlands the social inequities characteristic of urban places (see Donahue 2004, chap. 9, and Martin 1991: 228).

(2) A recent study by Amine Ouazad and Matthew Kahn has examined the risks specific to the mortgage market posed by environmental degradation and climate change. "It is less likely," they write, "that borrowers will continue to make mortgage payments if their homes are literally under water!" (Ouazad and Kahn 2019:86) Their article is about the threat climate change poses to the solvency of Fannie Mae and Freddy Mac today, but climate change is not new, and environmental degradation has been with us since the Serpent first appeared in the Garden.

In numerous publications, climate historian William R. Baron (1989) has identified 1750–1850 as a change-over period, an interval caught in the shift from one major climate regime to another. Before it was the Neo-glacial (or Little Ice Age), a cooler period with substantial polar anticyclones and other wind disturbances; after it, a warmer time of more even weather. In between was a period marked by strong vacillations. They included droughts, frequent snowstorms, and other unusual weather, dramatically altering growing season lengths: a variability even riskier than just the extreme weather itself. In short, the century was a hard and perilous time for farming.[9]

And risk there was: in more than half of the twenty-four years between 1750 and 1774 there were too few growing-degree days in Cambridge, Massachusetts, for the corn to mature at all. The most extreme instance of eccentric weather was 1815, which had the longest growing season by far of any year between 1750 and 1950 – 240 days between killing frosts! This, the "year without a winter," was followed the very next year by the "year without a summer," which had a growing season of only eighty days. In those two years, spring planting might happen any time between 11 March and 14 June, and the first killing frost (which would destroy at least half the crop) might come anytime between 29 August and 17 November. Risks on this scale – random, devastating, and uninsurable – dwarfed the risks of the market. In fact, in such an environment the market can become a risk-averse strategy to hedge against crop short-falls with higher crop prices.

(3) Improvements in market access become, then, critical buffers against risk. Those improvements, such as they were, happened along four axes: the straightening and surfacing of rutted country dirt roads, new roads to new market towns, and the concentration of market power among them.

There were two bursts of road-building in Massachusetts: the private turnpike era of 1790–1808 and the public road-building era of the 1820s and 1830s. The first of these brought major improvements in the straightening of roads, the second in the surfacing. Turnpikes and toll roads strove for a Roman straightness that considerably shortened the distance, but at the expense of steep grades that added weight and slowed transport, in proportion to the grade (Rothenberg 1992: 82–95). As to surfacing, little could be done until 1858 when the invention of the mechanical stone-crusher made macadam possible. Perhaps what speaks most unambiguously to the effectiveness of road improvement is that of the 1,827 marketing trips sampled for this study there is only one instance of paying a turnpike toll in the farm account books.

Farm account books provided the origins, destinations, and ton-mile costs of the marketing trips.[10] Ton-mile costs were estimated as the sum of the imputed wage of the driver, plus the costs of hiring the wagon and a team of oxen, per mile between farm and market and back. The distances traveled to markets were measured as the beeline distances between origin- and destination-pairs multiplied by 1.6.[11] The concentration of traffic to those market towns was measured by Gini coefficients ($0 < G < 1$), which by 1855 had declined to $G = .487$ in the east as the dominance of Boston and Salem fell away, while increasing to $G = .755$ in the west as Worcester recovered its standing as a Central Place.

Analysis of the Mortgage Sample

How did mortgage lending provide credit to the rural economy of colonial Massachusetts? I analyze a pooled sample of 1,529 mortgages: 1,191 issued by private lenders to private borrowers between 1642 and 1777; and 338 "public" (or Land Bank) mortgages issued by the province in three emissions between 1713 and 1741 as backing for a paper currency. All the documents are to be found in the Registry of Deeds of Middlesex County where they are bound among the true conveyances (deeds) in the basement of the County Courthouse.

Mortgages in the colonial period were all handwritten by clerks of the county courts, but their form and rhetoric were copied from the printed templates used in English law offices by scriveners and attorneys like William Bohun, whose manual *The Practising Attorney* was published in London in 1724 (see also Howe 1948). Mortgage contracts must be read carefully, because only one sentence – the "proviso" or "condition" – distinguishes a mortgage from an actual conveyance. In all respects other than the conditionality of the conveyance, the colonial mortgage was a deed of sale in which the borrower (the Mortgagor or Grantor) appears to be selling land he holds in fee simple to the lender (the Mortgagee or Grantee) for the amount of the loan. Thus:

> In the name of God, Amen, and of the Sovereign [James] in the [seventh] year of his reign. For and in consideration of the sum of [loan amount] in hand well and truly paid at or before the ensealing of these presents, I [Grantor], [husbandman, yeoman] of [Groton] do convey [land, structures] to [Grantee], [merchant] of [Charlestown], to have and to hold. This is followed by elaborate assurances that I, [the Grantor] stand rightly seized of and in the premises in a good and indefeasible title of inheritance in fee simple by virtue of which I have a good right and full power and lawful authority to sell, convey and alien the property. I then warrant to defend the premises to the behoof of [the Grantee] against any entrance upon it, by myself or my heirs and assigns, forever.

In the third paragraph of the document, when we are persuaded that the Grantor did indeed, very much mean to "sell, convey and alien" the property, a proviso transforms the deed into a mortgage in words that make it clear that he most decisively did not:

> PROVIDED always and upon condition nevertheless, and anything herein contained to the contrary notwithstanding. IF the said Grantor [the borrower] shall well and truly pay without fraud, coven, or delay unto the said Grantee [the lender] by [a date certain] the sum of [the loan] with lawful interest, then the above-written deed of sale [sic] and every clause and article therein contained shall cease, determine, be utterly null, void, and of no effect. ELSE the deed shall be, remain, and abide in full force strength and virtue, in which case the Grantee [the lender] shall have, hold, occupy, and possess the premises.

"Have, hold, occupy and possess," but notice: not "own." The distinction between possession and ownership – absolutely fundamental in mortgage law – will be discussed below, along with much other explanatory material.

Amount of Loan. A loan ("the consideration") was denominated in one or another of the several currencies that circulated in the Massachusetts

Bay colony during the colonial period, consisting, at first, of commodities, followed by sterling, pennyweight, and troy weight of silver, Spanish coins, Dutch guilders, bills of public credit (paper money) in one of several "tenors" – old, medium, and new – and finally, after 1750, in lawful money, a specie currency that returned the Massachusetts pound to the exchange rate (the so-called Proclamation Rate) of £133 Massachusetts per £100 sterling.[12] Considerable effort has been made to convert all currencies to Lawful Money according to ratios set by statute.

Conditions of Discharge. These include matters such as due date, currency of repayment, a schedule of amortization, the rate of interest, the indemnification of a third-party co-signer, and the attachment of a penal bond in the event of default. These will be discussed at length below. Suffice it to say at this point that in most instances interest rates were not specified in the mortgage deed; "lawful interest" somehow sufficed. But after 1696 wherever rates were specified, "lawful interest" was always 6 percent.

Date of Discharge. Although Massachusetts law as early as 1640 required that clerks record the date of ratifying (formally confirming) of mortgage deeds, it was not until 1692 that a public record of discharges was required by law. Consequently, less than one-third of the seventeenth-century mortgages in our sample were recorded as discharged. After 1692, the law required that a mortgagee, after receiving satisfaction, "shall acknowledge and cause such satisfaction and payment to be entered on the margin of the record, which shall thereafter discharge, defeat, and release such mortgage and perpetually bar all actions to be brought thereon" (Sullivan 1801: 96).[13]

Duration. Upon first encountering this sample the most startling discovery was that although most mortgage deeds in this sample were written for a term of twelve months,[14] they were held, on average, ninety-three months with no evidence at all of formal re-contracting! If overdue mortgages surprise us, it is because we expect that disappointed creditors had at least two remedies by law to use against delinquent debtors. One such, used with increasing frequency over time in our sample, was the penal bond; the other was to make the mortgage over into a perpetual annuity, which carried with it the possibility of renewal without formal re-contracting.

Occupations. Of the 1,191 mortgages in the private sample, 440 farmers were borrowers and 165 were lenders. In their case one may "read" much from the seasonal pattern of their borrowing: in the private sample there were twice as many mortgages ensealed in each of the months of March through October – the period of peak activity in agriculture – as in each of the months of November through February, early New England's "starving time." If not for consumption-smoothing, then they borrowed to clear land, build structures, erect fences, upgrade herds, lay in provisions in store, pay debts, pay taxes, move west, or to buy land for their sons, all of which strengthen the investment motive for mortgaging. Of the artisans in the sample,[15] 376 were borrowers and 193 were lenders. While artisans and farmers combined made up nearly three-quarters of the borrowers, they constituted only one-third of the lenders. The lenders on fully one-half of the mortgages came from an elite composed of merchants, professionals, esquires, gentlemen, and a few women. As might be expected, merchants and professionals, as members of an elite of sorts, provided significantly larger loans than did any other occupational category – as much as £73 more on average. But they also borrowed more than any other group. Here the merchants and the professional elite are seen to borrow on average twice as much as they lend. That the wealthy were net debtors is confirmed by my earlier finding (Rothenberg 1985): rich landowners' acreage determined the amounts they could borrow or lend, even when not put up as collateral for the loans (Rothenberg 1992: chapter 5).

Table 10.1. Number of mortgages by occupation of the parties.
© Winifred B. Rothenberg.

N = 1,529	Private Sample, n = 1,191		Public Sample, n = 338
Occupation	Mortgagors	Mortgagees	Mortgagors
Artisans	376	193	84
Farmers	440	165	215
Merchants	54	198	2
Professionals	56	271	8
Gentlemen	81	94	16
Officers	3	31	0
Women	31	88	1
Mariners	44	51	0
Service	46	28	2
Occupations known	1,131	1,119	328

Table 10.2. Mean nominal loan amount by occupation of the parties, in £s.
© Winifred B. Rothenberg.

	Farmer	Artisan	Merchant	Gentleman	Professional	Woman
Mortgagor	106	130	411	179	323	68
Mortgagee	116	116	214	161	157	106

Distance Between. Among the more interesting results have been those that came from analyses of the two distance variables, distance (in miles) between the towns of mortgagor and mortgagee, and distance (in miles) of mortgaged property from Boston, the heart of the capital market. Enforcement of contracts between neighbors was likely to be different from that between strangers, so that mitigation would increase with proximity and stringency would increase with distance. But I found the opposite: out-of-town borrowers had use of the loan 13 months longer than neighbors, and the incidence of penal bonds (discussed below), which appear on over a quarter of within-town mortgages, declines sharply as the distance between the parties increases. To coin a phrase, "proximity need not mean relating."

Of course, the opposite interpretation may fit the case even better, wherein debtors are more scrupulous to meet their obligations to neighbors than to strangers, if only because they belong to the same church, encounter one another frequently, and/or seek to "lock in" a relationship based on repeated reputational "games."

Distance from Boston. While a £1 increase in the size of the loan is associated with an increase of 0.12 acres in the collateral that secures it, a one-mile increase in the distance of the property from Boston, the heart of the capital market, required an increase of 5.4 acres in the collateral that secures it. We thus have an approximate measure of the von Thunen effect: that, other things being equal, land values decline along a gradient with distance from a central place.

Age. Reference was made earlier to Frank Lewis's one-period model of farm-making under borrowing constraints (Lewis 1999). In a second application of his model, the age – or at least the stage of life–of the borrower at the ensealing of the mortgage determines how he will allocate scarce household resources between present consumption and present-investment-toward-future consumption. The willingness to make that investment will depend on the intertemporal elasticity of substitution in consumption, and a variety of additional parameters the greatest of which is his life expectancy. Published life-tables suggest that an adult male in colonial Hingham, Andover, or Plymouth might well have expected to live into his late seventies (see Wells 2000: 162). We were able to link 329 mortgagors from our study sample to their probate documents[16] to determine dates of death, which when compared to the date of ratifying (confirming) their mortgages, gave a sense, at least, of the stage of life at which they committed to the mortgage contract. Alice Hanson Jones, in her study of the relation between the age and wealth of probated wealth-holders in 1774 (1980: 381 and Fig. 22 in Appendix C), found that both total physical wealth and net worth peaked at age sixty, fell slowly to age eighty, and thereafter declined sharply as the very old used *inter-vivos* transfers to secure that salt pork, clear cider, and a cord of chopped firewood were left regularly "at the door."

The Endowment of Adult Children. The inheritance of decedents' estates in the Bible commonwealth was governed at first by the Book of Deuteronomy, which found its way into the Body of Liberties in 1641, the colony's first constitution, and according to which intestate estates were to be passed by partible inheritance to all children with a double portion to the eldest son. But with completed family size averaging seven or eight children surviving into adulthood, it was clear that even a 250-acre farm would be subdivided away within two or three generations. That the double portion was removed by law in 1789 may have been a move, in the spirit of the Revolution, "to promote egalitarian ideals," but if so, those ideals quickly fell victim to still another set of "ideals": "the spirit of family capitalism." "In the degree to which the spirit of family capitalism required the *unequal* distribution of all property, the farm passed viable, entire, and intact to the eldest son" (Shammas, Salmon, and Dahlin 1987: 65, 42). Although that son must pay each of his siblings for their share, he had seven years in which to do it. In the meantime, it was the father's responsibility to find land for each of his remaining offspring, and, if necessary, to take on a mortgage to pay for it.[17] A borrowing constraint at this stage of a father's life would have constituted a serious barrier. There was, of course, another solution, and after the Revolution, Massachusetts families would be the first in the nation to adopt it: a sharp and sustained drop in the birth rate!

Penal Bonds. A penal bond secured a pledge to "save harmless" (i.e., indemnify) the co-signer on a loan if the primary borrower defaults. There were 380 penal bonds in this sample; of those, one-third were on mortgages between parties in the same town and two-thirds on mortgages between parties in different towns. Penal bonds made explicit what is never made explicit in the mortgage itself: the penalty for default amounted to twice the size of the loan, or in other words, the penalty for default was the whole value of the collateral. The penal bond for twice the amount of the loan was, in a manner of speaking, an "end run" around the limitations equity had placed on the mortgagee, enabling the lender to execute not against the debt – which, it will be recalled, was only half the value of the land – but against the whole value of the land (Maitland [1909, 1936] 2011: 182).

Discharges and Defaults. Given the several provisions fortifying the lender's position in a mortgage contract, why were so many in our sample either very much overdue or actually never discharged at all?! When the pooled sample of 1,191 private mortgages is divided into two sub-samples – the discharged and the undischarged – it becomes evident from a one-way analysis of variance that the means of variables in the two sub-samples differed significantly, and, incidentally, counterintuitively. Merchants and professionals in the set of *undischarged* mortgages were twice as large a share of borrowers as in the set of discharged mortgages; the loan amount was £37 larger; the mortgaged property had sixty-six more acres; the distance variables were 3 miles longer; borrowers were more often urban; lenders were more often non-urban; and the term of the loan was nearly ten months longer.

Given the "iron-clad" ultimatum written into the mortgage contract itself, into the commitment of co-signers, and into the penal bond that secures it, the toleration of "overdue-ness" is difficult to explain, especially in the case of the 321 mortgages – 27 percent – that were never dis-

Table 10.3. Mortgages discharged and undischarged, by occupation of the debtor. Percent of sub-sample. © Winifred B. Rothenberg.

	Farmers	Artisans	Gentlemen	Professionals	Merchants
Discharged	41.6	32.6	7.4	4.3	3.7
Undischarged	31.1	35.7	6.8	6.4	8.6
All	39.0	33.4	7.3	4.8	5.0

Note: Does not round to 100 because of the omission of some occupational categories.

Table 10.4. Discharged and undischarged mortgages, by percent urban/rural. Percent of sub-sample. © Winifred B. Rothenberg.

	Mortgagors		Mortgagees	
	Urban	Rural	Urban	Rural
Discharged	36	64	67.4	32.6
Undischarged	40	60	61.8	38.2

Note: "Urban" = residing in Boston, Cambridge, or Charlestown.

Table 10.5. Two sub-samples: Differences of means of selected variables. © Winifred B. Rothenberg.

	Discharged	Undischarged
Sub-sample size	860	321
Mean loan size, £s	131.65	169.04
Express Term, months	18.70	28.3
Mean acres mortgaged	59	125

charged at all! Why would a lender tolerate delay or outright delinquency when there are remedies through the law? Mortgage law was, after all, imbedded in a civil law system of jails, fines, debtors' prisons, indemnities, penal bonds, attachments, and – perhaps most effective of all in colonial Massachusetts – a culture of public shaming.

Perhaps the lender in these cases was evading court costs, which Claire Priest has found were heavy.[18] "To satisfy the average court fee in 1740, a skilled craftsman would have to work 5.7–5.8 days; and a farmer 7.8–8.0 days . . . In the 1780s, for a master tradesman, average courts costs in an uncontested debt action consumed the income of 9.2–9.8 days; for unskilled labor, 14.8–15.8 days in the summer and 19.7–21.0 days . . . in the fall" (Priest 1999: 2428), or the court would have to entertain the possibility that the defaults arose from a willingness on the part of lenders to partner with borrowers to re-contract the mortgage as a perpetual annuity. If, indeed, that is what they meant to do, the question is why? And that opens this study up to a discussion of the usury regime and the place of interest rates in it.

The Usury Regime

For a lender, mortgages had clear advantages over other investments: the debtor could not abscond with the collateral; the condition of the collateral and of its "improvement" could be easily monitored; and the growth of population, the proliferation of new market towns, and the improvement of market access worked, one assumes, to sustain an upward pressure on land values over time. But perhaps the most compelling reason for allowing a mortgage to be leveraged to a perpetual annuity was that the interest that continued to be paid on the mortgage was, at 6 percent, the highest the lender could have expected to earn on any alternative investment. But for that to be true, the usury law in colonial Massachusetts would have had to be binding, and this remains in doubt, a topic to which we will return.[19]

Usury theory has a long history. In the Bible, a firm distinction is – again and again and again – made between the "brotherhood" of the Hebrews and the "otherhood" of the Gentiles. "Unto a foreigner thou mayest lend upon interest; but unto thy brother thou shalt not lend upon interest; that the Lord thy God may bless thee in all that thou puttest thy hand unto, in the land whither thou goest in to possess it" (Deuteronomy 23:21).

When the Franciscans and Dominicans set about establishing their orders in the twelfth and thirteen centuries, a new brotherhood, that of believers in Christ, was folded into Deuteronomy's tent, while the brotherhood for which it was written was thrust out to become, forever, others (Nelson 1969: xxv).

Throughout the thirteenth century, the idea of equality as the proper end of all exchange was central in usury theory (Kaye 2014: 21–75). This principle is embodied in the concept of *mutuum* – literally "what had been mine becomes thine." When a person lends money, he transfers at the same time its substance, its use, and its ownership (*dominium*) to the borrower. If the usurer then charges the borrower for the use of the money loaned, he is either selling what does not yet exist or what is not his to sell, or he is selling the same thing twice, and in doing so he violates the equality built into both natural justice and nature itself.[20] Thereafter it followed from the notion of *mutuum* that to charge any interest within the Christian brotherhood is to demand more in repayment than the exact sum lent, robbing the borrower of that which, for the term of the loan, had become his, and thus sins against the principles of *aequalitis*, equality in exchange, commutative justice, and natural law. And is truly a mortal sin.

> At the same time, as the 13th century progressed, it was becoming ever clearer that the ideal numerical equality demanded by [Church law] was difficult, if not impossible, to impose upon credit contracts when they were embedded in the real world of economic exchange ... [W]ithin the disciplines of Roman and canon law ... the realization grew that if the lender was to be denied the expectation of reward [interest], he must at the same time be protected from damages associated with the act of lending. (Kaye 2014: 31–32)

There were two types of damages: the loss actually suffered (*damnum emergens*) and the loss of the imputed gains he might have made had he not lent it (*lucrum cessans*).

Hugh Rockoff has recently argued that usury laws were effective and "had a substantial impact on the structure of lending" (Rockoff 2001: 4). Many other historians, however, suspect that they were quite generally evaded, although it would be very difficult to prove, for directly in proportion as usury was condemned, so, we can assume, it was concealed: as rent, or as a discount, or lent in paper currency to be repaid in specie, or lent when money was cheap to be repaid when it was dear.[21]

Given the dearth of coin throughout the colonial period, a cap on the price of credit should have been unsustainable. True, a usurer convicted under Massachusetts law forfeited both principal and interest, but under the circumstances, was the risk not worth taking?

A usury ceiling should matter to us only if it distorted the workings of the colonial credit market, but there is no evidence that it did. In the short run, the efficiency of such a market can be tested in two ways: either through a flexible price response to fixed quantities, or a flexible quantity response to fixed prices. The first, price flexibility, is only a sufficient condition. The necessary condition is the responsiveness of demand and supply to price (Weitzman 1974). As Philip Hoffman, Gilles Postel-Vinay, and Jean-Laurent Rosenthal (2000) have shown, this – a "priceless market" for credit – functioned in Paris for two hundred of the most turbulent years of its history. To clear the credit market, the French relied not on market rates, but on notaries who culled the information from their wide networks to fix prices at rates that matched demand to supply.[22]

Equity of Redemption: An Opening for Judicial Conscience and Discretion

> To see a world in a grain of sand . . .
> – William Blake, "Auguries of Innocence"

If, as I claim at the beginning of this chapter, the capitalist transformation of Massachusetts' rural economy can be inferred from changes in the portfolio behavior of rural decedents, it should not surprise us to find a parallel transformation in the legal system.

> By 1820, the legal landscape in America bore only the faintest resemblance to what existed forty years earlier. While the words were often the same, the structure of thought had dramatically changed and with it the theory of law. Law was no longer conceived of as an eternal set of principles expressed in custom and derived from natural law . . . Instead, judges came to think of the common law as equally responsible with legislation for governing society and promoting socially desirable conduct. (Horwitz 1977: 30)

And "while the delegation of so explicit and self-conscious a legislative function to judges would have been inconceivable even two decades earlier, it was completely in tune with the emergence of *an instrumental conception of law as will*" (1977: 24, emphasis added).

A second change in the legal landscape was the emergence of an instrumental conception of property. William Blackstone in his *Commentaries*, in England, had defined property as "that sole and despotic dominion which one man claims and exercises over the external things of the world in total exclusion of the right of any other individual in the universe" (Blackstone [1766] 1979: 3). But dominion is rarely, if ever, sole and despotic. In Anglo-American property law it had been, since Roman times, contested, constrained, and curtailed by the ancient maxim *Sic utere tuo ut alienum non laedas* – use yours so as not to harm another's.

But by the mid-nineteenth century, as America was increasingly taken with the spirit of economic development, it was left to the courts to perform "the social engineering function of balancing the utility of economically productive activity against the harm" (Horwitz 1977: 102) that would accrue from its negative externalities (that is, from harms or damages beyond any to the persons or things most directly concerned). "Dominion over land began to be regarded as an absolute right to engage in any conduct on one's property regardless of its economic value ... While this trend only reached its culmination after the Civil War, its roots were deep in an antebellum change in the conception of property" (Horwitz 1977: 102).

At the juncture of law and property stands the mortgage and, most particularly, the doctrine of equitable redemption – an intricate body of legal doctrine that vests possession in the mortgagee, but ownership in the mortgagor (Sugarman and Warrington 1995: 118). I repeat: ownership in equity does remain in the mortgagor. That equity of redemption, imported from England to America, would remain an enduring part of the land law of the English-speaking world.

Since first enunciated in England in 1654, the concept of "equity of redemption" – basically safeguarding a mortgagor's right to redeem property upon payments of debts due in an allowable period of time – has been a linchpin of jurisprudence around the mortgage, both there and across the Atlantic, including in Massachusetts as in other colonies. The jurisprudence around equitable redemption, though, has swung between polarities that have bedeviled law courts and equity courts: equity/common law; seisin/dominium; the gage as lien on collateral/the gage as security for debt; possession/ownership; rights *in personem*/rights *in rem*; moveable/immoveable; corporeal/incorporeal; equitable estate of the mortgagor/legal estate of the mortgagee; status/contract; rules/exceptions; the spirit/the letter; find as to fact/find as to law; personality/realty; and substantive justice/procedural justice. The section below is an in-gathering of these ideas from a variety of legal sources to convey the issues that have arisen over centuries of jurisprudence around the equity of redemption.

The mortgage can be traced back, as we have suggested in this volume, to the very dawn of recorded history. A historical perspective on both the mortgage and the equity of redemption can be gleaned from a fascinating study of ancient Athens by John V.A. Fine in his book *Horoi: Studies in Mortgage, Real Security, and Land Tenure in Ancient Athens* (1951). According to

Fine, evidence of mortgaging has been unearthed in the Peloponnese as inscriptions on stone tablets called *horoi* that are thought to have marked the boundaries of encumbered land and are dated to between the fourth and seventh centuries BCE.

A harried peasant in need of money would borrow from a wealthy man, offering the only security he could provide – his own person. If the debtor was unable to pay the debt when the loan came due, the creditor was entitled to seize him as a slave. Mortgages in archaic Greece were secured by debt slavery because land was unalienable outside the family. Solon abolished debt slavery in or around 594 BCE, but the bar on alienation of land remained. To sell family land – to "commodify" land made sacred by ancestors and held in trust for descendants – threatened the very foundations of the society.

> In the course of the seventh century the production of olives and wine for export had supplanted cereal growing as the most profitable forms of agriculture in Attica. Orchards and vineyards, however, belonged to "long future" husbandry, a type of farming beyond the reach of the peasants who lacked the capital to tide them over the years until the trees and vines should become fruitful. Since the increasing use of money and the expansion of commerce were having a deleterious effect on the local prices of cereals, the small farmer was experiencing ever greater difficulty in maintaining himself on his little plot. The nobles, on the other hand with idle capital to invest were anxious to acquire more land which could be converted into orchards and vineyards. How was this land to be obtained as long as the principle of inalienability remained in force? ... To meet this situation a method was invented – undoubtedly by the land-grabbing nobles – which satisfied them and presumably was agreeable to the peasants. This device was really a legal fiction and, to use fourth century parlance, can be termed sale subject to redemption. In the seventh century it can be assumed that it worked as follows. The insolvent debtor, on the day of the maturity of the loan, was confronted with two possibilities: either he could pass into slavery or, as an alternative to this, he could transfer the possession of his land to his creditor. *The debtor, who retained a right of redemption,* would remain on the land as a rent paying tenant. This scheme satisfied all the necessary requirements of the times. The prohibition against alienating land was not violated because the peasant ... remained on his ancestral plot with the right of redemption, to which, in keeping with the legal fiction, no time limit was assigned. The creditor, again in conformity with the fiction, did not become outright owner of the land but he had what he most wanted – more acres which, if he desired, he could force his tenants to convert to olive and vine growing. And finally, the debtor escaped the horrors of slavery and remained on the land of his fathers. (Fine, 1951: 183, emphasis added)

Overturning that sacred ban against selling family land constituted a transformation so profound, Fine suggests, that it could be brought about only in the wake of a catastrophe. The Peloponnesian Wars and the famines and plagues that followed were indeed such catastrophes: one-third of the Athenian population perished. In the exodus of farmers who fled, whole families were wiped out, extinguishing their claims to family land. The bar to alienating property out of the family could not survive. It was, like the Black Death, an "axial moment" in world history. Out of the ashes, a market in land, the *sine qua non* of a mortgage market, emerged.

Let us skip ahead to several centuries of legal history in England, forming the basis of laws and customs by which land mortgagors, mortgagees, and others judging them in colonial Massachusetts were to be operating and adapting. Much of this history since medieval, feudal times took the form of debate and discussion about the nature of property, about transactions, and about what would eventually be called equity of redemption. "In the strange, half-timeless world of the traditional English landed estate, feudal concepts blissfully lingered long after feudal relations had been eradicated . . . Land was not just the most valuable form of property . . . it was a social-political nexus, a way of life, which the law treated with particular devotion" (Sugarman and Warrington 1995: 111).

The "peculiar devotion" of the English to land has been traced back to its sixth century Germanic roots. Frederick Pollock and Frederic William Maitland give us a description of how land was transferred from person to person in witnessed performances that varied both by time and local culture but involved acts such as transferring a twig or a piece of sod (symbolizing the land), a gauntlet (symbolizing a gloved hand that will fight to defend the territory), and a rod (symbolizing an obligation, perhaps for payment), and that also might have involved someone's leaping over a hedge (symbolizing transfer) (Pollock and Maitland [1895]1898: 85).

Common law, deeply rooted in medieval history, describes that part of canon law that flows from divinity, without human enactment, to all Englishmen (see Maitland [1909, 1936] 2011). Equity, on the other hand, is founded on abstract justice and on judicial discretion quite independent of law.

The courts have insisted that a mortgage does not give either party a lien on the collateral; it is merely a security for the money, not a pseudo-conveyance of land. Evidence of this is that the loan must not exceed one-half to two-thirds the value of the land. If the objective of the mortgage were truly a conveyance of land, the loan would at least equal the value of the land that stands security for it.

In the wording of the mortgage deed the mortgagee will seize the land if the mortgagor defaults on the loan, even by one day. But is the mortgagee's threat plausible when "once a mortgage always a mortgage, and nothing but a mortgage" (not a transfer of *ownership*) has stood for centuries as a firewall against predatory behavior by an acquisitive mortgagee?

Should the borrower default, the mortgage deed gives the lender "absolute legal title in the estate." But what is that "absolute *legal* title" worth when the lender cannot sell, or dispose of, or improve the estate while in possession because the courts allowed the interpretation that the borrower continues in equity, even if not in law, to hold *equitable* title as long as the clock is running on his right to redeem?[23]

The English mortgage was: "provisional," a "conditional conveyance," a "feigned transaction," "suppressio veri suggestio falsi." (see Maitland 1949: 191; [1909, 1936] 2011: 194). English equity gave the debtor an "equity estate" (a right to pursue the recovery of his land not only from the creditor but also from any purchaser of the land from the creditor), but not a "legal estate." The "duality of ownerships," legal and equitable, has been, in R. W. Turner's view, a unique and signal English contribution to legal thought (Turner 1931: xiii and 69).

The common law took no notice of equity of redemption. In 1759, the court held that it was "nothing at all" in the eye of the law. Mortga*gors* got an "estate sui generis," in equity but it was not a legal estate. The right upon which a mortga*gee* most frequently places his main reliance is given him by seizure and an extra-judicial power of sale, that is, a sale not ordered by the court. But so long as the mortgage remains un-foreclosed, the mortgagee is under an equitable obligation not to sell; if he attempts to sell, equity will stop him by injunction.

The mortgagor, on the other hand, although owner in equity of the land, may not lease it out during the term of the mortgage without consent of the mortgagee lest he deprive the mortgagee in some measure of the remedies due to him upon his taking possession of the estate. Nor could the mortgagee rent out the land while in possession because the mortgagor's right of redemption requires that he get back his land just as he had surrendered it.

The borrower always[24] has the right to redeem his equitable title out from under the lender without "clogs"?[25] Equity suffers no land to be lost if it can be redeemed in a "convenient time" – in one case thirty-three years, in another sixty years. "This justice was not an abstract principle." It turned upon what one deemed "just." "And for most judges most of the time, justice in this context meant the restoration of landed property to the original owner" (Sugarman and Warrington 1995: 118).

Equity of redemption was of no value at law. A mortgagor who made a covenant with the mortgagee to dig coal on land he possessed was held by the court of law to be "a perfect stranger." The mortgagor at law had no estate or interest whatever apart from possession. Hence a mortgagor in possession, if he wishes to sue a trespasser at law, must first persuade the mortgagee to join in action with him, or pay off his debts, interests, and costs before he has a right to sue the trespasser. During the term of the mortgage the mortgagor is at most a "tenant at sufferance," like one who overstays an agreed period of rent and has little right other than not to be injured deliberately by the landlord.[26]

If a mortgage is first and foremost a security for money, then why the collateralized land? Why the penal bonds? Why limit the loan to a fraction (half) of the value of the land? Why not allow the loan to equal 100 percent of the value of the collateral? In short, why the fortress that has been erected around a mere "security for money" when elsewhere in society there is a legal system that stands security against delinquent debts?

Equity has the power to make exceptions to the rules; common law does not. The rigor of the common law comes from its refusal to make exceptions, even when an exceptional case arises that cries out to set aside the letter of the law (think Antigone), and to follow the dictates of justice and the common good that are not known to strict law, but are apprehended only by the conscience and at the discretion of the judge. The broad range of a court of equity allows it to find the cracks in the law.

It is said that a court of equity determines according to the spirit, not the letter, of the law, for as in Corinthians (2:3:6), "the letter killeth but the Spirit giveth life." It is said that a court of equity is not constrained by rules, or precedents, or juries, or rules of evidence, but acts at the sole discretion of the judge. But government independent of law is tyranny.

In the event of a mortgagor's default, what the mortgagee is entitled to ask for is the debt and only the debt; not the collateral that stands security for the debt. The debt is, intentionally, only one-half to two-thirds the value of the collateral. The co-signer or surety, in the older sense, takes the place of current payment, and is relied upon by the mortgagee, but as a stand-in, must not be blamed or harmed in the case of a default (Wigmore 1897).

Once the notion came forward of land as a resource to be employed rather than an endowment to be enjoyed, debtors demanded that the profits earned by creditors from the fruits of the land while they are in possession should reduce the principal on the debt; while creditors demanded that the fruits of the land must not be allowed to reduce the principal on the debt: the pledge was of the land, not of its fruits.

The distinction between vifgage and mortgage hangs upon whether the fruits of the land can or cannot be used to reduce the debt. In the *mort*gage the gage is "dead": the fruits of the land cannot be used by the mortgagor to reduce the debt.

"Sequential transactions [and a mortgage certainly is one] in which the separation in time between the *quid* and the *quo* [the loan and the payback] encourages one party to renege are particularly vulnerable to acquisitive, rent-seeking behavior, unless that behavior can be refracted through institutions that foster the willingness *ex ante* to commit, and *ex post* to fulfill, contractual obligations" (Greif 2000: 256).

In the last quarter of the thirteenth century, a law of property in land was being developed with distinctions between movables and immovables, between corporeal things like land and incorporeal things like tithes, and, most important, between *seisin* and *dominium* – possession and ownership (Pollock and Maitland [1895] 1898: 153n1). Wrote Frederick Pollock and Frederic William Maitland:

> In the history of our law there is no idea more cardinal than that of seisin. Even in the law of the present day it plays a part which must be studied by every lawyer, but in the past, it was so important that we may almost say that the whole system of our law was law about seisin and its consequences. Seisin is possession . . . When we say that 'seisin is possession' we use the latter term in the sense in which lawyers use it, a sense in which possession is quite distinct from, and may be sharply opposed to, proprietary right. ([1895] 1898: 29)

They continue, "[S]o soon as there is any law worthy of the name, right and possession must emerge and be contrasted: so soon as any one has said 'You have got what belongs to me,' the germs of these two notions have appeared and can be *opposed to each other*" (Pollock and Maitland [1895] 1898: 33, emphasis added). And again,

> Why does our law protect possession? Why does law, when it has on its hands the difficult work of protecting ownership and other rights in things, prepare puzzles for itself by undertaking to protect something that is not ownership, something that will from time to time come into sharp collision with ownership? Is it not a main object of law that everyone should enjoy what is his own *de jure*, and if so, why are we to consecrate that *de facto* enjoyment which is signified by the term *possession*, and why, above all, why are we to protect the possessor even against the owner? ([1895] 1898: 40)

Because:

(1) To prove ownership is difficult; to prove possession comparatively easy.

(2) Ownership cannot be protected without protecting possession.
(3) To maintain peace and quiet, it has been found necessary to protect possession.
(4) One cannot disturb possession without being guilty of some injury that comes dangerously close to an assault.
(5) "The possessor has by the mere fact of his possession more right in the thing than the non-possessor has" (Pollock and Maitland [1895] 1898: 40).
(6) Possession could be defended by force, but ownership, more separate as a legal abstraction, may once have been something more like what we call contract than like what we call property, something more basic (Baker 1979).

One of the protections the legal system developed to safeguard land from capital was the equity of redemption. This "seemingly indestructible doctrine of land law" (first enunciated in *Duchess of Hamilton v. Countess of Dirlton*, in 1654) "played a role in the forging of English national identity and citizenship," giving claims of mortgagors' precedence over those of mortgagees (Sugarman and Warrington 1995: 112–13). Without equity of redemption – that is, possibility of paying off the debt and regaining the land – no mortgage. A foreshortened or eliminated equity of redemption, in a mortgage, is not really equity (Wyman 1908). That is, no mortgage can seem fair without it.

The mortgage deed is not, and never was intended to be, a conveyance. Ownership resides in the mortgagor, who can pursue equity of redemption beyond the lender all the way to an eventual purchaser. The rights of the landed were thus entrenched against those of the lenders "irrespective of the terms of the agreement [that is, of the terms of the contract] between the parties and their manifest intentions" (Sugarman and Warrington 1995: 111).

Some authors, though, comment on the equity of redemption as enduringly "so violent an interference in contract" (Sugarman and Warrington: 1995: 118); and on the complication and dilemma of "dual ownership" entailed by equity of redemption since the sixteenth and seventeenth centuries – something that the latter author sees as a continuing problem that one can only hope will somehow disappear. R. W. Turner has written, "if the creditor has the land only *qua* security for the debt, then he does not have it *qua* realty, then who does? The mortgagor, because otherwise the ownership of the land will be sunk, invested nowhere, which is not to be admitted, and therefore if it be in the mortgagee, it must remain in the mortgagor" (Turner 1931: 67).

"The real object of the [mortgage] transaction was the creation of a security for the debt . . . Time was not to be the essence of the agreement" (Sugarman and Warrington 1995: 113). Most judges in England generally believed it right to restore to original owners their landed property (1995: 118).

Colonial Novelty and Continuity

By way of summary, consider equitable redemption in terms of the interests it served in seventeenth-century England and in colonial Massachusetts, and the anomalous position it occupied in the eighteenth century in both, with respect to the common law and to emerging capitalism.

- Equitable redemption straddled the divide between the traditional and the instrumental, the old and the new.
- In its privileging of substantive justice over private contracts it was "old,"
- but in its procedural and substantive challenges to the common law courts it was "new."
- In preserving primogeniture and entailed estates against alienation it was "old,"
- but in mitigating the risks faced by landowners venturing their capital in new markets it was "new."
- In creating "a legal bulwark safeguarding land from the encroachments of capital" (Sugarman and Warrington 1995: 112) it was "old,"
- but in "helping to fashion the mortgage into a major vehicle for economic development" (1995: 112) it was "new."

Winifred B. Rothenberg is Associate Professor Emerita, Department of Economics, Tufts University. She received her PhD in American economic history from Brandeis University. She has taught at Amherst College, Brandeis, Boston University, and MIT; and at Tufts since 1986. She is the author of *From Market-Places to a Market Economy* (Chicago, 1992), and of a number of articles in the *Journal of Economic History* on the contribution of commodity markets (1979), capital markets (1985), and farm labor markets (1988) to economic growth in Massachusetts. Her chapter on mortgage credit in this volume "tops off" this long preoccupation.

NOTES

1. See also a review of Hernando de Soto's book *The Mystery of Capital* by Christopher Woodruff (2001: 1212–23).
2. See, for example, Karl Polanyi ([1944] 2001), where he argues that the rhetoric of "free labor markets" as it was used in debates to repeal the Poor Law, signaled the collapse of community and the abandonment of the laboring classes. As he might have said as in the song by Janis Joplin, "Me and Bobby McGee," but did not, "Freedom's just another name for nothing left to lose."
3. The question of the extent the farm mortgage was a productive investment deserves extended discussion, for it sits at the center of much of the popular outrage in US history. See, for example, Allan G. Bogue (1955: 1–6).
4. As will be seen later, where we analyze the sample data for this chapter, decedents who were living in the following towns – Auburn, Dracut, Dunstable, Pepperell, Tewksbury, Leicester, Lancaster, Rutland, Bolton, and Worcester – on land described in the mortgage documents as "wilderness," were living on the farming frontier of what was then Middlesex County.
5. Relative to an owner-operator, "the tenant will equate the marginal disutility of his effort with his *share* of the marginal product rather than with the total marginal product. Therefore, too little effort will be forthcoming from agents" (Stiglitz and Weiss 1981: 407).
6. See Stanley L. Engerman and Kenneth L. Sokoloff (2002: 69–71, Table 6 and its implications). This major monograph has given rise to a whole literature synthesizing economic development, environmental economics, the New Political Economy, and the New Institutional Economic History. Case in point: the 1860 Census (Atack, Bateman, and Weiss 2006). Sixty-seven percent of farmers in the northern tier of states in the American Midwest owned their own land, and those states have been, for most of the years since, the center of progressive politics in the United States. Compare that with Ireland where in the years before and after the famine, 0.1 percent of the Irish owned their own land, and until very recently it had long been among the least progressive countries in Western Europe. See Joel Mokyr (1985).
7. It is remarkable that immigration was not a significant factor in that population growth. Of the 9,364 British emigrants who came to the thirteen colonies between December 1773 and March 1776, only seventy-seven went to all the New England colonies combined! "They largely ignored New England," writes Bernard Bailyn (1986: 205 and 209).
8. The Massachusetts estimate is from John McCusker (2005, Table JJM.1.6). The English estimate is from Joel Mokyr (2009: 280, and Table 13.1). Mokyr's estimate is based on E. A. Wrigley and R. S. Schofield (1997: 614).
9. William R. Baron is the author of many articles that have appeared in *Climatic Change* 4; *Maine Historical Society Quarterly* 21; *Journal of Climate and Applied Meteorology* 23; *Climatic Change in Canada* 5; *Agricultural History* 63; and publications of Northern Arizona University. See, for instance, Baron's 1989 literature review focusing on the precariousness of farming in highly variable weather and periods of longer-term climate change.

10. Farm account books provided the data for the origins and destinations of the 1,827 marketing trips in this study. The distances traveled to markets were measured as the current map mileage multiplied by 1.6 to account for straightening. The concentration of those trips was measured as Gini coefficients, which by 1855 had declined to $g = 0.487$ in the east as the magnetic pull of the Boston and Salem central places fell away, while increasing to $g = 0.755$ in the west as the Worcester County market drew in magnetic strength after 1750.
11. The ratio 1.6 to 1 is the one Robert Fogel assumed to obtain between modern highway distances and beeline distances between towns on a map (1964: 67).
12. "Early in 1749 the legislature voted that after March 31, 1750, the treasurer should redeem outstanding bills in silver at the following rates: for every 45 shillings in old tenor bills, one piece of eight [= 6s.], and for every 11 shillings 3 pence in middle tenor and new tenor bills, one piece of eight ... One year was given for redemption. All subsequent contracts were payable in coined silver. In September 1749, the Boston colonists witnessed a novel sight. The silver freighted from England arrived in Boston; seventeen trucks laden with 217 chests of Spanish silver coins and ten trucks with 100 casks of copper coin were hauled up King Street and delivered at the office of the provincial treasurer. Approximately the paper currency was redeemed at the rate of 7 ½ paper to 1 specie" (Hart 1928: 212–13). John McCusker confirms these ratios at several places in his handbook (1978: 120, 133, and 133n48).
13. And if the mortgage was assigned (i.e., sold) to an assignee, that too must be recorded in the margin of the deed with the volume, number, and page on which the assignment is entered.
14. By the mid- to late nineteenth century the standard term was five years. The twenty- to thirty-year mortgage familiar to us now became standard only as a result of federal intervention in the mortgage market in the 1930s. See Kenneth Snowden and Walid Bu-Saba (1992).
15. Carpenters, blacksmiths, innkeepers, victuallers, glaziers, housewrights, curriers, tanners, tailors, potters, ropemakers, bakers, clothiers, cloth workers, cordwainers, joiners, feltmakers, saddlers, ferrymen, boatmen, tallow chandlers, weavers, lightermen, maltsters, sawyers, millwrights, coopers, shipwrights, masons, bricklayers, brick makers, block makers, gunsmiths, hatters, millers, clerks, a chocolate grinder, a goldsmith, a chaise maker, a glover, a perruque maker, a salter, a leather dresser, an oatmeal maker. They would have mortgaged to buy the tools of their trade, and forges, wherries, traces, nets, and looms, to purchase mill-rights and water-rights, to lay in a stock of raw materials, to build up an inventory of semi-finished goods, and perhaps most important, to build or expand a shop. It is noteworthy that in regressions attempting to explain Loan Amount, the presence of a dwelling or barn did not increase the value of the collateral, but the presence of a "shop" or "works" on the property was associated with a statistically significant increase of £106.7 in the amount of the loan.
16. What makes linking of this kind more than usually problematic is the small pool of first and last names in colonial Massachusetts, due, first, to the frequency, generation after generation, of Biblical and patrilineal first names,

and, second, to the slowing of immigration to Massachusetts to a mere trickle (see note 7).
17. "The costs of endowing children with either a start in adult life or a bequest in exchange for old age security drove the net cost of a northeastern child higher than in either of the other two regions" (the Midwest or the frontier) (Craig 1993: 92).
18. "Extremely costly" court fees discouraged creditors from litigating, even though all costs would be paid by the loser in the case. See Claire Priest (1999).
19. In Massachusetts, a usury ceiling was set by law at six percent in 1693 and remained on the books until 1873. A usurer under Massachusetts law forfeited both principal and interest if convicted, but given the severe strains on the colonial money supply, many have assumed that the risk was worth taking.
20. For the ideas in these paragraphs I am indebted to John Munro (2001) and Benjamin Nelson (1969), and to Joel Kaye (2014).
21. "High rates no doubt existed in commercial and personal transactions, but high interest rates were vigorously opposed by colonial law and custom and were therefore negotiated secretly and have not come down to us" (Homer 1963: 274–75).
22. For a discussion of social control under a regime of "fixed" prices in colonial Massachusetts, see Rothenberg (1992: 43–46).
23. New Jersey allowed twenty years for redemption. Massachusetts's three years is called a "drastic shortening" (Skilton 1943: 322).
24. "No American case, so far as the writer [Wyman] knows, has ever considered mere length of time as inconsistent with a mortgage transaction; indeed, we have countless corporate mortgages to secure bonds ranging in duration from twenty to *one thousand years*" (Wyman 1908: 471n3, emphasis added).
25. "The real test in the matter is not whether the mortgagor is subjected to various burdens during the currency of the mortgage, . . . but the true inquiry . . . is whether *after repayment of his loan* the mortgagor is free from interference with his enjoyment again of full ownership" (Wyman 1908: 472).
26. See Black's Law Dictionary ([1891] 2019) on a mortgagor as a "tenant at sufferance."

REFERENCES

Anderson, B. L. 1969. "The Attorney and the Early Capital Market in Lancashire." In *Liverpool and Merseyside: Essays in the Economic and Social History of the Port and its Hinterland*, ed. J. R. Harris, 50–77. New York: A.M. Kelley.

Atack, Jeremy, Fred Bateman, and Thomas Weiss, eds. 2006. *National Samples from the Census of Manufacturing: 1850, 1860, and 1870*. Inter-university Consortium for Political and Social Research [distributor]. Retrieved 13 March 2021 from https://doi.org/10.3886/ICPSR04048.v1.

Bailyn, Bernard. 1986. *Voyagers to the West: A Passage in the Peopling of America on the Eve of the Revolution*. New York: Alfred A Knopf.

Baker, John Hamilton. 1979. *An Introduction to English Legal History*, 2nd ed. London: Butterworths.

Baron, William R. 1989. "Retrieving American Climate History: A Bibliographic Essay." *Climate, Agriculture, and History. Agricultural History* 63(2): 7–35.

Black, Henry Campbell. [1891] 2019. *Black's Law Dictionary*, ed. Bryan Garner. St. Paul, MN: West Publishing.

Blackstone, William. [1766] 1979. *Commentaries on the Laws of England*, vol. 2, *Of the Rights of Things*. Chicago: University of Chicago Press.

Blake, William. 1982. "Auguries of Innocence." *The Complete Poetry and Prose of William Blake*, ed. David V. Erdman, 733–734. Garden City, NY: Anchor Books.

Bogue, Allan G. 1955. *Money at Interest: The Farm Mortgage on the Middle Border*. Lincoln: University of Nebraska Press.

Bohun, William. 1724. *The Practising Attorney, or Lawyer's Office: Containing the Business of Attorney in All Its Branches*. London: E.&R. Nutt & R. Gosling for J. Crockett.

Craig, Lee A. 1993. *To Sow One Acre More: Childbearing and Farm Productivity in the Antebellum North*. Baltimore, MD: Johns Hopkins University Press.

de Soto, Hernando de. 1989. *The Other Path: The Invisible Revolution in the Third World*. New York: HarperCollins.

———. 2000. *The Mystery of Capital: Why Capitalism Triumphs in the West and Fails Everywhere Else*. New York: Basic Books.

Donahue, Brian. 2004. *The Great Meadow: Farmers and the Land in Colonial Concord*. New Haven, CT: Yale University Press.

Engerman, Stanley L., and Kenneth L. Sokoloff. 2002. "Factor Endowments, Inequality, and Paths of Development among New World Economies." *Economia* 3(1): 41–88.

Fine, John V. A. 1951. *Horoi: Studies in Mortgage, Real Security, and Land Tenure in Ancient Athens*. Athens: American School of Classical Studies at Athens.

Fisher, Lynn M., and Abdullah Yavas. 2007. "The Value of Equitable Redemption in Commercial Mortgage Contracting." *Journal of Real Estate Finance and Economics* 35(4): 411–25.

Fogel, Robert. 1964. *Railroads and American Economic Growth: Essays in Econometric History*. Baltimore, MD: Johns Hopkins Press.

Greif, Avner. 2000. "The Fundamental Problem of Exchange: A Research Agenda in Historical Institutional Analysis." *European Review of Economic History* 4(3): 251–84.

Hart, Albert B. 1928 *Commonwealth History of Massachusetts*. vol. 2. New York: States History Co.

Hoffman, Philip, Gilles Postel-Vinay, and Jean-Laurent Rosenthal. 2000. *Priceless Markets: The Political Economy of Credit in Paris, 1660–1870*. Chicago: University of Chicago Press.

Holderness, B. A. 1975. "Credit in a Rural Community, 1660–1800: Some Neglected Aspects of Probate Inventories," *Midland History* 3(2): 94–116.

———. 1976. "Credit in English Rural Society before the Nineteenth Century, with special reference to the period 1650–1720." *Agricultural History Review* 24: 97–109.

Homer, Sidney. 1963. *A History of Interest Rates*. New Brunswick, NJ: Rutgers University Press.

Horwitz, Morton J. 1977. *Transformation of American Law: vol. 1: 1780–1860*. Cambridge, MA: Harvard University Press.

Howe, Mark DeWolfe. 1948. "The Recording of Deeds in the Colony of Massachusetts Bay." *Boston University Law Review* 28: 1–6.
Jones, Alice Hanson. 1980. *Wealth of a Nation to Be: The American Colonies on the Eve of the Revolution*. New York: Columbia University Press.
Kaye, Joel. 2014. *A History of Balance, 1250–1375: The Emergence of a New Model of Equilibrium and its Impact on Thought*. Cambridge: Cambridge University Press.
Lewis, Frank D. 1999. "A Life-Cycle Model of Farm Settlement with Imperfect Capital Markets: An Application to Upper Canada." Dept. of Economics, Queens University, May 1999. Republished in *Canadian Journal of Economics* 34 (2001): 174–95.
Lockridge, Kenneth. 1970. *A New England Town: Dedham, Massachusetts, The First Hundred Years, 1636–1736*. New York: W. W. Norton & Co.
Maitland, Frederic William. [1909; 1936 (2nd ed.)] 2011. *Equity: A Course of Lectures*. Cambridge: Cambridge University Press.
———. 1949. *Equity: A Course of Lectures*, revised ed. Cambridge: Cambridge University Press.
Martin, John Frederick. 1991. *Profits in the Wilderness: Entrepreneurship and the Founding of New England Towns in the Seventeenth Century*. Chapel Hill: University of North Carolina Press.
McCloskey, Donald N. 1991. "The Prudent Peasant: New Findings on Open Fields." *Journal of Economic History* 51(2): 343–355.
McCusker, John. 1978. *Money and Exchange in Europe and America, 1600–1775*. Chapel Hill: University of North Carolina Press.
———. 2005. "Population, by Race and by Colony or Locality, 1610–1780." In *Historical Statistics of the United States*, ed. Susan Carter, Scott Sigmund Gartner, Michael Haines, Alan Olmsted, Richard Sutch, and Gavin Wright, Table JJM.1.6. Cambridge: Cambridge University Press.
Mokyr, Joel. 1985. *Why Ireland Starved: An Analytical and Quantitative Study of Irish Poverty, 1800–1851*, revised ed. London: George Allen and Unwin.
———. 2009. *The Enlightened Economy: An Economic History of Britain, 1700–1850*. New Haven, CT: Yale University Press.
Munro, John. 2001. "The Origins of the Modern Financial Revolution: Responses to Impediments from Church and State in Western Europe, 1200–1600." Toronto: University of Toronto.
Nelson, Benjamin. 1969. *The Idea of Usury: From Tribal Brotherhood to Universal Otherhood*. Chicago: University of Chicago Press.
Ouazad, Amine, and Matthew Kahn. 2019. "Lenders' Response to Climate Risk Has Echoes of Subprime Crisis." *The New York Times*, 28 September 28, B6.
Park, K-Sue. 2016. "Money, Mortgages, and the Conquest of America." *Law & Social Inquiry* 41(4): 1006–35.
Polanyi, Karl. [1944] 2001. *The Great Transformation*, 2nd ed. Boston: Beacon.
Pollock, Frederick, and Frederic William Maitland. [1895] 1898. *History of English Law Before the Time of Edward I*, 2nd ed. Cambridge: Cambridge University Press.
Priest, Claire. 1999. "Colonial Courts and Secured Credit: Early American Commercial Litigation and Shays' Rebellion." *The Yale Law Journal* 108(8): 2413–50.
Rockoff, Hugh. 2001. "'Prodigals and Projectors': An Economic History of Usury Laws in the United States from Colonial Times to World War I." Prepared for

the Conference on Factor Endowments, Labor and Economic Growth in the Americas, 8 June 2001. Rochester, NY: University of Rochester.

Rothenberg, Winifred. 1985. "The Emergence of a Capital Market in Rural Massachusetts, 1730–1838." *Journal of Economic History* 45(4): 781–808.

———. 1992. *From Market-Places to a Market Economy: The Transformation of Rural Massachusetts, 1750–1850*. Chicago: University of Chicago Press.

Shammas, Carole, Marylynn Salmon, and Michel Dahlin. 1987. *Inheritance in America from Colonial Times to the Present*. New Brunswick, NJ: Rutgers University Press.

Skilton, Robert. 1943. "Developments in Mortgage Law and Practice," *Temple University Law Quarterly* 17: 315–84.

Snowden, Kenneth, and Walid Bu-Saba. 1992. "Mortgage Loan Duration before 1940." Unpublished working paper, University of North Carolina at Greensboro, and Boston College.

Stiglitz, Joseph E., and Andrew Weiss. 1981. "Credit Rationing in Markets with Imperfect Information." *American Economic Review* 71(3): 393–410.

Sugarman, David, and Ronnie Warrington. 1995. "Land Law, Citizenship, and the Invention of 'Englishness': The Strange World of Equity of Redemption." In *Early Modern Conceptions of Property*, ed. John Brewer & Susan Staves, 111–43. New York: Routledge.

Sullivan, James. 1801. *The History of Land Titles in Massachusetts*. Boston: I. Andrews and E. T. Andrews. (Reissued by HardPress, 2017.)

Sylla, Richard, Jack W. Wilson, and Robert Wright. 1997. "America's First Securities Markets, 1790–1830: Emergence, Development, Integration." Paper presented at the thirty-seventh annual Cliometrics Conference, 16–18 May. Toronto: University of Toronto.

Turner, R. W. 1931. *The Equity of Redemption: Its Nature, History and Connection with Equitable Estates Generally*. Cambridge: Cambridge University Press.

Weitzman, Martin L. 1974. "Prices vs. Quantities," *Review of Economic Studies* 41(4): 51–65.

Wells, Robert V. 2000. "Life Tables." In *A Population History of North America*, Michael R. Haines and Richard H. Steckel, 159–162. Cambridge: Cambridge University Press, 2000.

Wigmore, John H. 1897. "The Pledge Idea: A Study in Comparative Legal Ideas." *Harvard Law Review* 10(6): 321–50 (Jan. 25); 10(7): 389–417 (Feb. 25); 11(1): 8–39 (April 25).

Wilson, Thomas. 1965. *A Discourse upon Usury*, with an Introduction by R. H. Tawney [1572], Reprint. New York: Augustus M. Kelley.

Wood, Gordon S. 1994. "Inventing American Capitalism." *New York Review of Books* 41(11): 46.

Woodruff, Christopher. 2001. "Review of de Soto's *The Mystery of Capital*." *Journal of Economic Literature* 39 (December): 1215–23.

Wrigley, E. A., and R. S. Schofield. 1997. *English Population History from Family Reconstitution, 1580–1837*. Cambridge: Cambridge University Press.

Wyman, Bruce. 1908. "The Clog on the Equity of Redemption." *Harvard Law Review* 21(7): 459–75.

CHAPTER 11

 # When Land Takes Wing
The Concentration of Holdings and the Human-Animal Dimension

PARKER SHIPTON

Told of a bird with a mortgage, you might well think the speaker was joking. And yet, since it is from joking that so many of our deeper assumptions and subtler insights come to the surface, perhaps we ought to give a moment's attention to such a bird when one comes to our attention below. And to some of the kinds of people who could dream up and recount such a thing. Perhaps, when this is done, neither they nor it will seem quite so strange. Nor will the connection between the human mortgage and other animals.

The literature on mortgaging in social studies still lacks ample case histories of the countless farming people, herding people, and their families who have lost their homes and the land on which they lived. Yes, there are poems, short stories, novels, and some movies with powerful messages out about anxiety, desperation, and farm and home loss – in the vanguard, as usual, ahead of the academic humanists and social scientists. But the latter have begun catching up, as usually happens before too long. The mortgage finance crisis of 2007–2008 saw journalists, social workers, and filmmakers responding first. Memoir writers and scholars came soon after. The coronavirus crisis of 2019 and beyond has been teaching us again, as many people have found themselves without the work that had financed and maintained their homes.

What too few seem to think or remember, though, is that the topic of land, loans, and what links them is not just about humans. If the risks and rewards of borrowing, lending, and mortgaging are to be more fully understood, perhaps it is time to bring some other animals into the picture. This means looking over some fences, so to speak, that have separated economy from disciplines like zoology, agronomy, sociology, and ecology. And maybe using some literature, anthropology, and philosophy, useful at times for connecting such "fields."[1]

This chapter offers a simple contention: humans and other animals are inextricably tied together in the institution of the mortgage. Animals play an important part, moreover, in both the causes and effects of the transfers of control over land and homes that mortgaging can involve, and in further consequences, the ripple effects, of those changes. Elsewhere in this collection I have suggested that animals can play a metaphorical part in human imaginings and discourse about mortgaging, as they do for instance, by implication, in "house hunting," "fishing for a loan," or in the title of a recent book about mortgaging and "predatory bureaucracy." Below we see cases where humans have used specific animal imagery of specific kinds of animals – like the mockingbird – to teach each other lessons about land mortgaging.

Proceeding from fiction to fact, we then look for ways some of the thought, feeling, and actions of humans involved in mortgaging actually resemble any of those found among real animals. New animal science gives us some answers – ones that might a generation ago have seemed preposterous, but are supported by findings becoming well accepted in serious animal science. Human exceptionalism is now receding, though aspects of the mortgage remain distinctively human.

Finally, I suggest something more direct: animals and mortgages play key roles in each other's histories and future, and thus in those of humans too. Those roles range from the pragmatics of plowing to the psychology of pleasure, pain, and emotion. As landholdings become more concentrated into fewer hands, they increasingly involve animals kept in farms, feedlots, coops, and slaughterhouses, and thus the people working in those settings too. Directly or indirectly, they can involve each and all of us, insofar as we participate in markets for food and other animal products, consume the animal products and the chemicals mixed in with them, or remain susceptible to illnesses spread between humans and animals. But we need not go that far to ascertain some basic points.

Human-Animal Overlaps

How natural, we have asked, is mortgaging anyway? Humans seeking to find out about our "true nature" or cultural wellsprings, and who look not to philosophers or theologians for such things, tend to look to biology and ethology, the study of animal behavior, for evolutionary roots. Doing so, I shall suggest, may give us some clues, but few firm proofs, about the wellsprings of human habits in matters like the mortgage.

But let us first look more closely, taking the question piece by piece. Features we might share with other animals – some only lately becoming recognized and accepted as such – include capacities for territorial claiming, lending, trust, and deceit. Another is symbolic communication, including even some understanding of numbers. And there is another: fairness. This, too, is a concept and mode of understanding starting to appear, with careful observation, to be quite common among nonhuman species, as is forgiveness.[2]

Let us start with territory. One of the concepts most hotly debated in anthropology, for understanding humans, is territoriality: a term that sometimes connotes innate possessiveness or defensiveness, but can also have broader, looser meanings. Whether humans, and only certain humans, are the only beings who conceive of owning land, as distinct from just occupying or even possessing it, is an important, basic question. It comes up if we remember that many people, including Native American traditionalists (and New Age ecologists too) like to claim instead that land owns us; and that we owe it just as much as we can hope to hunt, fish, gather, or harvest from it. Or if we remember, as some East African people insist, that we were all conceived or born somewhere, so being without land to run or lie upon is an unnatural, artificial condition.

Territorial claiming and possessiveness are patterns over which humans certainly have no monopoly – although border-drawing, particularly at a distance, is probably our own invention. Most species of mammals and other animals cannot be called territorial, in the sense of defensiveness over turf or area of air or water. Humans, to the extent we can be, are well outnumbered here. But a few species are conspicuously, defensively territorial. Between our genetically two nearest species of kin, chimpanzees and bonobos, chimps are famous for patrolling the edges of their usual ranges or territories, and for getting gruesomely violent against intrusions or raids. They do this much more, indeed, than bonobos do, these latter being better at using matriarchal means and female bodily contact for peacemaking and peacekeeping. Blue wildebeests, when standing alone from age four or five years, turn aggressively territorial, using their horns as well as loud vocalizations for intimidation. Migratory male birds arriving in New England in spring use their songs (we still have no better name for them) as if to announce their presence and claims over place as well as to attract new or erstwhile mates arriving soon afterward. Various other species mark territory – as understood claimed right of range if not precisely bordered turf – by excretion (hippos, rhinos, red foxes) or paw print (dik-diks) and thus scent, or by claw marks (leopards).[3] Perciform jawfish fight over space around burrows, rather as human soldiers sometimes do in a dug-up battlefield. So while territorial exclusiveness and defensiveness characterize only a minority of animal species, they do have striking exemplars.

Comparisons of range and territory size begin to separate humans from other species. True, very few kinds of animals, notably golden eagles, seem to claim territories of many square miles; whereas others, like seagulls, seem to claim exclusive territories only within a few feet of their nests. But if nonhuman species usually called territorial actually conceive of precise lines of areal demarcation (or precise planar divisions, say, for those living more three-dimensionally in air or water) is highly doubtful; things that some humans do start looking more "unnatural."

What about the distribution over spaces claimed? Where animals of a single species vary widely in the amount of range or territory they may seem to claim – as humans so dramatically concentrate their land holdings into few hands, leaving others without in many parts of the world taken over by money and land titling – they usually do so not in the same environment. They tend to do so, that is, only in different places, as responses to very different environmental conditions, as between wetlands and dry, and as seems necessary for defending food supply. Not at all like the more conspicuous human land-accumulators, be these individual, familial, or corporate.[4]

In a few other ways, as when we bring in a time dimension, some particular kinds of animals resemble some humans in ways they treat territory. Wolves, for instance, are perceived to defend area formerly held by their parents and perhaps even ancestors.[5] But these, again, are outliers in nature. Most species of mammals (including wolves) seem to prefer the company of their conspecifics or mix with members of other species (whether for safety or comfort) to remaining alone in open space, for even short times, let alone long periods of time.[6]

Let us look next at lending. Is it really only humans who do this? You provide a dog with a ball; you could call that a kind of loan (with you as owner and the dog as possessor). The dog brings you the ball or a stick to throw: another kind of loan, you could say, with an evident expectation of return or of some continuing back-and-forth.[7] In this and numerous other ways, we can see that some animals are able to plan, just as many dogs will hold back on eating their full bowl when they know their humans will not return to feed them for a long while.

Animals other than humans were long deemed incapable of numerous cognitive functions like abstraction. Many people doubted in the past about planning, and carrying out complex sequences of actions, as well as of value-laden ones like begging, reciprocity, fairness, and deceit, and emotions like joy, sorrow, and grieving – all of which relate to borrowing, lending, land, belonging, and mortgaging. Upon more studies with mammals like apes, cetaceans, and elephants, as well as rats and mice, and with birds like corvids and parrots, things have changed fast within our lifetimes. The human-centric assumptions (human exceptionalism) about these abilities too have been quickly crumbling (see Dahaene et al. 2005; Dawkins 1993; de Waal 2016; Marzluff and Angell 2012; and Safina 2015 for a few examples of recent findings). We now need to be much more careful about such statements about human uniqueness, though our uniquely human language capacities do such a good job with deceit.

A mortgage always involves a mix of trust and mistrust, since if there were perfect trust no "collateral" land title or co-signature would be required. A lender trusts a borrower to repay so as not to put them through the hassles of foreclosure; a borrower trusts the lender to be reasonable when the time comes to extend a deadline. Both may have to trust witnesses or trust a judge or mediator to make a fair call. Trust is not something humans alone can claim. It is demonstrable among cleaner wrasses (small maritime fishes) who pluck parasites from much larger fishes, monkeys in zoos who clean hippo mouths, and the like: "We underestimate them, as we do most animals." But we humans are heavily invested in it. "Trust is the lubricant that makes a society run smoothly," as leading primatologist Frans de Waal writes; and many experiments have shown that "our species is more trusting than predicted by rational-choice theory." "We value trust to an extreme degree" (2009: 166, 167, 169).

Even if we mistrust other humans, we trust the land where they have lived, even if evicted, not to be poisoned, pit-trapped, or land-mined. Nor do other animals seem to booby-trap the homes or spaces out of which others force them. "Nature's real-estate changes hands all the time," writes de Waal; "potential homes range from holes drilled by woodpeckers to abandoned burrows" and hermit crabs changing shells in which to live as they grow. "Hermit crabs are not deal-makers, though, and in fact have no qualms evicting owners by force" (de Waal 2009: 170). In this last respect, they may seem to resemble creditors foreclosing on mortgages.

Here one might object that only humans understand numbers, and that mortgaging depends on numerical calculation. On the surface, the objection is reasonable enough. Experimental evidence is coming forth, though, that some other animals including rats can make quantitative calculations, for instance about multiple, shifted tunnels – beyond what most until recently imagined. They do not, admittedly, do math to the extent "Clever Hans" seemed to reach before it was proved that that famous horse was responding instead to subtle, unconscious gestural cues of his owner before crowds in shows. They do, though, demonstrate cognition significant and surprising anyway, as Oxford zoologist Marian Stamp Dawkins describes. (Dawkins 1993: 115–18; see also de Waal 2016). Others, including nutcrackers, some corvids (jays, crows, magpies, ravens), and other birds, seem able to remember caches of foods in the hundreds or thousands, and to visit them in ordered sequences (called trap-lining), as if not to duplicate effort and waste energy on ones where they have visited lately. This compares, in its way, to what lenders (or debt-purchasers) do when calculating whom to foreclose upon next, basing decisions on the sequence in which these borrowed. True, the animals are not counting money or months, as humans do – but they are doing some quite sophisticated quantitative and temporal reasoning. They are evolved to do it; their lives depend on it.

Where humans do split off from other species, and probably from all of them, is in monetization and in concepts like letter-of-law contracts and enduring debt: debts that may be recorded and held for decades or even, in some cultures, deemed heritable for generations. These are not things we have learned from the rest of nature. They are concepts and habits we have thought up and taught ourselves.[8]

Nonhuman animals did not invent the mortgage. We humans did, spinning imaginative creations of intellect and economic fabrications out of boundaries, pledges, contracts, loans, deadlines, laws, market securities, and financial derivatives. Most of these creations, when combined into such constructions as the mortgage, are ideas quite alien to the minds of other creatures, if not also still to many humans – maybe even most humans.[9] Alien and, as we have seen throughout this volume, not usually accepted as quite moral or fair.

Let us not, then, jump right to a conclusion that we learned all these things from other animals: that they taught us to be mortgagers or mortgagees. To look to species other than our own for indications about our true "inner" nature is, as I have suggested in these paragraphs, an endeavor likely to disappoint, especially when the questions move beyond comparison to causation. Even the species most closely related to us (chimps and bonobos) have evolved six million years on their own trajectories since their ancestry split from ours. These and others vary too widely in their propensities — to form gangs, aggregate into crowds, or disperse; to mark territory or not; to defend it or not — to say that we humans are in essence territorial or non-territorial beings by "descent" and thus by nature. Moreover, as we are quickly learning, many species, including primate species and large-brained ones, have too much cultural (as well as "personality") variability of their own, too much that is locally taught or emulated, too much that is "the way we do it here" themselves — to offer much firm clue for any other answers than "it's complex" or "it depends."[10]

To be more certain about what human customs like land mortgaging have to do with other animals, we need to begin taking other approaches. Let us take the fictional one waiting in the wings, so to speak — and then a more factual one.

When Land Takes Wing

A mortgage can be tragic, in its general tendencies and its experience for property losers and victims of eviction. But a story about it can also be comic at the same time, in that way that myths and legends can turn one transaction, one emotion, or one species into another. Here is that story from the southeast of the United States, relayed by ethnographer Shepard Krech from the Chickasaw people (and maybe also from African-American people nearby). Its subject is the mockingbird: the polyglot trickster, imitator, and master thief — also called, in their tongue, the *foshato'chi'* (mortgage-bird). "Mr. Mockingbird was conceived as the 'Master Bird,' because he was present in the 'first times,' because he sang, fought, and was a year-round resident — and because he figured significantly in financial affairs and financial ruin." In one story, recounting that in days when there was a pot of gold hidden underground beneath every stump, and when free African Americans were helping others unload their debts, Mr. Mockingbird did this too. He kept "recklessly" signing them on and signing them on, until his portfolio of debts was so valuable that the state insured him and threatened any who killed him with a fine of five dollars. "But Mr. Mockingbird, the most 'impudente' bird, denied that he was insured or that he cared, and he skipped and sang away. He had put his name on 'all the birds' notes' — on all their mortgages" (Krech 2012: 79). Like trickster figure animals, like derivatives traders.

The mortgage and the mockingbird may still seem far apart. Indeed they are. But it is not as though nonhuman animals had nothing to do with mortgaging. Nor does it stop with metaphoric uses, as in the phrase "predatory lending," increasingly used by scholarly critics of mortgaging.[11] The topic becomes more real still.

Let us pause to think about it a moment. What determines whether a borrower on a farm or ranch with animals is able to repay a loan on a schedule? Here are a few factors: whether the animals are owned and eaten or buried at home, or whether they are borrowed, lent, rented, or sold. Whether they are able to pull a plow or are too young, old, or sick. Whether they have just stepped into a hole and broken a leg, or maybe no less vital, whether their trainer or handler has shown up and done the job. Whether the artificial insemination is working, whether their milk is producing, whether someone who lent the cows or horses has just come to collect them. Whether the animals can carry a backload of human rider(s), crops, or other trade goods or pull a cart of them from market. Whether the slaughterhouse managers from the meat company honor their agreement to buy or visit the farm with a mobile slaughter truck, and whether the transporters transport the goods. Whether buyers in the markets are paying the price for meat, milk, leather, or wool the farmer expected when signing the glittering loan contract. Or whether a new synthetic substitute for leather, milk, or wool has just come onto the market to make the farm's selloff redundant. Or whether half the herd of cattle, flock of sheep, or barn-full of turkeys has just died in an animal disease (an epizootic) or a barn fire. In more ways than one can count, animals affect repayment prospects.

How many ways, then, can circumstances this varied not combine, producing boom or bust on the farm? And how likely is it that a farmer seeking to postpone foreclosure will able to convey this mixture of circumstances to the lender's collection agent? And would that agent be able to explain it all, specifically, accurately, and persuasively, to the manager – or, via that person and a chain of intermediaries, to the lending company's board of directors (who may live at a distance and may have never set foot on a farm)?

The Ripple—Past the Human Kind and Ken

Now to look at it the other way around. Many of those farm or ranch creatures and the ecosystems they inhabit are affected by land titling, by land transfers, and thus also by the mortgage system. This is true wherever mortgaging touches farming, and wherever there are animals, large or small, living on farms. Mortgaging is one of the main ways farming people leave the lands they farm and vice versa. Dispossession and eviction are hard to measure, as noted earlier, in terms of percentages of land sales in which they play a part; but they have had much to do with the drop in the percentage of Americans living on farms between 1900 and 2003 from about 40 percent to about 2 percent[12] – a sobering thought.

When small-scale family farms are yanked away from their owners and dwellers and relinquished, and when banks, other lending companies, and auctioneers then sell them off to larger agribusinesses and land speculators, a cascade of changes flows out over the landscape and those living in it. Newer, bigger, more crowded shelters are constructed, fewer and farther apart. Feeding, milking, and egg collecting get mechanized, seldom with pleasant effects on the animals forced into them. Planning horizons shorten, from multigenerational to annual and quarterly duration, as shareholders and executives answering to them have lately seemed to prefer. New chemicals – fertilizers, pesticides, herbicides, fungicides – with more damaging longer-term effects are likely to be applied, while at the other end, manure and effluent chemicals get pooled into ponds that run risks of runoff and noxious flooding.

More immediately, farm animals who once had individual names, habits, and (yes) even personalities – known, tended, and cared for more individually and closely by their owners – become animals merely given numbers instead (rather like prisoners, other slaves, or factory parts?) – mere inputs. Living, breathing, thinking, and feeling beings become units of production, likely to be pumped with growth hormones (carcinogenic, for humans later) and fed, sheltered, and shipped as cheaply as possible – commoditized – while still sentient, still conscious. Now, though, they are valued for little more than the quantity and quality of milk, meat, hides, and other body parts turned into many "by-products" – cosmetics from their fat, glue from their bones, and the like.

Not just their names and shelters, but just about everything in their daily conditions changes in these larger, corporate agribusinesses. Their feeding, brought indoors from grazing grounds, becomes more monotonous in diet, more forced in method, more automated, and more distantly scheduled in delivery. Milking too, increasingly mechanized, gets timed now more by clock schedules and the formulae of operations research, and less by the noticed condition of udders, sounds vocalized, or other bodily communication. The animal movements get more restricted and regimented, more out of touch with their own family sentiments or preferred herd sizes, and food enticements or gentle pokes for moving animals give way to electric prods.

Whether the creatures be kept now in solitary confinement in the dark for life (as with many veal calves), kept standing or crippled in their own urine and ammonia fumes, life in factory farms is not much like life around human homes. The animals' contact with real humans becomes hastier, more punctuated with prodding, branding, ear cutting, and electric shocking, albeit with still some hope of emergency care for some. Their bodies are injected with more growth hormones and antibiotics, their offspring yanked from them earlier, more suddenly, more callously. In short, their treatment and their lives change radically. More of the production process – much of the living and most of the killing – takes place behind closed doors: visitors, cameras, and recorders are barred from entering. Enough has been written about what happens there to animals (and, not just coincidentally, to workers acting upon them) – sometimes stretching words to their limits, sometimes challenging imagination – so that little needs to be added to it here. From the owners' and managers' perspectives, the heightened secrecy is not without reason.[13] It is well known, too, that large agribusinesses have powerful lobby groups (political action committees, PACs) in capital cities, ones that keep legislators from passing strict laws for farm animal care and well-being, and for allowing observer access to processing facilities.

The Dam of Denial: Cracking Through

Once these concerns bearing on animal minds and lives did not matter so much to scientists, social scientists, and philosophers. Now they do. Increasing numbers are refusing to dismiss them as irrelevancies. Or as kidding, a word that now, in a new light, takes its tragic as well as the comic sense. We may begin now to think more seriously, for instance, about what it means for caged-in, electric-prodded, milked, and slaughter-destined ruminants like goats, sheep, and cow mothers to have their suckling young yanked away from them, at younger and younger ages, with each one's bleating – harbinger of stress and trauma to come later for both – that may or may not be heard. Animals are docked of tails, torn of horns, or shorn of beaks without anesthetics. Male chicks are torn from their mothers too and killed (often put into a grinder), except for the few needed to sire new generations – they too may not be heard, or listened to, like the song of the mockingbird with whom we began.

The change in professional attitudes has come hard and slowly, over about the past four decades. The openness to animal minds and experience has not been altogether new. Charles Darwin (studying dogs, for instance; 1872) and Lewis Henry Morgan (studying beavers, their psyches, and environment-altering; 1868) devoted much attention to animal minds in the nineteenth century (as had others since Pythagoras and before). But the nearly century-long reign of Pavlovian and Skinnerian behaviorism, whose adherents sought so strenuously and dogmatically to reduce animals to stimulus-and-response mechanisms – running mazes, pecking levers, and receiving food pellets and electric shocks as positive or negative reinforcements of actions – cordoned off mention of thought or feeling among nonhuman beings, consigned animal feeling to silence as a taboo topic. Scientists and social scientists were debarred from publication, their careers damaged, with accusations of "anthropomorphism" each time they even mentioned the most common of sentiments like pain, pleasure, fear, or anxiety – and it still happens. But these are sentiments that we can now see clearly are common to all birds and mammals (and many other creatures besides). They are sentiments deriving from senses and from analogous brain and body parts, with neural and hormonal similarities too many to list.

Now that the sea change has begun its surge, a new and broader awareness has been coming to light. Now it is the neglect of kinship and bodily commonalities between humans and other animals (in skeletal structure, circulatory and respiratory function, and not least important, neural circuitry and hormonal makeup and function), the blinding from the clear signs of thought and feeling – the dismissal of real and mounting evidence – that are starting to be recognized instead as bad science. Just as the psychological, economic, and political causes of humans' economic and legal decisions, and all their neural and hormonal dimensions, are opening up for experimental and observational science, so too are the farther reaches of their political and economic effects, on humans and other beings, opening up again for cultural, philosophical, and other inquiry.

Human thought about other animals, especially about farm animals, is rife with inconsistencies, neglect, and denials. How many of us would be upset, how many of our children traumatized, if we but saw the conditions under which just one of the farm animals we consume lived and died – but are not too troubled each time a bag of groceries comes home, the meat appears on a plate, or the fork enters the mouth? But these inconsistencies and hypocrisies are themselves becoming the objects of careful study.[14] And in a field much less male-led than the lab science of the behaviorist period or the economics of the same decades – indeed largely pioneered in many respects by women scholars in disciplines ranging from biology to linguistics to philosophy – the studies of agronomy, animal sentience, farm and produce economies, nutrition, ecology, and ethics and morality are becoming more systemically connected. They are becoming linked, too, to the social and cultural studies that aim for a broader overview, taking animal as well as human well-being into consideration.[15]

Flight between Fields

So the gate is now opening for a new and different kind of study of land, finance, and mortgaging. Now, with new precedents coming together in many disciplines and beyond the academy, research can reach deeper into history, more probing in exploration of motives and methods, and farther reaching in terms of both causes and effects being studied.

Expect a lag. The published economic literature on farm mortgaging, in the mainstream academic journals in North America and elsewhere, is notable for scarcely mentioning people who borrow and repay or who do not and get dispossessed and evicted. It seldom even contains mention, either, of farms as homes, another term likely to elicit empathy, sympathy, anxiety, and other emotion. Never mind mention of the lives and minds of the nonhuman beings so directly affected, as already noted, by the changes of ownership and control over land and estates in foreclosures. These things will come as awareness of mortgage victimization and communication about animal lives affected rises.

It will take time. Just as behaviorist science held out for decades after pioneering women had lived with gorillas and chimps, embargoing talk of sentience and consciousness, so the mainstream economists still seeking scientific status may continue their denial of human and animal participants, with real lives, as part of their subjects, and keep discouraging and preventing their mention. But that dam, too, will break. It has already broken in fiction. In Charles Nordhoff and James Norman Hall's "A Cockfight in Tahiti" ([1940] 1994) for instance, a fighting rooster so hopefully (but vainly) named "mortgage lifter" – as though his winnings might lessen his owner's worries – has been in print for generations. (Alas, after raising confident hopes, this fictitious rooster lost his mortal combat in the ring, driving his owner's family deeper into poverty – as if to bring home, once more, the message of what a mortgage can so often mean.) For social studies and sciences too, land, animals, and human ideas like mortgaging do belong in the same books, the same paragraphs, the same sentences and questions. Once such mentions no longer seem so unusual or surprising, studies and publications on these things together are likely to multiply quickly.

That is what the longer view does to our thinking, does for our teaching and training. We remember to consider the many times and places where religious, legal, and moral leaders have rejected and condemned lending at interest and mortgaging as unfair gambles, and we ask whether they were so crazy to raise doubts. We slow down, back up, and notice that enticement for entrustment leads too often to entrapment, willful or not. We come to recognize that ideas like "realized assets" or "repossession" can also mean shock, family fragmentation, and enduring trauma. We recall that mortgage-backed securities and other fictitious financial concoctions, bank overreach, sporadic crises of confidence, and occasional but sudden, unpredicted market crashes threaten the very markets and financial systems whose managers and innovators gave rise to them in the first place. We take account of how small-scale, family-run farms can vanish and reappear in just a generation or two as new corporate and conglomerate agribusinesses that cover the landscape, purporting to manage farming and herding from a distance. We recall that the ecological, physical, and mental conditions they foment are new ones in world history, and newly threatening to more than our kind. We remember that many other animals (some with lives as long, brains as large, and abilities in this or that way no less impressive) have found so many ways to live their lives – on this our shared planet, for countless generations – somehow without the deadline-tied pledge, the mortgage, or anything of the sort. Is there, then, perhaps something that needs rethinking in the assumption, so common still among development optimists and program designers, that the mortgaging of land is so normal, natural, and necessary? Or might we still have something to learn – or to remember – from the other animals and the people who have lived their lives well enough without it?

Parker Shipton is Professor of Anthropology and African Studies, Boston University. Educated at Cornell, Oxford, and Cambridge, he has taught at Harvard and consulted for several international aid agencies. His books include *Bitter Money*, *The Nature of Entrustment*, *Mortgaging the Ancestors*, and *Credit between Cultures*. He has edited the book series *Peoples of Africa* and the *Blackwell Anthologies in Social and Cultural Anthropology* and co-edited *On the Human*, an online interdisciplinary forum of the National Humanities Center. A former President of the Association for Africanist Anthropology, he has received the Messenger-Chalmers Prize (Cornell), Curl Prize (Royal Anthropological Institute), and African Studies Association (Herskovits) Book Award.

NOTES

1. A fuller account of mortgaging and its cultural and political-economic dimensions over time, in an East African setting and rather more generally, can be found in Parker Shipton (2009); and a fuller account of human-animal entrustments in that context in another volume (2007). The present chapter is a first attempt at a bridging disciplines in terms of animals and the mortgage. But it is also an attempt to bridge observations from very rural locations, mostly in the 1980s and 1990s, and information gained from later reading in cities. Further contributions to the literature from authors with more or more recent experience in farms, ranches, animal transport facilities, feeding and fattening centers, or slaughterhouses – and with the people who work in and on them – are thus much welcomed. The earlier Shipton chapter in this volume cites some such literature. It also links culture and political economy with cultural linguistics, showing how metaphor inflects our understanding of mortgages by setting different frames of reference and evoking different kinds of motives, means, and outcomes.
2. On concepts of fairness as they are emerging in experimental studies of animals other than humans (as well as plenty more "anecdotal" evidence), see Frans de Waal (2009: chapter 6, especially 182–89, 195–200). On forgiveness, see for instance de Waal (2005). As he notes, "Forgiveness is sometimes touted as uniquely human, even uniquely Christian, but it may be a natural tendency for cooperative animals" (2005: 144). Much more on animal forgiveness can be found by word searches using also "peacemaking" and "reconciliation," as used for instance in Carl Safina (2020: 310–18, 323–24, and passim).
3. Some researchers have recently suggested that domestic dogs who urinate on particular, conspicuous places (trees, fire hydrants) and countermark in response to each other's leavings are not marking territory, as often supposed – but instead informing other dogs about themselves, for instance, about their health, height, sex, and/or phase in the estrus cycle. See Alexandra Horowitz (2017: 16–17). As she writes, in nonhuman animal territorial marking, "the means and placement are wonderfully more complicated than human flag-leaving" (2017: 14).
4. How far can it go? Consider the privately owned King Ranch in Texas, currently consisting of some 825,000 acres, spanning portions of six counties. (Its current owner has also been owner of the Los Angeles Rams football team.) That there is poverty in Texas and the surrounding areas hardly needs mention.
5. That wolves, a "fission-fusion" species in their aggregations, often defend territories of their matriarchs and families (but not usually from humans) is commonly found; that they defend those of their ancestors is harder to prove. For more on wolf minds and communications, see Carl Safina (2015: Part Two,

"Howls of Wolves," 137–240: esp. 145, 151–52, 222–23 on their territoriality). For more general discussions of territoriality, touching on many species as well as humans, a standard source (and source of debate) is Robert Ardrey ([1966] 1997); and see its Foreword by Irven deVore ([1966] 1997), emphasizing not just the hereditary but also socially and culturally acquired propensities of many species including humans. In my view, the book's title *The Territorial Imperative* might as well have been named *The Territorial Alternative*. A recent, more biologically based treatment of humanity's best and worst in spatial (and other) behavior, by a brain scientist and baboon specialist, is Robert Sapolsky (2018). A popular source on particular animal types is the *Species* Podcast of Macken Murphy "Species | The Podcast About Animals." Retrieved 25 March 2021 from speciespodcast.com.

6. This is of course true of humans too. Never mind the "solitary natural man" of Hobbes, Locke, Rousseau, and other social contract theorists – a pure fiction. Even Emerson, in his time "alone" by Walden Pond, let us not forget, made world news and textbook entries for the time, when in fact, he had still been into Concord town on weekends to visit his friends or buy nails.

7. Other transfers too might be classed as loans. You may offer that dog a fancy collar while assuming that if the dog dies, you will confer it then upon your next. Or you might offer feed to a cow, expecting for your part something later in return: the milk, and maybe the hide and more.

8. David Graeber's ambitious treatment of the history of debt (2014) is among the more thought-provoking. It brings our historic activities and obligations up before us in the mirror as something maybe not as "natural" as many have thought. His later work on bureaucracy (2016) can reinforce that point. Not being natural need not imply that holding others in debt or insisting on repayment be morally wrong to insist upon (any more than a charitable check or its cashing is wrong), but could be one interpretation.

9. Among the deeper treatments of what humans and other species share and do not share in symbolic communication, and in the brain and hormone functions that support it, is Terrence Deacon's tome (1997). This and his other writings seriously connect mind with matter and show how much these interdepend, and this one shows ways that nonhuman animal brains and modes of communication compare and contrast with our own. Among his main themes is that we humans have fashioned social and cultural environments, beyond those of natural selection, such that we can survive and reproduce only by emulating and learning from others. To the example of language, we could add the interrelated ones of landholding, finance, and law.

10. Some of the more comprehensive sources on the cultures of nonhuman animals – that is, in brief, their socially taught and learned values, attitudes, habits, and the limits of these, beyond or only conditioned by genetic proclivities – are those of Marian Stamp Dawkins (1993), Frans de Waal (2001), and Carl Safina (2015 and especially 2000); see also Robert Sapolsky (2018) and some of his other works. These compile many scientific and experiential findings and treat many species.

11. As in Noelle Stout (2019), where "predatory lending" and even "predatory bureaucracy," the latter in the title, are master tropes used to describe mortgage

machinations and misfortunes among Californians in the early 2000s. These reflect a longer-term trend in social and cultural anthropology toward skeptical interpretations of both capitalistic enterprise and bureaucracy as the discipline has increasingly tackled more economic and legal topics, including international economic development. See also, for instance, David Graeber (2014, 2016) again on debt and bureaucracy; and political scientist, historian, and anthropologist James Scott (2009) on continuing struggles against bureaucratic rule, especially in Southeast Asia (and his other works on the same in other contexts). Susanne Soederberg (2018) discusses mortgaging and evictions more specifically, but on global scale.

12. For these and related figures on the collapse of family farming in the United States and the takeover by industrial agriculture and animal keeping, see Bill Vorley (2003: 3), Peter Singer and Jim Mason (2006: 142). Figures comparable to these – sometimes reaching over 50 percent in 1900 and down by the century's end to 2 or 3 percent – have become fairly common. One caution is that the definition of a farm is quite flexible, given that many people who farm do other things as well for their livelihoods, and that some farms lie fallow for years. Still, the better part of United States farmland is now owned by just a handful of agribusinesses, while animals from other agribusinesses have been funneling to large-scale meat processors. *National Provisioner* lists annually the top one hundred meat producers in the United States, with some specific breakdown of their activities and products. "2021 Top 100 Meat and Poultry Processors." *National Provisioner* online. Retrieved 3 August 2021 from https://www.provisioneronline.com/2021-top-100-meat-and-poultry-processors.

13. An alarming exposition and analysis of both concealment and surveillance, paradoxically, in industrial animal killing and processing is that of Timothy Pachirat (2011). For other treatments of the combined abuse of animals and workers as reasons for secrecy, see Josh Berson (2019), Jonathan Safran Foer (2010), Barbara King (2017), Erin McKenna (2016), Peter Singer and Jim Mason (2006), Steve Striffler (2007), Anglea Stuesse (2016), Kendall Thu and E. Paul Durrenberger (1998), and Brad Weiss (2016). Exposés like "Meet Your Meat," made by activist group People for the Ethical Treatment of Animals (PETA) undercover in barns, coops, and slaughterhouses, succeed in gaining attention largely by focusing on individual animals. But then consider the ratios of cattle, sheep, goat, or pig minds to the number of human minds on any given farm, ranch, feedlot, or day's throughput in a slaughterhouse.

14. For psychological discussions of our striking, often paradoxical inconsistencies in attitudes and emotions about animals kept, killed, and eaten, see for starters Hal Herzog (2011) and Melanie Joy (2010). The roles of selective exposure, selective memory, and what social psychologist Leon Festinger earlier called "cognitive dissonance" and its reduction, for continuing self-esteem, remain recurrent themes in these and other psychological works on the topic. (For an anthropologist's bridge to these topics too, see John Edward Terrell and Gabriel Stowe Terrell 2020.) Jeremy Bentham's contention that every being with the capacity for suffering has rights has never lost relevance for philosophical discussion. It figures in the interest-based approach of Peter Singer (Singer and Mason 2006), the rights-based approaches of Tom Regan

(2004), and the potentiality-fulfillment approach of many neo-Aristotelians including Martha Nussbaum (Sunstein and Nussbaum 2005).

15. The past half century's gender shift in the scholarship involving and promoting animal well-being, toward women's acknowledged leadership, is one I would trace to the time of the famous work of primatologists Dyan Fossey, Jane Goodall, and the many they influenced, as well as to more general improvement in women's access to higher education and research of many kinds. For a moral-philosophical and multidisciplinary reader of human-animal studies, see Linda Kalof and Amy Fitzgerald (2016). For just a few volumes emblematic of the broader, more integrative "animal turn," devoting more attention to farmed animals, in anthropology, see Samantha Hurn (2012) and Barbara King (2018); in sociology, Amy Fitzgerald (2015); and in moral philosophy, Erin McKenna (2016). Other, more stridently activist-minded scholars offering socio-linguistic approaches to terms like "livestock" and "meat" include Carol J. Adams and Josephine Donovan (1995) and Joan Dunayer (2001). An especially successful pragmatic activist reformer for the interests of industrially farmed and slaughtered animals, though not a more thoroughgoing abolitionist like some of the others mentioned here, is Temple Grandin (2006).

REFERENCES

Adams, Carol J., and Josephine Donovan, eds. 1995. *Animals and Women: Feminist Theoretical Explorations*. Durham, NC: Duke University Press.

Ardrey, Robert. [1966] 1997. *The Territorial Imperative: A Personal Inquiry into the Animal Origins of Property and Nations*. New York: Kodansha International.

Berson, Josh. 2019. *The Meat Question: Animals, Humans, and the Deep History of Food*. Cambridge, MA: MIT Press.

Dahaene, Sanislas, Jean-René Duhamel, Marc D. Hauser, and Geacomo Rozolatti, eds. 2005. *From Monkey Brain to Human Brain: A Fyssen Foundation Symposium*. Cambridge, MA: MIT Press.

Darwin, Charles. 1872. *The Expression of the Emotions in Man and Animals*. London: John Murray.

Dawkins, Marian Stamp. 1993. *Through Our Eyes Only? The Search for Animal Consciousness*. Oxford: W.H. Freeman.

Deacon, Terrence. 1997. *The Symbolic Species: The Co-evolution of Language and the Human Brain*. New York: Penguin Books.

deVore, Irven. [1966] 1997. Foreword to *The Territorial Imperative: A Personal Inquiry into the Animal Origins of Property and Nations* by Robert Ardrey, ix–xviii. New York: Kodansha International.

de Waal, Frans. 2001. *The Ape and the Sushi Master: Cultural Lessons of a Primatologist*. New York: Basic Books.

———. 2005. *Our Inner Ape: A Leading Primatologist Explains Why We Are Who We Are*. New York: Riverhead Books (imprint of Penguin Books).

———. 2009. *The Age of Empathy: Nature's Lessons for a Kinder Society*. New York: Three Rivers Press.

———. 2016. *Are We Smart Enough to Know How Smart Animals Are?* New York: W.W. Norton.
Dunayer, Joan. 2001. *Animal Equality: Language and Liberation.* New York: Lantern Books.
Fitzgerald, Amy. 2015. *Animals as Food: (Re)connecting Production, Processing, Consumption, and Impacts.* East Lansing: Michigan State University Press.
Foer, Jonathan Safran. 2010. *Eating Animals.* Boston: Back Bay Books.
Graeber, David. 2014. *Debt: The First 5,000 Years.* New York: Melville House.
———. 2016. *Utopia of Rules: On Technology, Stupidity, and the Secret Joys of Bureaucracy.* New York: Melville House.
Grandin, Temple. 2006. *Animals in Translation.* New York: Harcourt.
Herzog, Hal. [2010] 2011. *Some We Love, Some We Hate, Some We Eat: Why It's So Hard to Think Straight about Animals.* New York: Harper Perennial (imprint of HarperCollins).
Horowitz, Alexandra. 2017. *Being a Dog: Following the Dog into the World of Smell.* New York: Scribner.
Hurn, Samantha. 2012. *Humans and Other Animals: Cross-Cultural Perspectives on Human-Animal Interactions.* London: Pluto Press.
Joy, Melanie. 2010. *Why We Love Dogs, Eat Pigs, and Wear Cows: An Introduction to Carnism, the Belief System that Allows Us to Eat Some Animals and Not Others.* San Francisco: Conari Press (imprint of Red Wheel/Weiser).
Kalof, Linda, and Amy Fitzgerald, eds. [2007] 2016. *The Animals Reader: The Essential Classic and Contemporary Writings.* London: Bloomsbury Academic.
King, Barbara. 2018. *Personalities on the Plate: The Lives and Minds of Animals We Eat.* Chicago: University of Chicago Press.
Krech, Shepard III. 2012. "Indigenous Ethnoörnithology in the American South." In *Indigenous Knowledge and the Environment in Africa and North America*," ed. David P. Gordon and Shepard Krech III, 69–93. Athens: Ohio University Press.
Marzluff, John, and Tony Angell. 2012. *Gifts of the Crow: How Perception, Emotion, and Thought Allow Smart Birds to Behave Like Humans.* New Haven, CT: Yale University Press.
McKenna, Erin. 2016. *Livestock: Food, Fiber, Friends.* Athens: University of Georgia Press.
Morgan, Lewis Henry. 1868. *The American Beaver and His Works.* Philadelphia, PA: J.B. Lippincott.
Nordhoff, Charles, and James Norman Hall. [1940] 1994. "A Cockfight in Tahiti." In *Cockfight: A Casebook*, ed. Alan Dundes, 30–37. Madison: University of Wisconsin Press.
Pachirat, Timothy. 2011. *Every Twelve Seconds: Industrial Slaughter and the Politics of Sight.* Durham, NC: Duke University Press.
Regan, Tom. 2004. *Empty Cages: Facing the Challenge of Animal Rights.* Lanham, MD: Rowman and Littlefield.
Safina, Carl. 2015. *Beyond Words: What Animals Think and Feel.* New York: Picador (imprint of Henry Holt and Co.).
———. 2020. *Becoming Wild: How Animal Cultures Raise Families, Create Beauty, and Achieve Peace.* New York: Henry Holt.

Sapolsky, Robert. 2018. *Behave: The Biology of Humans at Our Best and Worst*. New York: Penguin.

Scott, James C. 2009. *The Art of Not Being Governed: An Anarchist History of Upland Southeast Asia*. New Haven, CT: Yale University Press.

Shipton, Parker. 2007. *The Nature of Entrustment: Intimacy, Exchange, and the Sacred in Africa*. New Haven, CT: Yale University Press.

———. 2009. *Mortgaging the Ancestors: Ideologies of Attachment in Africa*. New Haven, CT: Yale University Press.

Singer, Peter, and Jim Mason. 2006. *The Ethics of What We Eat: Why Our Food Choices Matter*. Emmaus, PA: Rodale.

Soederberg, Susanne. 2018. "Evictions: A Global Capitalist Phenomenon." *Development and Change* 49(2): 286–301. https://doi.org/10.1111/dech.12383.

Stout, Noelle. 2019. *Dispossessed: How Predatory Bureaucracy Foreclosed on the Middle Class*. Berkeley: University of California Press.

Striffler, Steve. 2007. *Chicken: The Dangerous Transformation of America's Favorite Food*. New Haven, CT: Yale University Press.

Stuesse, Angela. 2016. *Scratching Out a Living: Latinos, Race, and Work in the Deep South*. Berkeley: University of California Press.

Sunstein, Cass, and Martha Nussbaum, eds. 2005. *Animal Rights: Current Debates and New Directions*. New York: Oxford University Press.

Terrell, John Edward, and Gabriel Stowe Terrell. 2020. *Understanding the Human Mind: Why You Shouldn't Trust What Your Brain is Telling You*. New York: Routledge.

Thu, Kendall M., and E. Paul Durrenberger, eds. 1998. *Pigs, Profits, and Rural Communities*. Albany: SUNY Press.

Vorley, Bill. 2003. *Food, Inc*. London: International Institute for Environment and Development.

Weiss, Brad. 2016. *Real Pigs: Shifting Values in the Field of Local Pork*. Durham, NC: Duke University Press.

CONCLUSION

 Envoi

PARKER SHIPTON

This has been a book of perspectives. Its subject, the mortgaging of land, has long been one of trial and error in many places and of uncertainty and debate. The angles taken by the authors of this book have been theoretical, practical, and personal. They are taken from many centuries, and from several continents. They come from a variety of contemporary scholarly disciplines bearing on human economy. The viewpoints represented include some historical, anthropological, economic, and legal. None of these disciplines, we insist, captures the land mortgage reality in its entirety – far from it. This is a matter for geographers, political scientists, and linguists; for agronomists, zoologists, and botanists alike – all of which must mean philosophers and others too. But most of all, perhaps, it is for people able to question and hop the disciplinary fences that can make such strained conclusions, such parodies of reason and breaches of common sense, into which the disciplines so often funnel us as scholars.

Humans farmed for over ten thousand years before any records of the mortgage appeared. Its invention is not a natural part of animal, agricultural, or necessarily even urban life. Rather than being a necessary or inevitable step on the way to whatever is called "civilization," we have shown that mortgaging can sometimes be publicly resisted (as in the Irish case here) or banned with regime changes, revolutions, and changes in official ideology; and that it can come back reinvented (as in the Romanian case). We have focused mostly on the principles and processes involved, in their variety. We have looked back at the old distinction between the *vif*gage, the "living pledge," and the *mort*gage, the "dead pledge." We have presented various ways people have thought about mortgaging, attempted to carry it out and live with it, and resisted, abolished, or restarted it. We have looked into the pledging of land in relation to other forms of loan "security," including the bondage of humans themselves – often the very epitome of *in*security for persons so treated as loan "collateral." Some forms of lending on land security have been short-term, others longer;

some tightly deadlined, some more flexible; and in some, as once in parts of Ghana, the land has been redeemable to pledgers or mortgagors after loss. We have considered landholding as not just possession or property, or even as just livelihood, but also to many, as home, social life, and belonging: the kinds of aspects that make space, place, and territory human in so many ways. We suggest there has been much change over time in what mortgaging means and how it works, and that the changes are continuing. Who has control of the land for the duration of a loan – the access to work it, the right to eat or profit from it, the power to rent it – depends, as chapters in this volume have shown, on what era and region we are talking about.

We have looked into the nature of the mortgage as an entrustment and counter-entrustment, both with possibilities of deceit, betrayal, and disappointment. It carries its helps and harms, its temptations and hazards, its deadlines, threats, and relaxations. We can only try to suggest something of the emotions of hope, pride, fear, shame, and forgiveness it involves. We can only hint at the distraints, distresses, and indeed devastations when it goes not according to plan, or even evolves (at the risk of sounding melodramatic) into a monster no one envisaged, threatening not just particular humans, but further, communities and other life forms.

Mortgaging always contains moral questions that ride not just on perspective but also on ideology, on world view. This means it also depends on enculturation and training early in life, on language and translation, and on simile and metaphor, things too rarely covered in studies of this custom and practice but ones ever central in human cognition.

The very question of mortgaging pries open some of the deepest and most basic questions that philosophers like to debate, and which others involved in other professions like development economics or policy work for indigenous peoples must also face if they are to do their jobs responsibly. Whether contemporary international traditions and options derive, or *should* derive, more from points on ancient maps or sources of ancient texts, like Athens, Rome, Jerusalem, or what is now Beijing, than from much wider influences from travel and trade involving other continents, is a kind of question all historians and social scientists must face. Much rethinking has lately been occurring as some are attempting to "decolonize" the understandings of cultures and traditions, and others attempt to uphold or build upon what they construe and cherish as "civilizations."

Mortgage can be for many an abstruse, intimidating topic. As we have seen, English speakers resort to multiple metaphorical framings, from diverse domains of experience, just to try to understand and communicate about it. Recondite legal concepts like "equity of redemption," differences between ownership and possession, and medieval archaisms like "novel seisin" can take careful explaining for laypeople and still leave much room for scholarly and juridical debate. Moreover, the words and phrases for land tenure vary enough between languages and dialects to cause confusion in translation or in word searches online. What Anglophones in the United States have called land "allotment," as recording boundaries and issuing private deeds, has usually been called in former British colonies "registration" or "titling" (and in Spanish *titulación*), but in former French ones *immatriculation*. Mortgage translates to French as *hypothèque* (Spanish, *hipoteca*), not an obvious cognate of the English term (as is the more seldom used "hypothecation") – and these are just from the same Indo-European language family. Translation hurdles mean, among other things, that lessons learned in one part of the world do not always transfer readily or effectively to other parts even when published. All these issues call for patient listening and extra effort at interpretation and empathy. They make study in situ and cross-cultural comparison both vital.

Whether oral traditions, as highly valued in Native North America, are to be deemed superior or inferior to written ones, and witnesses trusted over signatures or thumbprints when the very translations of agreements made between speakers of different tongues are open to question, is a question with few easy answers and much scope for disagreements and hardships. These can pile up atop others' hard feelings accrued over generations of invasions and ignored or reneged treaties. They remind anyone with a knowledge of history of drastic land losses in the few decades following "allotment" or privatization such as occurred in the late nineteenth-century United States: the drawing up of boundary lines and titles for individual holdings opened much Native-held land for lease, sale, and mortgage. In such cases, the very legitimacy of governments (tribal, state, national), and the histories of forced schooling and language extermination that came into being at different times, are likely to come into play in determining whose traditions are to be respected. The delicate negotiations and compromises between these on matters of economic importance, just as with (say) specially licensed casinos, always leave some parties more content than others.

These are not just matters of bygone days. At the time of this writing, new debates have opened up in policy matters concerning Native North American people (and other Indigenous people elsewhere) and their access to mortgages. Trust lands, as on reservations, have historically been exempt from eligibility for mortgage lending, and thus for related home dispossession or land eviction. But new voices, as I write, are emerging inside and outside of government bodies like the Bureau of Indian Affairs, claiming, in a voice more progressive-seeming than of yore, that access to mortgages need to be made more open and accessible to historically and currently underserved minorities. Policy makers may thus find themselves between a rock and a hard place.

The situation is also more complex than that – not just a matter of simple either/or decisions. The inclusion of sacred sites like ancestral graves, or lakes or forest groves deemed spiritual centers, in these sweeping decisions, as we can now appreciate, can raise strong feelings and strong resistance. These may remain only latent until aggrieved parties can find the means and the support, educational, financial, or militant, or the legal training to challenge established authority. Federal authorities in charge of agriculture, housing, and Native American affairs have lately been facing decisions about whether to offer guarantees to mortgage lenders, to borrowers, or both. These are not matters for abrupt, broadly categorical policy decisions like the ones foisted upon Native American people and others in the United States in the Indian Removal Act of 1830, the Homestead Act of 1862, or the General Allotment Act of 1887. They are matters for sensitivity to context and language, for more general discussions involving elders and juniors (that is, for attention to both memory and ambition) and different genders. They require considering and including voices from varied stakeholders including not just titleholders but also dependents. They are issues for cautious trying out of alternatives, and for careful observation of outcomes over extended periods – yes, even decades or generations, as that may be what fair decision-making takes.

From another angle too, that of class, mortgaging calls for caution. The twenty-first century histories of lender "redlining" in poor and ethnic minority neighborhoods, of the deliberate over-lending to people known to be unlikely to be able to repay, and of the packaging and resale of standing debts in derivative markets, and the huge human suffering all this has involved, all constitute warning flags about what can happen again. Here more and quicker policy decisions may need to be made and tried out to protect vulnerable populations at risk of being denied opportunities or brought up short in foreclosures and callous dispossessions and evictions. It is not just underprivileged people who can risk and lose land and home in mortgaging. Rich people can lose out by it too, as many have done in drought times in the American Midwest, or in the large, foreign-settled or resettled farm areas of Kenya or South Africa. But some people in less-privileged racial, ethnic, religious, or occupational categories frequently face a double disadvantage. They often find it harder to get a loan at all if they want or need one, and harder, once they have, to persuade creditors – particularly ones of more privileged categories who see themselves as different – to extend their deadlines for repayment.

As always, these considerations are ones not just of economic prospects and chances, but also of power and authority, and thus too of legal regulation and jurisdiction, administrative policy, and informal influences including bribes, kickbacks, and the like. These last are much more readily accepted and expected in some parts of the world than others. They are, then, matters of custom and culture no less. Where lenders' or officials' salaries are inadequate or do not arrive on time, or payments "upward" toward higher officials are expected or demanded, the intake of bribes or kickbacks by lower officials may be considered instead as prebendalism, that is, a more easily justified form of "corruption." Longer-distance regulation sometimes seems vague or even fictitious. Where regulation prohibits or has not yet allowed or encouraged land sale or mortgaging, the practices can sometimes arise anyway, by a more local initiative, as we have seen for instance in Senegal.

Recent scholarship in the social studies has suggested that much human hardship comes of lasting debt and indebtedness. We have seen that humans are not unique in our practices of loans, of the territoriality that some cultures allow, or in terms of the trust such as all humans and cooperative beings need. The very concept of lasting debt, though, is probably more typical of humans, to begin with, than of any other species (even if there are nonhuman beings that perform momentary or other brief acts we might call loans if we open our minds to them). If we are to bring the minds of other large-brained beings into our purview – for instance, those of elephants, dolphins, and whales, or even domestic dogs – we see much evidence of not just long memories, but also and especially forgiveness. Is there something here that humans might continue to learn from our fellow creatures, now that our scientific knowledge of our fellow beings is growing quickly – and now that scholars, scientists, and the reading public are increasingly learning to shed our special hubris, our arrogant erstwhile presumptions of superiority over the rest of life?

Or perhaps we can learn it from our own forebears. When looking back at some of the earliest writing traditions known, as in ancient Babylonia or Syria, we see evidence of widespread, categorical debt forgiveness (or jubilees) pronounced at times by rulers (ones typically deemed divine). These were pronounced in times of general rural and agricultural distress, for instance following droughts or other natural hardships, or just periodically or perhaps sometimes just in view of the rulers' own precarity under threats from within or outside their polities. In our own times, we have seen heads of state in Africa, for instance in Kenya, proclaiming moratoria on land mortgage foreclosures, as if to gain voters, as election times have approached. In pandemic times like that of this writing, moratoria on evictions have saved mortgagors and tenants deprived of accustomed livelihood from dispossession and homelessness, at least temporarily. Whether secularly rising socio-economic inequality, a trend hard to fathom as it occurs over a time period longer than our lifetimes, ought to justify more "clean slate" proclamations, as in ancient jubilees, remains a deep but vital question. These are issues morally and ethically debatable, for sure.

When differing world religions come into play, so too do different expectations about fairness in mortgage deals, just as with gambling or "gaming." These sometimes focus on participants having uneven knowledge of odds and likely outcomes: a particular long-term caution and prohibition in many Islamic faith communities especially, as for instance in the Pakistani case here. The cognate religions of the Abrahamic tradition (Judaism, Christianity, Islam) have shown much debate within each of them between different schools of thought, and much changing of minds over the centuries, about what is fair, what is usurious, what is owed or divinely approved or disapproved and needing forgiveness. (Changes in monetary currencies and their inflation and deflation only add to the dilemmas and disagreements about fair interest or unjust profiteering.) It would be rash and heartless for anyone to cast blame blithely and selectively on any one of these faiths for perceived abuses of the past, or for lagging behind the others in some supposed process of civilization or economic development. Whether faiths and scriptures from arid lands and herding communities can well serve as moral guides in contexts of farms, rainforests or wetlands millennia later is, a of course, a question with its own imponderables and debatables reaching beyond what can be considered here. But it is safe enough to say that the world is not just becoming secularized, as many social evolutionists once supposed, and that religious people most anywhere have felt mortgaging to be somehow a matter of conscience. It is also safe to say sectarianism splits apart schools of thought and diversifies moral orthodoxies. Just like ethnic and linguistic divisions, it requires open-minded learning and empathy, not to mention tolerance and forgiveness, for collaboration and harmony.

What motivates mortgagors and mortgagees in the first place, if we are to look at matters historically too, has turned out harder to answer than one might at first assume. A money loan (with a land counter-loan) that some call an investment, as we have seen, others might call a needy borrower's way out of a hungry season, famine, or period of physical incapacity. If the loan lasts for many years and one party can collect interest on the debt (or, in the case of a vifgage, the proceeds of the fruits of the land), then it might also be called an annuity for the recipient.

In modern times, in settings including towns and cities, what we now call a mortgage is a valued doorway for young people into housing otherwise well out of reach. The situation among those who can remain lastingly, gainfully employed differs sharply from the situation of farmers dependent on weather and water, correct crop choices, soil fertility maintenance, freedom from "pests," and possibly traction by healthy animals. It differs for people with lands heavily invested in cash crops, vulnerable to price vicissitudes should a foreign country take up growing the crop too in competition. For these agrarian borrowers, mortgaging land can be more like walking a minefield.

These pros and cons of mortgaging are matters of not just facts or figures but also of imagination, as we can now clearly see. And as such, they are also material for stories, verses, and movies that might, as many have already, contain their own lessons worth heeding.

The psychology of borrowing and lending, and of land contracts and evictions, has much relevance to our topic, but much still to be explored, given that rather few psychologists to date have considered these topics their specialties. The psychology of what I have called entrustment and obligation, and of dealings like land loans, leases, sales, mortgages, and evictions, should not be simply a matter of undergraduate students as experimental subjects in university labs. It can also, as recent explorations in "behavioral economics" have suggested (with their game theories, simulation scenarios, and such), be a matter for testing, interviewing, and focus-group exploration across cultures and in different continents. Will borrowing for investing in farming turn out easier than somehow holding out, saving, and waiting? Will near-term gain always tend to eclipse far-off rewards; and will the excitement of a cash windfall up front, or the anticipated pride of winning official recognition and approved contract, tilt the faculties of reason? Will kith or kin as lenders prove looser and more flexible about the timing of repayment of the loan than strangers at a distance – or if instead, they are added to contracts as co-signing guarantors, does their inclusion help mitigate the risks of land loss or jeopardize a relationship? And what about personal character? Will optimists or people with dramatic mood swings tend to borrow more heavily, and more riskily, than others, and more likely end up caught in foreclosure and eviction?

It is not only motives and allocation decisions that may come into focus, but also selective perception, selective memories, and moods. The same complex neuronal circuits and hormones that psychologists try to test in labs with brain scans or probes also play their part in decision-making most anywhere. The social psychology of organizing, respect, reform, and rebellion come into play wherever an authority imposes an eviction notice or a land auction, or (as it sometimes plays out in East African contexts) a group gangs up in a crowd with machetes to intimidate against such an auction, or the kin of an evicted farmer show up at the door of the next incumbent of that person's and that family's house. Exactly how, though, we are only beginning to find out.

Whether land and money will ever be truly interchangeable without emotions involved, where land and money both involve homes and livelihoods in such different ways, looks doubtful indeed. Whether borrower and lender will trust each other more when already acquainted – and thus lenders be more likely to want to lend without collateral or co-signatories, or to forgive later on – is likely, but exceptions are bound to occur. Whether courts of judgment ought to give priority to the letter of the law and contract, and to precedents – or to common sense and intuition – will find hardened advocates on both sides. Whether judicial provisions like "equity of redemption," for compassion or allowance for special circumstances, will do much to soften the blows of eviction, lost homes, and broken and traumatized families so common in cultures with rainfed farming that turn to land markets and mortgaging is sure to keep being debated for some time. Whether the pride of making a successful investment in cattle dip or tractor will motivate further investing, or whether the humiliation of a tractor sale or "repossession" and a move in view of neighbors' eyes will be something one can ever recover from is the sort of question for which we may need to rely on anecdotal evidence for now. But then, enough "anecdotes" can constitute serious data too.

Whether emotions and other mental conditions will ever really be reducible to pains and pleasures, and abstractable as costs and benefits – like the figures in economists' graphs or the amounts awarded in court-decided restitutions, will seldom, we can be sure, find everyone concerned in agreement. These are matters where the disciplines need better ways of talking to each other than their own siloed academic journals, and better ways of learning from each other.

Then someone will always need to ask what to do. Implementation of mortgage policies will always involve issues of context and character, and guesswork about likelihoods and outcomes. It will also require intuitive and moral judgments about what is usury or opportunity cost, what is fair contract enforcement and what is predatory lending, what is repossession and what is invasion. Policy making is never without categorical distinctions, based at best on educated guesses.

One of our main emphases in this collection has been on contexts where rainfed farming is an important part of land use. Here, as seen, borrowing money against land can be a tempting and handy way to ride out hard times, but deadlines make mortgage debt dangerous. Neighbors and members of communities, in places with land mortgaging, have many ways of relying on each other, and need them daily; but these do not always hold up as safety nets when a borrower gets into trouble. Here the history of the mortgage tends to be a cautionary tale.

Where farming is not rainfed, and where people have done more to smooth out such fluctuations and control such contingencies by means like irrigation canals or the piped water of towns and cities (and family farming may occur not in open fields but back yards or roofs), the verdicts on mortgaging as an institution are likely to differ. These settings have their own risks, of course, but different risks. Where mortgaging is used as way of buying one's first apartment or house as a young adult, as we have suggested, its outcomes will involve different risks and rewards from where it is used to install a cattle dip or to keep the beans alive. Some of these contexts will also involve land taxes, insurance, and pension annuities as parts of financial lives, others not. Whether it is people from one of these contexts who ought to be doing the planning for people in another, imposing their repayment deadlines, or passing judgments on them, we can only ask the reader to consider.

One of the enduring disciplinary orthodoxies within economic development circles, internationally, has been that farming people need credit to survive and prosper, and that private land titles helps them gain access to mortgages and thus to credit. But since this sort of credit means debt too, and since land individually titled can just as easily be lost as developed, much rethinking has been needed. Over the past several decades, economic analysts, planners and officials have devoted increasing attention to saving, as an alternative or supplement to borrowing. This is as it should be. Credit and indebtedness should not be standard go-to solutions for all contexts, but only one option – along with saving, investing, and of course sharing, both monetary and nonmonetary – available to farming people wishing some measure of economic autonomy and security. Saving is particularly to be desired, too, where trends toward monocropping or single-species animal keeping for markets have heightened profits but also risks of plague, or buyer refusal, and bust.

The study of landholding and mortgaging, and thus of belonging, requires skepticism of ideologies, but it also sometimes demands suspension of disbelief. If we are to conclude that ancestral spirits and apparitions in dreams are mere figments of superstition, then we will have little hope of understanding the mortgage and its sometimes violent outcomes where ancestors are spoken to, and sacrificed to, above dooryard graves. If we deem witchcraft or its accusation as mere hocus-pocus, to be ignored in any systematic study, we might miss the ways neighbors respond to purchasers before or after a land auction. If we deem world religions as mere archaisms, we may be left cold by doctrinal disputes and compromises where people seek advice from holy books and once a week leave their homes and farmsteads, convening to pray and think about money in terms of sin, forgiveness, or redemption – and then act upon each other's behavior.

We have suggested in this work some of the ideals of policy planners, especially ones attracted to capitalist or communist ideals. These hopes and faiths have had a way of turning into something like religions themselves. We have suggested how unrealistic both sorts can be, once the character of cultures and societies, and real human minds and behavior in them, are seriously explored. Real people mix and match and tinker between. Similarly, when we are dealing with extended distances of transactions between bank, parastatal, or other headquarters and their clients on farms, we are also dealing with chains of communication, where messages (about approved loan uses or deadlines, for instance) can transmute in series, like a "telephone game" where the sender and receiver at each end cannot recognize each other's message. Dangerously, too, responsibility for decisions diffuses between multiple parties in organizational hierarchies and multiple offices, so that, in the event of a cruel outcome like a home eviction, no one might feel personally responsible, whereas from another perspective, all participants in a broader system itself might be. In the recent histories of debts as derivatives, bundled and transferred not just by humans but also by machines using algorithms, the possibilities of misunderstandings and of unconcern multiply further.

The rules and expectations people hold about land, loans, and mortgaging take many forms, not all written or codified. There are, too, regulators' official but also personal perspectives to be explored, not least because jurists might know little about technology, finance, or farming but still need to make weighty decisions about their workings and their bounds. Nor is the locus of regulation likely to remain constant over generations. No, if history is any guide, it is likely to keep shifting between religious, legal, and other unnamed but locally live forms: ones like the general authority of elderhood and local experience, or the particular authorities of schooling and literacy, numeracy, and techno-savvy, where juniors may challenge or supplant elders. Sovereignty over the mortgage will remain slippery: hard to claim for sure, hard to hold onto for long, never likely to keep everyone happy.

We hope that this collection might serve to inspire more work on the land mortgage, not just of the kinds of work represented here but of others too. One is a more official kind: the tracings of policies, projects, and programs over time and space; the life histories of named institutions. But these will not be enough. Also needed are other related kinds of studies: local life and family histories, neighborhood studies, ones with the detailed works of particulars, personalities, and predicaments that focus on the words and sentiments of the persons involved and affected themselves, that illustrate and give further feel for our topic. These will involve their own twists and turns of circumstance and strategy, reason and rationalization.

Many kinds of comparisons and contrasts will be useful in further comparative work on the nature, working, and outcome of mortgaging. Some lines of analysis include the broad scales or continua between rural and urban, between farms, houses, and apartments, rainfed and irrigated farming, and animal keeping or grazing – and mixtures of these last. Farms kept as unified holdings with homes will differ from ones with plural lands, some only sometimes visited and easily mortgaged without risk to house and home. Farms with diverse crops and animals may not offer the bounty of cash crop rewards in boom times, but they offer more safety from price collapses by their plurality. Lands with permanent, transient, and invited or squatting residents, or no living occupants, must also be considered and distinguished. Each of these distinctions can be sliced from other angles of positions and social identities: by age, gender, class, faith community, kinship and friendship processes and networks, and so on; and along size ranges of amounts transferred. Methods of borrowing, repaying, and remitting money that switch from manual to electronic means, or methods of monitoring farms that begin to include cell phone cameras and drones, will alter too the social relations and the psychology of borrowing, lending, and surveillance; compliance, evasion, and rebellion. Each of these dimensions, furthermore, can be explored for issues of access and allocation, in responses and outcomes, and optimal strategies for best practices: for coping or optimization of outcomes. Where questions of costs and benefits, or more broadly construed helps and harms, come into mind, the seductive but also perilous concept of "efficiency" rears up. The question must never be forgotten: efficiency for whom?

What might seem expedient or efficient at one time scale can easily come to look different at another. We humans seem not particularly good at planning for long-term trends, that is, beyond a generation or two in duration. Arguably, we are not evolved for it. Just as the past century and a half of industrialization has resulted in alarming climate change that threatens humans and other life on earth, so, over the same period, has the mortgage contributed to the concentration of landholdings into fewer hands – the hands of larger corporations – to the industrialization of agriculture and animal care. So too, almost imperceptibly slowly, since occurring over longer than a generation, has the care of those animals and the less-privileged human workers involved degenerated in those industrialized facilities, into often horrifying practices lately obscured from public view, but with ancillary biochemical effects reaching deeply into the environment and into consumers' bodies and health. We in this volume urge a longer-term view of mortgaging and related developments in the human economy and ecology.

The meaning of empirical research will expand to include more of its original meaning – as being not just numerical but experiential. The records will include not just the written documents of cadasters and contracts, payments and receipts, but also the spoken words of witnesses who remember, forget, and remember selectively. The attentive observer, or participant-observer, will notice even the things that cannot be expressed so easily in words, but only in flickers of facial expression or silences. The careful researcher in the future will interview not just lenders and borrowers, but also people denied access to loans, and people who have moved away after eviction. These include ones relocated to shantytowns or "spontaneous" settlements, burgeoning partly as a result, who may have their own remembrances to tell. The people at the margins of the picture – the kith and kin of the mortgagors whose names do not go onto the contracts but whose lives and homes depend on the outcomes, need to be brought closer to the center of the picture. If the full emotional content of the mortgage topic is to be appreciated – content no less real (and often more realistic) than statistics and percentages, but involving different kinds of inquiry, more of these kinds of accounts too will be welcome.

Parker Shipton is Professor of Anthropology and African Studies, Boston University. Educated at Cornell, Oxford, and Cambridge, he has taught at Harvard and consulted for several international aid agencies. His books include *Bitter Money*, *The Nature of Entrustment*, *Mortgaging the Ancestors*, and *Credit between Cultures*. He has edited the book series *Peoples of Africa* and the *Blackwell Anthologies in Social and Cultural Anthropology* and co-edited *On* *the Human*, an online interdisciplinary forum of the National Humanities Center. A former President of the Association for Africanist Anthropology, he has received the Messenger-Chalmers Prize (Cornell), Curl Prize (Royal Anthropological Institute), and African Studies Association (Herskovits) Book Award.

Index

Note: Page references noted with an *f* are figures; page references noted with a *t* are tables.

Aalbers, Manuel, 11
Abhaile scheme (Ireland), 190, 203, 204, 205, 207, 208
absentee landownership, 76
abunu tenants, 107–8
Academy of the Agricultural Sciences and Forestry (AASF), 174
Acholi region (Uganda), 146. *See also* Uganda
Adwoa Mensah v. Afua Nkrumah and Another, 107–8
Africa, 21, 24, 43–44, 283, 285, 287; rural titling in Kenya, 38, 52; Ghana, 95 (*see also* Ghana); South Africa, 188–91 (*see also* South Africa); Uganda, 145 (*see also* Uganda)
African American borrowers, 18
agio (money-changing fees), 88
agreements: Native Americans and, 49; secured, 3
agricultural credit: development in, 176–79; Romania, 170–73. *See also* credit
agricultural debts, 74 *See also* debt
algorithms, 2; decision-making, 19, 22, 23; mortgage lending and, 15–21; redlining, 23
Allen, James, 18, 19
allocation decisions, 287
alternative repayment arrangements (ARAs), 191, 192
Alvin, Dave, 45
Alvin, Phil, 45
Amazeya jumui (leader of the soil), 154

amortization schedules, 239
Anglo-American property law, 244–54
animal-fattening activities, 126*f*, 127
animal-human dimension (of mortgages), 261–62; animals on human-occupied land (farms), 268–70; evolution of, 272–73; human-animal overlaps, 262–67; mockingbird allegory (debt), 267–68; treatment of animals, 270–72
animals, treatment of, 270–72
anthropomorphism, 271
Appel, Hannah, 23
applications, mortgages, 15
aquatic metaphors, 42
architectural metaphors, 42
Asante Region (Ghana), 96. *See also* Ghana
assets: family property, 107–12 (*see also* properties); in Ireland, 203; properties (*see* properties)
Asylia Gum Sarl, 138
automated calculative systems, 21
automation, 14. *See also* technologies

backyarders, 200
bankruptcies (in Romania), 171
banks, land, 176
bargaining, taxation, 134
Baron, William R., 236
Bartlett, Robert, 17
behaviorism, 271
Belinga, Samuel Eno, 99
Berry, Sara, 24, 40
Bible, 242, 251; usury laws and, 244, 245
big data, 18, 19, 20

birds: on farms, 272; migrations, 263; mockingbird allegory (debt), 267–68. *See also* animal-human dimension (of mortgages)
birth fees, 135f
Black borrowers, 17, 18
Black Marxism (Robinson), 190
Blackstone, William, 246
blockchain technology, 13. *See also* technologies
Bohun, William, 238
bolicup, 147
Bolt, Maxim, 97
Bonsu v. Manu, 104–5
boom and bust cycles (real estate), 201
border sticks, 174f
borrowers, 148f; defaults, 242; mortgages and, 66 (*see also* mortgages); risk and, 188 (*see also* risk)
borrowing: psychology of, 290; mortgages (*see* mortgages); in Senegal, 123–24. *See also* lending
Boston Consulting Group, 15
botanical metaphors, 42
bounded land, 45
Bractonian mortgages, 6
Bräutigam, Deborah, 121
bribes, 284
Broken Heartland (Davidson), 50
bundled rental checks, 14
buy-to-let homes, 202
Byzantine Empire, 86

Caesar, 85
Cambridge, Massachusetts, 236. *See also* Massachusetts
cancellation campaigns, debt, 23
Cape Town, South Africa, 193, 198. *See also* South Africa
capital formation, 119
capitalism, 190, 233–35, 289. *See also* United States
caretakers (land), 154
Carleton, Will, 51
cash payments, 124

catastrophes, 44
Central Bank of Ireland, 205, 207
Chancery courts, 22, 69, 70
Chauveau, Jean-Pierre, 156
chef de quartier, 129
Christianity, 40, 88, 210; Bible (*see* Bible); usury laws and, 245
Church banking orders, 87–88
church estates, 86
civilization, 280
Civil Rights Act of 1968, 16
Clark, John Bates, 89
classical rent theory, 88–89
Clean Slates, 74, 80. *See also* jubilee
climate, 235–36
Coben, Nate, 25, 200, 204, 206, 209, 210
Colin, Jean-Pierre, 156
collateral, 4, 42, 251, 265, 280
collectives, 140
colonial Massachusetts, 233–35. *See also* Massachusetts
Comaroff, John, 99
Commentaries (Blackstone), 246
commercialization, 95, 101
commercial silver loans, 77
commodification of land, 157–58
commodities, 10, 235
common law (England), 67, 68, 249
communication: animals and, 263; mortgages and, 43
communism, 289
Community Reinvestment Act of 1977, 16
Comneni Dynasty (1081–1184), 87
computer code, 21. *See also* technologies
conflicts, 5; contested property relations, 151–54; disputed land sales, 148–51; land, 144, 146
Constantine VII, 87
contemporary mortgage markets, 9–11
contested property relations, 151–54
contracting, 3–6
contract law, 7, 8
contracts, *abunu* tenants, 107–8

conveyance law, 7
co-signers, 251
counter-entrustment, 281
COVID-19 pandemic, 15
Crabbe, Samuel Azu, 99
crashes, markets, 39
credit, 5, 288; agricultural credit in Romania, 170–73; in colonial Massachusetts, 233–35 (*see also* Massachusetts); development in agricultural credit, 176–79; Ghana, 96–97; Guarantee Fund for Rural Credit, 176, 177; in Ireland, 203; markets, 13, 246; models, 15; northern Uganda, 146–48; relations, 98; scoring, 9, 18, 22, 23 (*see also* algorithms); in Senegal, 122, 124–27 (*see also* Senegal); sources of, 3; temporality of, 97
creditors: in Greece and Rome, 81; risk and, 188 (*see also* risk)
Crédits Agricoles, 127
creditworthiness, 23, 70, 127–31
crop choices, 286
Crusades, the, 87, 88
culinary metaphors, 42
custodians (land), 154
customary tenure, 145
customs, northern Uganda, 146–48
cycles of repayments, 130
Czech Republic, 11

Dahra, Senegal, 124, 129, 130, 140. *See also* Senegal
Danbom, David, 50
Darwin, Charles, 271
data storage, 20
Davidson, Osha, 50
Dawes Severalty Act of 1887, 48
Dawkins, Marian Stamp, 266
dead pledge, 6
death and wealth, 98, 99. *See also* inheritance
debt: agriculture, 74; cancellation, 23, 81; capacity, 122; circulation, 11; Ghana, 96–97; household, 23; housing, 2; *The Longue Durée*, 97–101;

mockingbird allegory, 267–68; mortgage loans, 1, 8; outstanding, 96; paying off, 96, 97; repayment, 6; security for, 253. *See also* loans
Debt and Dispossession (Dudley), 50
Debt Collective and Rolling Jubilee, 23
debtor-creditor relationships, 7
deceit, humans and, 265, 281
decentralized taxation, 131–37. *See also* taxation
decision-making algorithms, 19, 22, 23
decollectivization, 165, 170
deeds, mortgages, 253
defaults, borrowers, 242, 243, 250
de Glanvill, Randulf, 6
de Gramont, Diane, 136
depersonalized transactions, 22. *See also* transactions
de Soto, Hernando, 119, 222
de Waal, Frans, 265
digital land registries, 13
digital mortgage processing, 2, 13–15
digitization in Lahore, Pakistan, 217, 218, 222–24
discharge of mortgages, 239, 242, 243, 243t. *See also repayment*
Discount Benefit Scheme (South Africa), 199
discrimination, statistical, 18
discriminatory restrictions (United States), 16, 17
disempowerment, 22
dispossession, 22, 43, 47, 54, 110, 269
distraint, 54. *See also* dispossession; repossession
distressed mortgages (in Ireland), 200–211
documents, land titles, 173. *See also* titling
dominium (ownership), 245, 252
Dorondel, Stefan, 25, 164, 165, 171
Dourish, Paul, 227
downward mobility, 10
drought, 78, 137
Duchess of Hamilton v. Countess of Dirlton (1654), 253

Dudley, Katherine, 50
Dunn, Elizabeth, 204
Dynatoi (the powerful), 86–87

East Africa, 38, 144
Eastern Europe, 163. *See also* Europe
economic growth, 9
economic growth (in colonial Massachusetts), 233–35. *See also* Massachusetts
economies: credit and debt, 98; taxation and, 121 (*see also* taxation)
e-governance, 226–27
Egypt, 74, 77
emotional metaphors, 42
employment, 251, 286
England, 250; Chancery courts, 22, 69, 70; common law, 67, 68, 249; English law, 66, 71; mortgages as leases, 67; mortgages in, 6
enticement, 46–47
entrapment, 46–47
entrepreneurs, 137–39
entrustment, 46–47, 281
Equal Credit Opportunity Act of 1974, 16
equity, 9, 22; laws and, 68; of redemption, 69, 246–54, 282, 287; of taxation, 134
estates, 99. *See also* inheritance
Europe: England (*see* England); Ireland, 188–91 (*see also* Ireland); land mortgages in, 161–63; parliaments, 89; Romania, 161–63 (*see also* Romania)
Europeanization, 236
European Union, 161, 162, 177
evictions, 47–50, 54, 130, 283, 285
existential metaphors, 41

Faber, Jacob, 17
Fair Housing Act (1968), 16
fair lending, 15
fair prices, 87
false suggestion (*suggestio falsi*), 188
family property, 102, 107–12, 113, 269. *See also* properties

farmland: enticement/entrustment/entrapment, 46–47; history of mortgages and, 38–39; making a market out of, 39–41; metaphors (mortgages and), 41–45; mortgages and, 37; North America history, 48; property definitions, 47–50; risk of farming, 54; trauma and mortgages, 53–55; trust in mortgages, 50–53
farms, 288; birds on, 272; mortgages, 268–70; mortgages in Massachusetts, 235–36; in North America, 272
faunal metaphors, 42
Federal Home Loan Mortgage Corporation (Freddie Mac), 9
Federal Housing Administration, 16
Federal National Mortgage Association (Fannie Mae), 9
Federal Reserve Bank of New York, 1
fees, 131–37, 135*f*
Fernandez, Rodrigo, 11
Financed Linked Individual Subsidy Programme (FLISP), 190, 193, 194, 196, 197
Financial, Insurance, and Real Estate (FIRE) sector, 89–90
financial crashes (2008), 190
financial crisis (2007), 10
financial inclusion, 131–37
financialization, 9, 74–75, 188. *See also* land tenure
financial markets, access to, 2
financial modernity, 189
financial modernization (in Kenya), 96
financiers, farmers and, 51
Fine, John V.A., 247
FinTech, 2, 14, 17, 20
First Peoples, 39
fiscal inclusion, 131–37
Fjeldstad, Odd-Helge, 135
flat-rate poll taxes, 131
flooding, 78
foreclosures, 1, 21, 42, 52, 266; financial crisis (2007), 10;

foreclosure crisis (2008), 10; United States and, 22
forum-shopping, 165
foshato'chi' (mortgage-bird), 267
fragmentation patterns, 175, 176f, 273
freeholders, republic of, 202. *See also* Ireland
freehold-mortgages, 4
freehold tenure, 145. *See also* titling
freehold titles, 195
funerals, 98. *See also* inheritance
Fuster, Andreas, 14

gage (Germanic), 189. *See also* pledging
General Allotment Act of 1887, 48, 283
George, Henry, 89
Georgia, 13
Georgics (Virgil), 76
Germany, civil laws in, 12
Ghana, 4, 5, 13, 40, 281; *abunu* tenants, 107–8; credit, 96–97; debt, 96–97; family property, 102, 107–12; inheritance, 101–2; inheriting debt, 95–96 (*see also* credit; debt; inheritance); laws, 101; *The Longue Durée*, 97–101; pledge redemptions, 103–97; wills in, 96
Ghana Law Reports 1961, 105
gifts, 108. *See also* inheritance
Gilbert, Michelle, 99
Global Financial Crisis, 188, 189
Global North, 3
Global Property Guide, 136
Global South, 1, 3, 5, 11, 21, 120, 222
Government National Mortgage Association (Ginnie Mae), 9
Gracchus, Tiberius, 84
Graeber, David, 95, 96, 97, 99, 105, 113
grants, 67. *See also* land; mortgages
Great Britain: commercial bank lending in, 90; House of Lords, 89; Kenya and, 38; regulations in, 41. *See also* Europe
Great Depression, 16
Greece, creditors in Greece and Rome, 81
Greek Dark Age (1200–750 BCE), 80–82

gross domestic product (GDP), 1
growth, population, 235–36
Guarantee Fund for Rural Credit, 176, 177
guarantees, loans, 128. *See also* security
Guérin, Isabelle, 127
Gusterson, Hugh, 21
Guyer, Jane, 99

Hall, James Norman, 272
Hammurabi's laws, 79, 80
Hann, Chris, 164
Hart, Keith, 41
high-cost mortgage lending, 17
high-risk areas, 16
Historical Statistics of the United States (McCusker), 235
histories, 290; climate, 236; contemporary mortgage markets, 9–11; evolution of mortgages and titling, 21–23; of farmland and mortgages, 38–39; Lahore, Pakistan, 218–19; of land mortgage/reform in Romania, 167–68; legal histories (of mortgages), 66–72; markets in the United States, 233–34 (*see also* United States); Medieval European mortgages, 6–7; modern mortgages, 7–9; of mortgages, 21, 189, 248, 249; new technologies, 12–15; North America, 48; of pledging, 21; social embeddedness of land, 3–6; social histories (of mortgages), 66–72
Hoffman, Philip, 246
Holmes, Elizabeth, 128
Home Mortgage Disclosure Act of 1975, 16
Home Mortgage Disclosure Act of 2014, 17
homeownership, 1, 9, 189, 190
Home Owners' Loan Corporation, 16
Homestead Act of 1862, 283
Horoi: Studies in Mortgage, Real Security, and Land Tenure in Ancient Athens (Fine), 247
household debt, 23
House of Lords (Great Britain), 89

housing: options in South Africa, 194; seizure of homes, 21 (*see also* foreclosures)
Housing Act (Act No. 107 of 1997, Amendment Act No. 4 of 2001), 193
housing debt, 2
Hudson, Michael, 26, 40
human beings: customs of, 266; monetization and, 266. *See also* animal-human dimension (of mortgages)
hybrid worker-peasants, 165
hypothecation, 282. *See also* mortgage

ideology of kinship, 167
impôt du minimum fiscal, 131, 134, 140
improperty, 47. *See also* properties
inclusion, 131–37
income: in Ireland, 203; rental, 89, 90; taxes, 136
indebtedness, 146–48, 288
India, 220
Indian Home Loan Guarantee Program of the Department of Housing and Urban Development, 52
Indian Removal Act of 1830, 283
individualization, 127. *See also* titling
informal lending, 124
information processing, 20
inheritance, 5; family property, 107–12; Ghana, 101–2; of land, 44, 95; northern Uganda, 144–46; wealth and, 96
In re Krah (Deceased) Yankyeraah and Others v. Osei-Tutu and Another, 108–10
institutional lenders, 9
insurance, 123, 233
interest, 44; agriculture debts, 74; usury, 67
interest rates: hikes, 130; in Senegal, 126
International Monetary Fund, 163
interpersonal networks, 21. *See also* networks
Intestate Law of Succession, 102, 110

investments, 286; land as, 5 (*see also* land); mortgage-backed securities, 8; popularity of mortgages as, 22; Uganda, 144 (*see also* Uganda); wind turbines (in northern Uganda), 154–57
Ireland, 188–91; Abhaile scheme, 190, 203, 204, 205, 207, 208; distressed mortgages in, 200–211; Mortgage Arrears Resolution Process (Central Bank of Ireland), 205, 207
Irish Land Registry, 209
Islam, 40
Islamic Republic, 220

Jews, land ownership in England, 67
Jones, Alice Hanson, 241
jubilees, 284–85. *See also* clean slates
Judaism, 40
juggling practices, 125, 139
Juul, Kristine, 24, 38, 122

Kahn, Matthew, 236
Kane, Safiétou, 120
Karamoja region (northern Uganda), 144, 146, 154–57. *See also* Uganda
Keen, Michael, 121
Kenya, 283; financial modernization in, 96; mortgages and, 38, 39, 52; Western, 145
Keynes, John Maynard, 113
kickbacks, 284
Kidepo National Park (Uganda), 155
Kilkenny Trust, 209, 210
Krech, Shepard, 267
Kusk, Mette, 24
Kwame Kusi v. Andrews Abayie and Kwadwo Biewuo, 99–100
Kwame Mensah v. Abrokwa, 105–6

labor from the land, 84
Lahore, Pakistan, 216–18; digitization in, 217, 218, 222–24; e-governance, 226–27; history of, 218–19; land records, 222–24; liquidity in, 220–22; new technologies in, 224–26;

real estate in, 221; World Bank, 222–24
Lahore Development Authority (LDA), 219, 220, 221
land: access, 167; banks, 176; borders, 174; bounded, 45; categories of, 79–80; commercialization of, 95; commodification of, 157–58; conflicts, 144, 146; enticement/ entrustment/entrapment, 46–47; eviction, 283; farmland (*see* farmland); financialization, 74–75 (*see also* financialization); formalization in Romania, 163–67; fragmentation patterns, 175, 176*f*; grants, 67; inheritance of, 44, 95 (*see also* Ghana); Land Act of Uganda (1998), 145–46; land mortgages in Europe (*see also* Europe); leases, 4; liquidity, 223; loans in northern Uganda, 148–51; markets, 122; mortgages, 286 (*see also* mortgages); ownership in England (Jews), 67; postsocialist land reforms, 162, 163; privatization of, 164, 168; property definitions, 47–50; reforms, 164; registries, 13; rent, 89; restitution, 162; rights, 3, 4, 75; selling, 149*f*, 175; social embeddedness of, 3–6; taxation, 88, 288; titling, 4; transfers, 75 (*see also* transfers); trust and, 265; Uganda, 144 (*see also* Uganda); values, 70, 96; as wealth, 1, 71; wind turbines (in northern Uganda), 154–57
Land Act of Uganda (1998), 144
Land Bank mortgages, 237
Land Book, 172
landholders, 75; in Romania, 169; subordination of, 77
landholding systems, 165, 172, 289
landlords: landlord class (Rome), 76, 88; land rent and, 89; property management, 14
land mortgages (in Europe), 161–63
landownership, absentee, 76

land records (in Lahore, Pakistan), 222–24
Land Records Management and Information Systems (LRMIS), 222, 223, 224, 225, 226, 227
land size, restrictions on, 82–86
land tenure, 74–75; categories of land, 79–80; church banking orders, 87–88; classical rent theory, 88–89; exemptions from agrarian obligations, 78; fights to avoid taxation, 82–86; Financial, Insurance, and Real Estate (FIRE) sector, 89–90; fiscal origins of, 77; Greek Dark Age (1200–750 BCE), 80–82; for large institutions, 78–79; origins of, 75–76; reversing land transfers to the *Dynatoi* (the powerful), 86–87
land title documents, 173. See also titling
Langley, Paul, 11
language (about mortgages), 43
large institutions, land tenure for, 78–79
Lategan, Louis, 200
Latinx borrowers, 17, 18
The Law of Wills in Ghana (Crabbe), 99
laws: Anglo-American property law, 247; Chancery courts, 22, 69, 70; Civil Rights Act of 1968, 16; common law (England), 67, 68, 249; Community Reinvestment Act of 1977, 16; continuity of, 254; Dawes Severalty Act of 1887, 48; English law, 66, 71; Equal Credit Opportunity Act of 1974, 16; and equity, 68; Fair Housing Act (1968), 16; family property, 107–12 (*see also* properties); General Allotment Act of 1887, 48, 283; German civil laws, 12; Ghana, 101; Hammurabi's, 79, 80; Home Mortgage Disclosure Act of 1975, 16; Home Mortgage Disclosure Act of 2014, 17; Homestead Act of 1862, 283; Indian

Removal Act of 1830, 283; Intestate Law of Succession, 102, 110; Law of Pre-emption, 86; legal systems, 66; Licinio-Sextian law, 82; mortgage, 7, 8; Native Americans, 52; properties and, 247, 252; Romania, 166, 168, 169; usury, 244–46; as will, 246
LC1s (Local Council level 1), 154
leader of the soil (*Amazeya jumui*), 154
leasehold tenure, 145
leases, mortgages as, 67
legacies, family property, 107–12. *See also* inheritance; properties
legal histories (of mortgages), 66–72
legal pluralism, 101–2
legal systems, 66, 246–54
Lemanski, Charlotte, 195
lenders: profits, 67; as villains, 71, 72
lending, 1; informal, 124; predatory, 268; in Senegal, 122 (*see also* Senegal). *See also* mortgage lending
levies, 131–37
Lewis, Frank, 241
Licinio-Sextian law, 82
lines of credit. *See* credit
liquidity, 9; in Lahore, Pakistan, 220–22; land, 223
Littletonian gage, 6
livestock transactions, 125, 127, 133f
the living gage (*vifgage*), 189, 280
loans, 1; access to, 22; amounts, 238, 239, 240t; collateral, 280 (*see also* collateral); commercial silver, 77; Financed Linked Individual Subsidy Programme (FLISP), 190; guarantees, 128; land loans in northern Uganda, 148–51; liquidity, 171; modification, 205; profits, 40; repayments, 66, 68; in Senegal, 124; transactions, 6; Uganda, 144 (*see also* Uganda); uses of (in Senegal), 126f; warehouse, 206. *See also* mortgage lending; mortgages
Locke, John, 76
Lockridge, Kenneth, 236
The Longue Durée, 97–101
Lord's Resistance Army (LRA), 146, 148

Luo society, 96
Lycurgan reforms, 81
Lydon, Ghislaine, 98

machine learning technologies, 20
Madam Abena Adwapa v. John Amoah, 111–12
Madikizela, Bonginkosi, 196
mailo land, 145
Maitland, Frederic, 188, 189, 249, 252
Malthusian frontiers, 235
management of properties, 14
markets: access to, 235–36; commodities, 235; contemporary mortgage, 9–11; crashes, 39; credit, 13, 246; land, 122; land in Romania, 173–76; in the United States, 233–35 (*see also* United States); value-free economics, 89
marriage gifts, 98
marriages: fees, 135f
Massachusetts, 233–35; continuity of laws, 254; as a farming frontier, 234; farm mortgages in, 235–36; road-building in, 237; sample of mortgages in, 237–44; transformation of the legal system in, 246–54; usury laws, 244–46
McCaskie, Thomas, 97
McCloskey, Donald, 235
McCusker, John, 235
Medieval European mortgages, 6–7
Meinert, Lotte, 24
Melville, Herman, 39, 40
Menell, Clive, 194
MERS (Mortgage Electronic Registration System), 8, 9
Mesopotamia, 40, 74, 77
metaphors (mortgages and), 41–45
microfinance institutions (MFIs), 125, 127, 128, 130, 139
Micu, Cornel, 166
middle citizens, 195
military, land tenure for, 78–79
Mill, John Stuart, 88
misharum proclamations, 80
Mithridatic Wars (88–63 BC), 81

mockingbird allegory (debt), 267–68
models: credit, 15; originate-to-distribute business, 9
modernity: of capitalism, 190; financial, 189; political, 191
modern mortgages, 7–9
modification of loans, 205
modification programs: automated calculative systems, 21
Money Advice and Budgeting Service (MABS), 201, 203, 204, 208
money-changing fees (*agio*), 88
moneylenders, trust in, 50
Monkam, Nara, 135
morals, 23, 284, 285
Morgan, Lewis Henry, 271
Morse, Adair, 17
mortal sins, 245
Mortgage Arrears Resolution Process (Central Bank of Ireland), 205, 207
mortgage-backed securities, 8
mortgage-bird (*foshato'chi'*), 267
mortgage laws, 7, 8. See also laws
mortgage lending, 1–3; algorithms and, 15–21; contemporary mortgage markets, 9–11; high-cost, 17; Medieval European mortgages, 6–7; modern mortgages, 7–9; new technologies, 12–15; processes, 14; social embeddedness of land, 3–6
mortgages: access to, 22; age, 241; animal-human dimension of, 261–62 (*see also* animal-human dimension [of mortgages]); applications, 15; automated calculative systems, 21; Bractonian, 6; collateral (*see also* collateral; security); in colonial Massachusetts, 233–35 (*see also* Massachusetts); communication and, 43; conditions of discharge, 239; deeds, 253; definitions, 66; digital mortgage processing, 2; discharge of, 239, 242, 243, 243t; distance between, 241; distance from Boston, 241; distressed mortgages in Ireland, 200–211; duration of, 239;
endowment of adult children, 242; in England, 6; enticement/entrustment/entrapment, 46–47; evading in South Africa, 191–200; evolution of, 21–23; farmland and, 37 (*see also* farmland); farm mortgages in Massachusetts, 235–36; farms, 268–70; financial crisis (2007), 10; foreclosures, 52 (*see also* foreclosures); freehold-mortgages, 4; histories of, 21, 189, 248, 249; interest, 44 (*see also* interest); Kenya and, 38, 39; Land Bank, 237; land mortgages in Europe, 161–63 (*see also* Europe); land values and, 70; as last resorts, 69; as leases, 67; legal histories of, 66–72; Medieval European, 6–7; metaphors (mortgages and), 41–45; mockingbird allegory (debt), 267–68; modern, 7–9; objectives of, 249; occupations, 239, 240, 240t; origins of, 40; overview of, 280; payments to, 70; penal bonds, 242; renegotiation, 205; in Senegal, 119–23, 123–24 (*see also* Senegal); social histories of, 66–72; split, 206; standardization of, 10; transfers, 49 (*see also* transfers); trauma and, 53–55; trust in, 50–53, 265
mortgagors, 69, 246–54, 29. See also borrowers
motives, 287
movies, 71
mutuum, concept of (what had been mine becomes thine), 245

Nana Baffoe Ababio and Adansi Boye v. Kwabena Num, Kwaku Asiedu, and Yaa Akyaa, 110–11
Nana Wireko Ababio (Kaasehene) v. Nana Kwabena Ofori (Chief of Nkontonko), 106–7
National Bank of Romania, 172
National Housing Forum (1992–94 [South Africa]), 195
National Land Register, 174

Native Americans, 39, 49, 282; farming and, 48; laws, 52; politics, 52
natural catastrophes, 44
nature, 262. *See also* animal-human dimension (of mortgages)
The Nature of Entrustment (Shipton), 97
Ndambu, Jules, 128
Near East, 74
negotiations, 124
neoliberalism, 21. *See also* capitalism
networks, transactions and, 21
new technologies, 12–15, 216
Nordhoff, Charles, 272
North America, 39, 233; farms in, 272; histories, 48; Native Americans, 282
northern Uganda, 144; commodification of land, 157–58; contested property relations, 151–54; credit, 146–48; customs, 146–48; indebtedness, 146–48; inheritance in, 144–46; land loans in, 148–51; property in, 144–46; wind turbines in, 154–57. *See also* Uganda
not-for-sale signs, 151–54, 153*f*
Nwokeji, Ugo, 98

Oheneba Kofi Duo v. Kwame Manhyia, 103–4
old city Lahore, 216, 218, 219. *See also* Lahore, Pakistan
Oppenheimer, Harry, 194
Organisation for Economic Co-operation and Development (OECD), 1, 202
originate-to-distribute business model, 9
Ouazad, Amine, 236
outstanding debt, 96
ownership: absentee landownership, 76; churches and, 86; Jews in England, 67; leases and, 67; proof of, 252–53; records, 5; security of property, 75
ownership (*dominium*), 245, 252. *See also* titling

Pakistan: corruption in, 217; independence of (1947), 219; Lahore (*see* Lahore, Pakistan)
palaces, land tenure for, 78–79
parliaments (Europe), 89
patwaris, 26, 217, 222, 223, 225, 227
pawning, land, 3, 4
paying off debt, 96, 97. *See also* debt
payments: *abunu* tenants, 107–8; cash, 124; to mortgages, 70
pencil redlining, 18
Perry, Donna, 127
Piketty, Thomas, 121
plays, 71
pledging, 280; English law and, 66; histories of, 21; land, 3–6 (*See also* land); origins of, 40; pledge redemptions, 103–7
pneumatic metaphors, 42
Polanyi, Karl, 39
policy-making, 288
policy reforms, 20
political modernity, 191
politics, Native Americans, 52
Pollock, Frederick, 189, 249, 252
poll taxes, 131, 138
Popular Banks, 168
population growth, 235–36
possession (*seisin*), 252
Postel-Vinay, Gilles, 246
postsocialist land reforms, 161
the powerful (*Dynatoi*), 86–87
The Practising Attorney (Bohun), 238
predatory lending, 268
private entrepreneurs, 137–39
privatization of land, 164, 168
processes, mortgage lending, 14
profits, 21, 43, 98; lenders, 67; loans, 40
programming, 21
promising, 3
properties: Anglo-American property law, 247; contested property relations, 151–54; definitions, 47–50, 246; family property, 102, 107–12, 113; forfeiting, 6; laws and, 247, 252;

management, 14; Mesopotamia, 77; northern Uganda, 144–46; rights, 122, 161, 165; rise in prices (Africa), 135; security of property ownership, 75; self-squired property, 108; tax transfers, 175. *See also* housing; land; mortgages

property taxes, 134–37

prosperity, promotion of, 119

public shaming, 244

Punjab Land Records Authority (PLRA), 224, 225, 226, 227

qua security, 253. *See also* security

Quicken Loans, 14, 15

Radical Ricardians, 88

Rahman, Tariq, 25

ranges, animal and human, 264

Ravnborg, Helle Munk, 147

Rawlings, J. J., 102

real estate: boom and bust cycles, 201; categories of land, 79–80; in Lahore, Pakistan, 221. *See also* land; properties

records, ownership, 5

redemption: equity of, 69, 246–54, 282, 287; pledge, 103–7

redlined communities, 16, 18

redlining, 23, 283

reforms, 2; land, 164; land titling, 4; Lycurgan, 81; policies, 20; postsocialist land, 162, 163; postsocialist policies/reforms in Romania, 168–70; Uganda, 144

registration procedures, 12, 282

registries, land, 13

regulations, 41. *See also* laws

relationships: debtor-creditor, 7; family property, 107–12 (*see also* properties)

religions, 40

religious metaphors, 42

renegotiation of mortgages, 205

rent: buy-to-let homes, 202; classical rent theory, 88–89; land, 89

rental houses (South Africa), 199

rental income, 89, 90

repayments, 125; cycles, 130; failure to pay, 129; land grants, 67; loans, 66, 68. *See also* discharge

repossession, 287. *See also* dispossession; distraint; displacement

reputations, 127. *See also* creditworthiness

restitution, land, 162

revenues, tax, 136. *See also* taxation

revolutions, capitalism, 190

rights: land, 3, 4, 75; properties, 122, 161, 165

risk, 283; categories, 9; creditworthiness, 127–31 (*see also* creditworthiness); fair lending, 15; of farming, 54 (*see also* farmland); hedging, 235; high-risk areas, 16; investments and, 188 (*see also* investments); in Senegal, 119–23 (*see also* Senegal)

risk-taking, 8

road-building in Massachusetts, 237

Robinson, Cedric, 190

Robinson, J., 194

Rocket Mortgage (Quicken), 15

Rockoff, Hugh, 245

Rodima-Taylor, Daivi, 25

Romania, 171, 179–81; agricultural credit, 170–73; development in agricultural credit, 176–79; history of land mortgage/reform in, 167–68; land formalization in, 163–67; land mortgages in, 161–63; land titling in, 173–76; laws, 166, 168, 169; postsocialist policies/reforms in, 168–70; Soviet era in, 167

Romanos II, 87

Rome: creditors in Greece and, 81; fights to avoid taxation, 82–86; landlord class and, 75, 76, 88

Rosenthal, Jean-Laurent, 246

Rothenberg, Winifred, 40

Rupert, Anton, 194

rural titling (in Africa), 38. *See also* titling
Rusu, Marioara, 25

Saif, Umar, 224
Salvian, 85
Samec, Tomas, 11
saving groups, 125
schedules, amortization, 239
scoring, credit, 9, 18, 22, 23. *See also* algorithms
secured agreements, 3
secure tenure, 47
securities: mortgage-backed, 8; popularity of mortgages as, 22
security, 251, 280; for debt, 253; pledging land as, 66 (*see also* pledging); of property ownership, 75. *See also* collateral
seisin (possession), 252
self-squired property, 108
Senegal: borrowing in, 123–24; credit in, 124–27; creditworthiness, 127–31; examples of taxation, 137–39; interest rates in, 126; mortgages in, 119–23, 123–24; property taxes, 134–37; small taxes, 134–37; taxation in, 131–37; Technical Director of Dahra Municipality, 132; titling in, 124
Şerban, Stelu, 164, 165
shantytowns, 291
Shipton, Parker, 26, 95, 145, 180
signatories, Native Americans, 49
silver, commercial silver loans, 77
sins, 245
smallholders, 75
small taxes, 134–37
Smith, Adam, 88
Smith, Brian Cantwell, 227
social histories (of mortgages), 66–72
socialism, 163, 171. *See also* Romania
Sod-Busting (Danbom), 50
somatic metaphors, 42
sous-préfet, 138
South Africa, 38, 188–91; Discount Benefit Scheme, 199; evading mortgages in, 191–200; Financed Linked Individual Subsidy Programme (FLISP), 190, 193, 194, 196, 197; National Housing Forum (1992–94), 195; rental houses, 199; unemployment, 200
South African Human Rights Commission, 198
split mortgages, 206
Standard Financial Statements (SFS), 203
Stanton, Richard, 17
statistical discrimination, 18
status, 127. *See also* creditworthiness
status quo ante (of land tenure), 80
Stout, Noelle, 21
subsidies: European Union, 177; Financed Linked Individual Subsidy Programme (FLISP), 190, 193, 194, 196, 197
subsidized housing projects (RDP), 191, 193, 195, 196
suggestio falsi (false suggestion), 188
Sulla, 84
suppressio veri (suppression of truth), 188
surety, 251. *See also* collateral
Sweden, 13

taxation, 78, 79, 133f; bargaining, 121, 134; churches and, 86; equity of, 134; examples of, 137–39; fights to avoid, 82–86; flat-rate poll taxes, 131; income taxes, 136; land, 88, 288; poll taxes, 138; property taxes, 134–37; rates, 89; in Senegal, 119–23, 131–37 (*see also* Senegal); small taxes, 134–37
Technical Director of Dahra Municipality, 132
technologies: digital land registry, 13, 226–7; digital mortgage processing, 2; machine learning, 20; new, 12–15
temples, 78–79, 83
tenure, land, 145–46. *See also* land tenure

territoriality, human and animal, 263, 264, 284
theories, classical rent theory, 88–89
titling, 282; collateral, 265; evolution of, 21–23; freehold titles, 195; land, 4; land titling in Romania, 173–76; Native Americans and, 48; new technologies, 12–15; rural titling in Africa, 38; in Senegal, 124; Torrens title system, 12; transfers of titles, 68 (*see also* mortgages)
tolls in Massachusetts, 237
tontines (saving groups), 125
Torrens title system, 12
Toynbee, Arnold, 83, 87
transactions: credit, 5 (*see also* credit); depersonalized, 22; family property, 107–12; livestock, 125, 127, 133f; loans, 6 (*see also* loans); networks and, 21. *See also* mortgages
transfers: mortgages, 49; pledges, 48 (*see also* pledging); reversing land transfers to the *Dynatoi* (the powerful), 86–87; of titles, 68 (*see also* mortgages). *See also* mortgages
trauma, mortgages and, 53–55
trust in mortgages, 50–53, 265
trusts, 208, 209
Turner, R. W., 253

Uganda, 144; commodification of land, 157–58; Kidepo National Park, 155; reforms, 144. *See also* northern Uganda
unemployment (in South Africa), 200
United States: commercial bank lending in, 90; discriminatory restrictions, 16, 17; financial crisis (2007), 10; foreclosures in, 22; homeownership in, 9; Massachusetts, 233–35 (*see also* Massachusetts); mortgage loans in, 1, 8. *See also* North America
Urban Foundation (UF), 194, 195
usury, 67, 244–46. *See also* interest

value-free economics, 89
values, land, 70, 96
Van Erp, Sjef, 8
Verdery, Katherine, 167
Vidal, Lorenzo, 23
vifgage (the living gage), 189, 280
villains, lenders as, 71, 72
violence, 53–55
voluntary sales, 128

Waddilove, David, 7, 69, 70, 71
Wallace, Nancy, 17
warehouse loans, 206
wealth, 83; family property, 113 (*see also* family property); inheritance and, 96; land as, 71
wealth-in-people, 99
West Africa, 38, 97–101, 135. *See also* Africa; Ghana
Western Cape Department of Human Settlements, 197f
Western Kenya, 145
widows, dispossession of, 110
wills, 96, 108. *See also* inheritance
wind turbines (in northern Uganda), 154–57, 156f
World Bank, 41, 119, 163, 216, 217, 222–24
Wrapp, Melissa, 25, 191, 192, 196, 198, 199

Xhosa, 199, 200. *See also* South Africa

Yeboah and Others v. Kwakye, 110

www.ingramcontent.com/pod-product-compliance
Lightning Source LLC
Chambersburg PA
CBHW051528020426
42333CB00016B/1830